Spring Microservices in Action, Second Edition

Spring Microservices in Action

SECOND EDITION

JOHN CARNELL AND ILLARY HUAYLUPO SÁNCHEZ

MANNING

SHELTER ISLAND

Manning Publications Co.
20 Baldwin Road
PO Box 761
Shelter Island, NY 11964

Development editor:	Leslie Trites
Technical development editor:	Robert Wenner
Review editor:	Aleksandar Dragosavljević
Production editor:	Deirdre Hiam
Copy editor:	Frances Buran
Proofreader:	Katie Tennant
Technical proofreader:	Stephan Pirnbaum
Typesetter:	Gordan Salinovic
Cover designer:	Marija Tudor

ISBN 9781617296956
Printed in the United States of America

I dedicate this book to all women
who are currently pursuing STEM careers.

With hard work, everything is possible.

brief contents

contents

preface

This book is part of a dream to contribute to the development of the field I am most passionate about—computer science, and particularly, software development. These fields show their extraordinary importance in the interconnected and global present. We see the incredible transformations of these disciplines every day, in all areas of human activities. But why write about microservices architecture when there are a lot of other topics to write about?

The word "microservices" has a lot of interpretations. But in this book, I define a microservice as a distributed, loosely coupled software service that carries out a small number of well-defined tasks. Microservices crept up as an alternative to monolithic applications to help combat the traditional problems of complexity in a large code base by decomposing that down into small, well-defined pieces.

During my 13 years of experience, I have dedicated myself to software development, working with different languages and different types of software architectures. When I started, I used architectures that today are practically obsolete. The contemporary world forces us to update continually, and innovation in the software development field advances at an accelerated pace. Because of this search for up-to-date knowledge and practices, I decided to get involved in the world of microservices some years ago. Since then, it is the architecture I have used the most because of the advantages it provides (advantages such as scalability, speed, and maintainability). Successfully venturing into the microservices field prompted me to take on the task of writing this book as an opportunity to systematize and share what I have learned.

As a software developer, I discovered how important it is to continually research and apply new knowledge to development. Before undertaking this book, I decided to share my findings and started publishing microservices articles on the blog platform of a software development company I worked for in Costa Rica, my home country. While I was writing these articles, I realized I had found a new passion and purpose in my professional career. A few months after writing one of my articles, I received an email from Manning Publications, offering me the opportunity to write the second edition of this book that I share with you today.

The first edition of this book was written by John Carnell, a consummate professional with many years of software development experience. I wrote this second edition from this basis, combined with my own interpretation and understanding. The second edition of *Spring Microservices in Action* will allow you to implement diverse design patterns that will help you create a successful microservices architecture using Spring. It's a framework that offers out-of-the-box solutions for many of the common development problems you will run into as a microservice developer. Now, let's start this incredible journey into the world of microservices with Spring.

acknowledgments

I am deeply grateful for the opportunity to work on this book, which has allowed me to share my knowledge and to learn at the same time. I am also grateful to Manning Publications for trusting my work and allowing me to share it with so many people; most importantly, to Michael Stephens for offering me this fantastic opportunity; to John Carnell for his support, work, and knowledge; to Robert Wenner, my technical development editor, for his valuable contributions; and to Lesley Trites, my editor, for accompanying me throughout the process with her valuable help.

I would also like to thank Stephan Pirnbaum and John Guthrie, who, as my technical reviewers, checked my work and ensured the book's overall quality. Thanks go also to my project editor, Deirdre Hiam; my copyeditor, Frances Buran; my proofreader, Katie Tennant; my reviewing editor, Aleks Dragosavljevic; and to all the reviewers (Aditya Kumar, Al Pezewski, Alex Lucas, Arpit Khandelwal, Bonnie Malec, Christopher Kardell, David Morgan, Gilberto Taccari, Harinath Kuntamukkala, Iain Campbell, Kapil Dev S, Konstantin Eremin, Krzysztof Kamyczek, Marko Umek, Matthew Greene, Philippe Vialatte, Pierre-Michel Ansel, Ronald Borman, Satej Kumar Sahu, Stephan Pirnbaum, Tan Wee, Todd Cook, and Víctor Durán)—your suggestions helped make this a better book.

I want to thank my mom, dad, and my entire family, who supported me and encouraged me to pursue my dreams, and who, by their dedication to work as an example, helped me become the professional I am today. My gratitude also goes out to Eli, who was always by my side on those long days of work, and to my friends, who always trusted me and encouraged me throughout this process.

Last, but not least, I thank each and every one of you for buying this book and allowing me to share my knowledge with you. I hope you enjoy reading it as much as I did writing it. I hope it becomes a valuable contribution to your professional careers.

about this book

Spring Microservices in Action, Second Edition, is written for the practicing Java/Spring developer who needs hands-on advice and examples of how to build and operationalize microservice-based applications. When we wrote this book, we wanted to maintain the same central idea as in the first edition. We wanted it to be based on core microservice patterns aligned with Spring Boot and Spring Cloud's latest practices and examples. In almost every chapter, you will find specific microservice design patterns, along with examples of the Spring Cloud implementations.

Who should read this book

- You are a Java developer who has some experience (1–3 years) with building distributed applications.
- You have some background (1+ years) with Spring.
- You are interested in learning how to build microservice-based applications.
- You are interested in how you can leverage microservices for building cloud-based applications.
- You want to know if Java and Spring are relevant technologies for building microservice-based applications.
- You are interested in seeing what goes into deploying a microservice-based application to the cloud.

How this book is organized: A roadmap

This book consists of 12 chapters and 3 appendixes:

- Chapter 1 introduces you to why microservices architecture is an important and relevant approach to building applications, especially cloud-based applications.
- Chapter 2 walks you through the Spring Cloud technologies that we'll use and provides a guide on how to build cloud-native microservices following the twelve-factor application best practices. This chapter also walks you through how to build your first REST-based microservice using Spring Boot.
- Chapter 3 shows you how to look at your microservices through the eyes of an architect, application engineer, or DevOps engineer and provides a guide on how to implement some of the microservice best practices in your first REST-based microservice.
- Chapter 4 walks you through the container world, highlighting the main differences between containers and virtual machines (VMs). This chapter also shows you how to containerize your microservices using several Maven plugins and Docker commands.
- Chapter 5 introduces you to how to manage the configuration of your microservices using Spring Cloud Config. Spring Cloud Config helps guarantee that your service configurations are centralized in a single repository, versioned, and repeatable across all instances of your services.
- Chapter 6 introduces you to the service discovery routing pattern. You will learn how to use Spring Cloud and Netflix's Eureka service to abstract the location of your services away from the clients consuming them. You'll also learn how to implement client-side load balancing using the Spring Cloud LoadBalancer and a Netflix Feign client.
- Chapter 7 is about protecting the consumers of your microservices when one or more microservice instances are down or in a degraded state. This chapter demonstrates how to use Spring Cloud and Resilience4j to implement the circuit breaker, fallback, and bulkhead patterns.
- Chapter 8 covers the service gateway routing pattern. Using Spring Cloud Gateway, we build a single entry point to call all our microservices. We will demonstrate how to use the Spring Cloud Gateway filters to build policies that can be enforced against all services flowing through the service gateway.
- Chapter 9 covers how to implement service authentication and authorization using Keycloak. In this chapter, we cover some basic principles of OAuth2 and how to use Spring and Keycloak to protect your microservices architecture.
- Chapter 10 looks at how we can introduce asynchronous messaging into our microservices using Spring Cloud Stream and Apache Kafka. This chapter also shows you how to use Redis to cache lookups.
- Chapter 11 shows how to implement common logging patterns like log correlation, log aggregation, and tracing with Spring Cloud Sleuth, Zipkin, and the ELK Stack.

- Chapter 12 is the cornerstone project for this book. We take the services we have built throughout the book and deploy them to an Amazon Elastic Kubernetes Service (Amazon EKS). We also discuss how to automate the build and deployment of your microservices using tools like Jenkins.
- Appendix A shows additional microservices architecture best practices and explains the Richardson Maturity Model.
- Appendix B contains supplemental material on OAuth2. OAuth2 is an extremely flexible authentication model, and this chapter provides a brief overview of the different ways in which you can use OAuth2 to protect your application and its corresponding microservices.
- Appendix C covers how to monitor your Spring Boot microservices using several technologies such as Spring Boot Actuator, Micrometer, Prometheus, and Grafana.

In general, developers should read chapters 1, 2, and 3, which provide essential information about best practices and about implementing microservices using Spring Boot with Java 11. If you're a reader who's new to Docker, we highly recommend reading chapter 4 carefully because it briefly introduces all the Docker concepts used throughout the book.

The rest of the book discusses several microservice patterns, such as service discovery, distributed tracing, API Gateway, and more. The approach of this book is to read the chapters in order and follow the code examples for the chapters. But in case someone wants to skip the examples, they can download the code from the GitHub repository at https://github.com/ihuaylupo/manning-smia.

About the code

This book contains code in almost every chapter, both in numbered listings and in line with normal text. In both cases, source code is formatted in a `fixed-width font like this` to separate it from ordinary text. All code examples are available in my GitHub repository at https://github.com/ihuaylupo/manning-smia.

Each chapter has a different folder in the repository. Note also that all the code in this book is built to run with Java 11 using Maven as the main build tool and Docker as the container tool. In the README.md file for each chapter, you can find the following information:

- A brief introduction to the chapter
- The tools required for the initial configuration
- A "how to use" section
- The build command for the examples
- The run command for the examples
- Contact and contributing information

One of the core concepts we followed throughout the entire book is that the code examples in each chapter should be able to run completely independent of any of the other chapters. What does this mean? You should be able to grab the code from chapter 10, for example, and run it without following the examples in the previous chapters. You'll see that for every service built in each chapter there is a corresponding Docker image. Each chapter uses Docker Compose to execute the Docker images in order to guarantee that you have a reproducible run-time environment for each chapter.

In many cases, the original source code has been reformatted; we've added line breaks and reworked indentation to accommodate the available page space in the book. In rare cases, even this was not enough, and listings include line-continuation markers (➡). Additionally, comments in the source code have often been removed from the listings when the code is described in the text. Code annotations accompany many of the listings, highlighting important concepts.

liveBook discussion forum

Purchase of *Spring Microservices in Action, Second Edition*, includes free access to a private web forum run by Manning Publications, where you can make comments about the book, ask technical questions, and receive help from the authors and from other users. To access the forum, go to https://livebook.manning.com/book/spring-microservices-in-action-second-edition/discussion. You can also learn more about Manning's forums and the rules of conduct at https://livebook.manning.com/#!/discussion.

Manning's commitment to our readers is to provide a venue where a meaningful dialogue between individual readers and between readers and authors can take place. It is not a commitment to any specific amount of participation on the part of the authors, whose contribution to the forum remains voluntary (and unpaid). We suggest you try asking them some challenging questions lest their interest stray! The forum and the archives of previous discussions will be accessible from the publisher's website as long as the book is in print.

about the authors

JOHN CARNELL is a software architect and leads the Developer Engagement team for Genesys Cloud. John spends the majority of his day teaching Genesys Cloud customers and internal developers how to deliver cloud-based contact center and telephony solutions and best practices for cloud-based development. He works hands-on building telephony-based microservices using the AWS platform. His day-to-day job is to design and build microservices across a number of technology platforms including Java, Clojure, and Go. John is a prolific speaker and writer. He regularly speaks at local user groups and was a regular speaker on "The No Fluff Just Stuff Software Symposium." Over the last 20 years, John has authored, coauthored, and functioned as a technical reviewer for a number of Java-based technology books and industry publications. John holds a BA from Marquette University and an MBA from the University of Wisconsin in Oshkosh. John is a passionate technologist who constantly explores new technologies and programming languages. When John is not speaking, writing, or coding, he lives in Cary, North Carolina, with his wife, Janet, his three children (Christopher, Agatha, and Jack), and yes, his dog, Vader.

ILLARY HUAYLUPO SÁNCHEZ is a software engineer who graduated from Cenfotec University and holds an MBA focused on IT management from the Latin American University of Science and Technology (ULACIT) in Costa Rica. Her knowledge of software development is quite extensive. She has experience working with Java and other programming languages such as Python, C#, Node.js, and with other technologies such as various databases, frameworks, cloud services, and more. Currently, Illary works as a Senior Software Engineer at Microsoft, San Jose, Costa Rica, where she spends most of her time researching and developing a variety of trendy and up-to-date projects. In her professional portfolio, we also find that she has 12 years of experience as an Oracle Certified Developer and has worked as a Senior Software Engineer in large companies such as IBM, Gorilla Logic, Cargill, and BAC Credomatic (a prestigious Latin American bank). Illary likes challenges and is always willing to learn new programming languages and new technologies. During her free time, she likes to play the bass guitar and spend time with her family and friends. Illary can be reached at illaryhs@gmail.com.

About the cover illustration

The figure on the cover of Spring Microservices in Action is captioned a "A Man from Croatia." This illustration is taken from a recent reprint of Balthasar Hacquet's Images and Descriptions of Southwestern and Eastern Wenda, Illyrians, and Slavs, published by the Ethnographic Museum in Split, Croatia, in 2008. Hacquet (1739–1815) was an Austrian physician and scientist who spent many years studying the botany, geology, and ethnography of many parts of the Austrian Empire, as well as the Veneto, the Julian Alps, and the western Balkans, inhabited in the past by peoples of the Illyrian tribes. Hand drawn illustrations accompany the many scientific papers and books that Hacquet published. The rich diversity of the drawings in Hacquet's publications speaks vividly of the uniqueness and individuality of the eastern Alpine and northwestern Balkan regions just 200 years ago.

This was a time when the dress codes of two villages separated by a few miles identified people uniquely as belonging to one or the other, and when members of a social class or trade could be easily distinguished by what they were wearing. Dress codes have changed since then and the diversity by region, so rich at the time, has faded away. It is now often hard to tell the inhabitant of one continent from another, and today the inhabitants of the picturesque towns and villages in the Slovenian Alps or Balkan coastal towns are not readily distinguishable from the residents of other parts of Europe.

We at Manning celebrate the inventiveness, the initiative, and the fun of the computer business with book covers based on costumes from two centuries ago, brought back to life by illustrations such as this one.

Welcome to
the cloud, Spring

This chapter covers

- Understanding microservices architectures
- Understanding why companies use microservices
- Using Spring, Spring Boot, and Spring Cloud for building microservices
- Understanding the cloud and cloud-based computing models

Implementing any new architecture is not an easy task; it comes with many challenges such as application scalability, service discovery, monitoring, distributed tracing, security, management, and more. This book will introduce you to the world of microservices in Spring, teach you how to tackle all those challenges, and show you the trade-offs to consider when considering microservices for your business applications. As you go, you'll learn how to build microservice applications using technologies such as Spring Cloud, Spring Boot, Swagger, Docker, Kubernetes, ELK (Elasticsearch, Logstash, and Kibana), Stack, Grafana, Prometheus, and more.

If you are a Java developer, this book will provide a smooth migration path from building traditional Spring applications to microservice applications that can be deployed to the cloud. This book uses practical examples, diagrams, and descriptive texts to provide further details of how to implement microservice architectures.

In the end, you will have learned how to implement technologies and techniques such as client load balancing, dynamic scaling, distributed tracing, and more, to create flexible, modern, and autonomous microservice-based business applications with Spring Boot and Spring Cloud. You will also be able to create your own build/deployment pipelines to achieve continuous delivery and integration with your business by applying technologies such as Kubernetes, Jenkins, and Docker.

1.1   *The evolution towards a microservices architecture*

Software architecture refers to all the fundamental parts that establish the structure, operation, and interaction between the software components. This book explains how to create a microservice architecture that consists of loosely coupled software services that carry out a small number of well-defined tasks and communicate using messages over a network. Let's start by considering the differences between microservices and some other common architectures.

1.1.1   *N-tier architecture*

One common type of enterprise architecture is the multi-layered or n-tier architecture. With this design, an applications is divided into multiple layers, each with their own responsibilities and functions, such as UI, services, data, testing, and so forth. For example, as you create your application, you make a specific project or solution for the UI, then another one for the services, another for the data layer, and so on. In the end, you will have several projects that, combined, create an entire application. For large enterprise systems, n-tier applications have many advantages, including these:

- N-tier applications offer good separation of concerns, making it possible to consider areas like UI (user interface), data, and business logic separately.
- It's easy for teams to work independently on different components of n-tier applications.
- Because this is a well-understood enterprise architecture, it's relatively easy to find skilled developers for n-tier projects.

N-tier applications also have drawbacks, such as these:

- You must stop and restart the entire application when you want to make a change.
- Messages tend to pass up and down through the layers, which can be inefficient.
- Once it's deployed, refactoring a large n-tier application can be difficult.

Although some of the topics we'll discuss in this book relate directly to n-tier applications, we will focus more directly on distinguishing microservices from another common architecture, often called the monolith.

1.1.2 What's a monolithic architecture?

Many small-to-medium web-based applications are built using a monolithic architectural style. In a monolithic architecture, an application is delivered as a single deployable software artifact. All of the UI, business, and database access logic are packaged together into a unique application and deployed to an application server. Figure 1.1 shows the basic architecture of this application.

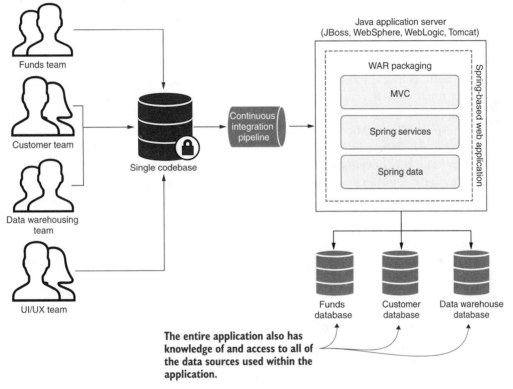

Figure 1.1 **Monolithic applications force multiple development teams to synchronize their delivery date because their code needs to be built, tested, and deployed as an entire unit.**

While an application might be deployed as a single unit of work, often there are multiple development teams working on a single application. Each development team is responsible for their own discrete piece of the application that usually targets specific customers. For example, imagine a scenario where we have an in-house, custom-built customer relations management (CRM) application that involves the coordination of multiple teams, including UI/UX, customer, data warehouse, and financial players, or more.

Although monolithic applications are sometimes described in negative terms by proponents of microservices architecture, these are often a great choice. Monoliths are easier to build and deploy than more complex architectures like n-tier or microservices. If your use case is well defined and unlikely to change, it can be a good decision to start with a monolith.

When an application begins to increase in size and complexity, however, monoliths can become difficult to manage. Each change to a monolith can have a cascading effect on other parts of the application, which may make it time consuming and expensive, especially in a production system. Our third option, the microservices architecture, offers the potential of greater flexibility and maintainability.

1.1.3   *What's a microservice?*

The concept of a microservice initially crept into the software development community's consciousness as a direct response to many of the challenges of trying to scale (both technically and organizationally) large monolithic applications. A *microservice* is a small, loosely coupled, distributed service. Microservices let you take an extensive application and decompose it into easy-to-manage components with narrowly defined responsibilities. Microservices help combat the traditional problems of complexity in a large codebase by decomposing it down into small, well-defined pieces.

The key concepts you need to embrace as you think about microservices are *decomposing* and *unbundling*. The functionality of your applications should be entirely independent of one another. If we take the CRM application mentioned previously and decompose it into microservices, it might look something like figure 1.2.

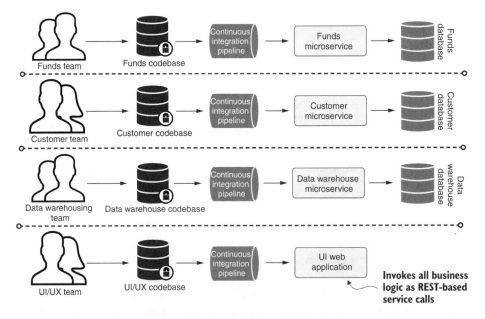

Figure 1.2   Using a microservice architecture, a CRM application is decomposed into a set of completely independent microservices, allowing each development team to move at its own pace.

Figure 1.2 shows how each team completely owns their service code and service infrastructure. They can build, deploy, and test independently of each other because their code, source control repository, and infrastructure (app server and database) are now entirely independent of the different parts of the application. To recap, a microservice architecture has the following characteristics:

- Application logic is broken down into small-grained components with well-defined, coordinate boundaries of responsibility.
- Each component has a small domain of responsibility and is deployed independently of the others. A single microservice is responsible for one part of a business domain.
- Microservices employ lightweight communication protocols such as HTTP and JSON (JavaScript Object Notation) for exchanging data between the service consumer and service provider.
- Because microservice applications always communicate with a technology-neutral format (JSON is the most common), the underlying technical implementation of the service is irrelevant. This means that an application built using a microservice approach can be constructed with multiple languages and technologies.
- Microservices—by their small, independent, and distributed nature—allow organizations to have smaller development teams with well-defined areas of responsibility. These teams might work toward a single goal, such as delivering an application, but each team is responsible only for the services on which they're working.

Figure 1.3 compares a monolithic design with a microservices approach for a typical small e-commerce application.

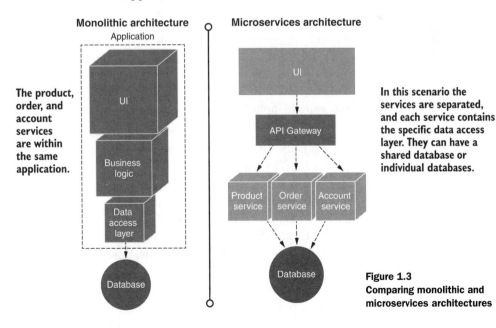

Figure 1.3 Comparing monolithic and microservices architectures

1.1.4 *Why change the way we build applications?*

Companies that used to serve local markets are suddenly finding that they can reach out to a global customer base. However, with a broader global customer base also comes worldwide competition. More competition impacts the way developers need to think about building applications. For example:

- *Complexity has gone way up.* Customers expect that all parts of an organization know who they are. But "siloed" applications that talk to a single database and don't integrate with other applications are no longer the norm. Today's applications need to communicate with multiple services and databases, residing not only inside a company's data center but also within external internet service providers.
- *Customers want faster delivery.* Customers no longer want to wait for the next annual release of a software package. Instead, they expect the features in a software product to be unbundled so that new functionality can be released quickly in a matter of weeks (or even days).
- *Customers also demand reliable performance and scalability.* Global applications make it extremely difficult to predict how many transactions are going to be handled by an application and when that transaction volume is going to hit. Applications need to scale up quickly across multiple servers, then scale back down seamlessly when the volume has passed.
- *Customers expect their applications to be available.* Because customers are one click away from a competitor, a company's applications must be highly resilient. Failures or problems in one part of the application shouldn't bring down the entire application.

To meet these expectations, we, as application developers, have to embrace the enigma that to build highly scalable and highly redundant applications, we need to break our applications into small services that can be built and deployed independently of one another. If we "unbundle" our applications into smaller services and move these away from a single monolithic artifact, we can build systems that are

- *Flexible*—Decoupled services can be composed and rearranged to quickly deliver new functionality. The smaller the unit of code that one is working with, the less complicated it is to change and the less time it takes to test and deploy the code.
- *Resilient*—Decoupled services mean an application is no longer a single "ball of mud," where a degradation in one part of the application causes the entire application to fail. Failures can be localized to a small part of the application and contained before the entire application shuts down. This also enables the application to degrade gracefully in case of an unrecoverable error.
- *Scalable*—Decoupled services can easily be distributed horizontally across multiple servers, making it possible to scale the features/services appropriately. With a monolithic application, where all the logic for the application is intertwined,

the *entire* application needs to scale back, even if only a small part of the application is the bottleneck. With small services, scaling is localized and much more cost effective.

To this end, we begin our discussion of microservices. Keep the following in mind as we start our journey:

Small, Simple, and Decoupled Services = Scalable, Resilient, and Flexible Applications

It's important to understand that systems and organizations can benefit from a microservices approach. To obtain benefits in the organization, we can apply *Conway's law* in reverse. This law indicates several points that can improve the communication and structure of a company.

Conway's law (which first appeared in April, 1968, written by Melvin R. Conway in the article, "How Do Committees Invent") states that "Organizations which design systems . . . are constrained to produce designs which are copies of the communication structures of these organizations." Basically, what that indicates is that the way teams communicate within the team and with other teams is directly reflected in the code they produce.

If we apply Conway's law in reverse (also known as *inverse Conway maneuver*) and design the company structure based on a microservice architecture, the communication, stability, and organizational structure of our applications improve by creating loosely coupled and autonomous teams to implement the microservices.

1.2   *Microservices with Spring*

Spring has become the most popular development framework for building Java-based applications. At its core, Spring is based on the concept of dependency injection. A *dependency injection framework* allows you to more efficiently manage large Java projects by externalizing the relationship between objects within your application through convention (and annotations) rather than hardcoding those objects to "know" about each other. Spring sits as an intermediary between the different Java classes of your application and manages their dependencies. Spring essentially lets you assemble your code like a set of Lego bricks that snap together.

What's impressive about the Spring framework, and a testament to its development community, is its ability to stay relevant and to reinvent itself. The Spring developers quickly saw that many development teams were moving away from monolithic applications where the application's presentation, business, and data access logic were packaged together and deployed as a single artifact. Instead, they noticed that development teams were moving to highly distributed models where small services can be quickly deployed to the cloud. In response to this shift, the Spring developers launched two projects: Spring Boot and Spring Cloud.

Spring Boot is a re-envisioning of the Spring framework. While it embraces core features of Spring, Spring Boot strips away many of the "enterprise" features found in Spring and instead delivers a framework geared toward Java-based, REST-oriented (Representational State Transfer) microservices. With a few simple annotations, a Java developer can quickly build a REST service that can be packaged and deployed without the need for an external application container.

> **NOTE** While we cover REST in more detail in chapter 3, the core concept behind REST is that your services should embrace the use of HTTP verbs (GET, POST, PUT, and DELETE) to represent the core actions of the service and should use a lightweight, web-oriented data serialization protocol, such as JSON, for requesting and receiving data from the service.

The key features of Spring Boot include the following:

- An embedded web server to avoid complexity in deploying the application: Tomcat (default), Jetty, or Undertow.

  This is one essential component of Spring Boot; the chosen web server is part of the deployable JAR. For Spring Boot applications, the only requisite to deploy the app is to have Java installed on the server.
- A suggested configuration to start quickly with a project (starters).
- An automatic configuration for Spring functionally—whenever it's possible.
- A wide range of features ready for production (such as metrics, security, status verification, externalized configuration, and more).

Using Spring Boot offers the following benefits for our microservices:

- Reduces development time and increases efficiency and productivity
- Offers an embedded HTTP server to run web applications
- Allows you to avoid writing a lot of boilerplate code
- Facilitates integration with the Spring Ecosystem (includes Spring Data, Spring Security, Spring Cloud, and more)
- Provides a set of various development plugins

Because microservices have become one of the more common architectural patterns for building cloud-based applications, the Spring development community gives us Spring Cloud. The Spring Cloud framework makes it simple to operationalize and deploy microservices to a private or public cloud. Spring Cloud wraps several popular cloud-management microservice frameworks in a common framework. It makes the use and deployment of these technologies as easy as is annotating your code. We cover the different components within Spring Cloud in the next chapter.

1.3   *What are we building?*

This book offers a step-by-step guide on creating a complete microservices architecture using Spring Boot, Spring Cloud, and other useful and modern technologies. Figure 1.4 shows a high-level overview of some of the services and technology integrations that we will use throughout the book.

Figure 1.4 describes a client request to update and retrieve the organization's information in the microservice architecture that we will create. To start the request,

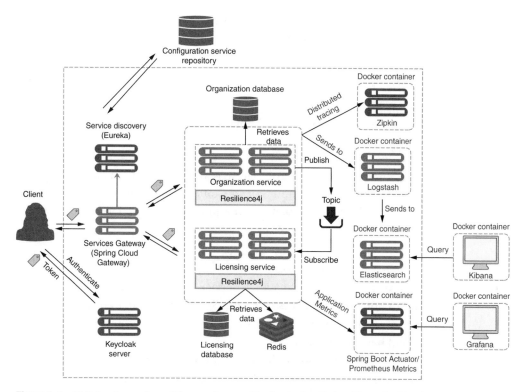

Figure 1.4 High-level overview of the services and technologies that we'll use in this book

the client first needs to authenticate with Keycloak to get an access token. Once the token is obtained, the client makes a request to the Spring Cloud API Gateway. The API Gateway service is the entry point to our entire architecture; this service communicates with the Eureka service discovery to retrieve the locations of the organization and licensing services and then calls the specific microservice.

Once the request arrives at the organization service, it validates the access token against Keycloak to see if the user has permission to continue the process. Once validated, the organization service updates and retrieves its information from the organization database and sends it back to the client as an HTTP response. As an alternative path, once the organization information is updated, the organization service adds a message to the Kafka topic so the licensing service is aware of the change.

When the message arrives at the licensing service, Redis stores the specific information in Redis's in-memory database. Throughout this process, the architecture uses distributed tracing from Zipkin, Elasticsearch, and Logstash to manage and display the logs and employs Spring Boot Actuator, Prometheus, and Grafana to expose and display the application metrics.

As we move forward, we will see topics such as Spring Boot, Spring Cloud, Elasticsearch, Logstash, Kibana, Prometheus, Grafana, and Kafka, among others. All these technologies may sound complicated, but we will see how to create and integrate the different components that make up the diagram in figure 1.4 as we progress through the book.

1.4   *What is this book about?*

The scope of this book is broad. It covers everything from basic definitions to more complex implementations to create a microservices architecture.

1.4.1   *What you'll learn in this book*

This book is about building microservice-based applications using a variety of Spring projects, such as Spring Boot and Spring Cloud, which can be deployed locally in a private cloud run by your company or in a public cloud such as Amazon, Google, or Azure. This book covers the following topics:

- What a microservice is, best practices, and design considerations that go into building a microservice-based application
- When you shouldn't build a microservice-based application
- How to build microservices using the Spring Boot framework
- The core operational patterns to support microservice applications, particularly a cloud-base application
- What Docker is and how to integrate it with a microservice-based application
- How you can use Spring Cloud to implement the operational patterns described later in this chapter
- How to create application metrics and visualize these in a monitoring tool
- How to achieve distributed tracing with Zipkin and Sleuth
- How to manage application logs with the ELK Stack
- How to take what you've learned and build a deployment pipeline that can be used to deploy your services locally, to a private internally managed cloud, or to a public cloud provider

By the time you're done reading this book, you should have the knowledge needed to build and deploy a Spring Boot microservice. You'll also understand the key design decisions needed to operationalize your microservices. You'll realize how service configuration management, service discovery, messaging, logging and tracing, and security all fit together to deliver a robust microservice environment. Finally, you'll see how your microservices can be deployed using different technologies.

1.4.2   *Why is this book relevant to you?*

I suspect that if you have reached this point, it is because you

- Are a Java developer or have a strong grasp of Java
- Have a background in Spring
- Are interested in learning how to build microservice-based applications

- Are interested in how to use microservices to build cloud-based applications
- Want to know if Java and Spring are relevant technologies for building microservice-based applications
- Want to know what the cutting-edge technologies are to achieve a microservice architecture
- Are interested in seeing what goes into deploying a microservice-based application to the cloud

This book offers a detailed guide on how to implement a microservices architecture in Java. It provides descriptive and visual information and a lot of hands-on code examples to give you a programmatic guide on how to implement this architecture using the latest versions of different Spring projects like Spring Boot and Spring Cloud.

Additionally, this book provides an introduction to the microservice patterns, best practices, and infrastructure technologies that go hand in hand with this type of architecture, simulating a real-world application development environment. Let's shift gears for a moment and walk through building a simple microservice using Spring Boot.

1.5 Cloud and microservice-based applications

In this section, we'll see how to create a microservice using Spring Boot and learn why the cloud is relevant to microservice-based applications.

1.5.1 Building a microservice with Spring Boot

This section will not provide a detailed walk-through of much of the code you'll use to create microservices, but is just a brief introduction on how to create a service to show you how easy it is to use Spring Boot. For this, we're going to create a simple REST service for "Hello World" with one main endpoint that uses the GET HTTP verb. This service endpoint will receive request parameters and URL parameters (also known as *path variables*). Figure 1.5 shows what the REST service will do and the general flow of how a Spring Boot microservice processes a user's request.

This example is by no means exhaustive or even illustrative of how you should build a production-level microservice, but it should cause you to pause because of how little code it takes to write it. We won't go through how to set up the project build files or the details of the code until chapter 2. If you'd like to see the Maven pom.xml file and the actual code, you can find it in the chapter 1 section of the downloadable code.

> **NOTE** You can retrieve all the source code for chapter 1 from the GitHub repository for the book at https://github.com/ihuaylupo/manning-smia/tree/master/chapter1.

For this example, we have a single Java class called Application, which you'll find in the class file, com/huaylupo/spmia/ch01/SimpleApplication/Application.java. We

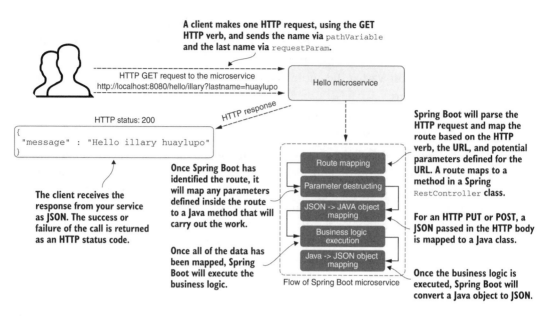

Figure 1.5   Spring Boot abstracts away the common REST microservice tasks (routing to business logic, parsing HTTP parameters from the URL, mapping JSON to and from Java objects) and lets the developer focus on the business logic for the service. This figure shows three different ways to pass parameters to our controller.

will use this class to expose a REST endpoint called /hello. The following listing shows the code for the Application class.

Listing 1.1   Hello World with Spring Boot: a (very) simple Spring microservice

Tells Spring Boot that this class is the entry point for the Spring Boot service

```
import org.springframework.boot.SpringApplication;
import org.springframework.boot.autoconfigure.SpringBootApplication;
import org.springframework.web.bind.annotation.GetMapping;
import org.springframework.web.bind.annotation.PathVariable;
import org.springframework.web.bind.annotation.PostMapping;
import org.springframework.web.bind.annotation.RequestBody;
import org.springframework.web.bind.annotation.RequestMapping;
import org.springframework.web.bind.annotation.RequestParam;
import org.springframework.web.bind.annotation.RestController;

@SpringBootApplication
@RestController
@RequestMapping(value="hello")
public class Application {

    public static void main(String[] args) {
        SpringApplication.run(Application.class, args);
    }

    @GetMapping(value="/{firstName}")
```

Tells Spring Boot to expose the code in this class as a Spring RestController

Prefaces all URLs exposed in this application with a /hello prefix

Exposes an endpoint as a GET-based REST that takes two parameters in its firstName (via @PathVariable) and lastName (via @RequestParam)

```
    public String helloGET(
      @PathVariable("firstName") String firstName,
      @RequestParam("lastName") String lastName) {
      return String.format(
            "{\"message\":\"Hello %s %s\"}",
                firstName, lastName);
    }
}

class HelloRequest{

  private String firstName;
  private String lastName;

  public String getFirstName() {
    return firstName;
  }
  public void setFirstName(String firstName) {
    this.firstName = firstName;
  }
  public String getLastName() {
    return lastName;
  }
  public void setLastName(String lastName) {
    this.lastName = lastName;
  }

}
```

> **Maps the firstName and lastName parameters to the two variables passed into the hello function**

> **Returns a simple JSON string that we manually build (in chapter 2, we won't create any JSON)**

> **Contains the fields of the JSON structure sent by the user**

In listing 1.1, you're basically exposing one endpoint with a GET HTTP verb that takes two parameters (firstName and lastName) on the URL: one from the path variable (@PathVariable) and another one as the request parameter (@RequestParam). The endpoint returns a simple JSON string that has a payload containing the message "Hello firstName lastName". To call the GET endpoint /hello/illary?lastName=huaylupo on your service, the return call would be

```
{"message":"Hello illary huaylupo"}
```

Let's start the Spring Boot application. In order to do this, let's execute the following command on the command line. This Maven command uses a Spring Boot plugin defined in the pom.xml file to start the application using an embedded Tomcat server. Once you execute the mvn spring-boot:run command and everything starts correctly, you should see what's shown in figure 1.6 in your command-line window.

```
mvn spring-boot:run
```

> **NOTE** If you are running the command from the command line, make sure you are in the root directory. The root directory is the one that contains the pom.xml file. Otherwise, you will run into this error: No plugin found for prefix 'spring-boot' in the current project and in the plugin groups.

Java vs. Groovy and Maven vs. Gradle

The Spring Boot framework supports both Java and the Groovy programming languages. Spring Boot also supports both Maven and Gradle build tools. Gradle introduces a Groovy-based DSL (domain specific language) to declare the project configuration instead of an XML file like Maven. Although Gradle is powerful, flexible, and top-rated, Maven is still used by the Java developer community. This book, therefore, only contains examples in Maven to keep it manageable and the material focused, and it is intended to reach the largest audience possible.

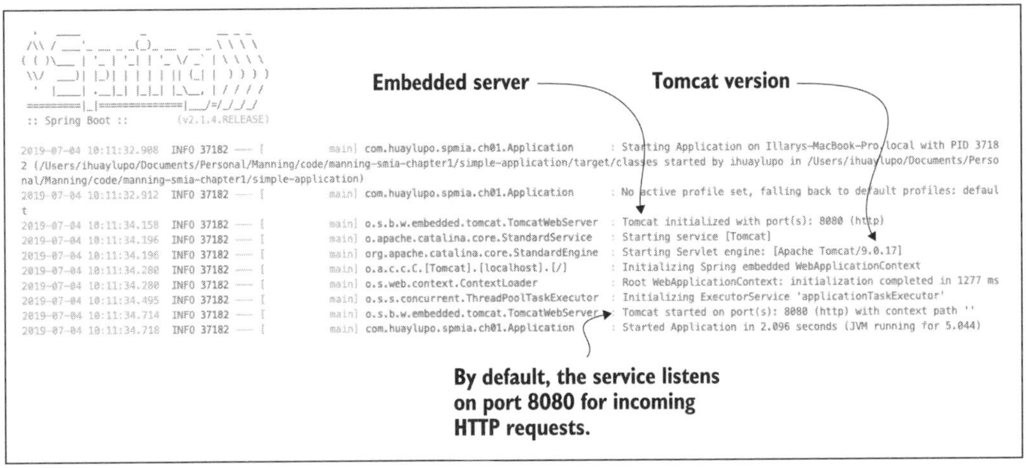

Figure 1.6   The Spring Boot service communicates the service port via the console.

To execute the services, you need to use a browser-based REST tool. You'll find many tools, both graphical and command-line, for invoking REST-based services. For this book, we will use Postman (https://www.getpostman.com/). Figures 1.7 and 1.8 show two different Postman calls to the endpoints with the results returned from the services.

Figure 1.8 shows a brief example of how to make a call using the POST HTTP verb. It is essential that we mention this is only for demonstration purposes. In the following chapters, you'll see that the POST method is preferred when it involves creating new records in our service.

This simple example code doesn't demonstrate the full power of Spring Boot, nor the best practices to create a service. But what it shows is that you can write a full HTTP JSON REST-based service with route-mapping of the URL and parameters in Java with a few lines of code. Although Java is a powerful language, it has acquired a reputation for being wordy compared with other languages. With Spring, however, we can accomplish a lot with just a few lines of code. Next, let's walk through why and when a microservice approach is justified for building applications.

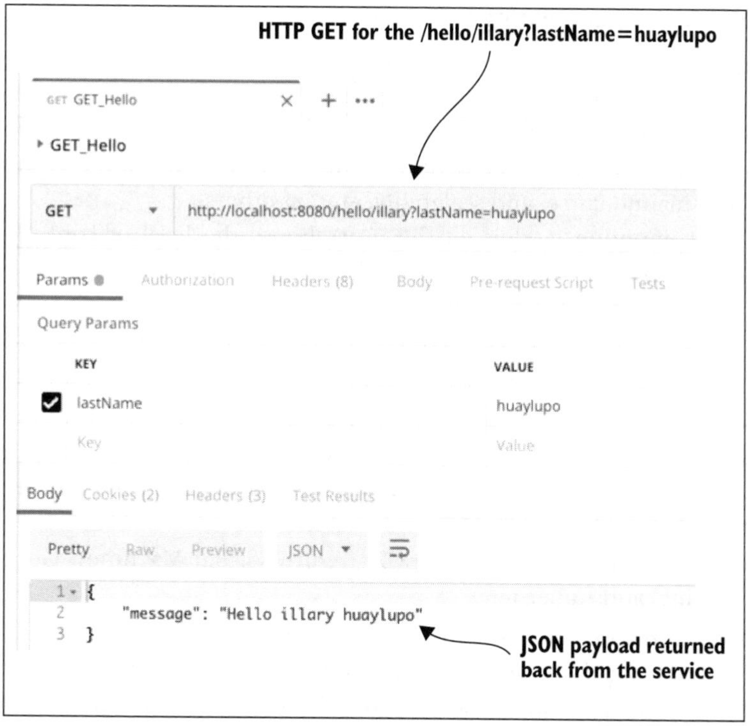

Figure 1.7 The response from the GET `/hello` endpoint shows the data you've requested represented as a JSON payload.

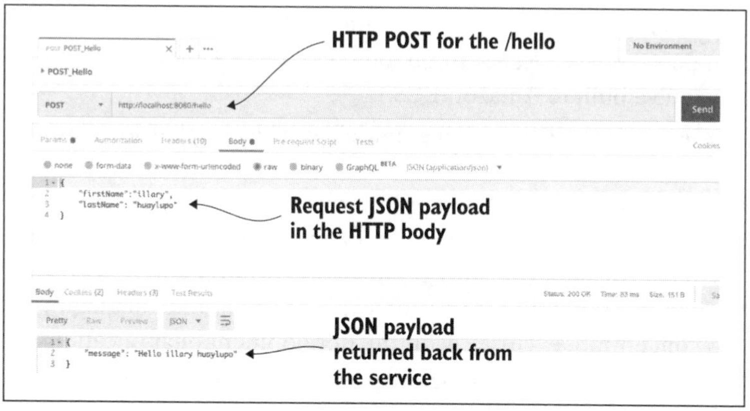

Figure 1.8 The response from the POST `/hello` endpoint shows the request and the response data represented as a JSON payload.

1.5.2   *What exactly is cloud computing?*

Cloud computing is the delivery of computing and virtualized IT services—databases, networking, software, servers, analytics, and more—through the internet to provide a flexible, secure, and easy-to-use environment. Cloud computing offers significant advantages in the internal management of a company, such as low initial investment, ease of use and maintenance, and scalability, among others.

The cloud computing models let the user choose the level of control over the information and services that these provide. These models are known by their acronyms, and are generically referred to as *XaaS*—an acronym that means *anything as a service*. The following lists the most common cloud computing models. Figure 1.9 shows the differences between these models.

- *Infrastructure as a Service (IaaS)*—The vendor provides the infrastructure that lets you access computing resources such as servers, storage, and networks. In this model, the user is responsible for everything related to the maintenance of the infrastructure and the scalability of the application.

  IaaS platforms include AWS (EC2), Azure Virtual Machines, Google Compute Engine, and Kubernetes.

- *Container as a Service (CaaS)*—An intermediate model between the IaaS and the PaaS, it refers to a form of container-based virtualization. Unlike an IaaS model, where a developer manages the virtual machine to which the service is deployed, with CaaS, you deploy your microservices in a lightweight, portable virtual container (such as Docker) to a cloud provider. The cloud provider runs the virtual server the container is running on, as well as the provider's comprehensive tools for building, deploying, monitoring, and scaling containers.

  CaaS platforms include Google Container Engine (GKE) and Amazon's Elastic Container Service (ECS). In chapter 11, we'll see how to deploy the microservices you've built to Amazon ECS.

- *Platform as a Service (PaaS)*—This model provides a platform and an environment that allow users to focus on the development, execution, and maintenance of the application. The applications can be created with tools that are provided by the vendor (for example, operating system, database management systems, technical support, storage, hosting, network, and more). Users do not need to invest in a physical infrastructure, nor spend time managing it, allowing them to concentrate exclusively on the development of applications.

  PaaS platforms include Google App Engine, Cloud Foundry, Heroku, and AWS Elastic Beanstalk.

- *Function as a Service (FaaS)*—Also known as serverless architecture, despite the name, this architecture doesn't mean running specific code without a server. What it means is a way of executing functionalities in the cloud in which the vendor provides all the required servers. Serverless architecture allows us to focus only on the development of services without having to worry about scaling, provisioning, and server administration. Instead, we can solely concentrate on uploading our functions without handling any administration infrastructure.

FaaS platforms include AWS (Lambda), Google Cloud Function, and Azure functions.

- *Software as a Service (SaaS)*—Also known as software on demand, this model allows users to use a specific application without having to deploy or to maintain it. In most cases, the access is through a web browser. Everything is managed by the service provider: application, data, operating system, virtualization, servers, storage, and network. The user just hires the service and uses the software.

  SaaS platforms include Salesforce, SAP, and Google Business.

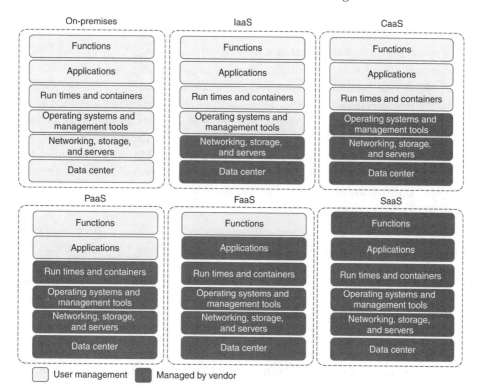

Figure 1.9　**The different cloud computing models come down to who's responsible for what: user management or cloud vendor.**

NOTE　If you're not careful, FaaS-based platforms can lock your code into a cloud vendor platform because your code is deployed to a vendor-specific runtime engine. With a FaaS-based model, you might be writing your service using a general programming language (Java, Python, JavaScript, and so on), but you're still tying yourself to the underlying vendor's APIs and runtime engine that your function will be deployed to.

1.5.3   *Why the cloud and microservices?*

One of the core concepts of a microservice architecture is that each service is packaged and deployed as its own discrete and independent artifact. Service instances should be brought up quickly, and each should be indistinguishable from another. When writing a microservice, sooner or later you're going to have to decide whether your service is going to be deployed to one of the following:

- *Physical server*—While you can build and deploy your microservices to a physical machine(s), few organizations do this because physical servers are constrained. You can't quickly ramp up the capacity of a physical server, and it can become extremely costly to scale your microservice horizontally across multiple physical servers.
- *Virtual machine images*—One of the key benefits of microservices is their ability to quickly start up and shut down instances in response to scalability and service failure events. Virtual machines (VMs) are the heart and soul of the major cloud providers.
- *Virtual container*—Virtual containers are a natural extension of deploying your microservices on a VM image. Rather than deploying a service to a full VM, many developers deploy their services as Docker containers (or equivalent container technology) to the cloud. Virtual containers run inside a VM, and using a virtual container, you can segregate a single VM into a series of self-contained processes that share the same image. A microservice can be packaged, and multiple instances of the service can then be quickly deployed and started in either an IaaS private or public cloud.

The advantage of cloud-based microservice centers around the concept of *elasticity*. Cloud service providers allow you to quickly spin up new VMs and containers in a matter of minutes. If your capacity needs for your services drop, you can spin down containers to avoid additional costs. Using a cloud provider to deploy your microservices gives you significantly more horizontal scalability (adding more servers and service instances) for your applications.

Server elasticity also means that your applications can be more resilient. If one of your microservices is having problems and is failing over, spinning up new service instances can keep your application alive long enough for your development team to gracefully resolve the issue.

For this book, all the microservices and corresponding service infrastructure will be deployed to a CaaS-based cloud provider using Docker containers. This is a common deployment topology for microservices. The most common characteristics of CaaS cloud providers are as follows:

- *Simplified infrastructure management*—CaaS cloud providers give you the ability to have more control over your services. New services can be started and stopped with simple API calls.
- *Massive horizontal scalability*—CaaS cloud providers allow you to quickly and succinctly start one or more instances of a service. This capability means you can quickly scale services and route around misbehaving or failing servers.
- *High redundancy through geographic distribution*—By necessity, CaaS providers have multiple data centers. By deploying your microservices using a CaaS cloud provider, you can gain a higher level of redundancy beyond using clusters in a data center.

Why not PaaS-based microservices?

Earlier in the chapter I discussed five types of cloud platforms—Infrastructure as a Service (IaaS), Container as a Service (CaaS), Platform as a Service (PaaS), Function as a Service (FaaS), and Software as a Service (SaaS). This book focuses specifically on building microservices using a CaaS approach. While certain cloud providers will let you abstract away the deployment infrastructure of your microservice, this book will teach you how to remain vendor independent and deploy all parts of the application (including the servers).

For instance, Cloud Foundry, AWS Elastic Beanstalk, Google App Engine, and Heroku give you the ability to deploy your services without having to know about the underlying application container. These provide a web interface and command-line interface (CLI) to allow you to deploy your application as a WAR or JAR file. Setting up and tuning the application server and the corresponding Java container are abstracted away from you. While this is convenient, each cloud provider's platform has different idiosyncrasies related to its individual PaaS solution.

The services built in this book are packaged as Docker containers; the main reason is that Docker is deployable to all major cloud providers. In later chapters, we'll see what Docker is and learn how to integrate Docker to run all the services and infrastructure used in this book.

1.6 Microservices are more than writing the code

While the concepts around building individual microservices are easy to understand, running and supporting a robust microservice application (especially when running in the cloud) involves more than just writing the code for the service. Figure 1.10 shows some guidelines to consider while writing or building a microservice.

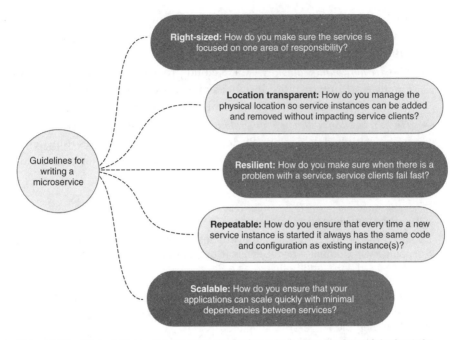

Figure 1.10 Microservices are more than the business logic. You need to think about the environment where you'll run the services and how the services will scale and be resilient.

Writing a robust service includes considering several topics. Let's walk through the items show in figure 1.10 in more detail:

- *Right-sized*—How you ensure that your microservices are properly sized so that you don't have a microservice take on too much responsibility. Remember, properly sized, a service allows you to make changes to an application quickly and reduces the overall risk of an outage to the entire application.
- *Location transparent*—How you manage the physical details of service invocation. When in a microservice application, multiple service instances can quickly start and shut down.
- *Resilient*—How you protect your microservice consumers and the overall integrity of your application by routing around failing services and ensuring that you take a "fail-fast" approach.
- *Repeatable*—How you ensure that every new instance of your service brought up is guaranteed to have the same configuration and codebase as all the other service instances in production.
- *Scalable*—How you establish a communication that minimizes the direct dependencies between your services and ensures that you can gracefully scale your microservices.

This book takes a patterns-based approach as we look at these items in more detail. With a patterns-based approach, we'll look at common designs that can be used across different technology implementations. While we've chosen to use Spring Boot and Spring Cloud to implement the patterns we're going to use in this book, nothing will keep you from taking the concepts presented here and using these with other technology platforms. Specifically, we'll cover the following microservice patterns:

- Core development pattern
- Client resiliency patterns
- Logging and tracing patterns
- Build and deployment pattern

- Routing patterns
- Security patterns
- Application metrics patterns

It's important to understand that there isn't a formal definition of how to create a microservice. In the next section, you'll see a list of common aspects you need to take into consideration while building a microservice.

1.7 *Core microservice development pattern*

The core microservice development pattern addresses the basics of building a microservice. Figure 1.11 highlights the topics we'll cover around basic service design.

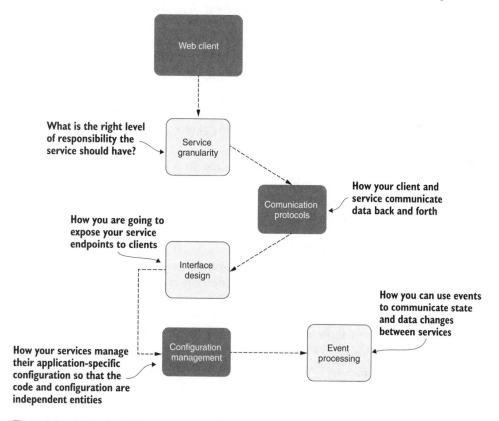

Figure 1.11 When designing your microservice, you need to think about how the service will be consumed and communicated with.

The following patterns (shown in figure 1.11) show the basics of building a microservice:

- *Service granularity*—How do you approach decomposing a business domain down into microservices so that each microservice has the right level of responsibility? Making a service too coarse-grained with responsibilities that overlap into different business-problems domains makes the service difficult to maintain and change over time. Making the service too fine-grained increases the overall complexity of the application and turns the service into a "dumb" data abstraction layer with no logic except for that needed to access the data store. Service granularity is covered in chapter 3.

- *Communication protocols*—How will developers communicate with your service? The first step is to define whether you want a synchronous or asynchronous protocol. For synchronous, the most common communication is HTTP-based REST using XML (Extensible Markup Language), JSON (JavaScript Object Notation), or a binary protocol such as Thrift to send data back and forth to your microservices. For asynchronous, the most popular protocol is AMQP (Advanced Message Queuing Protocol) using a one-to-one (queue) or a one-to-many (topic) with message brokers such as RabbitMQ, Apache Kafka, and Amazon Simple Queue Service (SQS). In later chapters, we'll learn about the communication protocols.

- *Interface design*—What's the best way to design the actual service interfaces that developers are going to use to call your service? How do you structure your services? What are the best practices? Best practices and interface design are covered in the next chapters.

- *Configuration management of service*—How do you manage the configuration of your microservice so that it moves between different environments in the cloud? This can be managed with externalized configuration and profiles as seen in chapter 5.

- *Event processing between services*—How do you decouple your microservice using events so that you minimize hardcoded dependencies between your services and increase the resiliency of your application? We'll use an event-driven architecture with Spring Cloud Stream as covered in chapter 10.

1.8   *Microservice routing patterns*

The microservice routing patterns deal with how a client application that wants to consume a microservice discovers the location of the service and is routed over to it. In a cloud-based application, it is possible to have hundreds of microservice instances running. To enforce security and content policies, it is required to abstract the physical IP address of those services and have a single point of entry for the service calls. How? The following patterns are going to answer that question:

- *Service discovery*—With service discovery and its key feature, service registry, you can make your microservice discoverable so client applications can find them without having the location of the service hardcoded into their application. How? We explain this in chapter 6. Remember the service discovery is an internal service, not a client-facing service.

Note that in this book, we use Netflix Eureka Service Discovery, but there are other service registries such as etcd, Consul, and Apache Zookeeper. Also, some systems do not have an explicit service registry. Instead these use an interservice communication infrastructure known as a *service mesh*.

- *Service routing*—With an API Gateway, you can provide a single entry point for all of your services so that security policies and routing rules are applied uniformly to multiple services and service instances in your microservices applications. How? With the Spring Cloud API Gateway, as we explain in chapter 8.

Figure 1.12 shows how service discovery and service routing appear to have a hardcoded sequence of events between them (first comes service routing and then service discovery). However, the two patterns aren't dependent on one another. For instance, we can implement service discovery without service routing, and we can implement service routing without service discovery (even though its implementation is more difficult).

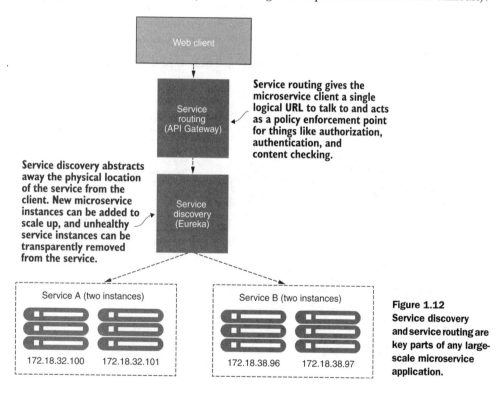

Figure 1.12 Service discovery and service routing are key parts of any large-scale microservice application.

1.9 *Microservice client resiliency*

Because microservice architectures are highly distributed, you have to be extremely sensitive in how you prevent a problem in a single service (or service instance) from cascading up and out to the consumers of the service. To this end, we'll cover four client resiliency patterns:

- *Client-side load balancing*—How you cache the location of your service instances on the service so that calls to multiple instances of a microservice are load balanced to all the health instances of that microservice.
- *Circuit breaker pattern*—How you prevent a client from continuing to call a service that's failing or suffering performance problems. When a service is running slowly, it consumes resources on the client calling it. You want these microservice calls to fail fast so that the calling client can quickly respond and take appropriate action.
- *Fallback pattern*—When a service call fails, how you provide a "plug-in" mechanism that allows the service client to try to carry out its work through alternative means other than the microservice being called.
- *Bulkhead pattern*—Microservice applications use multiple distributed resources to carry out their work. This pattern refers to how you compartmentalize these calls so that the misbehavior of one service call doesn't negatively impact the rest of the application.

Figure 1.13 shows how these patterns protect the service consumer from being impacted when a service is misbehaving. These topics are covered in chapter 7.

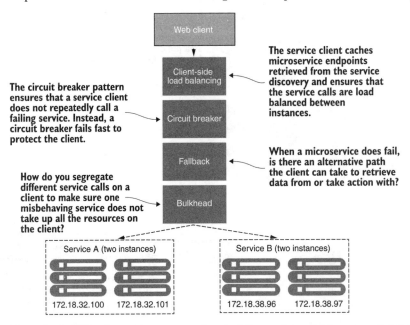

Figure 1.13   With microservices, you must protect the service caller from a poorly behaving service. Remember, a slow or down service can cause disruptions beyond the immediate service.

1.10 *Microservice security patterns*

To ensure that the microservices are not open to the public, it is important to apply the following security patterns to the architecture in order to ensure that only granted requests with proper credentials can invoke the services. Figure 1.14 shows how you can implement these three patterns to build an authentication service that can protect your microservices:

- *Authentication*—How you determine the service client calling the service is who they say they are.
- *Authorization*—How you determine whether the service client calling a microservice is allowed to undertake the action they're trying to take.
- *Credential management and propagation*—How you prevent a service client from constantly having to present their credentials for service calls involved in a transaction. To achieve this, we'll look at how you can use token-based security standards such as OAuth2 and JSON Web Tokens (JWT) to obtain a token that can be passed from service call to service call to authenticate and authorize the user.

What is OAuth 2.0?

OAuth2 is a token-based security framework that allows a user to authenticate themselves with a third-party authentication service. If the user successfully authenticates, they will be presented with a token that *must* be sent with every request.

The main goal behind OAuth2 is that when multiple services are called to fulfill a user's request, the user can be authenticated by each service without having to present their credentials to each service processing their request. While OAuth is covered in chapter 9, it's worthwhile to read the OAuth 2.0 documentation by Aaron Parecki (https://www.oauth.com/).

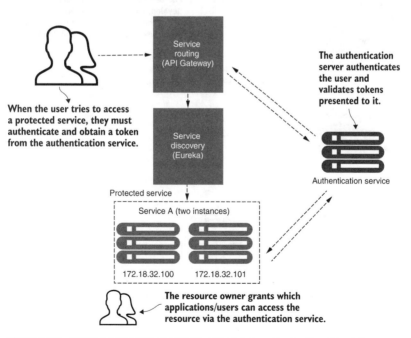

Figure 1.14 Using a token-based security scheme, you can implement service authentication and authorization without passing around client credentials.

1.11   *Microservice logging and tracing patterns*

The downside of a microservice architecture is that it's much more difficult to debug, trace, and monitor the issues because one simple action can trigger numerous microservice calls within your application. Further chapters will cover how to implement distributed tracing with Spring Cloud Sleuth, Zipkin, and the ELK Stack. For this reason, we'll look at the following three core logging and tracing patterns to achieve distributed tracing:

- *Log correlation*—How you tie together all the logs produced between services for a single user transaction. With this pattern, we'll look at how to implement a correlation ID, which is a unique identifier that's carried across all service calls in a transaction and that can be used to tie together log entries produced from each service.
- *Log aggregation*—With this pattern, we'll look at how to pull together all of the logs produced by your microservices (and their individual instances) into a single queryable database across all the services involved and understand the performance characteristics of the services in the transaction.
- *Microservice tracing*—We'll explore how to visualize the flow of a client transaction across all the services involved and understand the performance characteristics of the transaction's services.

Figure 1.15 shows how these patterns fit together. We'll cover the logging and tracing patterns in greater detail in chapter 11.

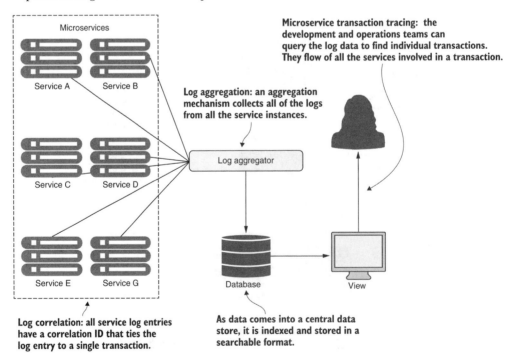

Figure 1.15   A well-thought-out logging and tracing strategy makes debugging transactions across multiple services manageable.

1.12   *Application metrics pattern*

The application metrics pattern deals with how the application is going to monitor metrics and warn of possible causes of failure within our applications. This pattern shows how the metrics service is responsible for getting (scraping), storing, and querying business-related data in order to prevent potential performance issues in our services. This pattern contains the following three main components:

- *Metrics*—How you create critical information about the health of your application and how to expose those metrics
- *Metrics service*—Where you can store and query the application metrics
- *Metrics visualization suite*—Where you can visualize business-related time data for the application and infrastructure

Figure 1.16 shows how the metrics generated by the microservices are highly dependent on the metrics service and the visualization suite. It would be useless to have metrics that generate and show infinite information if there is no way to understand and analyze that information. The metrics service can obtain the metrics using the pull or push style:

- With the push style, the service instance invokes a service API exposed by the metrics service in order to send the application data.
- With the pull style, the metrics service asks or queries a function to fetch the application data.

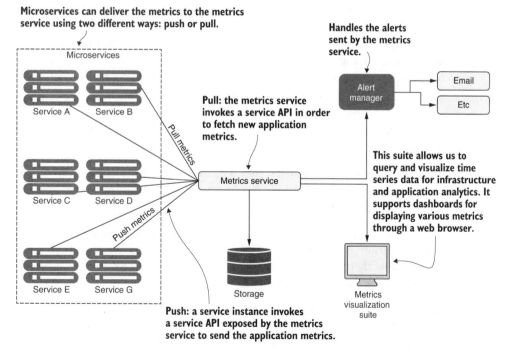

Figure 1.16   Metrics are pulled or pushed from the microservices and collected and stored in the metrics service to be shown using a metrics visualization suite and an alert management tool.

It's important to understand that monitoring metrics is an essential aspect of the micro-services architectures and that the monitoring requirements in these kinds of architec-tures tend to be higher than monolithic structures due to their high distribution.

1.13 *Microservice build/deployment patterns*

One of the core parts of a microservice architecture is that each instance of a micro-service should be identical to all its other instances. You can't allow *configuration drift* (something changes on a server after it's been deployed) to occur because this can introduce instability in your applications.

The goal with this pattern is to integrate the configuration of your infrastructure right into your build/deployment process so that you no longer deploy software arti-facts such as Java WAR or EAR files to an already running piece of infrastructure. Instead, you want to build and compile your microservice and the virtual server image it's running on as part of the build process. Then, when your microservice gets deployed, the entire machine image with the server running on it gets deployed. Figure 1.17 illustrates this process. At the end of the book, we'll look at how to create your build/deployment pipeline. In chapter 12, we cover the following patterns and topics:

- *Build and deployment pipelines*—How you create a repeatable build and deploy-ment process that emphasizes one-button builds and deployment to any envi-ronment in your organization.
- *Infrastructure as code*—How you treat the provisioning of your services as code that can be executed and managed under source control.
- *Immutable servers*—Once a microservice image is created, how you ensure that it's never changed after it has been deployed.
- *Phoenix servers*—How you ensure that servers that run individual containers get torn down on a regular basis and re-created from an immutable image. The longer a server is running, the more opportunity there is for configuration drift. A configuration drift can occur when ad hoc changes to a system configu-ration are unrecorded.

Our goal with these patterns and topics is to ruthlessly expose and stamp out configu-ration drift as quickly as possible before it can hit your upper environments (stage or production).

> **NOTE** For the code examples in this book (except in chapter 12), everything will run locally on your desktop machine. The first chapters can be run natively directly from the command line. Starting in chapter 3, all the code will be compiled and run as Docker containers.

Now that we've covered the patterns that we will use throughout the book, let's continue with the second chapter. In the next chapter, we'll cover the Spring Cloud technologies that we will use, some best practices for designing a cloud microservice–oriented application, and the first steps to creating our first microservice using Spring Boot and Java.

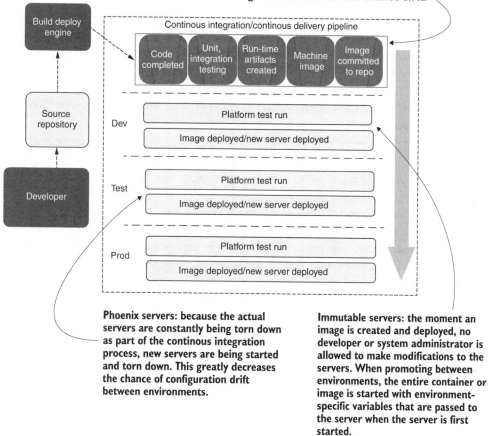

Figure 1.17 You want the deployment of the microservice and the server it's running on to be one atomic artifact that's deployed as a whole between environments.

Summary

- Monolithic architectures have all processes tightly coupled, and these run as a single service.
- Microservices are extremely small pieces of functionality responsible for one specific area of scope.
- Spring Boot allows you to create both types of architectures.
- Monolithic architectures tend to be ideal for simple, lightweight applications, and microservices architectures are usually better for developing complex and

evolving applications. In the end, selecting the software architecture depends entirely on your project size, time, and requirements, among other factors.

- Spring Boot simplifies the building of REST-based/JSON microservices. Its goal is to make it possible for you to build microservices quickly with nothing more than a few annotations.

- Writing microservices is easy, but fully operationalizing these for production requires additional forethought. There are several categories of microservice development patterns, including core development, routing patterns, client resiliency, security, application metrics, and build/deployment patterns.

- The microservice routing patterns deal with how a client application that wants to consume a microservice discovers the location of the service and is routed over to it.

- To prevent a problem in a service instance from cascading up and out to the consumers of the service, use the client resiliency patterns. These include the circuit breaker pattern to avoid making calls to a failing service, the fallback pattern to create alternative paths in order to retrieve data or execute a specific action when a service fails, the client load-balancing pattern to scale and remove all possible bottlenecks or points of failure scenarios, and the bulkhead pattern to limit the number of concurrent calls to a service in order to stop poor performance calls negatively affecting other services.

- OAuth 2.0 is the most common user authorization protocol and is an excellent choice for securing a microservice architecture.

- The build/deployment pattern allows you to integrate the configuration of your infrastructure right into your build/deployment process so that you no longer deploy software artifacts such as Java WAR or EAR files to an already running piece of infrastructure.

Exploring
the microservices world
with Spring Cloud

2

This chapter covers

- Learning about Spring Cloud's technologies
- Understanding the principles of cloud-native applications
- Applying the twelve-factor app best practices
- Using Spring Cloud to build microservices

Designing, implementing, and maintaining microservices quickly become a problem if these processes are not managed correctly. When we start working with microservice solutions, it is essential to apply *best practices* to keep the architecture as efficient and scalable as possible to avoid performance issues, bottlenecks, or operational problems. Adhering to best practices also makes it easier for new developers to come up to speed with our systems. As we continue our discussion of microservices architectures, it's important to keep the following in mind:

The more distributed a system is, the more places it can fail.

By this we mean that with a microservice architecture, we have more points of failure. That's because instead of having a single monolith application, we now have an ecosystem of multiple individual services that interact with each other. This is the main reason why developers often encounter different administration and synchronization challenges or points of failure when creating microservice applications or architectures. To avoid possible points of failure, we will use Spring Cloud. Spring Cloud offers a set of features (service registration and discovery, circuit breakers, monitoring, and others) that will allow us to quickly build microservice architectures with minimal configurations.

This chapter briefly introduces the Spring Cloud technologies that we will use throughout this book. This is a high-level overview; as you use the different technologies, we'll give you the details on each as needed. Because we will use microservices throughout the next chapters, it is crucial to understand the concept of microservices, their benefits, and their development patterns.

2.1 *What is Spring Cloud?*

Implementing all of the patterns we explained in the first chapter from scratch would be a tremendous amount of work. Fortunately, for us, the Spring team has integrated a wide number of battle-tested open source projects into a single Spring subproject collectively known as Spring Cloud (https://projects.spring.io/spring-cloud/).

Spring Cloud is a collection of tools that wraps the work of open source companies such as VMware, HashiCorp, and Netflix in delivery patterns. Spring Cloud simplifies setting up and configuring our projects and provides solutions to the most commonly encountered patterns into our Spring application. We can then focus on writing code, not on getting buried in the details of configuring all the infrastructure that goes into building and deploying a microservice application. Figure 2.1 maps the patterns listed in the previous chapter to the Spring Cloud projects that implement them.

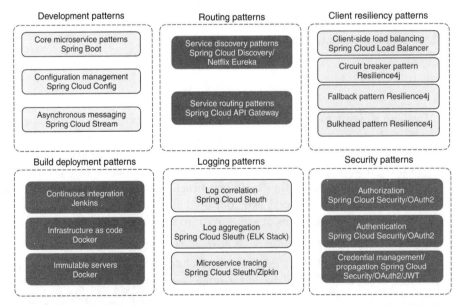

Figure 2.1 With Spring Cloud, we can map the technologies we're going to use directly to the microservice patterns we've explored so far.

2.1.1 Spring Cloud Config

Spring Cloud Config handles the management of the application configuration data through a centralized service. Your application configuration data (particularly your environment-specific configuration data) is then cleanly separated from your deployed microservice. This ensures that no matter how many microservice instances you bring up, they'll always have the same configuration. Spring Cloud Config has its own property management repository but also integrates with open source projects like these:

- *Git* (https://git-scm.com/)—An open source version control system that lets you manage and track changes to any text file. Spring Cloud Config integrates with a Git backend repository and reads the application's configuration data from the repository.
- *Consul* (https://www.consul.io/)—An open source service discovery that allows service instances to register themselves with a service. Service clients can then query Consul to find the location of their service instances. Consul also includes a key-value store database that Spring Cloud Config uses to store application configuration data.
- *Eureka* (https://github.com/Netflix/eureka)—An open source Netflix project that, like Consul, offers similar service discovery capabilities. Eureka also has a key-value database that can be used with Spring Cloud Config.

2.1.2 Spring Cloud Service Discovery

With Spring Cloud Service Discovery, you can abstract away the physical location (IP and/or server name) of where your servers are deployed from the clients consuming the service. Service consumers invoke business logic for the servers through a logical name rather than a physical location. Spring Cloud Service Discovery also handles the registration and deregistration of service instances as these are started and shut down. Spring Cloud Service Discovery can be implemented using the following services:

- Consul (https:// www.consul.io/)
- Zookeeper (https://spring.io/projects/spring-cloud-zookeeper)
- Eureka (https://github.com/Netflix/eureka) as its service discovery engine

NOTE Although Consul and Zookeeper are powerful and flexible, the Java developer community still uses Eureka. This book contains examples with Eureka to keep it manageable and material focused, and to reach the largest audience possible. If you're interested in Consul or Zookeeper, make sure you read appendixes C and D. In appendix C, we added an example of how we can use Consul as a service discovery, and in appendix D, we added an example of how to use Zookeeper.

2.1.3 Spring Cloud LoadBalancer and Resilience4j

Spring Cloud integrates heavily with several open source projects. For microservice client resiliency patterns, Spring Cloud wraps the Resilience4j library and the Spring Cloud

LoadBalancer project to make using these within your own microservices trivial to implement. You'll find the Resilience4j library here: https://github.com/resilience4j/resilience4j. By using the Resilience4j libraries, you can quickly implement service client resiliency patterns such as circuit breaker, retry, bulkhead, and more.

While the Spring Cloud LoadBalancer project simplifies integrating with service discovery agents such as Eureka, it also provides client-side load balancing of calls from a service consumer. This makes it possible for a client to continue making service calls even if the service discovery agent is temporarily unavailable.

2.1.4 Spring Cloud API Gateway

The API Gateway provides service-routing capabilities for your microservice application. Like the name says, it is a service gateway that proxies service requests and makes sure that all calls to your microservices go through a single "front door" before the targeted service is invoked. With this centralization of service calls, you can enforce standard service policies such as security authorization, authentication, content filtering, and routing rules. You can implement the API Gateway using Spring Cloud Gateway (https://spring.io/projects/spring-cloud-gateway).

> **NOTE** In this book, we use the Spring Cloud API Gateway that was built with Spring Framework 5 Project Reactor (allowing integration with Spring Web Flux) and Spring Boot 2 to better integrate our Spring projects.

2.1.5 Spring Cloud Stream

Spring Cloud Stream (https://cloud.spring.io/spring-cloud-stream) is an enabling technology that lets you easily integrate lightweight message processing into your microservice. Using Spring Cloud Stream, you can build intelligent microservices that use asynchronous events as these occur in your application. You can also quickly integrate your microservices with message brokers such as RabbitMQ (https://www.rabbitmq.com) and Kafka (http://kafka.apache.org).

2.1.6 Spring Cloud Sleuth

Spring Cloud Sleuth (https://cloud.spring.io/spring-cloud-sleuth/) lets you integrate unique tracking identifiers into the HTTP calls and message channels (RabbitMQ, Apache Kafka) used within your application. These tracking numbers, sometimes referred to as correlation or trace IDs, allow you to track a transaction as it flows across the different services in your application. With Spring Cloud Sleuth, trace IDs are automatically added to any logging statements you make in your microservice.

The real beauty of Spring Cloud Sleuth is seen when it's combined with logging-aggregation technology tools like the ELK Stack (https://www.elastic.co/what-is/elk-stack) and tracking tools like Zipkin (http://zipkin.io). Open Zipkin takes data produced by Spring Cloud Sleuth and allows you to visualize the flow of your service calls involved for a single transaction. The ELK Stack is the acronym for three open source projects:

- Elasticsearch (https://www.elastic.co) is a search and analytics engine.
- Logstash (https://www.elastic.co/products/logstash) is a server-side, data-processing pipeline that consumes data and then transforms it in order to send it to a "stash."
- Kibana (https://www.elastic.co/products/kibana) is a client UI that allows the user to query and visualize the data of the whole stack.

2.1.7 Spring Cloud Security

Spring Cloud Security (https://cloud.spring.io/spring-cloud-security/) is an authentication and authorization framework that controls who can access your services and what they can do with them. Because Spring Cloud Security is token-based, it allows services to communicate with one another through a token issued by an authentication server. Each service receiving an HTTP call can check the provided token to validate the user's identity and their access rights. Spring Cloud Security also supports JSON Web Tokens (JWT). JWT (https://jwt.io) standardizes the format for creating an OAuth2 token and normalizes digital signatures for a generated token.

2.2 Spring Cloud by example

In the last section, we explained all the different Spring Cloud technologies that you're going to use to build your microservices. Because each of these technologies is an independent service, it will take more than one chapter to explain all of the details. However, as we wrap up this chapter, we want to leave you with a small code example that again demonstrates how easy it is to integrate these technologies into your own microservice developments.

Unlike the first code example in listing 1.1, you can't run this example because we first need to set up and configure a number of supporting services. Don't worry though; the setup costs for these Spring Cloud services are a one-time expense. Once they're set up, your individual microservices can use these capabilities over and over again. We couldn't fit all that goodness into a single code example at the beginning of the book. The following listing quickly demonstrates how we can integrate service discovery and client-side load balancing for remote services in our Hello World example.

Listing 2.1 Hello World service using Spring Cloud

```
package com.optima.growth.simpleservice;

import org.springframework.boot.SpringApplication;
import org.springframework.boot.autoconfigure.SpringBootApplication;
import org.springframework.cloud.netflix.eureka.EnableEurekaClient;
import org.springframework.http.HttpMethod;
import org.springframework.http.ResponseEntity;
import org.springframework.web.bind.annotation.PathVariable;
import org.springframework.web.bind.annotation.RequestMapping;
import org.springframework.web.bind.annotation.RequestMethod;
import org.springframework.web.bind.annotation.RestController;
```

```java
import org.springframework.web.client.RestTemplate;

@SpringBootApplication
@RestController
@RequestMapping(value="hello")
@EnableEurekaClient
public class Application {

    public static void main(String[] args) {
        SpringApplication.run(ContactServerAppApplication.class, args);
    }

    public String helloRemoteServiceCall(String firstName,String lastName){
        RestTemplate restTemplate = new RestTemplate();
        ResponseEntity<String> restExchange =
            restTemplate.exchange(
                "http://logical-service-id/name/" + "{firstName}/
                {lastName}", HttpMethod.GET, null, String.class,
        firstName, lastName);
        return restExchange.getBody();
    }

    @RequestMapping(value="/{firstName}/{lastName}",
                    method = RequestMethod.GET)
    public String hello(@PathVariable("firstName") String firstName,
                        @PathVariable("lastName") String lastName) {
        return helloRemoteServiceCall(firstName, lastName);
    }
}
```

Tells the service to register with a Eureka service discovery agent to look up the location of remote services

Uses a decorated RestTemplate class to take a "logical" service ID, and Eureka under the covers will look up the service's physical location

This code has a lot packed into it, so let's walk through it. Keep in mind that this listing is only an example and isn't found in the chapter 2 GitHub repository source code. We've included it here to give you a taste of what's to come later in the book.

The first thing to notice is the @EnableEurekaClient annotation. This annotation tells your microservice to register itself with a Eureka service discovery agent because you're going to use service discovery to look up remote REST service endpoints. Note that the configuration happens in a property file, giving the simple service the location and port number of a Eureka server to contact.

The second thing to notice is what's occurring inside the helloRemoteService-Call method. The @EnableEurekaClient annotation tells Spring Boot that you are enabling the Eureka client. It is important to highlight that this annotation is optional if you already have the spring-cloud-starter-netflix-eureka-client dependency in your pom.xml. The RestTemplate class lets you pass in a logical service ID for the service you're trying to invoke, for example:

```
ResponseEntity<String> restExchange = restTemplate.exchange
    (http://logical-service-id/name/{firstName}/{lastName}
```

Under the covers, the RestTemplate class contacts the Eureka service and looks up the physical location of one or more of the named service instances. As a consumer of the service, your code doesn't need to know where that service is located.

The RestTemplate class also uses the Spring Cloud LoadBalancer library. This library retrieves a list of all the physical endpoints associated with a service. Every time the service is called by the client, it "round-robins" the call to different service instances without having to go through a centralized load balancer. By eliminating a centralized load balancer and moving it to the client, you eliminate another failure point (the load balancer going down) in your application infrastructure.

We hope that you're impressed now: you've added a significant number of capabilities to your microservice with only a few annotations. That's the real beauty behind Spring Cloud. You, as a developer, get to take advantage of battle-hardened microservice capabilities from premier cloud companies like Netflix and Consul. Spring Cloud simplifies their use to literally nothing more than a few simple annotations and configuration entries. Before we start building our first microservice, let's look at the best practices for implementing a cloud-native microservice.

2.3 *How to build a cloud-native microservice*

In this section, we pause to understand the best practices for designing cloud microservice applications. In the previous chapter, we explained the difference between the cloud computing models, but what exactly is the cloud? The cloud is not a place; instead, it is a technology resource management system that lets you replace local machines and private data centers by using a virtual infrastructure. There are several levels or types of cloud applications, but in this section, we only focus on two types of cloud applications—cloud-ready and cloud-native.

A *cloud-ready* application is an application that was once used on a computer or on an onsite server. With the arrival of the cloud, these types of applications have moved from static to dynamic environments with the aim of running in the cloud. For example, a cloud-unready application could be a local on-premises application that only contains one specific database configuration, which must be customized in each installation environment (development, stage, production). In order to make an application like this cloud-ready, we need to externalize the application's configuration so that it quickly adapts to different environments. By doing this, we can ensure the application will run on multiple environments without changing any source code during the builds.

A *cloud-native* application (figure 2.2) is designed specifically for a cloud computing architecture to take advantage of all of its benefits and services. When creating this type of application, developers divide the functions into microservices with scalable components like containers, enabling these to run on several servers. These services are then managed by virtual infrastructures through the DevOps processes with continuous delivery workflows.

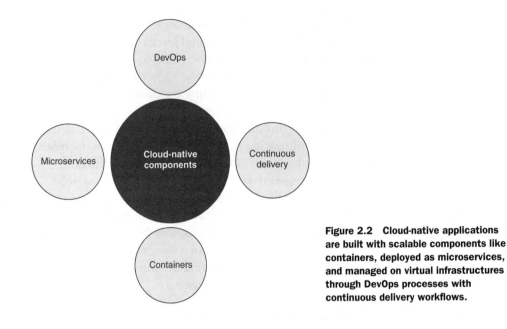

Figure 2.2   Cloud-native applications are built with scalable components like containers, deployed as microservices, and managed on virtual infrastructures through DevOps processes with continuous delivery workflows.

It's important to understand that cloud-ready applications do *not* require any change or conversion to work in the cloud. They are designed to deal with the unavailability of downstream components. The four principles of native cloud development are

- *DevOps is the acronym for development (Dev) and operations (Ops)*. It refers to a software development methodology that focuses on communication, collaboration, and integration among software developers and IT operations. The main goal is to automate the software delivery processes and infrastructure changes at lower costs.
- *Microservices are small, loosely coupled, distributed services*. These allow you to take a large application and decompose it into easy-to-manage components with narrowly defined responsibilities. They also help combat the traditional problems of complexity in a large codebase by decomposing it down into small, well-defined pieces.
- *Continuous delivery is a software development practice*. With this practice, the process of delivering software is automated to allow short-term deliveries to a production environment.
- *Containers are a natural extension of deploying your microservices on a virtual machine (VM) image*. Rather than deploying a service to a full VM, many developers deploy their services as Docker containers (or similar container technology) to the cloud.

In this book, because we'll focus on creating microservices, we should remember that, by definition, these are cloud-native. This means that a microservice application can be executed on multiple cloud providers while obtaining all of the benefits of the cloud services.

In order to face the challenges of creating cloud-native microservices, we will use Heroku's best practice guide—called *the twelve-factor app*—in order to build high-quality microservices. The twelve-factor app (https://12factor.net/) enables us to build and develop cloud-native applications (microservices). We can see this methodology as a collection of development and designing practices that focus on dynamic scaling and fundamental points while building a distributed service.

This methodology was created in 2002 by several Heroku developers. The main goal was to provide 12 best practices when building microservices. We chose the twelve-factor document because it is one of the most complete guides to follow when creating cloud-native applications. This guide not only provides a common vocabulary about the most common problems observed in the development of modern applications, it also offers robust solutions to tackle these problems. Figure 2.3 shows the best practices covered by the twelve-factor manifesto.

NOTE In this chapter, we will give you a high-level overview of each best practice because, as you continue reading, you'll see how we intend to use the twelve-factor methodology throughout. Further, we'll apply those practices to examples with the Spring Cloud projects and other technologies.

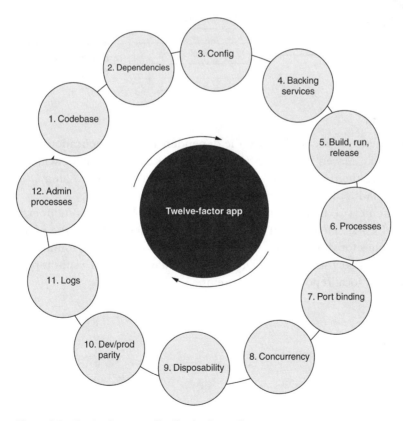

Figure 2.3　Twelve-factor application best practices

2.3.1   *Codebase*

With this practice, each microservice should have a single, source-controlled codebase. Also, it is essential to highlight that the server provisioning information should be in version control as well. Remember, *version control* is the management of changes to a file or set of files.

The codebase can have multiple instances of deployment environments (such as development, testing, staging, production, and so forth), but it's not shared with any other microservice. This is an important guideline because if we share the codebase for all the microservices, we would end up producing a lot of immutable releases that belong to different environments. Figure 2.4 shows a single codebase with many deployments.

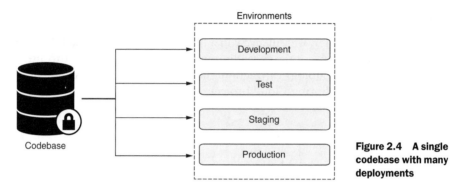

Figure 2.4   A single codebase with many deployments

2.3.2   *Dependencies*

This best practice explicitly declares the dependencies your application uses through build tools like Maven or Gradle (Java). Third-party JAR dependencies should be declared using their specific version numbers. This allows you to always build your microservices with the same library version.

If you are new to the build tools concept, figure 2.5 can help you understand how a build tool works. First, Maven reads the dependencies stored in the pom.xml file, then it searches for those on the local repository. If these are not found, then it proceeds to download the dependencies from the Maven central repository, inserting those into your local repository for future use.

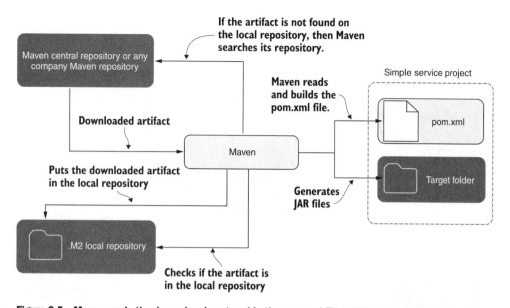

Figure 2.5   Maven reads the dependencies stored in the pom.xml file and then searches for them in a local repository. If the dependencies are not found, then Maven downloads the dependencies from the Maven repository, inserting them into your local repository.

2.3.3   Config

This practice refers to how you store your application configurations (especially your environment-specific configurations). Never add embedded configurations to your source code! Instead, it's best to maintain your configuration completely separate from your deployable microservice.

Imagine this scenario: you want to update a configuration for a specific microservice that has been replicated 100 times on a server. If you keep the configuration packaged within the microservice, you'll need to redeploy each of the 100 instances to make the change. However, microservices can load the external configuration and use a cloud service to reload that configuration at run time without having to restart the microservice. Figure 2.6 shows an example of how your environment should look.

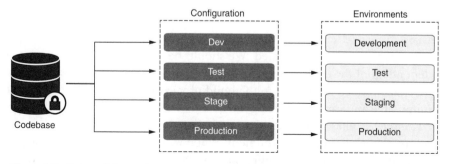

Figure 2.6   Externalizing environment-specific configurations

2.3.4   *Backing services*

Your microservice will often communicate over a network with databases, API RESTful services, other servers, or messaging systems. When it does, you should ensure that you can swap your deployment implementations between local and third-party connections without any changes to the application code. In chapter 12, we'll see how to move the microservices from a locally managed database to one managed by Amazon. Figure 2.7 shows an example of some backing services that our applications might have.

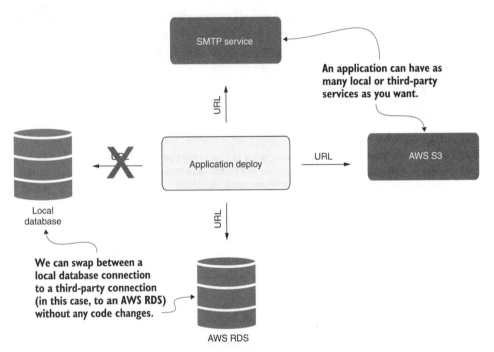

Figure 2.7   A backing service is any service that the application consumes over the network. When deploying the application, you should be able to swap a local connection to a third-party without any changes to the code.

2.3.5   *Build, release, run*

This best practice reminds us to keep our build, release, and run stages of application deployment completely separated. We should be able to build microservices that are independent of the environment on which they run. Once our code is built, any runtime changes need to go back to the build process and be redeployed. A built service is immutable and cannot be changed.

The release phase is in charge of combining the built service with a specific configuration for each targeted environment. When we do not separate the different stages, this can lead to problems and differences in the code that are not traceable or, at best, are hard to trace. For example, if we modify a service already deployed in production, the change will not be logged in the repository, and two situations can occur: changes get lost with newer versions of the service or we are forced to copy the changes to the new version of the service. Figure 2.8 shows a high-level architectural example for this best practice.

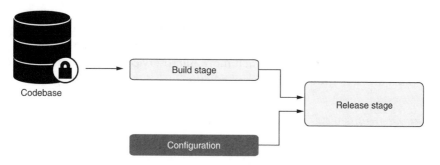

Figure 2.8 **It's in our best practice to strictly separate the build, release, and run stages of the microservice.**

2.3.6 *Processes*

Your microservices should always be stateless and should only contain the necessary information to carry out the requested transaction. Microservices can be killed and replaced at any time without the fear that a loss of a service instance will result in data loss. If there is a specific requirement to store a state, it must be done through an in-memory cache such as Redis or a backing database. Figure 2.9 shows how stateless microservices work.

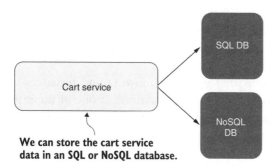

We can store the cart service data in an **SQL** or **NoSQL** database.

Figure 2.9 **Stateless microservices don't store any session data (state) on the server. These services use SQL or NoSQL databases to store all the information.**

2.3.7 *Port binding*

Port binding means to publish services through a specific port. In a microservices architecture, a microservice is completely self-contained with the run-time engine for the service packaged in the service executable. You should run the service without the need for a separate web or application server. The service should start by itself on the command line and be accessed immediately through an exposed HTTP port.

2.3.8 Concurrency

The concurrency best practice explains that cloud-native applications should scale out using the process model. What does this mean? Let's imagine, rather than making a single significant process larger, we can create multiple processes and then distribute the service's load or application among different processes.

Vertical scaling (scale up) refers to increasing the hardware infrastructure (CPU, RAM). Horizontal scaling (scale out) refers to adding more instances of the application. When you need to scale, launch more microservice instances and scale out and not up. Figure 2.10 shows the difference between both types of scaling.

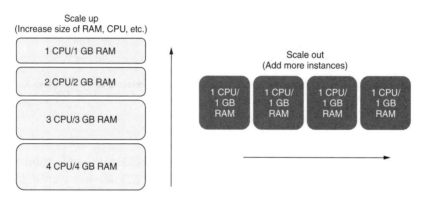

Figure 2.10 **Differences between scaling up and scaling out**

2.3.9 Disposability

Microservices are disposable and can start and stop on demand in order to facilitate elastic scaling and to quickly deploy application code and configuration changes. Ideally, startup should last a few seconds from the moment the launch command executes until the process is ready to receive requests.

What we mean by disposable is that we can remove failing instances with new instances without affecting any other services. For example, if one of the instances of the microservice is failing because of a failure in the underlying hardware, we can shut down that instance without affecting other microservices and start another one somewhere else if needed.

2.3.10 Dev/prod parity

This best practice refers to having different environments (for example, development, staging, production) as analogous as possible. The environments should always contain similar versions of deployed code, as well as the infrastructure and services. This can be done with continuous deployment, which automates the deployment process as much as possible, allowing a microservice to be deployed between environments in short periods of time.

As soon as code is committed, it should be tested and then promoted as quickly as possible from development all the way to production. This guideline is essential if we want to avoid deployment errors. Having similar development and production environments allows us to control all the possible scenarios we might have while deploying and executing our application.

2.3.11 Logs

Logs are a stream of events. As these are written, logs should be managed by tools such as Logstash (https://www.elastic.co/logstash) or Fluentd (https://www.fluentd.org/), which collect the logs and write those to a central location. The microservice should never be concerned about the mechanisms of how this happens. It only needs to focus on writing the log entries into the standard output (stdout).

In chapter 11, we will demonstrate how to provide an autoconfiguration for sending these logs to the ELK Stack (Elasticsearch, Logstash, and Kibana). Figure 2.11 shows how logging works in a microservice architecture using this stack.

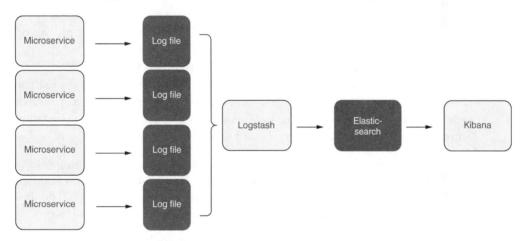

Figure 2.11   Managing the microservice logs with the ELK architecture

2.3.12 Admin processes

Developers will often have to do administrative tasks for their services (data migration or conversion, for example). These tasks should never be ad hoc and instead should be done via scripts that are managed and maintained through a source code repository. The scripts should be repeatable and non-changing (the script code isn't modified for each environment) across each environment they're run against. It's important to have defined the types of tasks we need to take into consideration while running our microservice, so that if we have multiple microservices with these scripts, we are able to execute all of the administrative tasks without having to do this manually.

> **NOTE** If you're interested in reading more about Heroku's twelve-factor manifesto, visit the twelve-factor app website (https://12factor.net/).

In chapter 8, we will explain how to implement these features using the Spring Cloud API Gateway. Now that we have seen what the best practices are, we can continue with the next section, where we'll start building our first microservice with Spring Boot and Spring Cloud.

2.4   *Making sure our examples are relevant*

We want to make sure this book provides examples that you can relate to as you go about your day-to-day job. To this end, we've structured the chapters in this book and the corresponding code examples around a software product of a fictitious company called Optima Growth.

Optima Growth is a software development company whose core product, Optima Stock (that we'll refer to as O-stock), provides an enterprise-grade asset management application. It furnishes coverage for all the critical elements: inventory, software delivery, license management, compliance, cost, and resource management. Its primary goal is to enable organizations to gain an accurate point-in-time picture of their software assets. The company is approximately 12 years old.

The company wants to rebuild their core product, O-stock. While much of the business logic for the application will remain in place, the application itself will be broken down from a monolithic architecture to a much smaller microservice design, whose pieces can be deployed independently to the cloud. The replatforming involved with O-stock can be a "make or break" moment for the company.

> **NOTE** The examples in this book won't build the entire O-stock application. Instead, we'll build specific microservices from the problem domain at hand and then create the infrastructure that will support these services. We'll do this by using various Spring Cloud (and some non–Spring Cloud) technologies.

The ability to successfully adopt a cloud-based microservice architecture will impact all parts of the technical organization, including the architecture, engineering (development), and operations teams. Input will be needed from each group and, in the end, these groups are probably going to need reorganization as the team reevaluates their responsibilities in this new environment. Let's start our journey with Optima Growth as we begin the fundamental work of identifying and building several of the microservices used in O-stock. Then we'll build these services using Spring Boot.

> **NOTE** We understand that the architecture of an asset management system is complex. Therefore, in this book, we will only use some of its basic concepts, focusing on creating a complete microservice architecture with a simple system as an example. Creating a complete software asset management application is beyond the scope of this book.

2.5   Building a microservice with Spring Boot and Java

In this section, we will build the skeleton of a microservice called *licensing service* for the Optima Growth company mentioned in the previous section. We'll create all of the microservices using Spring Boot.

Spring Boot, as previously mentioned, is an abstraction layer over the Spring libraries that allows us to quickly build Groovy- and Java-based web applications and microservices with significantly less ceremony and configuration than in a full-blown Spring application. For the licensing service example, we'll use Java as our core programming language and Apache Maven as our build tool. Over the next sections, we will

1 Create the basic skeleton of the microservice and a Maven script to build the application
2 Implement a Spring bootstrap class that will start the Spring container for the microservice and initiate the kick-off of any initialization work for the class

2.5.1   Setting up the environment

To start building our microservices, you should have the following components:

- Java 11 (http://mng.bz/ZP4m)
- Maven 3.5.4 or later (https://maven.apache.org/download.cgi)
- Spring Tools 4 (https://spring.io/tools) or you can download it within your selected Integrated Development Environment (IDE)
- IDEs such as
  - Eclipse (https://www.eclipse.org/downloads/)
  - IntelliJ IDEA (https://www.jetbrains.com/idea/download/)
  - NetBeans (https://netbeans.org/features/index.html)

NOTE All of the code listings from now on will be created using Spring Framework 5 and Spring Boot 2. It is important to understand that we're not going to explain all the features of Spring Boot, we're just going to highlight the essential ones in order to create the microservice. Another important fact is that we'll use Java 11 in this book in order to reach the largest audience possible.

2.5.2   Getting started with the skeleton project

To begin, you'll create a skeleton project for O-stock's licensing service using Spring Initializr. Spring Initializr (https://start.spring.io/) enables you to create a new Spring Boot project with the possibility of choosing dependencies from an extensive list. Also, it allows you to change specific project configurations that you are about to create. Figures 2.12 and 2.13 show how the Spring Initializr page should look like for the licensing service.

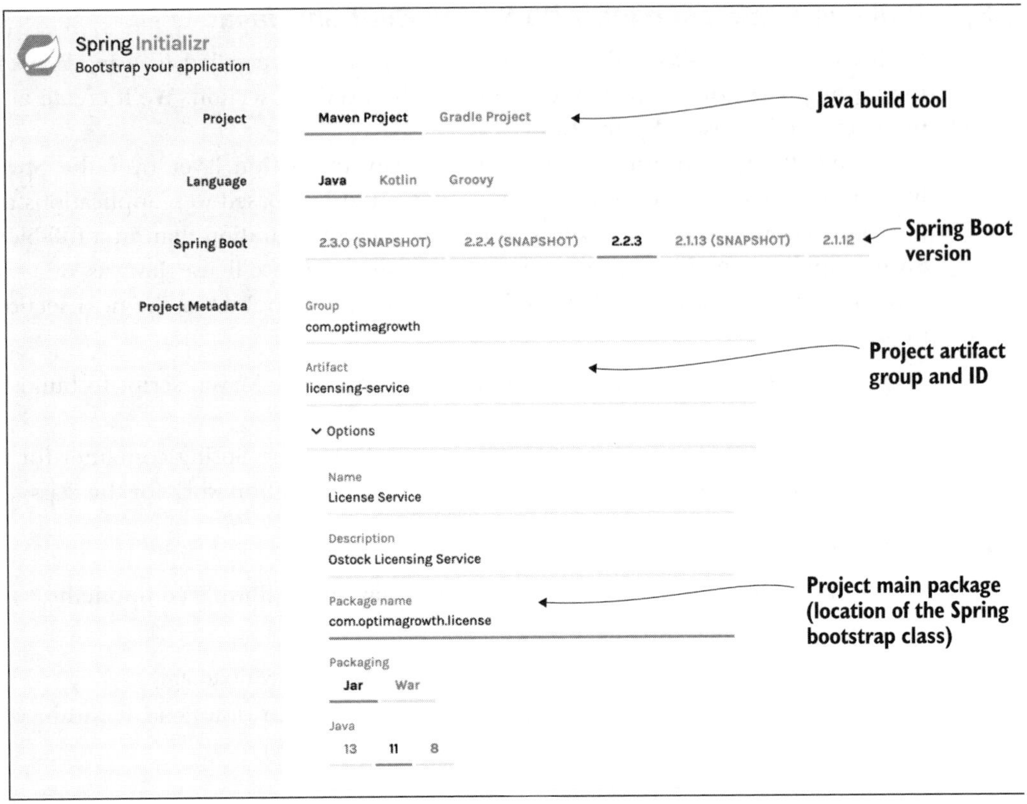

Spring Initializr
Bootstrap your application

Project	**Maven Project** Gradle Project	← Java build tool
Language	**Java** Kotlin Groovy	
Spring Boot	2.3.0 (SNAPSHOT) 2.2.4 (SNAPSHOT) **2.2.3** 2.1.13 (SNAPSHOT) 2.1.12	← **Spring Boot version**

Project Metadata

Group
com.optimagrowth

Artifact
licensing-service   ← **Project artifact group and ID**

⌄ Options

   Name
   License Service

   Description
   Ostock Licensing Service

   Package name
   com.optimagrowth.license   ← **Project main package (location of the Spring bootstrap class)**

   Packaging
   Jar   War

   Java
   13   **11**   8

Figure 2.12   Spring Initializr dependencies for the licensing service

Dependencies   🔍 ☰   **2 selected**

Search dependencies to add

Web, Security, JPA, Actuator, Devtools...

Selected dependencies

Spring Web
Build web, including RESTful, applications
using Spring MVC. Uses Apache Tomcat as the   ✓
default embedded container.

Spring Boot Actuator
Supports built in (or custom) endpoints that let
you monitor and manage your application -   ✓
such as application health, metrics, sessions,
etc.

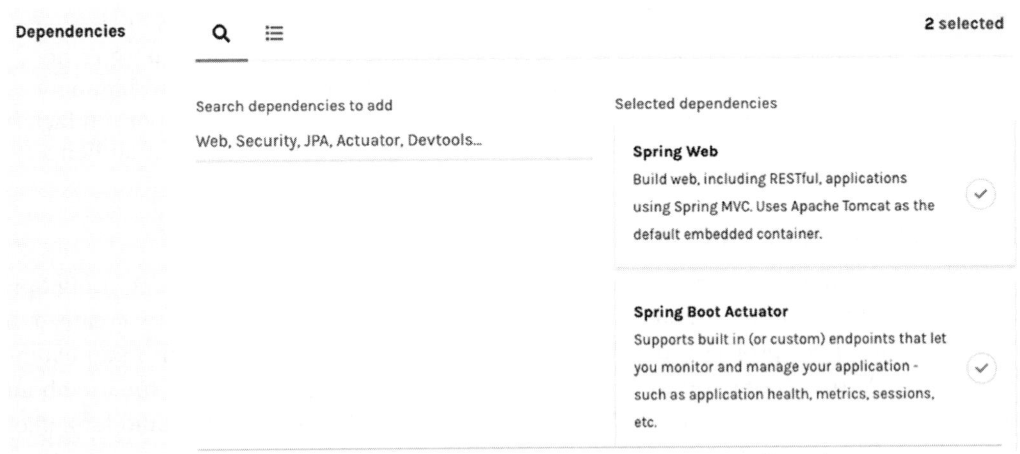

Figure 2.13   Spring Initializr configuration for the licensing service

NOTE You can also pull down the source code from the GitHub repository here: https://github.com/ihuaylupo/manning-smia/tree/master/chapter2.

Once you've created and imported the project as a Maven project into your preferred IDE, let's add the following packages:

```
com.optimagrowth.license.controller
com.optimagrowth.license.model
com.optimagrowth.license.service
```

Figure 2.14 shows the initial project structure for the licensing service in your IDE. Listing 2.2 then shows how your pom.xml file for our licensing service should look.

Licensing-service
• src/main/java
  • com.optimagrowth.license
    • com.optimagrowth.license.controller
    • com.optimagrowth.license.model
    • com.optimagrowth.license.service
• src/main/resources
    • static
    • templates
    • application.properties
• src/test/java
• com.optimagrowth.license
• src
• target
• pom.xml

Figure 2.14 Licensing project structure for O-stock with the bootstrap class, application properties, tests, and pom.xml

NOTE An in-depth discussion of how to test our microservices is outside of the scope of this book. If you're interested in diving into more detail on how to create unit, integration, and platform tests, we highly recommend Alex Soto Bueno, Andy Gumbrecht, and Jason Porter's book, *Testing Java Microservices* (Manning, 2018).

Listing 2.2 Maven pom file for the licensing service

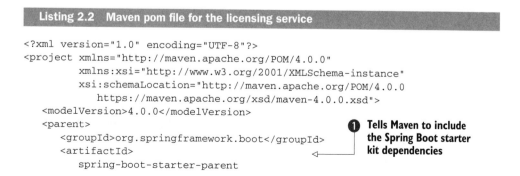

```xml
<?xml version="1.0" encoding="UTF-8"?>
<project xmlns="http://maven.apache.org/POM/4.0.0"
         xmlns:xsi="http://www.w3.org/2001/XMLSchema-instance"
         xsi:schemaLocation="http://maven.apache.org/POM/4.0.0
            https://maven.apache.org/xsd/maven-4.0.0.xsd">
    <modelVersion>4.0.0</modelVersion>
    <parent>
      <groupId>org.springframework.boot</groupId>
      <artifactId>
        spring-boot-starter-parent
```

❶ Tells Maven to include the Spring Boot starter kit dependencies

```
      </artifactId>
      <version>2.2.3.RELEASE</version>
      <relativePath/> <!-- lookup parent from repository -->
   </parent>
   <groupId>com.optimagrowth</groupId>
   <artifactId>licensing-service</artifactId>
   <version>0.0.1-SNAPSHOT</version>
   <name>License Service</name>
   <description>Ostock Licensing Service</description>

   <properties>
      <java.version>11</java.version>
   </properties>

   <dependencies>
      <dependency>
         <groupId>org.springframework.boot</groupId>
         <artifactId>
            spring-boot-starter-actuator
         </artifactId>
      </dependency>
      <dependency>
         <groupId>org.springframework.boot</groupId>
         <artifactId>
            spring-boot-starter-web
         </artifactId>
      </dependency>
      <dependency>
         <groupId>org.springframework.boot</groupId>
         <artifactId>spring-boot-starter-test</artifactId>
         <scope>test</scope>
         <exclusions>
            <exclusion>
               <groupId>org.junit.vintage</groupId>
               <artifactId>junit-vintage-engine</artifactId>
            </exclusion>
         </exclusions>
      </dependency>
      <dependency>
         <groupId>org.projectlombok</groupId>
         <artifactId>lombok</artifactId>
         <scope>provided</scope>
      </dependency>
   </dependencies>
      <build>
      <plugins>
         <plugin>
            <groupId>org.springframework.boot</groupId>
            <artifactId>
               spring-boot-maven-plugin
            </artifactId>
         </plugin>
      </plugins>
   </build>
</project>
```

2 By default, pom adds Java 6. To use Spring 5, we override it with Java 11.

3 Tells Maven to include the Spring Actuator dependencies

4 Tells Maven to include the Spring Boot Web dependencies

5 Tells Maven to include Spring-specific Maven plugins for building and deploying Spring Boot applications.

NOTE A Spring Boot project doesn't need to set the individual Spring dependencies explicitly. These dependencies are automatically pulled from the Spring Boot core artifact defined in the pom file. Spring Boot v2.x builds use Spring framework 5.

We won't go through the entire file in detail, but we'll look at a few key areas. Spring Boot is broken into many individual projects. The philosophy is that you shouldn't have to "pull down the world" if you aren't going to use different pieces of Spring Boot in your application. This also allows the various Spring Boot projects to release new versions of code independently of one another.

To help simplify the life of the developers, the Spring Boot team gathered related dependent projects into various "starter" kits. In the listing, ❶ of the Maven pom file tells Maven that you need to pull down a specific version of the Spring Boot framework (in our case, 2.2.3). In ❷, you specify the version of Java you're going to use, and in ❸ and ❹, you identify that you're pulling down the Spring Actuator and Spring Boot Web starter kits. Note that the Spring Actuator dependency is not required, but we will use several Actuator endpoints in the next chapters, so that's why we add it at this point. These two projects are the heart of almost any Spring Boot REST-based service. You'll find that as you build more functionality into your services, the list of these dependent projects becomes longer.

Spring also provides Maven plugins that simplify the build and deployment of Spring Boot applications. In ❺ of the pom file, you tell your Maven build script to install the latest Spring Boot Maven plugin. This plugin contains several add-on tasks (for example, `spring-boot:run`) that simplify your interaction between Maven and Spring Boot.

In order to check the Spring dependencies pulled by Spring Boot into our licensing service, we can use the Maven goal `dependency:tree`. Figure 2.15 shows the dependency tree for the licensing service.

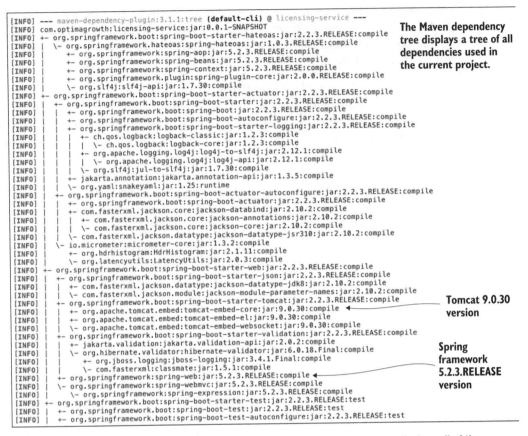

```
[INFO] --- maven-dependency-plugin:3.1.1:tree (default-cli) @ licensing-service ---
[INFO] com.optimagrowth:licensing-service:jar:0.0.1-SNAPSHOT
[INFO] +- org.springframework.boot:spring-boot-starter-hateoas:jar:2.2.3.RELEASE:compile
[INFO] |  \- org.springframework.hateoas:spring-hateoas:jar:1.0.3.RELEASE:compile
[INFO] |     +- org.springframework:spring-aop:jar:5.2.3.RELEASE:compile
[INFO] |     +- org.springframework:spring-beans:jar:5.2.3.RELEASE:compile
[INFO] |     +- org.springframework:spring-context:jar:5.2.3.RELEASE:compile
[INFO] |     +- org.springframework.plugin:spring-plugin-core:jar:2.0.0.RELEASE:compile
[INFO] |     \- org.slf4j:slf4j-api:jar:1.7.30:compile
[INFO] +- org.springframework.boot:spring-boot-starter-actuator:jar:2.2.3.RELEASE:compile
[INFO] |  +- org.springframework.boot:spring-boot-starter:jar:2.2.3.RELEASE:compile
[INFO] |  |  +- org.springframework.boot:spring-boot:jar:2.2.3.RELEASE:compile
[INFO] |  |  +- org.springframework.boot:spring-boot-autoconfigure:jar:2.2.3.RELEASE:compile
[INFO] |  |  +- org.springframework.boot:spring-boot-starter-logging:jar:2.2.3.RELEASE:compile
[INFO] |  |  |  +- ch.qos.logback:logback-classic:jar:1.2.3:compile
[INFO] |  |  |  |  \- ch.qos.logback:logback-core:jar:1.2.3:compile
[INFO] |  |  |  +- org.apache.logging.log4j:log4j-to-slf4j:jar:2.12.1:compile
[INFO] |  |  |  |  \- org.apache.logging.log4j:log4j-api:jar:2.12.1:compile
[INFO] |  |  |  \- org.slf4j:jul-to-slf4j:jar:1.7.30:compile
[INFO] |  |  +- jakarta.annotation:jakarta.annotation-api:jar:1.3.5:compile
[INFO] |  |  \- org.yaml:snakeyaml:jar:1.25:runtime
[INFO] |  +- org.springframework.boot:spring-boot-actuator-autoconfigure:jar:2.2.3.RELEASE:compile
[INFO] |  +- org.springframework.boot:spring-boot-actuator:jar:2.2.3.RELEASE:compile
[INFO] |  +- com.fasterxml.jackson.core:jackson-databind:jar:2.10.2:compile
[INFO] |  |  +- com.fasterxml.jackson.core:jackson-annotations:jar:2.10.2:compile
[INFO] |  |  \- com.fasterxml.jackson.core:jackson-core:jar:2.10.2:compile
[INFO] |  \- com.fasterxml.jackson.datatype:jackson-datatype-jsr310:jar:2.10.2:compile
[INFO] |  \- io.micrometer:micrometer-core:jar:1.3.2:compile
[INFO] |     +- org.hdrhistogram:HdrHistogram:jar:2.1.11:compile
[INFO] |     \- org.latencyutils:LatencyUtils:jar:2.0.3:compile
[INFO] +- org.springframework.boot:spring-boot-starter-web:jar:2.2.3.RELEASE:compile
[INFO] |  +- org.springframework.boot:spring-boot-starter-json:jar:2.2.3.RELEASE:compile
[INFO] |  |  +- com.fasterxml.jackson.datatype:jackson-datatype-jdk8:jar:2.10.2:compile
[INFO] |  |  \- com.fasterxml.jackson.module:jackson-module-parameter-names:jar:2.10.2:compile
[INFO] |  +- org.springframework.boot:spring-boot-starter-tomcat:jar:2.2.3.RELEASE:compile
[INFO] |  |  +- org.apache.tomcat.embed:tomcat-embed-core:jar:9.0.30:compile
[INFO] |  |  +- org.apache.tomcat.embed:tomcat-embed-el:jar:9.0.30:compile
[INFO] |  |  \- org.apache.tomcat.embed:tomcat-embed-websocket:jar:9.0.30:compile
[INFO] |  +- org.springframework.boot:spring-boot-starter-validation:jar:2.2.3.RELEASE:compile
[INFO] |  |  +- jakarta.validation:jakarta.validation-api:jar:2.0.2:compile
[INFO] |  |  \- org.hibernate.validator:hibernate-validator:jar:6.0.18.Final:compile
[INFO] |  |     +- org.jboss.logging:jboss-logging:jar:3.4.1.Final:compile
[INFO] |  |     \- com.fasterxml:classmate:jar:1.5.1:compile
[INFO] |  +- org.springframework:spring-web:jar:5.2.3.RELEASE:compile
[INFO] |  \- org.springframework:spring-webmvc:jar:5.2.3.RELEASE:compile
[INFO] |     \- org.springframework:spring-expression:jar:5.2.3.RELEASE:compile
[INFO] +- org.springframework.boot:spring-boot-starter-test:jar:2.2.3.RELEASE:test
[INFO] |  +- org.springframework.boot:spring-boot-test:jar:2.2.3.RELEASE:test
[INFO] |  +- org.springframework.boot:spring-boot-test-autoconfigure:jar:2.2.3.RELEASE:test
```

The Maven dependency tree displays a tree of all dependencies used in the current project.

Tomcat 9.0.30 version

Spring framework 5.2.3.RELEASE version

Figure 2.15 Dependency tree for O-stock's licensing service. The dependency tree displays all of the dependencies declared and used in the service.

2.5.3 *Booting your Spring Boot application: Writing the bootstrap class*

Our goal in this section is to get a simple microservice up and running in Spring Boot and then iterate over it to deliver some functionality. To this end, you need to create two classes in your licensing service microservice:

- A Spring bootstrap class, which Spring Boot uses to start up and initialize the application
- A Spring controller class, which exposes the HTTP endpoints that can be invoked on the microservice

As you'll soon see, Spring Boot uses annotations to simplify setting up and configuring the service. This becomes evident as you look at the bootstrap class in the following code listing. You'll find this bootstrap class is in the LicenseServiceApplication.java file located in src/main/java/com/optimagrowth/license.

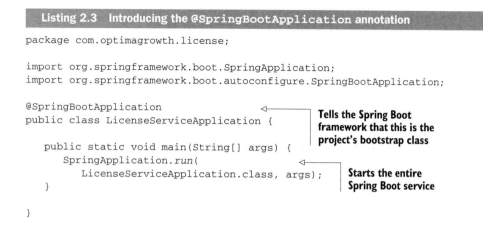

Listing 2.3　Introducing the `@SpringBootApplication` annotation

```
package com.optimagrowth.license;

import org.springframework.boot.SpringApplication;
import org.springframework.boot.autoconfigure.SpringBootApplication;

@SpringBootApplication
public class LicenseServiceApplication {

    public static void main(String[] args) {
        SpringApplication.run(
            LicenseServiceApplication.class, args);
    }

}
```

Tells the Spring Boot framework that this is the project's bootstrap class

Starts the entire Spring Boot service

The first thing to note in this code is the use of the `@SpringBootApplication` annotation. Spring Boot uses this annotation to tell the Spring container that this class is the source of bean definitions. In a Spring Boot application, you can define Spring beans by

1 Annotating a Java class with a `@Component`, `@Service`, or `@Repository` annotation tag
2 Annotating a class with a `@Configuration` tag and then defining a factory method for each Spring bean you want to build with a `@Bean` tag

NOTE A Spring bean is an object that the Spring framework manages at run time with the Inversion of Control (IoC) container. These are created and added to a "repository of objects" so you can get them later.

Under the covers, the `@SpringBootApplication` annotation marks the application class in listing 2.3 as a configuration class. It then begins autoscanning all the classes on the Java classpath for other Spring beans.

The second thing to note in listing 2.3 is the `main()` method in the `LicenseService-Application` class. The `SpringApplication.run(LicenseServiceApplication .class, args)` call in the `main()` method starts the Spring container and returns a Spring `ApplicationContext` object. (We aren't doing anything with the `Application-Context`, so it isn't shown in the code.)

The easiest thing to remember about the `@SpringBootApplication` annotation and the corresponding `LicenseServiceApplication` class is that it's the bootstrap class for the entire microservice. Core initialization logic for the service should be placed in this class.

Now that we know how to create the skeleton and the bootstrap class for our microservice, let's continue with the next chapter. In the next chapter, we will explain some of the critical roles we must consider while we are building a microservice and how those roles are involved in the creation of the O-stock scenario. Also, we will explain some additional technologies to make our microservices more flexible and robust.

Summary

- Spring Cloud is a collection of open source technologies from companies like Netflix and HashiCorp. This technology is "wrapped" with Spring annotations to significantly simplify the setup and configuration of these services.
- Cloud-native applications are built with scalable components like containers, deployed as microservices, and managed on virtual infrastructures through DevOps processes with continuous delivery workflows.
- DevOps is the acronym for development (Dev) and operations (Ops). It refers to a software development methodology that focuses on communication, collaboration, and integration between software developers and IT operations. The primary goal is to automate the process of software delivery and infrastructure changes at lower costs.
- The twelve-factor application manifesto, framed by Heroku, provides best practices you should implement when building cloud-native microservices.
- The best practices of the twelve-factor application manifesto include codebase, dependencies, configuration, backing services, build/release runs, processes, port binding, concurrency, disposability, dev/prod parity, logs, and admin processes.
- The Spring Initializr allows you to create a new Spring Boot project while choosing dependencies from an extensive list.
- Spring Boot is the ideal framework for building microservices because it lets you build a REST-based JSON service with a few simple annotations.

Building microservices with Spring Boot

This chapter covers

- Understanding how microservices fit into a cloud architecture
- Decomposing a business domain into a set of microservices
- Understanding the perspectives for building microservice apps
- Learning when not to use microservices
- Implementing a microservice

To successfully design and build microservices, you need to approach them as if you're a police detective interviewing witnesses to a crime. Although each witness sees the same event, their interpretation of the crime is shaped by their background, what's important to them (for example, what motivates them), and what environmental pressures were brought to bear at the moment they witnessed the event. Witnesses each have their own perspective (and bias) on what they consider essential.

Like successful police detectives trying to get to the truth, the journey to build a successful microservice architecture involves incorporating the perspectives of multiple individuals within your software development organization. Because it takes more than technical people to deliver an entire application, we believe that the foundation for successful microservice development starts with the perspectives of three critical roles:

- *The architect*—Sees the big picture, decomposes an application into individual microservices, and then understands how the microservices interact to deliver a solution.
- *The software developer*—Writes the code and understands how the language and development frameworks will be used to deliver a microservice.
- *The DevOps engineer*—Determines how the services are deployed and managed throughout production and non-production environments. The watchwords for the DevOps engineer are *consistency* and *repeatability* in every environment.

In this chapter, we will demonstrate how to design and build a set of microservices from the perspective of each of these roles. This chapter will give you the foundation you need to identify potential microservices within your own business application and then to understand the operational attributes that need to be in place to deploy a microservice. By the end of this chapter, you'll have a service that can be packaged and deployed to the cloud using the skeleton project we created in the chapter 2.

3.1   The architect's story: Designing the microservice architecture

An architect's role in a software project is to provide a working model of the problem that needs to be solved. The architect provides the scaffolding against which developers will build their code so that all the pieces of the application fit together. When building a microservice, a project's architect focuses on three key tasks:

- Decomposing the business problem
- Establishing service granularity
- Defining the service interfaces

3.1.1   Decomposing the business problem

In the face of complexity, most people try to break down the problem on which they're working into manageable chunks. They do this so they don't have to fit all the details of the problem in their heads. They may break the problem down into a few essential parts and then look for the relationships that exist among these parts.

In a microservices architecture, the process is much the same. The architect breaks the business problem into chunks that represent discrete domains of activity. These chunks encapsulate the business rules and the data logic associated with a particular part of the business domain. For example, an architect might look at a business flow that needs to be carried out by code and realize that it needs both customer and product information.

TIP   The presence of two discrete data domains is a good indication that multiple microservices are at play. How the two different parts of the business transaction interact usually becomes the service interface for the microservice.

Breaking down a business domain is an art form rather than black-and-white science. You can use the following guidelines for identifying and decomposing a business problem into microservice candidates:

- *Describe the business problem and notice the nouns you use to describe it.* Using the same nouns over and over in describing the problem is usually a good indication of a core business domain and an opportunity for a microservice. Examples of target nouns for the O-stock application might be something like *contract, licenses,* and *assets.*

- *Pay attention to the verbs.* Verbs highlight actions and often represent the natural contours of a problem domain. If you find yourself saying "transaction *X* needs to get data from thing *A* and thing *B*," that usually indicates that multiple services are at play.

  If you apply this approach to the O-stock application, you might look for statements like, "When Mike from desktop services sets up a new PC, he looks up the number of licenses available for software *X* and, if licenses are available, installs the software. He then updates the number of licenses used in his tracking spreadsheet." The key verbs here are *looks* and *updates.*

- *Look for data cohesion.* As you break your business problem down into discrete pieces, look for pieces of data that are highly related to one another. If suddenly, during the course of your conversation, you're reading or updating data that is radically different from what you've discussed, you potentially have another service candidate. Microservices must completely own their data.

Let's take these guidelines and apply them to a real-world problem, like the one for the O-stock software that is used for managing software assets. (We first mentioned this application in chapter 2.)

As a reminder, O-stock is Optima Growth's monolithic web application that is deployed to a Java EE application server residing within a customer's data center. Our goal is to tease apart the existing monolithic application into a set of services. To achieve this, we'll start by interviewing the users and some of the business stakeholders of the O-stock application, discussing how they interact with and use the application. Figure 3.1 summarizes and highlights a number of nouns and verbs of some of the conversations with different business customers.

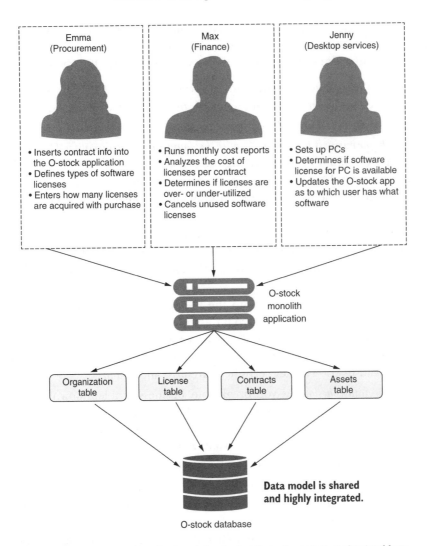
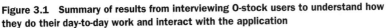

Figure 3.1   Summary of results from interviewing O-stock users to understand how they do their day-to-day work and interact with the application

Looking at how the users of O-stock interact with the application and answering the following questions, we can identify the data model for the application. By doing this, we can decompose the O-stock problem domain into microservice candidates.

- Where are we going to store the contract info managed by Emma?
- Where are we going to store and how are we going to manage the license information (cost, license type, license owner, and license contract)?
- Jenny sets up the licenses on the PCs. Where are we going to store the assets?

- Taking into consideration all the previously mentioned concepts, we can see that the license belongs to an organization that has several assets, right? So, where are we going to store the organization information?

Figure 3.2 shows a simplified data model based on the conversations with Optima Growth's customers. Based on the business interviews and the data model, the microservice candidates are *organization, license, contract,* and *assets.*

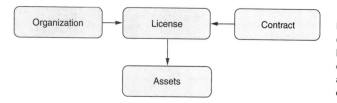

Figure 3.2 **A simplified O-stock data model. An organization can have many licenses, the licenses can be applied to one or several assets, and each license has a contract.**

3.1.2 *Establishing service granularity*

Once we have a simplified data model, we can begin the process of defining what microservices we are going to need in the application. As the data model in figure 3.2 illustrates, we can see the four potential microservices based on the following elements:

- Assets
- License
- Contract
- Organization

The goal is to take these major pieces of functionality and extract them into entirely self-contained units that we can build and deploy independently of each other. These units can optionally share or have individual databases. However, extracting services from the data model involves more than repackaging code into separate projects. It also involves teasing out the actual database tables the services will access and only allowing each service to access the tables in its specific domain. Figure 3.3 shows how the application code and the data model become "chunked" into individual pieces.

> **NOTE** We created individual databases for each service, but you can also share databases between the services.

After we break down a problem domain into its discrete pieces, we will often find ourselves struggling to determine whether we've achieved the right level of *granularity* for our services. A microservice that is too coarse- or fine-grained will have several telltale attributes, which we'll discuss shortly.

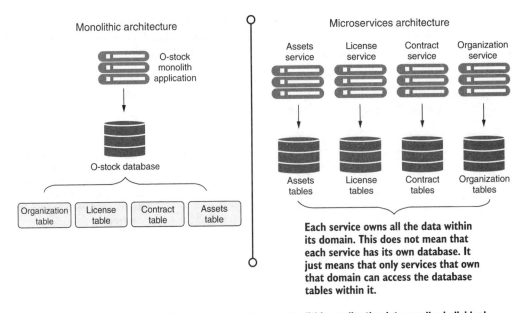

Figure 3.3   The O-stock application broken down from a monolithic application into smaller individual services that are deployed independently of one another

When we build a microservice architecture, the question of granularity is essential. This is why we want to explain the following concepts to determine the correct answer to what is the right level of granularity:

- *It's better to start broad with our microservice and refactor to smaller services.* It is easy to go overboard when you begin your microservice journey and make everything a microservice. But decomposing the problem domain into small services often leads to premature complexity because microservices devolve into nothing more than fine-grained data services.

- *Focus first on how our services interact with one another.* This helps to establish the coarse-grained interfaces of your problem domain. It is easier to refactor from being too coarse-grained than from being too fine-grained.

- *Service responsibilities change over time as our understanding of the problem domain grows.* Often, a microservice gains responsibilities as new application functionalities are requested. What starts as a single microservice might grow into multiple services, with the original microservice acting as an orchestration layer for these new services and encapsulating their functionality from other parts of the application.

What smells as a bad microservice? How do you know whether your microservices are the right size? If a microservice is too coarse-grained, you'll likely see the following:

- *A service with too many responsibilities.* The general flow of the business logic in the service is complicated and seems to be enforcing an overly diverse array of rules.

- *A service that manages data across a large number of tables.* A microservice is the record for the data it manages. If you find yourself persisting data to multiple tables or reaching out to tables outside of the service database, this is a clue that the service is too big. We like to use the guideline that a microservice should own no more than three to five tables. Any more, and your service is likely to have too much responsibility.

- *A service with too many test cases.* Services can grow in size and responsibility over time. If you have a service that started with a small number of test cases and ended up with hundreds of unit and integration tests, you might need to refactor.

What about a microservice that's too fine-grained?

- *The microservices in one part of the problem domain breed like rabbits.* If everything becomes a microservice, composing business logic out of the services becomes complex and difficult. That's because the number of services needed to get a piece of work done grows tremendously. A common smell is when you have dozens of microservices in an application, and each service interacts with only a single database table.

- *Your microservices are heavily interdependent on one another.* You find that microservices in one part of the problem domain keep calling back and forth between each other to complete a single user request.

- *Your microservices become a collection of simple CRUD (Create, Replace, Update, Delete) services.* Microservices are an expression of business logic and not an abstraction layer over your data sources. If your microservices do nothing but CRUD-related logic, they're probably too fine-grained.

A microservices architecture should be developed with an evolutionary thought process, where you know that you aren't going to get the design right the first time. That is why it's better to start with your first set of services being more coarse-grained than fine-grained.

It is also essential not to be dogmatic with your design. You may run into physical constraints on your services. For example, you'll need to make an aggregation service that joins data together because two separate services will be too chatty, or no clear boundaries exist between the domain lines of a service. In the end, take a pragmatic approach and deliver rather than wasting time trying to get the design perfect and then have nothing to show for your efforts.

3.1.3 Defining the service interfaces

The last part of the architect's input is about defining how the microservices in your application will talk to one another. When building business logic with microservices, the interfaces for the services should be intuitive, and developers should get a rhythm of how all the services work in the application by fully understanding one or two of the services in the application. In general, we can use the following guidelines for implementing service interface design:

- *Embrace the REST philosophy.* This is one of the best practices (see appendix A), along with the Richardson Maturity Model (see the next sidebar). The REST approach to service is, at heart, the embracing of HTTP as the invocation protocol for the services, using standard HTTP verbs (GET, PUT, POST, and DELETE). Model your basic behaviors around these HTTP verbs.
- *Use URIs to communicate intent.* The URIs you use as endpoints for the service should describe the different resources in your problem domain and provide a basic mechanism for relationships of resources within it.
- *Use JSON for your requests and responses.* JSON is an extremely lightweight data-serialization protocol, and it's much easier to consume than XML.
- *Use HTTP status codes to communicate results.* The HTTP protocol has a rich body of standard response codes to indicate the success or failure of a service. Learn these status codes and, most importantly, use these consistently across all your services.

All the basic guidelines point to one thing: making your service interfaces easy to understand and consumable. You want a developer to sit down, look at the service interfaces, and start using them. If a microservice isn't easy to consume, developers will go out of their way to work around it and subvert the intention of the architecture.

3.2 When not to use microservices

We've spent this chapter talking about why microservices are a powerful architectural pattern for building applications. But we haven't touched on when you *shouldn't* use microservices to build your applications. Let's walk through these "should nots":

- Complexity when building distributed systems
- Virtual server or container sprawl
- Application type
- Data transactions and consistency

3.2.1 Complexity when building distributed systems

Because microservices are distributed and fine-grained (small), these introduce a level of complexity into your application that's not found in more monolithic applications. Microservice architectures require a high degree of operational maturity. Don't consider using microservices unless your organization is willing to invest in the automation and operational work (monitoring, scaling, and so on) that a highly distributed application needs to be successful.

3.2.2   *Server or container sprawl*

One of the most common deployment models for microservices is to have one microservice instance deployed in one container. In a large microservice-based application, you might end up with 50 to 100 servers or containers (usually virtual) that must be built and maintained in production alone. Even with the lower cost of running these services in the cloud, the operational complexity of managing and monitoring these services can be tremendous.

> **NOTE** The flexibility of microservices has to be weighed against the cost of running all of those servers. You can also have different alternatives, such as considering functional developments like lambdas or adding more microservice instances on the same server.

3.2.3   *Application type*

Microservices are geared toward reusability and are extremely useful for building large applications that need to be highly resilient and scalable. This is one of the reasons why so many cloud-based companies have adopted microservices. If you're building small, departmental-level applications, or applications with a small user base, the complexity associated with building a distributed model like a microservice might generate more expense than it's worth.

3.2.4   *Data transactions and consistency*

As you begin looking at microservices, you need to think through the data usage patterns of your services and service consumers. A microservice wraps around and abstracts away a small number of tables and works well as a mechanism for performing "operational" tasks like creating, adding, and performing simple (non-complex) queries against a data store.

If your application needs to do complex data aggregation or transformation across multiple data sources, the distributed nature of microservices will make this work difficult. Your microservices will invariably take on too much responsibility and can also become vulnerable to performance problems.

3.3   *The developer's tale: Building a microservice with Spring Boot and Java*

In this section, we'll explore the developer's priorities in building the licensing microservice from the O-stock domain model.

> **NOTE** We created the skeleton of the licensing service in the previous chapter. In case you didn't follow the code listings in that chapter, you can download the source code from https://github.com/ihuaylupo/manning-smia/tree/master/chapter2.

Over the next several sections, we'll

1   Implement a Spring Boot controller class for mapping an endpoint to expose the licensing service endpoints
2   Implement internationalization so that the messages can be adapted to different languages
3   Implement Spring HATEOAS to provide enough information so the user can interact with the server

3.3.1   *Building the doorway into the microservice: The Spring Boot controller*

Now that we've gotten the build script out of the way (see chapter 2) and have implemented a simple Spring Boot bootstrap class, you can write your first code that will do something. This code will be your controller class. In a Spring Boot application, the controller class exposes the service endpoints and maps the data from an incoming HTTP request to a Java method that processes the request.

> **Give it a REST**
>
> All the microservices in this book follow the Richardson Maturity Model (http://mng .bz/JD5Z). All the services you build will have the following characteristics:
>
> - *Use HTTP/HTTPS as the invocation protocol for the service*—An HTTP endpoint exposes the service, and the HTTP protocol carries data to and from the service.
> - *Map the behavior of the service to standard HTTP verbs*—REST emphasizes having services that map their behavior to the HTTP verbs POST, GET, PUT, and DELETE. These verbs map to the CRUD functions found in most services.
> - *Use JSON as the serialization format for all data going to and from the service*—This isn't a hard-and-fast principle for REST-based microservices, but JSON has become "lingua franca" for serializing data that's submitted and returned by a microservice. You can use XML, but many REST-based applications make use of JavaScript and JSON. JSON is the native format for serializing and deserializing data consumed by JavaScript-based web front ends and services.
> - *Use HTTP status codes to communicate the status of a service call*—The HTTP protocol uses a rich set of status codes to indicate the success or failure of a service. REST-based services take advantage of these HTTP status codes and other web-based infrastructures, such as reverse proxies and caches. These can be integrated with your microservices with relative ease.
>
> HTTP is the language of the web. Using HTTP as the philosophical framework for building your service is key to building services in the cloud.

You'll find your first controller class located in src/main/java/com/optimagrowth/ license/controller/LicenseController.java. The `LicenseController` class exposes four HTTP endpoints that will map to the POST, GET, PUT, DELETE verbs.

Let's walk through this controller class and see how Spring Boot provides a set of annotations that help to keep the effort needed to expose your service endpoints to a minimum and allow you to focus on building the business logic for the service. We'll start by looking at the basic controller class definition without any class methods in it just yet. The following listing shows the controller class for O-stock's licensing service.

Listing 3.1   Marking the `LicenseServiceController` as a Spring `RestController`

```
package com.optimagrowth.license.controller;

import java.util.Random;

import org.springframework.http.ResponseEntity;
import org.springframework.web.bind.annotation.PathVariable;
import org.springframework.web.bind.annotation.PostMapping;
import org.springframework.web.bind.annotation.PutMapping;
import org.springframework.web.bind.annotation.RequestBody;
import org.springframework.web.bind.annotation.RequestMapping;
import org.springframework.web.bind.annotation.RequestMethod;
import org.springframework.web.bind.annotation.RestController;

import com.optimagrowth.license.model.License;

@RestController
@RequestMapping(value="v1/organization/
                {organizationId}/license")

public class LicenseController {
}
```

Tells Spring Boot that this is a REST-based service and it will automatically serialize/deserialize service requests/responses via JSON.

Exposes all the HTTP endpoints in this class with a prefix of /v1/organization/{organizationId}/license

We'll begin our exploration by looking at the `@RestController` annotation. The `@RestController` is a class-level Java annotation that tells the Spring container that this Java class will be used for a REST-based service. This annotation automatically handles the serialization of data passed into the services as either JSON or XML (by default, this class serializes returned data into JSON). Unlike the traditional Spring `@Controller` annotation, `@RestController` doesn't require you to return a `ResponseBody` class from your method in the controller class. This is all handled by the presence of the `@RestController` annotation, which includes the `@ResponseBody` annotation.

Why JSON for microservices?

We can use multiple protocols to send data back and forth between HTTP-based microservices. But JSON has emerged as the de facto standard for several reasons:

- *Compared to other protocols like XML-based SOAP (Simple Object Access Protocol), JSON is extremely lightweight.* You can express your data without having much textual overhead.

(continued)

- *JSON is easily read and consumed by a human being.* This is an underrated quality for choosing a serialization protocol. When a problem arises, it's critical for developers to look at a chunk of JSON and to quickly process what's in it. The simplicity of the protocol makes this incredibly easy to do.
- *JSON is the default serialization protocol used in JavaScript.* Since the dramatic rise of JavaScript as a programming language and the equally dramatic rise of Single Page Internet Applications (SPIA) that rely heavily on JavaScript, JSON has become a natural fit for building REST-based applications, which is what the front-end web clients use to call services.
- Other mechanisms and protocols, however, are more efficient than JSON for communicating between services. The Apache Thrift (http://thrift.apache.org) framework allows you to build multilanguage services that can communicate with one another using a binary protocol. The Apache Avro protocol (http://avro.apache.org) is a data serialization protocol that converts data back and forth to a binary format between client and server calls. If you need to minimize the size of the data you're sending across the wire, we recommend you look at these protocols. But it has been our experience that using straight-up JSON in your microservices works effectively and doesn't interject another layer of communication to debug between your service consumers and service clients.

You can use the `@RequestMapping` annotation (the second annotation in listing 3.1) as a class-level and method-level annotation and to tell the Spring container the HTTP endpoint that the service is going to expose to the user. When you use `@RequestMapping` as the class-level annotation, you're establishing the root of the URL for all the other endpoints exposed by the controller. `@RequestMapping(value="v1/organization/{organizationId}/ license")` uses the `value` attribute to establish the root of the URL for all endpoints exposed in the `Controller` class. All service endpoints exposed in this controller will start with

```
v1/organization/{organizationId}/license
```

as the root of their endpoint. The `{organizationId}` is a placeholder that indicates how you expect the URL to be parameterized with an `organizationId` passed in every call. The use of `organizationId` in the URL allows you to differentiate between the different customers who might use your service.

Before we add the first method to the controller, let's explore the model and the service class that we'll use in the services we're about to create. Listing 3.2 shows the POJO class that encapsulates the license data.

NOTE Encapsulation is one of the main principles of object-oriented programming, and in order to achieve encapsulation in Java, we must declare the variables of a class as private and then provide public getters and setters to read and write the values of those variables.

Listing 3.2   Exploring the license model

```
package com.optimagrowth.license.model;

import lombok.Getter;
import lombok.Setter;
import lombok.ToString;


@Getter @Setter @ToString
public class License {

    private int id;
    private String licenseId;
    private String description;
    private String organizationId;
    private String productName;
    private String licenseType;
}
```

A Plain Old Java Object (POJO) that contains the license info

Lombok

Lombok is a small library that allows us to reduce the amount of boilerplate Java code written in the Java classes of our project. Lombok generates code such as getters and setters for string methods, constructors, and so forth.

In this book, we will use Lombok throughout the code examples in order to keep the code more readable, but we will not get into the details of how to use it. If you are interested in knowing more about Lombok, we highly recommend you look at the following Baeldung.com articles:

- https://www.baeldung.com/intro-to-project-lombok
- https://www.baeldung.com/lombok-ide

In case you want to install Lombok on the Spring Tools Suite 4, you must download and execute Lombok and link it to the IDE.

The following listing shows the service class that we'll use to develop the logic of the different services we are going to create on the controller class.

Listing 3.3   Exploring the `LicenseService` class

```
package com.optimagrowth.license.service;

import java.util.Random;

import org.springframework.stereotype.Service;
import org.springframework.util.StringUtils;

import com.optimagrowth.license.model.License;
```

```
@Service
public class LicenseService {

    public License getLicense(String licenseId, String organizationId){
        License license = new License();
        license.setId(new Random().nextInt(1000));
        license.setLicenseId(licenseId);
        license.setOrganizationId(organizationId);
        license.setDescription("Software product");
        license.setProductName("Ostock");
        license.setLicenseType("full");

        return license;
    }

    public String createLicense(License license, String organizationId){
        String responseMessage = null;
        if(license != null) {
           license.setOrganizationId(organizationId);
            responseMessage = String.format("This is the post and the
                                    object is: %s", license.toString());
        }

        return responseMessage;
    }

    public String updateLicense(License license, String organizationId){
        String responseMessage = null;
        if (license != null) {
           license.setOrganizationId(organizationId);
           responseMessage = String.format("This is the put and
                        the object is: %s", license.toString());
        }

        return responseMessage;
    }

    public String deleteLicense(String licenseId, String organizationId){
        String responseMessage = null;
        responseMessage = String.format("Deleting license with id %s for
                       the organization %s",licenseId, organizationId);
        return responseMessage;

    }
}
```

This service class contains a set of dummy services returning hardcoded data to give you an idea of how the skeleton of a microservice should look. As you continue reading, you'll continue working on this service, and we'll delve further into how to structure it. For now, let's add the first method to the controller. This method implements the GET verb used in a REST call and returns a single License class instance as shown in the next code listing.

Listing 3.4　Exposing an individual GET HTTP endpoint

```
package com.optimagrowth.license.controller;

import org.springframework.http.ResponseEntity;
import org.springframework.web.bind.annotation.PathVariable;
import org.springframework.web.bind.annotation.PostMapping;
import org.springframework.web.bind.annotation.PutMapping;
import org.springframework.web.bind.annotation.RequestBody;
import org.springframework.web.bind.annotation.RequestMapping;
import org.springframework.web.bind.annotation.RequestMethod;
import org.springframework.web.bind.annotation.RestController;

import com.optimagrowth.license.model.License;
import com.optimagrowth.license.service.LicenseService;

@RestController
@RequestMapping(value="v1/organization/{organizationId}/license")
public class LicenseController {

    @Autowired
        private LicenseService licenseService;

    @GetMapping(value="/{licenseId}")
        public ResponseEntity<License> getLicense(
            @PathVariable("organizationId") String organizationId,
            @PathVariable("licenseId") String licenseId) {

        License license = licenseService
                .getLicense(licenseId,organizationId);
            return ResponseEntity.ok(license);
    }
}
```

Annotations (callouts):
- **Get method to retrieve the license data** → (points to `@GetMapping`)
- **Maps two parameters (organizationId and licenseId) from the URL to @GetMapping's parameters**
- **ResponseEntity represents the entire HTTP response.**

The first thing we do in this listing was to annotate the getLicense() method with a @GetMapping annotation. Here we can use also the @RequestMapping(value="/{licenseId}", method = RequestMethod.GET) annotation that passes two parameters (value and method) to the annotation. With a method-level @GetMapping annotation, we can build the following endpoint for the getLicense() method:

```
v1/organization/{organizationId}/license/{licenseId}
```

Why? If we go back and take a look at the top of the class, we specified a root-level annotation to match all HTTP requests coming to the controller: first, we added the root-level annotation value, and then, the method-level value. The second parameter of the annotation, method, specifies the HTTP verb used to match the method. In the getLicense() method, we match on the GET method as presented by the Request-Method.GET enumeration.

The second thing to note in listing 3.4 is that we use the @PathVariable annotation in the parameter body of the getLicense() method. This annotation maps the parameter values passed in the incoming URL (as denoted by the {parameterName} syntax) to the parameters of your method. For the GET service in listing 3.4, we map two parameters from the URL (organizationId and licenseId) to two parameter-level variables in the method, like so:

```
@PathVariable("organizationId") String organizationId
@PathVariable("licenseId") String licenseId
```

Finally, let's examine the ResponseEntity return object. The ResponseEntity represents the entire HTTP response, including the status code, the headers, and the body. In the previous listing, it allows us to return the License object as the body and the 200(OK) status code as the HTTP response of the service.

Now that you understand how to create an endpoint using the HTTP GET verb, let's continue by adding POST, PUT, and DELETE methods to create, update, and delete License class instances. The following listing shows how to do this.

Listing 3.5   Exposing individual HTTP endpoints

```
package com.optimagrowth.license.controller;

import org.springframework.beans.factory.annotation.Autowired;
import org.springframework.http.ResponseEntity;
import org.springframework.web.bind.annotation.DeleteMapping;
import org.springframework.web.bind.annotation.PathVariable;
import org.springframework.web.bind.annotation.PostMapping;
import org.springframework.web.bind.annotation.PutMapping;
import org.springframework.web.bind.annotation.RequestBody;
import org.springframework.web.bind.annotation.RequestMapping;
import org.springframework.web.bind.annotation.RequestMethod;
import org.springframework.web.bind.annotation.RestController;

import com.optimagrowth.license.model.License;
import com.optimagrowth.license.service.LicenseService;

@RestController
@RequestMapping(value="v1/organization/{organizationId}/license")
public class LicenseController {

    @Autowired
    private LicenseService licenseService;

    @RequestMapping(value="/{licenseId}",method = RequestMethod.GET)
    public ResponseEntity<License> getLicense(
        @PathVariable("organizationId") String organizationId,
        @PathVariable("licenseId") String licenseId) {

        License license = licenseService.getLicense(licenseId,
                                            organizationId);
        return ResponseEntity.ok(license);
    }

    @PutMapping    <⎯⎯  Put method to update a license
```

```
public ResponseEntity<String> updateLicense(
        @PathVariable("organizationId")
        String organizationId,
        @RequestBody License request) {
    return ResponseEntity.ok(licenseService.updateLicense(request,
                        organizationId));
}

@PostMapping
public ResponseEntity<String> createLicense(
        @PathVariable("organizationId") String organizationId,
        @RequestBody License request) {
    return ResponseEntity.ok(licenseService.createLicense(request,
                        organizationId));
}

@DeleteMapping(value="/{licenseId}")
public ResponseEntity<String> deleteLicense(
        @PathVariable("organizationId") String organizationId,
        @PathVariable("licenseId") String licenseId) {
    return ResponseEntity.ok(licenseService.deleteLicense(licenseId,
                        organizationId));
}
}
```

Maps the HTTP request body to a License object — @RequestBody License request

Post method to insert a license — @PostMapping

Delete method to delete a license — @DeleteMapping(value="/{licenseId}")

In listing 3.5, we first annotate the updateLicense() method with a method-level @PutMapping annotation. This annotation acts as a shortcut for the @Request-Mapping (method = RequestMethod.PUT) annotation, which we haven't used yet.

The next thing to note is that we use the @PathVariable and the @RequestBody annotations in the parameter body of the updateLicense() method. @RequestBody maps the HTTPRequest body to a transfer object (in this case, the License object). In the updateLicense() method, we map to the createLicense method from two parameters (one from the URL and the other from the HTTPRequest body) to the following two parameter-level variables:

```
@PathVariable("organizationId") String organizationId
@RequestBody License request
```

And finally, in listing 3.5 note that we use the @PostMapping and the @DeleteMapping annotations. The @PostMapping annotation is a method-level annotation that acts as a shortcut for

```
@RequestMapping(method = RequestMethod.POST)
```

@DeleteMapping(value="/{licenseId}") is also a method-level annotation and acts as a shortcut for

```
@RequestMapping(value="/{licenseId}",method = RequestMethod.DELETE)
```

Endpoint names matter

Before you get too far down the path of writing microservices, make sure that you (and potentially other teams in your organization) establish standards for the endpoints you want to exposed via your services. The URLs (Uniform Resource Locator) for the microservice should be used to clearly communicate the intent of the service, the resources the service manages, and the relationships that exist between the resources managed within the service. We've found the following guidelines useful for naming service endpoints:

- *Use clear URL names that establish what resource the service represents.* Having a canonical format for defining URLs will help your API feel more intuitive and easier to use—and be consistent in your naming conventions.
- *Use the URL to establish relationships between resources.* Often times, you'll have a parent-child relationship between resources within your microservices where the child doesn't exist outside the context of the parent. Hence, you might not have a separate microservice for the child. Use the URLs to express these relationships. If you find that your URLs tend to be long and nested, your microservice may be doing too much.
- *Establish a versioning scheme for URLs early.* The URL and its corresponding endpoints represent a contract between the service owner and the consumer of the service. One common pattern is to prepend all endpoints with a version number. Establish your versioning scheme early and stick to it. It's extremely difficult to retrofit versioning to URLS (for example, using /v1/ in the URL mappings) after you already have several consumers using them.

At this point, you have several services. From a command-line window, go to your project root directory, where you'll find pom.xml, and execute the following Maven command. (Figure 3.4 shows the expected output of this command.)

```
mvn spring-boot:run
```

The license server starting on port 8080

```
c.o.license.LicenseServiceApplication      : No active profile set, falling back to default profiles: default
o.s.b.w.embedded.tomcat.TomcatWebServer    : Tomcat initialized with port(s): 8080 (http)
o.apache.catalina.core.StandardService     : Starting service [Tomcat]
org.apache.catalina.core.StandardEngine    : Starting Servlet engine: [Apache Tomcat/9.0.30]
o.a.c.c.C.[Tomcat].[localhost].[/]         : Initializing Spring embedded WebApplicationContext
o.s.web.context.ContextLoader              : Root WebApplicationContext: initialization completed in 662 ms
o.s.s.concurrent.ThreadPoolTaskExecutor    : Initializing ExecutorService 'applicationTaskExecutor'
o.s.b.a.e.web.EndpointLinksResolver        : Exposing 1 endpoint(s) beneath base path '/v1'
o.s.b.w.embedded.tomcat.TomcatWebServer    : Tomcat started on port(s): 8080 (http) with context path ''
c.o.license.LicenseServiceApplication      : Started LicenseServiceApplication in 1.732 seconds (JVM running for 1.969)
```

Figure 3.4   Output showing that the licensing service successfully starts

Once the service is started, you can directly select the exposed endpoints. We highly recommend using a Chrome-based tool like Postman or cURL for calling the service. Figure 3.5 shows how to call the GET and DELETE services on an endpoint.

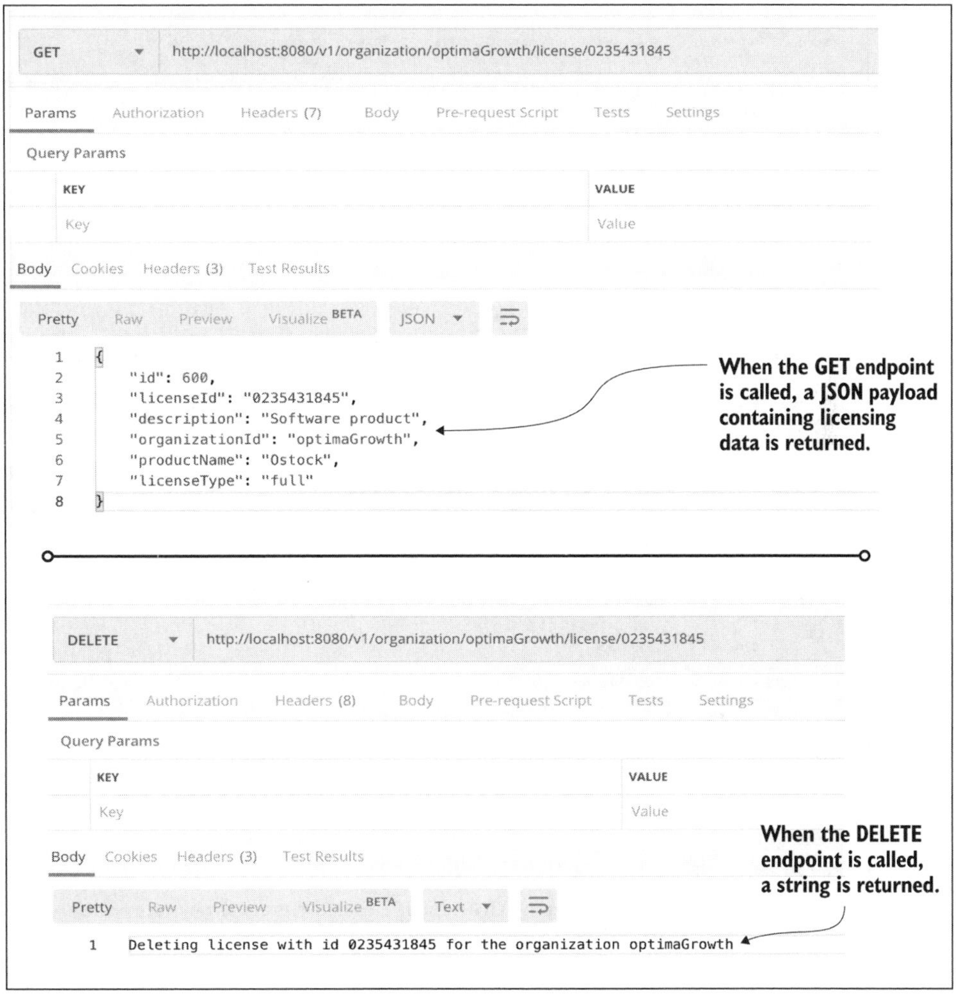

Figure 3.5   Your licensing GET and DELETE services called with Postman

Figure 3.6 shows how to call the POST and PUT services using the `http://local-host:8080/v1/organization/optimaGrowth/license` endpoint.

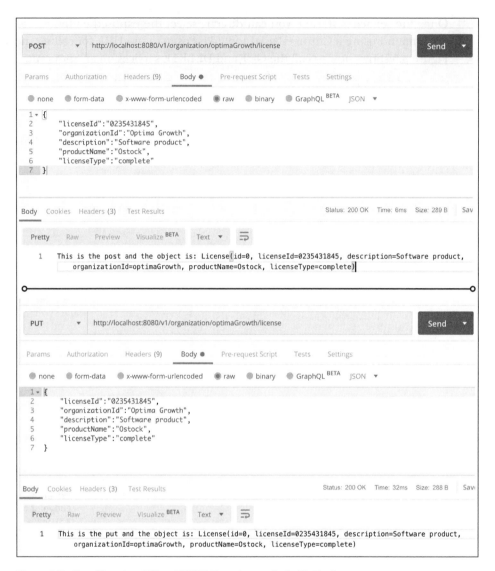

Figure 3.6   Your licensing GET and DELETE services called with Postman

Once we have implemented the methods for the PUT, DELETE, POST, and GET HTTP verbs, we can move on with internalization.

3.3.2   *Adding internationalization into the licensing service*

Internationalization is an essential requirement to enable your application to adapt to different languages. The main goal here is to develop applications that offer content in multiple formats and languages. In this section, we will explain how to add internalization to the licensing service we previously created.

First, we'll update the bootstrap class `LicenseServiceApplication.java` to create a `LocaleResolver` and a `ResourceBundleMessageSource` for our license service. The following listing shows how the bootstrap class should look.

Listing 3.6   Creating beans for the bootstrap class

```
package com.optimagrowth.license;

import java.util.Locale;

import org.springframework.boot.SpringApplication;
import org.springframework.boot.autoconfigure.SpringBootApplication;
import org.springframework.context.annotation.Bean;
import org.springframework.context.support.ResourceBundleMessageSource;
import org.springframework.web.servlet.LocaleResolver;
import org.springframework.web.servlet.i18n.SessionLocaleResolver;

@SpringBootApplication
public class LicenseServiceApplication {

    public static void main(String[] args) {
        SpringApplication.run(LicenseServiceApplication.class, args);
    }

    @Bean
    public LocaleResolver localeResolver() {
        SessionLocaleResolver localeResolver = new SessionLocaleResolver();
        localeResolver.setDefaultLocale(Locale.US);
        return localeResolver;
    }
    @Bean
    public ResourceBundleMessageSource messageSource() {
        ResourceBundleMessageSource messageSource =
                            new ResourceBundleMessageSource();
        messageSource.setUseCodeAsDefaultMessage(true);

        messageSource.setBasenames("messages");
        return messageSource;
    }
}
```

Sets US as the default locale

Sets the base name of the languages properties files

Doesn't throw an error if a message isn't found, instead it returns the message code

The first thing to note in listing 3.6 is that we set `Locale.US` as the default locale. If we don't set a `Locale` when we retrieve the message, the `messageSource` will use the default locale set as the `LocaleResolver`. Next, note the following call:

```
messageSource.setUseCodeAsDefaultMessage(true)
```

When a message is not found, this option returns the message code `'license.creates .message'` instead of an error like this one:

```
"No message found under code 'license.creates.message' for locale 'es'
```

Finally, the `messageSource.setBasenames("messages")` call sets `messages` as the base name of the message source file. For example, if we were in Italy, we would use the `Locale.IT`, and we would have a file called messages_it.properties. In case we don't find a message in a specific language, the message source will search on the default message file called messages.properties.

Now, let's configure the messages. For this example, we will use English and Spanish messages. To achieve this, we need to create the following files under the /src/main/resources source folder:

- messages_en.properties
- messages_es.properties
- messages.properties

The following two listings show how the messages_en.properties and the messages_es.properties files should look.

Listing 3.7   Exploring the messages_en.properties file

```
license.create.message = License created %s
license.update.message = License %s updated
license.delete.message = Deleting license with
                id %s for the organization %s
```

Listing 3.8   Exploring the messages_es.properties file

```
license.create.message = Licencia creada %s
license.update.message = Licencia %s creada
license.delete.message = Eliminando licencia con
                id %s para la organization %s license
```

Now that we've implemented the messages and the `@Beans` annotation, we can update the code in our controller or service to call the message resource. The following listing shows how this is done.

Listing 3.9   Updating the service to look for the messages on the `MessageSource`

```
@Autowired
MessageSource messages;

public String createLicense(License license,
                    String organizationId,
                    Locale locale){                    Receives the Locale as
        String responseMessage = null;               a method parameter
        if (license != null) {
            license.setOrganizationId(organizationId);
            responseMessage = String.format(messages.getMessage(
                        "license.create.message", null,locale),
                        license.toString());         Sets the received locale to
        }                                            retrieve the specific message
```

```
        return responseMessage;
}

public String updateLicense(License license, String organizationId){
    String responseMessage = null;
    if (license != null) {
        license.setOrganizationId(organizationId);
        responseMessage = String.format(messages.getMessage(
                        "license.update.message", null, null),
                        license.toString());
    }

    return responseMessage;
}
```

Sends a null locale to retrieve
the specific message

There are three important things to highlight from the code in listing 3.9. The first is that we can receive the `Locale` from the `Controller` itself. The second is that we can call the `messages.getMessage("license.create.message",null,locale)` using the locale we received by parameters, and the third thing to note is that we can call the `messages.getMessage("license.update.message", null, null)` without sending any locale. In this particular scenario, the application will use the default locale we previously defined in the bootstrap class. Now let's update our `createLicense()` method on the controller to receive the language from the request `Accept-Language` header with this code:

```
@PostMapping
public ResponseEntity<String> createLicense(
    @PathVariable("organizationId") String organizationId,
    @RequestBody License request,
    @RequestHeader(value = "Accept-Language",required = false)
                Locale locale){
  return ResponseEntity.ok(licenseService.createLicense(
                    request, organizationId, locale));
}
```

A few things to note from this code is that here we use the `@RequestHeader` annotation. The `@RequestHeader` annotation maps method parameters with request header values. In the `createLicense()` method, we retrieve the locale from the request header `Accept-Language`. This service parameter is not required, so if it's not specified, we will use the default locale. Figure 3.7 shows you how to send the `Accept-Language` request header from Postman.

> **NOTE** There isn't a well-defined rule on how to use `locale`. Our recommendation is to analyze your architecture and select the option that is most suitable for you. For example, if the front-end application handles the locale, then receiving the locale as a parameter in the controller method is the best option. But if you are managing the locale in the backend, you can use a default locale.

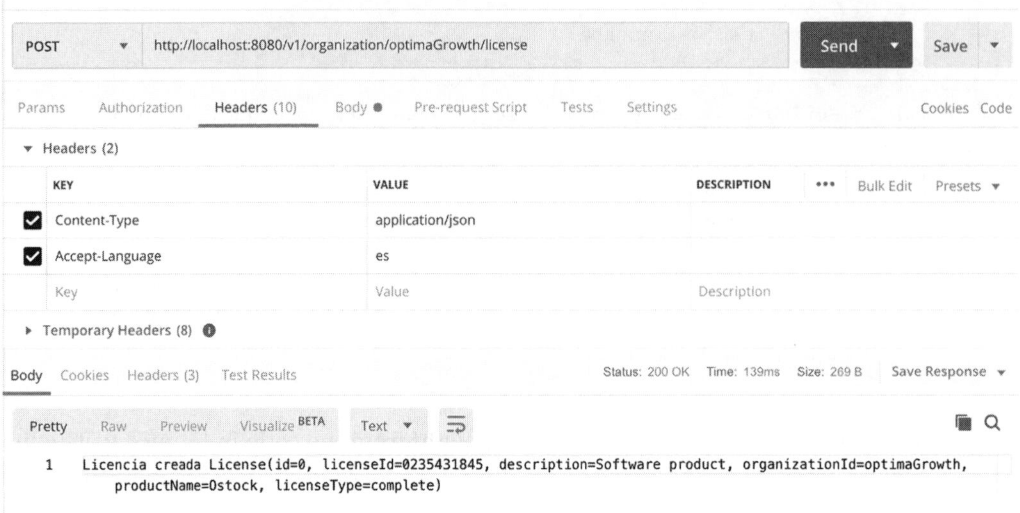

Figure 3.7   Setting the `Accept-Language` header in the POST create license service

3.3.3   *Implementing Spring HATEOAS to display related links*

HATEOAS stands for Hypermedia as the Engine of Application State. Spring HATEOAS is a small project that allows us to create APIs that follow the HATEOAS principle of displaying the related links for a given resource. The HATEOAS principle states that an API should provide a guide to the client by returning information about possible next steps with each service response. This project isn't a core or a must-have feature, but if you want to have a complete guide for all of the API services of a given resource, it is an excellent option.

With Spring HATEOAS, you can quickly create model classes for links to resource representation models. It also provides a link builder API to create specific links that point to Spring MVC controller methods. The following code snippet shows an example of how HATEOAS should look for the license service:

```
"_links": {
    "self" : {
        "href" : "http://localhost:8080/v1/organization/
                  optimaGrowth/license/0235431845"
    },
    "createLicense" : {
        "href" : "http://localhost:8080/v1/organization/
                  optimaGrowth/license"
    },
    "updateLicense" : {
        "href" : "http://localhost:8080/v1/organization/
                  optimaGrowth/license"
    },
```

```
    "deleteLicense" : {
        "href" : "http://localhost:8080/v1/organization/
                  optimaGrowth/license/0235431845"
    }
}
```

In this section, we will show you how to implement Spring HATEOAS in the license service. The first thing we must do to send the links related to a resource in the response is to add the HATEOAS dependency into our pom.xml file, like this:

```
<dependency>
    <groupId>org.springframework.boot</groupId>
    <artifactId>spring-boot-starter-hateoas</artifactId>
</dependency>
```

Once we have the dependency, we need to update the License class in order to extend from RepresentationModel<License>. The following listing shows how to do this.

Listing 3.10 Extending from `RepresentationModel`

```
package com.optimagrowth.license.model;

import org.springframework.hateoas.RepresentationModel;

import lombok.Getter;
import lombok.Setter;
import lombok.ToString;


@Getter @Setter @ToString
public class License extends RepresentationModel<License> {

    private int id;
    private String licenseId;
    private String description;
    private String organizationId;
    private String productName;
    private String licenseType;

}
```

RepresentationModel<License> gives us the ability to add links to the License model class. Now that we have everything set up, let's create the HATEOS configuration to retrieve the links for the LicenseController class. The next listing shows how this is done. For this example, we're only going to change the getLicense() method in the LicenseController class.

Listing 3.11   Adding links to the `LicenseController`

```
@RequestMapping(value="/{licenseId}",method = RequestMethod.GET)
public ResponseEntity<License> getLicense(
        @PathVariable("organizationId") String organizationId,
        @PathVariable("licenseId") String licenseId) {

    License license = licenseService.getLicense(licenseId,
                                        organizationId);
    license.add(linkTo(methodOn(LicenseController.class)
        .getLicense(organizationId, license.getLicenseId()))
        .withSelfRel(),
        linkTo(methodOn(LicenseController.class)
        .createLicense(organizationId, license, null))
        .withRel("createLicense"),
        linkTo(methodOn(LicenseController.class)
        .updateLicense(organizationId, license))
        .withRel("updateLicense"),
        linkTo(methodOn(LicenseController.class)
        .deleteLicense(organizationId, license.getLicenseId()))
        .withRel("deleteLicense"));
    return ResponseEntity.ok(license);
}
```

The method `add()` is a method of the `RepresentationModel`. The `linkTo` method inspects the `License` controller class and obtains the root mapping, and the `methodOn` method obtains the method mapping by doing a dummy invocation of the target method. Both methods are static methods of `org.springframework.hateoas.server` `.mvc.WebMvcLinkBuilder`. `WebMvcLinkBuilder` is a utility class for creating links on the controller classes. Figure 3.8 shows the links on the response body of the `get-License()` service. To retrieve those, you must call the GET HTTP method.

At this point, you have a running skeleton of a service. But from a development perspective, this service isn't complete. A good microservice design doesn't eschew segregating the service into well-defined business logic and data access layers. As you progress in later chapters, you'll continue to iterate on this service and delve further into how to structure it. For now, let's switch to the final perspective: exploring how a DevOps engineer would operationalize the service and package it for deployment to the cloud.

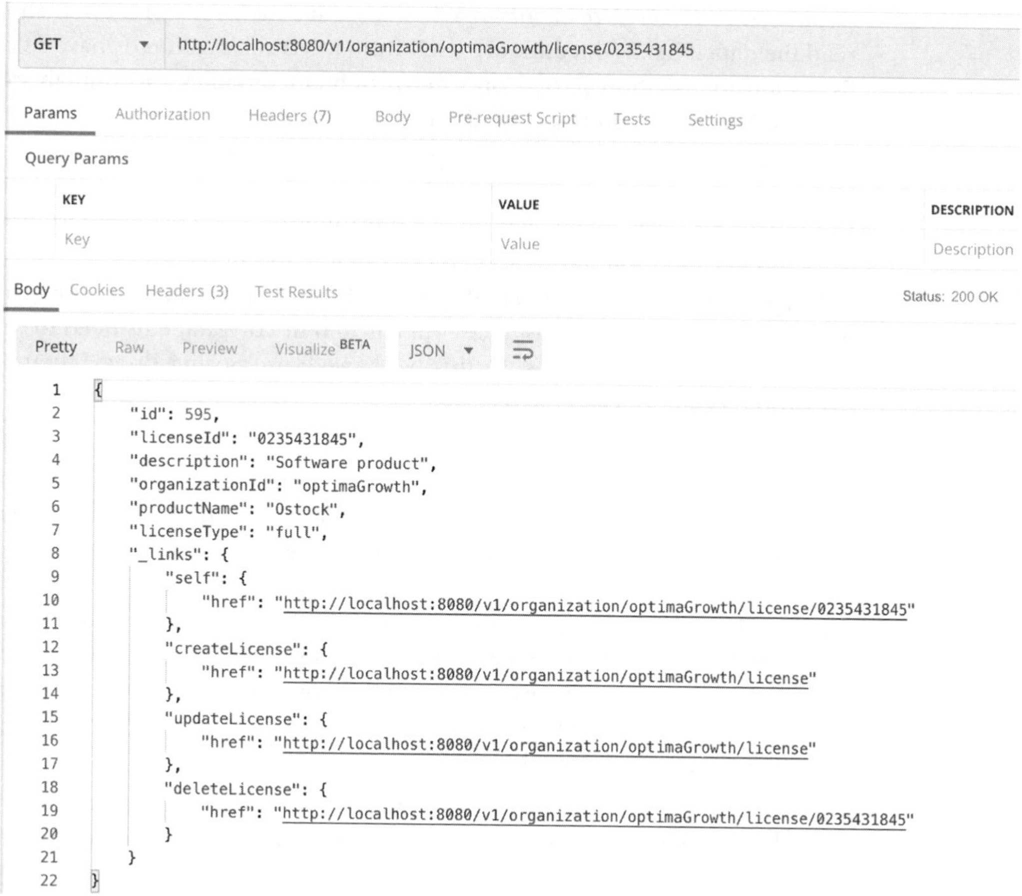

```
GET           ▼    http://localhost:8080/v1/organization/optimaGrowth/license/0235431845
```

Params   Authorization   Headers (7)   Body   Pre-request Script   Tests   Settings

Query Params

KEY	VALUE	DESCRIPTION
Key	Value	Description

Body   Cookies   Headers (3)   Test Results   Status: 200 OK

Pretty   Raw   Preview   Visualize ^BETA   JSON ▼   ⇥

```
 1   {
 2       "id": 595,
 3       "licenseId": "0235431845",
 4       "description": "Software product",
 5       "organizationId": "optimaGrowth",
 6       "productName": "Ostock",
 7       "licenseType": "full",
 8       "_links": {
 9           "self": {
10               "href": "http://localhost:8080/v1/organization/optimaGrowth/license/0235431845"
11           },
12           "createLicense": {
13               "href": "http://localhost:8080/v1/organization/optimaGrowth/license"
14           },
15           "updateLicense": {
16               "href": "http://localhost:8080/v1/organization/optimaGrowth/license"
17           },
18           "deleteLicense": {
19               "href": "http://localhost:8080/v1/organization/optimaGrowth/license/0235431845"
20           }
21       }
22   }
```

Figure 3.8   HATEOAS links on the response body of the HTTP GET license service

3.4 *The DevOps story: Building for the rigors of runtime*

While DevOps is a rich and emerging IT field, for the DevOps engineer, the design of the microservice is all about managing the service after it goes into production. Writing the code is often the easy part. Keeping it running is the hard part. We'll start our microservice development effort with four principles and build on these later in the book:

- *A microservice should be self-contained.* It should also be independently deployable with multiple instances of the service being started up and torn down with a single software artifact.

- *A microservice should be configurable.* When a service instance starts up, it should read the data it needs to configure itself from a central location or have its configuration information passed on as environment variables. No human intervention should be required to configure the service.

- *A microservice instance needs to be transparent to the client.* The client should never know the exact location of a service. Instead, a microservice client should talk to a service discovery agent. That allows the application to locate an instance of a microservice without having to know its physical location.

- *A microservice should communicate its health.* This is a critical part of your cloud architecture. Microservice instances will fail, and discovery agents need to route around bad service instances. In this book, we'll use Spring Boot Actuator to display the health of each microservice.

These four principles expose the paradox that can exist with microservice development. Microservices are smaller in size and scope, but their use introduces more moving parts in an application because microservices are distributed and run independently of each other in their own containers. This introduces a high degree of coordination and more opportunities for failure points in the application.

From a DevOps perspective, you must address the operational needs of a microservice up front and translate these four principles into a standard set of lifecycle events that occur every time a microservice is built and deployed to an environment. The four principles can be mapped to the following operational lifecycles. Figure 3.9 shows how these four steps fit together.

- *Service assembly*—How you package and deploy your service to guarantee repeatability and consistency so that the same service code and run time are deployed exactly the same way.

- *Service bootstrapping*—How you separate your application and environment-specific configuration code from the run-time code so that you can start and deploy a microservice instance quickly in any environment without human intervention.

- *Service registration/discovery*—When a new microservice instance is deployed, how you make the new service instance discoverable by other application clients.

- *Service monitoring*—In a microservice environment, it's common for multiple instances of the same service to be running due to high availability needs. From a DevOps perspective, you need to monitor microservice instances and ensure that any faults are routed around failing service instances, and that these are taken down.

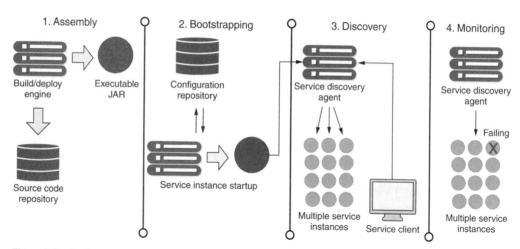

Figure 3.9 **A microservice goes through multiple steps in its lifecycle.**

3.4.1 *Service assembly: Packaging and deploying your microservices*

From a DevOps perspective, one of the key concepts behind a microservice architecture is that multiple instances of a microservice can be deployed quickly in response to a changed application environment (for example, a sudden influx of user requests, problems within the infrastructure, and so on). To accomplish this, a microservice needs to be packaged and installable as a single artifact with all of its dependencies defined within it. These dependencies must also include the run-time engine (for example, an HTTP server or application container) that hosts the microservice.

The process of consistently building, packaging, and deploying is the service assembly (step 1 in figure 3.9). Figure 3.10 shows additional details about this step.

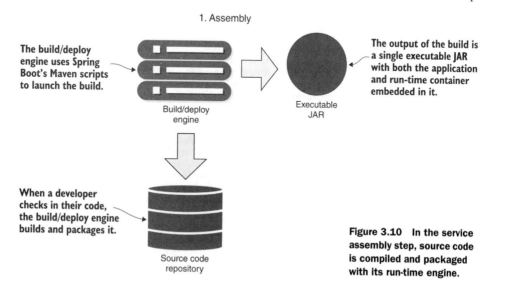

Figure 3.10 **In the service assembly step, source code is compiled and packaged with its run-time engine.**

Fortunately, almost all Java microservice frameworks will include a run-time engine that you can package and deploy with the code. For instance, in the Spring Boot example in figure 3.10, Maven and Spring Boot build an executable Java JAR file that has an embedded Tomcat engine built right into the JAR. In the following command-line example, we build the licensing service as an executable JAR and then start the JAR from the command line:

```
mvn clean package && java -jar target/licensing-service-0.0.1-SNAPSHOT.jar
```

For certain operations teams, the concept of embedding a run-time environment right in the JAR file is a major shift in the way they think about deploying applications. In a traditional Java web-based application, the application is deployed to an application server. This model implies that the application server is an entity in and of itself and would often be managed by a team of system administrators who oversee the server's configuration independently of the applications being deployed to them.

This separation of the application server configuration from the application introduces failure points in the deployment process. This is because in many organizations, the configuration of the application servers isn't kept under source control and is managed through a combination of the user interface and home-grown management scripts. It's too easy for configuration drift to creep into the application server environment and suddenly cause what on the surface appears to be random outages.

3.4.2 *Service bootstrapping: Managing configuration of your microservices*

Service bootstrapping (step 2 in figure 3.9) occurs when the microservice first starts and needs to load its application configuration information. Figure 3.11 provides more context for the bootstrapping process.

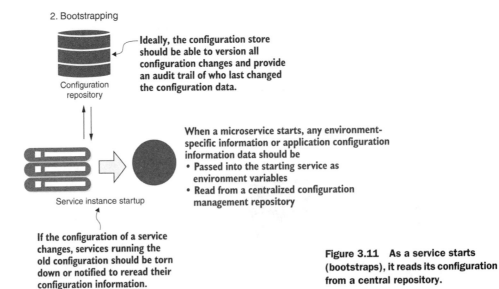

2. Bootstrapping

Configuration repository

Ideally, the configuration store should be able to version all configuration changes and provide an audit trail of who last changed the configuration data.

Service instance startup

When a microservice starts, any environment-specific information or application configuration information data should be
• Passed into the starting service as environment variables
• Read from a centralized configuration management repository

If the configuration of a service changes, services running the old configuration should be torn down or notified to reread their configuration information.

Figure 3.11 As a service starts (bootstraps), it reads its configuration from a central repository.

As any application developer knows, there will be times when you need to make the run-time behavior of the application configurable. Usually this involves reading your application configuration data from a property file deployed with the application or reading the data out of a data store like a relational database.

Microservices often run into the same type of configuration requirements. The difference is that in a microservice application running in the cloud, you might have hundreds or even thousands of microservice instances running. Further complicating this is that the services might be spread across the globe. With a high number of geographically dispersed services, it becomes unfeasible to redeploy your services to pick up new configuration data. Storing the data in a data store external to the service solves this problem. But microservices in the cloud offer a set of unique challenges:

- Configuration data tends to be simple in structure and is usually read frequently and written infrequently. Relational databases are overkill in this situation because they're designed to manage much more complicated data models than a simple set of key-value pairs.
- Because the data is accessed on a regular basis but changes infrequently, the data must be readable with a low level of latency.
- The data store has to be highly available and close to the services reading the data. A configuration data store can't go down completely because it would become a single point of failure for your application.

In chapter 5, we'll show how to manage your microservice application configuration data using things like a simple key-value data store.

3.4.3 *Service registration and discovery: How clients communicate with your microservices*

From a microservice consumer perspective, a microservice should be location-transparent because in a cloud-based environment, servers are ephemeral. *Ephemeral* means that the servers that a service is hosted on usually have shorter lives than a service running in a corporate data center. Cloud-based services can be started and torn down quickly with an entirely new IP address assigned to the server on which the services are running.

By insisting that services are treated as short-lived disposable objects, microservice architectures can achieve a high degree of scalability and availability by having multiple instances of a service running. Service demand and resiliency can be managed as quickly as the situation warrants. Each service has a unique and impermanent IP address assigned to it. The downside to ephemeral services is that with services constantly coming up and down, managing a large pool of these services manually or by hand is an invitation to an outage.

A microservice instance needs to register itself with a third-party agent. This registration process is called *service discovery* (see step 3 in figure 3.9, then see figure 3.12 for details on this process). When a microservice instance registers with a service discovery agent, it tells the discovery agent two things: the physical IP address (or domain address of the service instance) and a logical name that an application can use to look up the service. Certain service discovery agents also require a URL sent back to the registering service, which can be used by the service discovery agent to perform health checks. The service client then communicates with the discovery agent to look up the service's location.

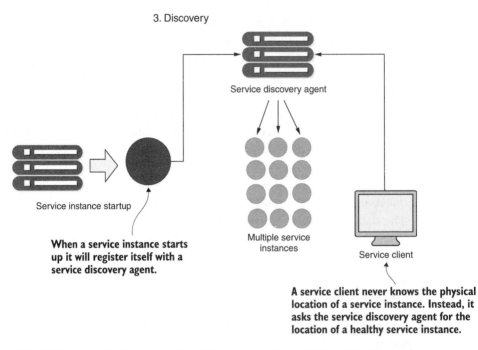

Figure 3.12   A service discovery agent abstracts away the physical location of a service.

3.4.4   *Communicating a microservice's health*

A service discovery agent doesn't act only as a traffic cop that guides the client to the location of the service. In a cloud-based microservice application, you'll often have multiple instances of a running service. Sooner or later, one of those service instances will fail. The service discovery agent monitors the health of each service instance registered with it and removes any failing service instances from its routing tables to ensure that clients aren't sent a service instance that has failed.

After a microservice comes up, the service discovery agent will continue to monitor and ping the health check interface to ensure that that service is available. This is step 4 in figure 3.9; figure 3.13 provides context for this step.

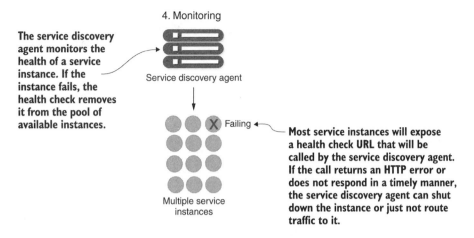

4. Monitoring

The service discovery agent monitors the health of a service instance. If the instance fails, the health check removes it from the pool of available instances.

Service discovery agent

X Failing

Multiple service instances

Most service instances will expose a health check URL that will be called by the service discovery agent. If the call returns an HTTP error or does not respond in a timely manner, the service discovery agent can shut down the instance or just not route traffic to it.

Figure 3.13   The service discovery agent uses the exposed health URL to check the microservice state.

By building a consistent health check interface, you can use cloud-based monitoring tools to detect problems and respond to these appropriately. If the service discovery agent discovers a problem with a service instance, it can take corrective action such as shutting down the ailing instance or bringing additional service instances up.

In a microservice environment that uses REST, the simplest way to build a health check interface is to expose an HTTP endpoint that can return a JSON payload and HTTP status code. In a non-Spring Boot-based microservice, it's often the developer's responsibility to write an endpoint that returns the health of the service.

In Spring Boot, exposing an endpoint is trivial and involves nothing more than modifying your Maven build file to include the Spring Actuator module. Spring Actuator provides out-of-the-box operational endpoints that help you understand and manage the health of your service. To use Spring Actuator, you need to include the following dependencies in your Maven build file:

```
<dependency>
    <groupId>org.springframework.boot</groupId>
    <artifactId>spring-boot-starter-actuator</artifactId>
</dependency>
```

If you reach the `http://localhost:8080/actuator/health` endpoint on the licensing service, you should see health data returned. Figure 3.14 provides an example of the data returned.

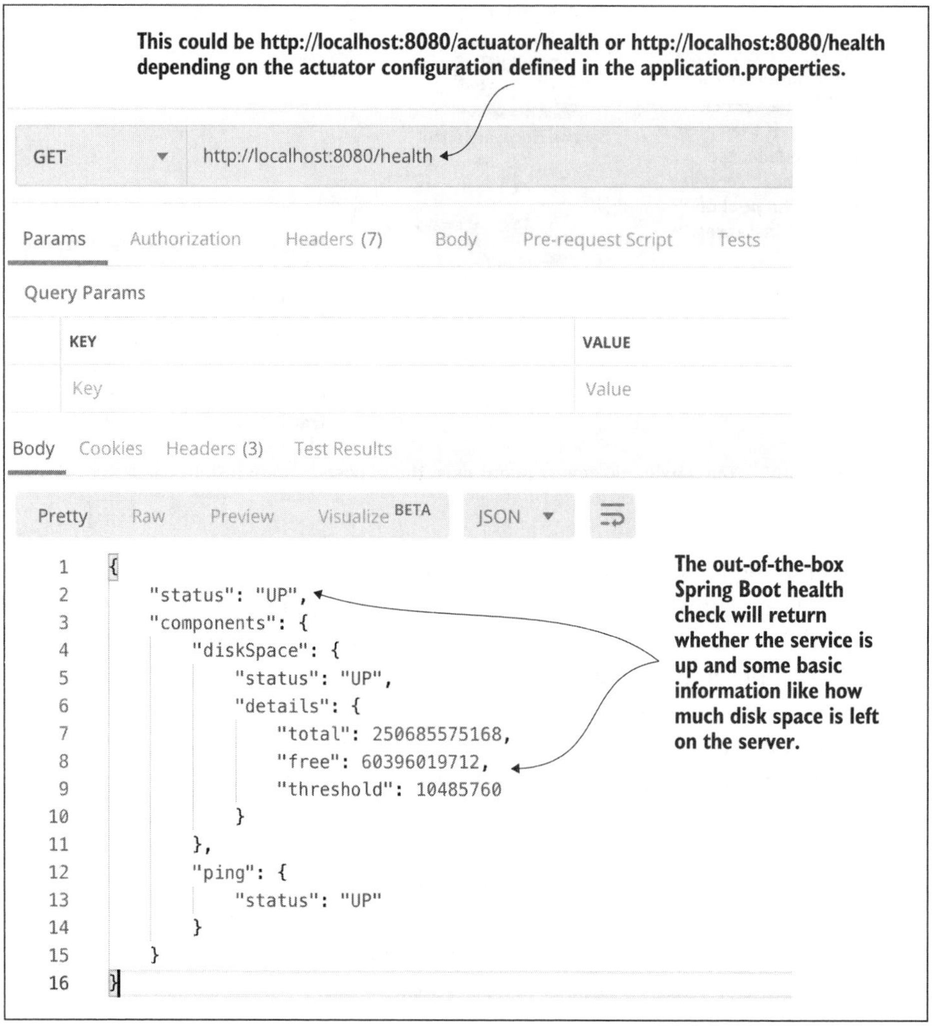

This could be http://localhost:8080/actuator/health or http://localhost:8080/health depending on the actuator configuration defined in the application.properties.

```
GET          ▼    http://localhost:8080/health
```

Params   Authorization   Headers (7)   Body   Pre-request Script   Tests

Query Params

KEY	VALUE
Key	Value

Body   Cookies   Headers (3)   Test Results

Pretty   Raw   Preview   Visualize BETA   JSON ▼

```
 1  {
 2      "status": "UP",
 3      "components": {
 4          "diskSpace": {
 5              "status": "UP",
 6              "details": {
 7                  "total": 250685575168,
 8                  "free": 60396019712,
 9                  "threshold": 10485760
10              }
11          },
12          "ping": {
13              "status": "UP"
14          }
15      }
16  }
```

The out-of-the-box Spring Boot health check will return whether the service is up and some basic information like how much disk space is left on the server.

Figure 3.14 A health check on each service instance allows monitoring tools to determine if the service instance is running.

As you can see in figure 3.14, the health check can be more than an indicator of what's up and what's down. It also can give information about the state of the server on which the microservice instance is running. Spring Actuator lets you change the default configuration via the application properties file. For example:

```
management.endpoints.web.base-path=/
management.endpoints.enabled-by-default=false
management.endpoint.health.enabled=true
management.endpoint.health.show-details=always
management.health.db.enabled=false
management.health.diskspace.enabled=true
```

The first line allows you to set the base path for all Actuator services (for example, the health endpoint is now exposed in the `http://localhost:8080/health` URL). The remaining lines allow you to disable the default services and enable the services you want to use.

> **NOTE** If you are interested in knowing all of the services exposed by Spring Actuator, we recommend you read the following Spring document: https://docs.spring.io/spring-boot/docs/current/reference/html/production-ready-endpoints.html.

3.5   *Pulling the perspectives together*

Microservices in the cloud seem deceptively simple. But to be successful with them, you need to have an integrated view that pulls the perspective of the architect, the developer, and the DevOps engineer together into a cohesive vision. The key takeaways for each of these perspectives are as follows:

- *Architect*—Focus on the natural contours of your business problem. Describe your business problem domain and listen to the story you're telling. Target microservice candidates will emerge. Remember, too, that it's better to start with a coarse-grained microservice and refactor back to smaller services than it is to start with a large group of small services. Microservice architectures, like most good architectures, are emergent and not preplanned to the minute.
- *Software engineer (aka developer)*—The fact that the service is small doesn't mean good design principles get thrown out the window. Focus on building a layered service, where each layer in the service has discrete responsibilities. Avoid the temptation to build frameworks in your code and try to make each microservice completely independent. Premature framework design and adoption can have massive maintenance costs later in the lifecycle of the application.
- *DevOps engineer*—Services don't exist in a vacuum. Establish the lifecycle of your services early. The DevOps perspective needs to focus not only on how to automate the building and deployment of a service, but also on how to monitor the health of the service and react when something goes wrong. Operationalizing a service often takes more work and forethought than writing business logic. In appendix C, we'll explain how to achieve this with Prometheus and Grafana.

Summary

- To be successful with microservices, you need to integrate three team perspectives: the architect, the developer, and the DevOps.
- Microservices, while a powerful architectural paradigm, have their benefits and trade-offs. Not all applications should be microservice applications.
- From an architect's perspective, microservices are small, self-contained, and distributed. Microservices should have narrow boundaries and manage a small set of data.

- From a developer's perspective, microservices are typically built using a REST-style design, with JSON as the payload for sending and receiving data from the service.
- The main goal of internationalization is to develop applications that offer content in multiple formats and languages.
- HATEOAS stands for Hypermedia as the Engine of Application State. Spring HATEOAS is a small project that allows us to create APIs that follow the HATEOAS principle of displaying the related links for a given resource.
- From a DevOps perspective, how a microservice is packaged, deployed, and monitored is of critical importance.
- Out of the box, Spring Boot allows you to deliver a service as a single executable JAR file. An embedded Tomcat server in the produced JAR file hosts the service.
- Spring Actuator, which is included with the Spring Boot framework, exposes information about the operational health of the service along with information about the run time of the service.

Welcome to Docker 4

This chapter covers

- Understanding the importance of containers
- Recognizing how containers fit into a microservices architecture
- Understanding the differences between a VM and a container
- Using Docker and its main components
- Integrating Docker with microservices

To continue successfully building our microservices, we need to address the portability issue: how are we going to execute our microservices in different technology locations? *Portability* is the ability to use or move software to different environments.

In recent years, the concept of containers has gained more and more popularity, going from a "nice-to-have" to a "must-have" in software architecture. The use of containers is an agile and useful way to migrate and execute any software development from one platform to another (for example, from the developer's machine to a physical or virtual enterprise server). We can replace the traditional models of web servers with smaller and much more adaptable virtualized software containers that offer advantages such as speed, portability, and scalability to our microservices.

This chapter provides a brief introduction to containers using Docker, a technology we selected because we can use it with all the major cloud providers. We will explain what Docker is, how to use its core components, and how to integrate Docker with our microservices. By the end of the chapter, you will be able to run Docker, create your own images with Maven, and execute your microservices within a container. Also, you'll notice you no longer have to worry about installing all the prerequisites your microservices need to run; the only requirement is that you have an environment with Docker installed.

> **NOTE**   In this chapter, we will only explain what we are going to use throughout the book. If you are interested in knowing more about Docker, we highly recommend you check out the excellent book, *Docker in Action*, 2nd ed., by Jeff Nickoloff, Stephen Kuenzli, and Bret Fisher (Manning, 2019). The authors provide an exhaustive overview of what Docker is and how it works.

4.1   *Containers or virtual machines?*

In many companies, virtual machines (VMs) are still the de facto standard for software deployment. In this section, we'll look at the main differences between VMs and containers.

A VM is a software environment that allows us to emulate the operation of a computer within another computer. These are based on a hypervisor that emulates the complete physical machine, allocating the desired amount of system memory, processor cores, disk storage, and other technological resources such as networks, PCI add-ons, and so forth. On the other hand, a container is a package that contains a virtual operating system (OS) that allows us to run an application with its dependent elements in an isolated and independent environment.

Both technologies have similarities, like the existence of a hypervisor or container engine that allows the execution of both technologies, but the way they implement them makes VMs and containers very different. In figure 4.1, you can see the main differences between VMs and containers.

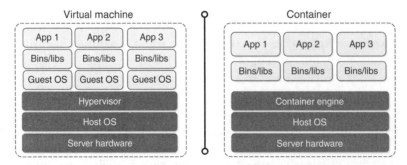

Figure 4.1   **Main differences between VMs and containers. Containers don't need the guest OS or the hypervisor to assign resources; instead, they use a container engine.**

If we analyze figure 4.1, at first glance, we can see that there isn't that much difference. After all, only the guest OS layer has disappeared in the container, and the hypervisor is replaced by the container's engine. However, the differences between VMs and containers are still enormous.

In a VM, we must set how many physical resources we'll need in advance; for example, how many virtual processors or how many GBs of RAM and disk space we are going to use. Defining those values can be a tricky task, and we must be careful to take into consideration the following:

- Processors can be shared between different VMs.
- Disk space in the VM can be set to use only what it needs. You can define a disk max size, but it will only use the actively consumed space on your machine.
- Reserved memory is total and can't be shared between VMs.

With containers, we can also set the memory and the CPU that we'll need by using Kubernetes, but this isn't required. In case you don't specify these values, the container engine will assign the necessary resources for the container to function correctly. Because containers don't need a complete OS, but can reuse the underlying one, this reduces the load the physical machine must support, as well as the storage space used and the time needed to launch the application. Therefore, containers are much lighter than VMs.

In the end, both technologies have their benefits and drawbacks, and the ultimate decision depends on your specific needs. For example, if you want to handle a variety of operating systems, manage multiple applications on a single server, and execute an application that requires the functionalities of an OS, VMs are a better solution.

In this book, we've chosen to use containers due to the cloud architecture we are building. Instead of virtualizing the hardware as with the VM approach, we will use containers to only virtualize the OS level, which creates a much lighter and faster alternative than what we would be able to run on premises and on every major cloud provider.

Nowadays, performance and portability are critical concepts for decision making in a company. It's important, therefore, to know the benefits of the technologies we are going to use. In this case, with the use of containers with our microservices, we will have these benefits:

- Containers can run everywhere, which facilitates development and implementation and increases portability.
- Containers provide the ability to create predictable environments that are entirely isolated from other applications.
- Containers can be started and stopped faster than VMs, which makes them cloud-native feasible.
- Containers are scalable and can be actively scheduled and managed to optimize resource utilization, increasing the performance and maintainability of the application running within.
- We can realize a maximum number of applications on a minimum number of servers.

Now that we understand the difference between VMs and containers, let's take a closer look at Docker.

4.2   *What is Docker?*

Docker is a popular open source container engine based on Linux, created by Solomon Hykes, founder and CEO of dotCloud in March, 2013. Docker started as a nice-to-have technology that was responsible for launching and managing containers within our applications. This technology allowed us to share the resources of a physical machine with different containers instead of exposing different hardware resources like VMs.

The support that big companies like IBM, Microsoft, and Google gave to Docker allowed for the conversion of a new technology into a fundamental tool for software developers. Nowadays, Docker continues to grow and currently represents one of the most widely used tools to deploy software with containers on any server.

> **DEFINITION** A *container* represents a logical packaging mechanism, providing applications with everything they need to run.

To understand better how Docker works, it's essential to note that the Docker Engine is the core piece of the entire Docker system. What is the Docker Engine? It is an application that follows the client-server pattern architecture. This application is installed in the host machine and contains the following three critical components: server, REST API, and command-line interface (CLI). Figure 4.2 illustrates these Docker components, as well as others.

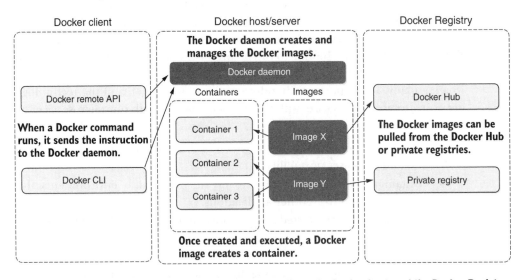

Figure 4.2   Docker architecture composed of the Docker client, the Docker host, and the Docker Registry.

The Docker Engine contains the following components:

- *Docker daemon*—A server, called dockerd, that allows us to create and manage the Docker images. The REST API sends instructions to the daemon, and the CLI client enters the Docker commands.
- *Docker client*—Docker users interact with Docker via a client. When a Docker command runs, the client is in charge of sending the instruction to the daemon.
- *Docker Registry*—The location where Docker images are stored. These registries can be either public or private. The Docker Hub is the default place for the public registries, but you can also create your own private registry.
- *Docker images*—These are read-only templates with several instructions to create a Docker container. The images can be pulled from the Docker Hub, and you can use them as is, or you can modify them by adding additional instructions. Also, you can create new images by using a Dockerfile. Later on, in this chapter, we will explain how to use Dockerfiles.
- *Docker containers*—Once created and executed with the docker run command, a Docker image creates a container. The application and its environment run inside this container. In order to start, stop, and delete a Docker container, you can use the Docker API or the CLI.
- *Docker volumes*—Docker volumes are the preferred mechanism to store data generated by Docker and used by the Docker containers. They can be managed using the Docker API or the Docker CLI.
- *Docker networks*—The Docker networks allow us to attach the containers to as many networks as we like. We can see the networks as a means to communicate with isolated containers. Docker contains the following five network driver types: bridge, host, overlay, none, and macvlan.

Figure 4.3 shows a diagram of how Docker works. Note that the Docker daemon is responsible for all the container's actions. As shown in figure 4.3, we can see that the daemon receives the commands from the Docker client; these commands can be sent via the CLI or the REST APIs. In the diagram, we can see how the Docker images found in the registries create the containers.

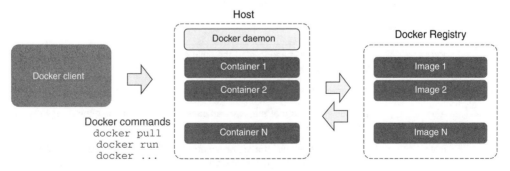

Figure 4.3   The Docker client sends Docker commands to the Docker daemon, and the Docker daemon creates the containers based on the Docker images.

> **NOTE** In this book, we won't teach you how to install Docker. If you don't have
> Docker already installed on your computer, we highly recommend you look at
> the following documentation, which contains all the steps to install and config-
> ure Docker in Windows, macOS, or Linux: https://docs.docker.com/install/.

In the next sections, we will explain how Docker's components work and how to integrate them with our license microservice. In case you didn't follow the example in
chapters 1 and 3, you can apply what we're about to explain to any Java Maven project
you have.

4.3 *Dockerfiles*

A *Dockerfile* is a simple text file that contains a list of instructions and commands that
the Docker client calls to create and prepare an image. This file automates the image
creation process for you. The commands used in the Dockerfile are similar to Linux
commands, which makes the Dockerfile easier to understand.

The following code snippet presents a brief example of how a Dockerfile looks. In
section 4.5.1, we will show you how to create custom Dockerfiles for your own microservices. Figure 4.4 shows how the Docker image creation workflow should look.

```
FROM openjdk:11-slim
ARG JAR_FILE=target/*.jar
COPY ${JAR_FILE} app.jar
ENTRYPOINT ["java","-jar","/app.jar"]
```

**Figure 4.4 Once the Dockerfile is created, you run the `docker build` command to build a Docker
image. Then, once the Docker image is ready, you use the `run` command to create the containers.**

Table 4.1 shows the most common Dockerfile commands that we'll use in our Dockerfiles. See also listing 4.1 for an example Dockerfile.

Table 4.1 Dockerfile commands

FROM	Defines a base image to start the build process. In other words, the FROM command specifies the Docker image that you'll use in your Docker run time.
LABEL	Adds metadata to an image. This is a key-value pair.
ARG	Defines variables that the user can pass to the builder using the docker build command.
COPY	Copies new files, directories, or remote file URLs from a source and adds them to the filesystem of the image we are creating at the specified destination path (for example, COPY ${JAR_FILE} app.jar).

Table 4.1   Dockerfile commands

VOLUME	Creates a mount point in our container. When we create a new container using the same image, we will create a new volume that will be isolated from the previous one.
RUN	Takes the command and its arguments to run a container from the image. We often use this for installing software packages.
CMD	Provides arguments to the ENTRYPOINT. This command is similar to the docker run command, but this command gets executed only after a container is instantiated.
ADD	Copies and adds the files from a source to a destination within the container.
ENTRYPOINT	Configures a container that will run as an executable.
ENV	Sets the environment variables.

4.4   *Docker Compose*

Docker Compose simplifies the use of Docker by allowing us to create scripts that facilitate the design and the construction of services. With Docker Compose, you can run multiple containers as a single service or you can create different containers simultaneously. To use Docker Compose, follow these steps:

1 Install Docker Compose if you don't have it already installed. You can access this tool at https://docs.docker.com/compose/install/.
2 Create a YAML file to configure your application services. You should name this file docker-compose.yml.
3 Check the validity of the file using the following command: docker-compose config.
4 Start the services using the following command: docker-compose up.

A docker-compose.yml file should look like that shown in the following listing. Later, in this chapter, we will explain how to create our docker-compose.yml file.

Listing 4.1   A sample docker-compose.yml file

```
version: <docker-compose-version>
services:
  database:
    image: <database-docker-image-name>
    ports:
      - "<databasePort>:<databasePort>"
    environment:
      POSTGRES_USER: <databaseUser>
      POSTGRES_PASSWORD: <databasePassword>
      POSTGRES_DB:<databaseName>

  <service-name>:
    image: <service-docker-image-name>
    ports:
      - "<applicationPort>:<applicationPort>"
    environment:
```

```
        PROFILE: <profile-name>
        DATABASESERVER_PORT: "<databasePort>"
    container_name: <container_name>
        networks:
        backend:
        aliases:
          - "alias"

networks:
  backend:
      driver: bridge
```

Table 4.2 shows the instructions that we will use in the docker-compose.yml file. Then table 4.3 lists the `docker-compose` commands that we will use throughout the book.

Table 4.2 Docker Compose instructions

`version`	Specifies the version of the Docker Compose tool.
`service`	Specifies which services to deploy. The service name becomes the DNS entry for the Docker instance when started and is how other services access it.
`image`	Specifies the tool to run a container using the specified image.
`port`	Defines the port number on the started Docker container that will be exposed to the outside world. Maps the internal and the external port.
`environment`	Passes the environment variables to the starting Docker image.
`network`	Specifies a custom network, allowing us to create complex topologies. The default type is `bridge`, so if we don't specify another type of network (`host`, `overlay`, `macvlan`, or `none`), we will create a bridge. The bridge network allows us to maintain the container's connection to the same network. Note that the bridge network only applies to the containers running on the same Docker daemon host.
`alias`	Specifies an alternative hostname for the service on the network.

Table 4.3 Docker Compose commands

`docker-compose up -d`	Builds the images for your application and starts the services you define. This command downloads all the necessary images and then deploys these and starts the container. The `-d` parameter indicates to run Docker in the background.
`docker-compose logs`	Lets you view all the information about your latest deployment.
`docker-compose logs <service_id>`	Lets you view the logs for a specific service. To view the licensing service deployment, for example, use this command: `docker-compose logs licenseService`.
`docker-compose ps`	Outputs the list of all the containers you have deployed in your system.

Table 4.3   Docker Compose commands

`docker-compose stop`	Stops your services once you have finished with them. This also stops the containers.
`docker-compose down`	Shuts down everything and removes all containers.

4.5   *Integrating Docker with our microservices*

Now that we understand the main components of Docker, let's integrate Docker with our licensing microservice to create a more portable, scalable, and manageable microservice. To achieve this integration, let's start by adding the Docker Maven plugin to our licensing service created in the previous chapter. In case you didn't follow the code listings there, you can download the code created in chapter 3 from the following link:

https://github.com/ihuaylupo/manning-smia/tree/master/chapter3

4.5.1   *Building the Docker Image*

To begin, we'll build a Docker image by adding the Docker Maven plugin to the pom.xml of our licensing service. This plugin will allow us to manage the Docker images and containers from our Maven pom.xml file. The following listing shows how your pom file should look.

Listing 4.2   Adding `dockerfile-maven-plugin` to pom.xml

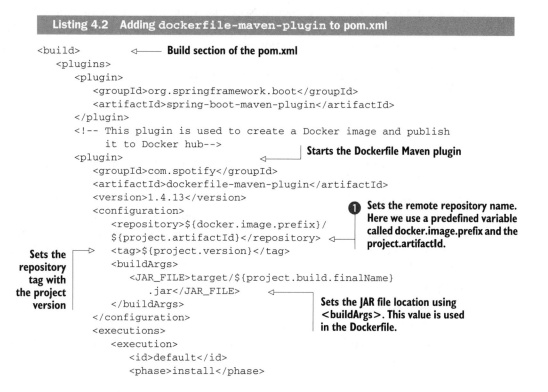

```
<build>              ←——  Build section of the pom.xml
    <plugins>
        <plugin>
            <groupId>org.springframework.boot</groupId>
            <artifactId>spring-boot-maven-plugin</artifactId>
        </plugin>
        <!-- This plugin is used to create a Docker image and publish
             it to Docker hub-->
        <plugin>                            ←——  Starts the Dockerfile Maven plugin
            <groupId>com.spotify</groupId>
            <artifactId>dockerfile-maven-plugin</artifactId>
            <version>1.4.13</version>
            <configuration>
                <repository>${docker.image.prefix}/
                ${project.artifactId}</repository>  ←——  ❶ Sets the remote repository name. Here we use a predefined variable called docker.image.prefix and the project.artifactId.
                <tag>${project.version}</tag>       ←——  Sets the repository tag with the project version
                <buildArgs>
                    <JAR_FILE>target/${project.build.finalName}
                        .jar</JAR_FILE>   ←——  Sets the JAR file location using <buildArgs>. This value is used in the Dockerfile.
                </buildArgs>
            </configuration>
            <executions>
                <execution>
                    <id>default</id>
                    <phase>install</phase>
```

```
        <goals>
            <goal>build</goal>
            <goal>push</goal>
        </goals>
      </execution>
    </executions>
  </plugin>
 </plugins>
</build>
```

Now that we have the plugin in our pom.xml file, we can continue the process by creating the variable `docker.image.prefix` mentioned in the previous code listing ❶. This variable will indicate what prefix to use for our image. The following listing shows how to add the variable into the pom.xml.

Listing 4.3   Adding the `docker.image.prefix` variable

```
<properties>
  <java.version>11</java.version>
  <docker.image.prefix>ostock</docker.image.prefix>   ◁─┐  Sets the value for the
</properties>                                            docker.image.prefix variable
```

There are several ways to define the value for the `docker.image.prefix` variable. Listing 4.3 shows but one option. Another way is to directly send the value using the `-d` option in the Maven JVM arguments. Note that if you don't create this variable in the `<properties>` section of the pom.xml, when you execute the command to package and create the Docker image, the following error is thrown:

```
Failed to execute goal com.spotify:dockerfile-maven-plugin:1.4.0:build
(default-cli) on project licensing-service: Execution default-cli of goal
com.spotify:dockerfile-maven-plugin:1.4.0:build failed: The template variable
'docker.image.prefix' has no value
```

Now that we've imported the plugin into the pom.xml, let's continue by adding the Dockerfile to our project. In the next sections, we will show you how to create a basic Dockerfile and a multistage build Dockerfile. Note that you can use both Dockerfiles because both files allow you to execute your microservice. The main difference between them is that with the basic Dockerfile, you'll copy the entire JAR file of your Spring Boot microservice, and with the multistage build, you'll copy only what's essential to the application. In this book, we chose to use the multistage build to optimize the Docker image that we will create, but feel free to use the option that best suits your needs.

BASIC DOCKERFILE

In this Dockerfile, we will copy the Spring Boot JAR file into the Docker image and then execute the application JAR. The following listing shows how to achieve this with a few simple steps.

Listing 4.4 A basic Dockerfile

```
#Start with a base image containing Java runtime
FROM openjdk:11-slim

# Add Maintainer Info
LABEL maintainer="Illary Huaylupo <illaryhs@gmail.com>"

# The application's jar file
ARG JAR_FILE

# Add the application's jar to the container
COPY ${JAR_FILE} app.jar

#execute the application
ENTRYPOINT ["java","-jar","/app.jar"]
```

Specifies the Docker image to use in our
Docker run time (in this case, openjdk:11-slim)

Defines the JAR_FILE variable
set by dockerfile-maven-plugin

Copies the JAR file to the filesystem
of the image named app.jar

Targets the licensing service application in
the image when the container is created

MULTISTAGE BUILD DOCKERFILE

In the Dockerfile for this section, we use a multistage build. Why multistage? This will allow us to discard anything that isn't essential to the execution of the application. For example, with Spring Boot, instead of copying the entire target directory to the Docker image, we only need to copy what's necessary to run the Spring Boot application. This practice will optimize the Docker image we create. The following listing shows how your Dockerfile should look.

Listing 4.5 A Dockerfile with a multistage build

```
#stage 1
#Start with a base image containing Java runtime
FROM openjdk:11-slim as build

# Add Maintainer Info
LABEL maintainer="Illary Huaylupo <illaryhs@gmail.com>"

# The application's jar file
ARG JAR_FILE

# Add the application's jar to the container
COPY ${JAR_FILE} app.jar

#unpackage jar file
RUN mkdir -p target/dependency &&
    (cd target/dependency; jar -xf /app.jar)

#stage 2
#Same Java runtime
FROM openjdk:11-slim

#Add volume pointing to /tmp
VOLUME /tmp
```

Unpacks the app.jar copied
previously into the filesystem
of the build image

This new image contains the different
layers of a Spring Boot app instead of
the complete JAR file.

```
#Copy unpackaged application to new container
ARG DEPENDENCY=/target/dependency
COPY --from=build ${DEPENDENCY}/BOOT-INF/lib /app/lib
COPY --from=build ${DEPENDENCY}/META-INF /app/META-INF
COPY --from=build ${DEPENDENCY}/BOOT-INF/classes /app

#execute the application
ENTRYPOINT ["java","-cp","app:app/lib/*","com.optimagrowth.license.
           LicenseServiceApplication"]
```

Copies the different layers from the first image named build

Targets the licensing service in the image when the container is created

We won't go through the entire multistage Docker file in detail, but we'll note a few key areas. In stage 1, using the FROM command, the Dockerfile creates an image called build from the openJDK image that is optimized for Java applications. This image is in charge of creating and unpacking the JAR application file.

NOTE The image we use already has the Java 11 JDK installed on it.

Next, the Dockerfile obtains the value for the JAR_FILE variable that we set in the <configuration> <buildArgs> section of the pom.xml. Then, we copy the JAR file into the image filesystem as app.jar and unpack it to expose the different layers that a Spring Boot application contains. Once the different layers are exposed, the Dockerfile creates another image that will only contain the layers instead of the complete application JAR. After that, in stage 2, the Dockerfile copies the different layers into the new image.

NOTE If we don't change the project's dependencies, the BOOT-INF/lib folder doesn't change. This folder contains all of the internal and external dependencies needed to run the application.

Finally, the ENTRYPOINT command allows us to target the licensing service application in the new image when the container is created. To understand more about the multistage build process, you can take a look inside the Spring Boot application fat JAR by executing the following command on the target folder of your microservice:

```
jar tf jar-file
```

For example, for the licensing service, the command should look like the following:

```
jar tf licensing-service-0.0.1-SNAPSHOT.jar
```

In case you don't have the JAR file in the target folder, execute the following Maven command on the root of the pom.xml file of your project:

```
mvn clean package
```

Now that we have our Maven environment set up, let's build our Docker image. To achieve this, you will need to execute the following command:

```
mvn package dockerfile:build
```

NOTE Verify that you have at least version 18.06.0 or greater of the Docker Engine on your local machine in order to guarantee that all the Docker code examples will run successfully. To find your Docker version, execute the `docker version` command.

Once the Docker image is built, you should see something like that shown in figure 4.5.

```
--- dockerfile-maven-plugin:1.4.13:build (default-cli) @ licensing-service ---
dockerfile: null
contextDirectory: /Users/illary.huaylupo/Documents/Personal/Manning/code/manning-smia/chapter4/licensing-service
Building Docker context /Users/illary.huaylupo/Documents/Personal/Manning/code/manning-smia/chapter4/licensing-s
Path(dockerfile): null
Path(contextDirectory): /Users/illary.huaylupo/Documents/Personal/Manning/code/manning-smia/chapter4/licensing-s

Image will be built as ostock/licensing-service:0.0.1-SNAPSHOT

Step 1/12 : FROM openjdk:11-slim as build ◄──────────────────────── Dockerfile steps

Pulling from library/openjdk
Digest: sha256:225e03d0955b1cd6da39003db94f0e655b112b76bd65a29e06e8dd98e9030bf5
Status: Image is up to date for openjdk:11-slim
 ---> 6085fd745c24
Step 2/12 : LABEL maintainer="Illary Huaylupo <illaryhs@gmail.com>"

 ---> Running in 371380f9e53e
Removing intermediate container 371380f9e53e
 ---> 57a44e0e985b
Step 3/12 : ARG JAR_FILE

 ---> Running in 4655b1862836
Removing intermediate container 4655b1862836
 ---> 71e6835e40fc
Step 4/12 : COPY ${JAR_FILE} app.jar

 ---> dee44fe0de6c
Step 5/12 : RUN mkdir -p target/dependency && (cd target/dependency; jar -xf /app.jar)

 ---> Running in 9c23dabae835
Removing intermediate container 9c23dabae835
 ---> f0aa2ff9fedc
Step 6/12 : FROM openjdk:11-slim

Pulling from library/openjdk
Digest: sha256:225e03d0955b1cd6da39003db94f0e655b112b76bd65a29e06e8dd98e9030bf5
Status: Image is up to date for openjdk:11-slim
 ---> 6085fd745c24
Step 7/12 : VOLUME /tmp

 ---> Using cache
 ---> bf23ae387bbd
Step 8/12 : ARG DEPENDENCY=/target/dependency

 ---> Running in 9b6a06b1b495
Removing intermediate container 9b6a06b1b495
 ---> 5dab66558903
Step 9/12 : COPY --from=build ${DEPENDENCY}/BOOT-INF/lib /app/lib

 ---> bb8ecadb4040
Step 10/12 : COPY --from=build ${DEPENDENCY}/META-INF /app/META-INF

 ---> 06ddb7fc4d1e
Step 11/12 : COPY --from=build ${DEPENDENCY}/BOOT-INF/classes /app

 ---> 5ae10ed09222
Step 12/12 : ENTRYPOINT ["java","-cp","app:app/lib/*","com.optimagrowth.license.LicenseServiceApplication"]

 ---> Running in 464f8b4b4a45
Removing intermediate container 464f8b4b4a45
 ---> 52cef232a505
Successfully built 52cef232a505
Successfully tagged ostock/licensing-service:0.0.1-SNAPSHOT ◄─────────── Image ID

Detected build of image with id 52cef232a505 ◄───────────
Building jar: /Users/illary.huaylupo/Documents/Personal/Manning/code/manning-smia/chapter4/licensing-service/
target/licensing-service-0.0.1-SNAPSHOT-docker-info.jar
Successfully built ostock/licensing-service:0.0.1-SNAPSHOT ◄───────────
------------------------------------------------------------------------ Image name
BUILD SUCCESS
------------------------------------------------------------------------
Total time:  21.505 s
Finished at: 2019-12-30T12:18:45-06:00
------------------------------------------------------------------------
```

Figure 4.5 Docker image built with the Maven plugin by executing the `mvn package dockerfile:build` command

Now that we have the Docker image, we can see it in the list of the Docker images on our system. To list all of the Docker images, we need to execute the `docker images` command. If everything runs correctly, you should see something like this:

```
REPOSITORY              TAG             IMAGE ID      CREATED        SIZE
ostock/licensing-service 0.0.1-SNAPSHOT  231fc4a87903  1 minute ago  149MB
```

Once we have the Docker image, we can run it by using the following command:

```
docker run ostock/licensing-service:0.0.1-SNAPSHOT
```

You can also use the -d option in the `docker run` command to run the container in the background. For example, like this:

```
docker run -d ostock/licensing-service:0.0.1-SNAPSHOT
```

This `docker run` command starts the container. In order to see all the running containers in your system, you can execute the `docker ps` command. That command opens all the running containers with their corresponding ID, image, command, creation date, status, port, and name. If you need to stop the container, you can execute the following command with the corresponding container ID:

```
docker stop <container_id>
```

4.5.2 *Creating Docker images with Spring Boot*

In this section, we will give you a brief overview of how to create Docker images using the new features released in Spring Boot v2.3. Note that in order to use these new features, you must

- Have Docker and Docker Compose installed.
- Have a Spring Boot application with a version equal to or greater than 2.3 in your microservice.

These new features help improve the Buildpack support and layered JARs. To create a Docker image using the new features, add the following. Make sure your pom.xml file contains the `spring-boot-starter-parent` version 2.3 or greater.

```
<parent>
<groupId>org.springframework.boot</groupId>
<artifactId>spring-boot-starter-parent</artifactId>
<version>2.4.0</version>
<relativePath/> <!-- lookup parent from repository -->
</parent>
```

BUILDPACKS

Buildpacks are tools that provide application and framework dependencies, transforming our source code into a runnable application image. In other words, Buildpacks detect and obtain everything the application needs to run.

Spring Boot 2.3.0 introduces support for building Docker images using Cloud Native Buildpacks. This support was added to the Maven and Gradle plugins using the `spring-boot:build-image` goal for Maven and the `bootBuildImage` task for Gradle. For more information, see the following links:

- Spring Boot Maven Plugin at https://docs.spring.io/spring-boot/docs/ 2.3.0.M1/maven-plugin/html/
- Spring Boot Gradle Plugin at https://docs.spring.io/spring-boot/docs/ 2.3.0.M1/gradle-plugin/reference/html/

In this book, we will only explain how to use the Maven scenario. To build the image using this new feature, execute the following command from the root directory of your Spring Boot microservice:

```
./mvnw spring-boot:build-image
```

Once the command executes, you should be able to see output similar to that shown in the next code snippet:

```
[INFO]      [creator]      Setting default process type 'web'
[INFO]      [creator]      *** Images (045116f040d2):
[INFO]      [creator]      docker.io/library/licensing-service:0.0.1-SNAPSHOT
[INFO]
[INFO] Successfully built image 'docker.io/library/
➥ licensing-service:0.0.1-SNAPSHOT'
```

If you want to customize the name of the image created, you can add the following plugin to your pom.xml file and then define the name under the configuration section:

```
<plugin>
    <groupId>org.springframework.boot</groupId>
    <artifactId>spring-boot-maven-plugin</artifactId>
    <configuration>
    <image>
        <name>${docker.image.prefix}/${project.artifactId}:latest</name>
    </image>
    </configuration>
</plugin>
```

Once the image is successfully built, you can execute the following command to start the container via Docker:

```
docker run -it -p8080:8080 docker.io/library/
➥ licensing-service:0.0.1-SNAPSHOT
```

LAYERED JARS

Spring Boot introduced a new JAR layout called layered JARs. In this format, the /lib and /classes folders are split up and categorized into layers. This layering was created to separate code based on how likely it is to change between the builds, leaving the necessary information for the build. This is another excellent option to use in case you don't want to use the Buildpacks. To extract the layers of our microservice, let's execute the following steps:

1 Add the layer configuration into the pom.xml file
2 Package the application
3 Execute the `jarmode` system property with the `layertools` JAR mode
4 Create the Dockerfile
5 Build and run the image

The first step adds the layer configuration to the Spring Boot Maven plugin in pom.xml, for example:

```
<plugin>
    <groupId>org.springframework.boot</groupId>
    <artifactId>spring-boot-maven-plugin</artifactId>
    <configuration>
            <layers>
            <enabled>true</enabled>
        </layers>
    </configuration>
</plugin>yp
```

Once we have the configuration set up in our pom.xml file, we can execute the following command to rebuild our Spring Boot JAR:

```
mvn clean package
```

Once the JAR file is created, we can execute the following command in the root directory of our application to display the layers and the order in which these should be added to our Dockerfile:

```
java -Djarmode=layertools -jar target/
    licensing-service-0.0.1-SNAPSHOT.jar list
```

And, once executed, you should see output similar to the following code snippet:

```
dependencies
spring-boot-loader
snapshot-dependencies
application
```

Now that we have the layer information, let's continue with the fourth step, which is creating our Dockerfile. The following listing shows you how.

Listing 4.6   Creating a Dockerfile file with layered JARS

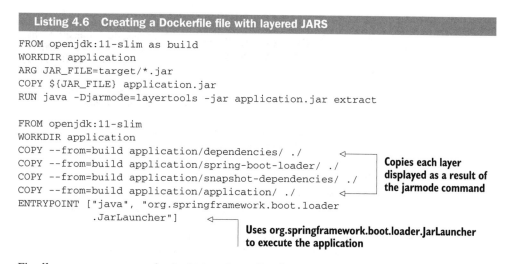

```
FROM openjdk:11-slim as build
WORKDIR application
ARG JAR_FILE=target/*.jar
COPY ${JAR_FILE} application.jar
RUN java -Djarmode=layertools -jar application.jar extract

FROM openjdk:11-slim
WORKDIR application
COPY --from=build application/dependencies/ ./
COPY --from=build application/spring-boot-loader/ ./
COPY --from=build application/snapshot-dependencies/ ./
COPY --from=build application/application/ ./
ENTRYPOINT ["java", "org.springframework.boot.loader
          .JarLauncher"]
```

Copies each layer displayed as a result of the jarmode command

Uses org.springframework.boot.loader.JarLauncher to execute the application

Finally, we can execute the `build` and `run` Docker commands in the root directory of our microservice:

```
docker build . --tag licensing-service
docker run -it -p8080:8080 licensing-service:latest
```

4.5.3 *Launching the services with Docker Compose*

Docker Compose is installed as part of the Docker installation process. It's a service orchestration tool that allows you to define services as a group and then to launch these together as a single unit. Docker Compose includes capabilities for also defining environment variables for each service.

Docker Compose uses a YAML file for defining the services that are going to be launched. For example, each chapter in this book has a file called <<*chapter*>>/docker-compose.yml. This file contains the service definitions used to launch the services for the chapter.

Let's create our first docker-compose.yml file. The following listing shows what your docker-compose.yml should look like.

Listing 4.7   The docker-compose.yml file

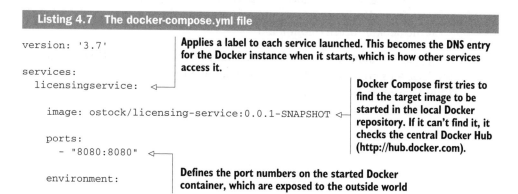

```
version: '3.7'

services:
  licensingservice:

    image: ostock/licensing-service:0.0.1-SNAPSHOT

    ports:
      - "8080:8080"

    environment:
```

Applies a label to each service launched. This becomes the DNS entry for the Docker instance when it starts, which is how other services access it.

Docker Compose first tries to find the target image to be started in the local Docker repository. If it can't find it, it checks the central Docker Hub (http://hub.docker.com).

Defines the port numbers on the started Docker container, which are exposed to the outside world

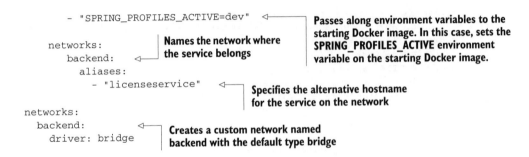

```
      - "SPRING_PROFILES_ACTIVE=dev"   ◁──────┐
                                               │
  networks:                ┌─ Names the network where
    backend:      ◁────────┘   the service belongs
      aliases:
        - "licenseservice"   ◁───┐
                                  │
networks:
  backend:      ◁──────┐
    driver: bridge      │
```

- "SPRING_PROFILES_ACTIVE=dev" — Passes along environment variables to the starting Docker image. In this case, sets the **SPRING_PROFILES_ACTIVE** environment variable on the starting Docker image.

backend: — Names the network where the service belongs

- "licenseservice" — Specifies the alternative hostname for the service on the network

driver: bridge — Creates a custom network named backend with the default type bridge

Now that we have a docker-compose.yml, we can start our services by executing the docker-compose up command in the directory where the docker-compose.yml file is located. Once it executes, you should see a result similar to that shown figure 4.6.

NOTE If you are not yet familiar with the SPRING_PROFILES_ACTIVE variable, don't worry about it. We'll cover this in the next chapter, where we'll manage different profiles in our microservice.

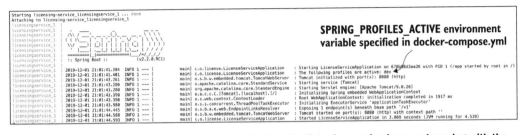

Figure 4.6   The Docker Compose console log, showing that the licensing service is up and running with the SPRING_PROFILES_ACTIVE variable specified in docker-compose.yml

Once you start the container, you can execute the docker ps command to see all the containers that are running.

NOTE All the Docker containers used in this book are *ephemeral*—they won't retain their state after they're started and stopped. Keep this in mind if you start playing with code and you see your data disappear after your restart your containers. If you are interested in how to save the container state, take a look at the docker commit command.

Now that we know what containers are and how to integrate Docker with our micro-services, let's continue with the next chapter. In that chapter, we'll create our Spring Cloud configuration server.

Summary

- Containers allow us to execute successfully the software we are developing in any environment—from the developer's machine to a physical or virtual enterprise server.

- A virtual machine (VM) allows us to emulate the operation of a computer within another computer. This is based on a hypervisor that mimics the complete physical machine, allocating the desired amount of system memory, processor cores, disk storage, and other resources such as networks, PCI add-ons, and so forth.

- Containers are another operating system (OS) virtualization method that allows you to run an application with its dependent elements in an isolated and independent environment.

- The use of containers reduces general costs by creating lightweight VMs that speed up the run/execution process, therefore reducing the costs of each project.

- Docker is a popular open source container engine based on Linux containers. It was created by Solomon Hykes, founder and CEO of dotCloud in 2013.

- Docker is composed of the following components: Docker Engines, clients, Registries, images, containers, volumes, and networks.

- A Dockerfile is a simple text file that contains a list of instructions and commands that the Docker client calls to create and prepare an image. This file automates the image creation process. The commands used in the Dockerfile are similar to Linux commands, which makes the Dockerfile commands easier to understand.

- Docker Compose is a service orchestration tool that allows you to define services as a group and then launch them together as a single unit.

- Docker Compose is installed as part of the Docker installation process.

- The Dockerfile Maven plugin integrates Maven with Docker.

5

Controlling your configuration with the Spring Cloud Configuration Server

This chapter covers

- Separating the service configuration from the service code
- Configuring a Spring Cloud Configuration Server
- Integrating a Spring Boot microservice with a configuration server
- Encrypting sensitive properties
- Integrating the Spring Cloud Configuration Server with HashiCorp Vault

Software developers always hear about the importance of keeping the application configuration separate from the code. In most scenarios, this means not using hardcoded values in the code. Forgetting this principle can make changing an application more complicated because every time a change to the configuration is made, the application has to be recompiled and/or redeployed.

Completely separating the configuration information from the application code allows developers and operations to make changes to their configurations without going through a recompile process. But it also introduces complexity, because now developers have another artifact to manage and deploy with the application.

Many developers turn to property files (YAML, JSON, or XML) to store their configuration information. Configuring your application in these files becomes a simple task, so easy that most developers never do more than placing their configuration file under source control (if that) and deploying the file as part of their application. This approach might work with a small number of applications, but it quickly falls apart when dealing with cloud-based applications that can contain hundreds of microservices, where each microservice, in turn, might have multiple service instances running. Suddenly, an easy and straightforward process becomes a big deal, and an entire team has to wrestle with all of the configuration files.

For example, let's imagine we have hundreds of microservices, and each microservice contains different configurations for three environments. If we don't manage those files outside the application, every time there is a change, we must search for the file in the code repository, follow the integration process (if there is one), and restart the application. To avoid this catastrophic scenario, as a best practice for cloud-based microservices development, we should consider the following:

- Completely separate the configuration of an application from the actual code being deployed.
- Build immutable application images that never change as these are promoted through your environments.
- Inject any application configuration information at server startup through either environment variables or a centralized repository that the microservices read on startup.

This chapter introduces you to the core principles and patterns needed to manage application configuration data in a cloud-based microservice application. We'll then build a configuration server, integrate the server with Spring and with Spring Boot clients, and then learn about protecting our more sensitive configurations.

5.1 On managing configuration (and complexity)

Managing application configuration is critical for microservices running in the cloud because microservice instances need to be launched quickly with minimal human intervention. When a person needs to manually configure or touch a service to get it deployed, this becomes an opportunity for configuration drift, an unexpected outage, and a lag time in responding to scalability challenges within the application. Let's begin our discussion about application configuration management by establishing four principles we want to follow:

- *Segregate*—We need to completely separate the service configuration informa-tion from the actual physical deployment of a service. In fact, application con-figuration shouldn't be deployed with the service instance. Instead, configuration information should either be passed as environment variables to the starting service or read from a centralized repository when the service starts.

- *Abstract*—We also need to abstract access to configuration data behind a service interface. Instead of writing code that directly reads the service repository, whether file-based or a JDBC database, we should use a REST-based JSON ser-vice to retrieve the application's configuration data.

- *Centralize*—Because a cloud-based application might literally have hundreds of services, it's critical to minimize the number of different repositories used to hold configuration data. Centralize your application configuration into as few repositories as possible.

- *Harden*—Because your application configuration information is going to be completely segregated from your deployed service and centralized, it's critical that the solution you utilize and implement be highly available and redundant.

One of the key things to remember is that when you separate your configuration information outside of your actual code, you're creating an external dependency that will need to be managed and version controlled. We can't emphasize enough that the application configuration data needs to be tracked and version controlled because mismanaged application configuration is a fertile breeding ground for difficult-to-detect bugs and unplanned outages.

5.1.1   *Your configuration management architecture*

As you'll remember from the previous chapters, the loading of configuration manage-ment for a microservice occurs during the bootstrapping phase of the microservice. As a reminder, figure 5.1 shows the microservice lifecycle.

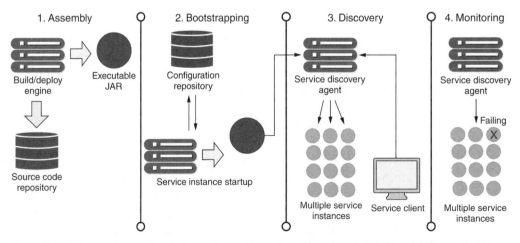

Figure 5.1   When a microservice starts up, it goes through multiple steps in its lifecycle. The application configuration data is read during the service's bootstrapping phase.

Let's take the four principles we laid out in section 5.1 (segregate, abstract, centralize, and harden) and see how these apply when the service is bootstrapped. Figure 5.2 presents the bootstrapping process in more detail and shows how a configuration service plays a critical role in this step.

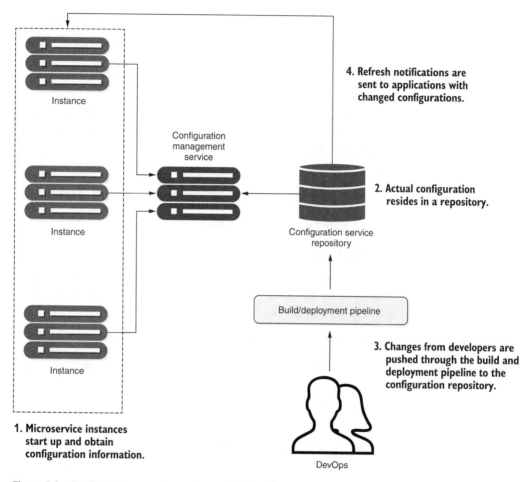

Figure 5.2 Configuration management conceptual architecture

In figure 5.2, several activities are taking place. Here's a rundown for each step in the figure:

1 When a microservice instance comes up, it calls a service endpoint to read its configuration information, which is specific to the environment it's operating in. The connection information for the configuration management (connection credentials, service endpoint, and so on) then passes into the microservice as it starts.

2   The actual configuration resides in a repository. Based on the implementation of your configuration repository, you can choose different ways to hold your configuration data. This can include files under source control, relational databases, or key-value data stores.

3   The actual management of the application configuration data occurs independently of how the application is deployed. Changes to configuration management are typically handled through the build and deployment pipeline, where modifications can be tagged with version information and deployed through the different environments (development, staging, production, and so forth).

4   When the configuration management changes, the services that use that application configuration data must be notified of the alteration and refresh their copy of the application data.

At this point, we've worked through the conceptual architecture that illustrates the different pieces of a configuration management pattern and how these pieces fit together. Now we will look at the different solutions to achieve configuration management and then look at a concrete implementation.

5.1.2   Implementation choices

Fortunately, you can choose from a large number of battle-tested open source projects to implement a configuration management solution. Let's look at several of the different choices available and compare them. Table 5.1 lays out the options.

Table 5.1   Open source projects for implementing a configuration management system

Project name	Description	Characteristics
etcd	Written in Go. Used for service discovery and key-value management. Uses the raft protocol (https://raft.github.io/) for its distributed computing model.	Very fast and scalable Distributable Command-line driven Easy to use and set up
Eureka	Written by Netflix. Extremely battle-tested. Used for both service discovery and key-value management.	Distributed key-value store Flexible but takes some effort to set up Offers dynamic client refresh out of the box
Consul	Written by HashiCorp. Similar to etcd and Eureka but uses a different algorithm for its distributed computing model.	Fast Offers native service discovery with the option to integrate directly with DNS Doesn't offer client dynamic refresh out of the box

Table 5.1 Open source projects for implementing a configuration management system

Project name	Description	Characteristics
Zookeeper	An Apache project. Offers distributed locking capabilities. Often used as a configuration management solution for accessing key-value data.	Oldest, most battle-tested of the solutions Most complex to use Can be used for configuration management, but consider only if you're already using Zookeeper in other pieces of your architecture
Spring Cloud Configuration Server	An open source project. Offers a general configuration management solution with different backends.	Non-distributed key-value store Offers tight integration for Spring and non-Spring services Can use multiple backends for storing configuration data including a shared filesystem, Eureka, Consul, or Git

All the solutions in table 5.1 can easily be used to build a configuration management solution. For the examples in this chapter, and throughout the rest of the book, we'll use the Spring Cloud Configuration Server (often called the Spring Cloud Config Server or, simply, the Config Server), which adapts perfectly to our Spring microservices architecture. We chose this solution because

- The Spring Cloud Configuration Server is easy to set up and use.
- Spring Cloud Config integrates tightly with Spring Boot. You can literally read all of your application's configuration data with a few simple-to-use annotations.
- The Config Server offers multiple backends for storing configuration data.
- Of all of the solutions in table 5.1, the Config Server can integrate directly with the Git source control platform and with the HashiCorp Vault. We will explain these topics later on this chapter.

For the rest of this chapter, we'll do the following:

1 Set up a Spring Cloud Configuration Server. We'll demonstrate three different mechanisms for serving application configuration data—one using the filesystem, another using a Git repository, and another using the HashiCorp Vault.
2 Continue to build the licensing service to retrieve data from a database.
3 Hook the Spring Cloud Config service into your licensing service to serve up the application's configuration data.

5.2 *Building our Spring Cloud Configuration Server*

The Spring Cloud Configuration Server is a REST-based application that is built on top of Spring Boot. The Config Server doesn't come as a standalone server. Instead, you can choose to either embed it in an existing Spring Boot application or start a new Spring Boot project with the server embedded in it. The best practice is to keep things separated.

The first thing we need to do to build our configuration server is to create a Spring Boot project with Spring Initializr (https://start.spring.io/). To achieve this, we'll implement the following steps in the Initializr's form. Once filled in, your Spring Initializr form should look like that shown in figures 5.3 and 5.4. In the form, you'll

1 Select Maven as the project type.
2 Select Java as the language.
3 Select the latest or more stable Spring version.
4 Write com.optimagrowth as the group and configserver as the artifact.
5 Expand the options list and write.
   a Configuration Server as its name.
   b Configuration server as its description.
   c com.optimagrowth.configserver as its package name.
6 Select JAR Packaging.
7 Select Java 11 as the Java version.
8 Add the Config Server and Spring Boot Actuator dependencies.

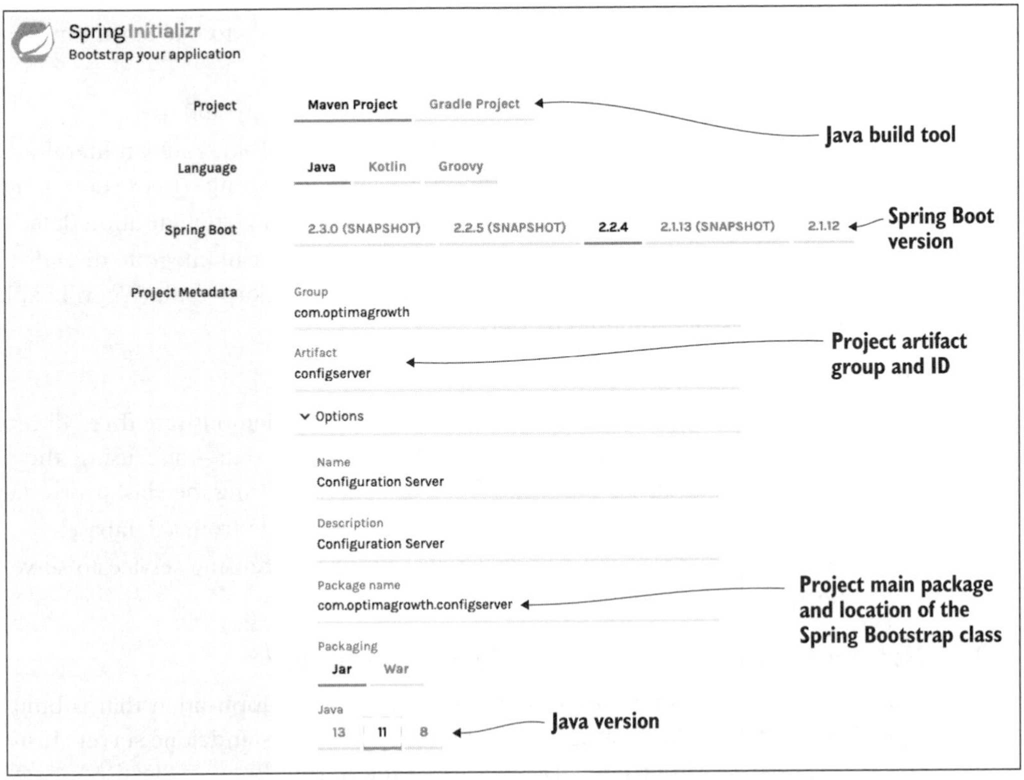

Figure 5.3   Spring Initializr configuration for the Spring Configuration Server

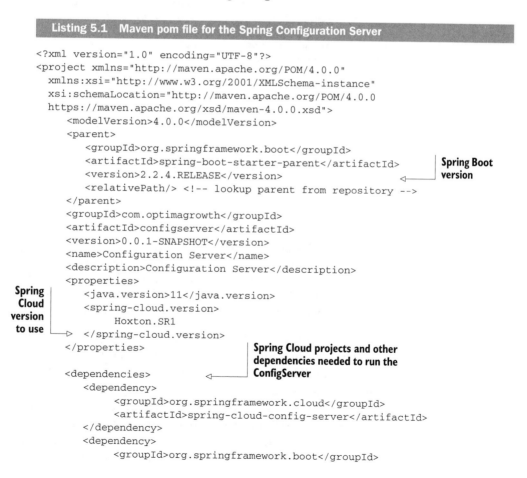

Figure 5.4 Spring Initializr Config Server and Spring Boot Actuator dependencies

Once you've created and imported the form as a Maven project into your preferred IDE, you should have a pom.xml file in the root of the config server project directory that looks like the code in the following listing.

Listing 5.1 Maven pom file for the Spring Configuration Server

```xml
<?xml version="1.0" encoding="UTF-8"?>
<project xmlns="http://maven.apache.org/POM/4.0.0"
  xmlns:xsi="http://www.w3.org/2001/XMLSchema-instance"
  xsi:schemaLocation="http://maven.apache.org/POM/4.0.0
  https://maven.apache.org/xsd/maven-4.0.0.xsd">
    <modelVersion>4.0.0</modelVersion>
    <parent>
        <groupId>org.springframework.boot</groupId>
        <artifactId>spring-boot-starter-parent</artifactId>
        <version>2.2.4.RELEASE</version>          ◁——— Spring Boot version
        <relativePath/> <!-- lookup parent from repository -->
    </parent>
    <groupId>com.optimagrowth</groupId>
    <artifactId>configserver</artifactId>
    <version>0.0.1-SNAPSHOT</version>
    <name>Configuration Server</name>
    <description>Configuration Server</description>
    <properties>
        <java.version>11</java.version>
        <spring-cloud.version>
            Hoxton.SR1
        </spring-cloud.version>         ◁——— Spring Cloud version to use
    </properties>
                                        Spring Cloud projects and other
                                        dependencies needed to run the
    <dependencies>           ◁——————    ConfigServer
        <dependency>
            <groupId>org.springframework.cloud</groupId>
            <artifactId>spring-cloud-config-server</artifactId>
        </dependency>
        <dependency>
            <groupId>org.springframework.boot</groupId>
```

```
                    <artifactId>spring-boot-starter-actuator</artifactId>
                </dependency>
                <dependency>
                    <groupId>org.springframework.boot</groupId>
                    <artifactId>spring-boot-starter-test</artifactId>
                    <scope>test</scope>
                    <exclusions>
                        <exclusion>
                            <groupId>org.junit.vintage</groupId>
                            <artifactId>
                                junit-vintage-engine
                            </artifactId>
                        </exclusion>
                    </exclusions>
                </dependency>
            </dependencies>
            <dependencyManagement>        ◁──┐ Spring Cloud BOM (Bill
                <dependencies>                 │ of Materials) definition
                    <dependency>
                        <groupId>org.springframework.cloud</groupId>
                        <artifactId>spring-cloud-dependencies</artifactId>
                        <version>${spring-cloud.version}</version>
                        <type>pom</type>
                        <scope>import</scope>
                    </dependency>
                </dependencies>
            </dependencyManagement>

            <build>
                <plugins>
                    <plugin>
                        <groupId>org.springframework.boot</groupId>
                        <artifactId>spring-boot-maven-plugin</artifactId>
                    </plugin>
                </plugins>
            </build>
        </project>
```

NOTE All the pom.xml files should contain Docker dependencies and configurations, but in order to save space, we won't add those lines to the code listings. If you want to take a look at the Docker configuration for the configuration server, visit the chapter 5 folder in the GitHub repository: https://github.com/ihuaylupo/manning-smia/tree/master/chapter5.

We won't go through the entire pom file in detail, but we'll note a few key areas to begin with. In the Maven file in listing 5.1, we can see four important parts. The first is the Spring Boot version, and the next is the Spring Cloud version that we are going to use. In this example, we use version Hoxton.SR1 of Spring Cloud. The third point highlighted in the listing is the specific dependencies that we'll use in the service, and the last point is the Spring Cloud Config parent BOM (Bill of Materials) that we'll use.

This parent BOM contains all the third-party libraries and dependencies that are used in the cloud project and the version numbers of the individual projects that make up that version. In this example, we use the version defined previously in the `<properties>` section of the pom file. By using a BOM definition, we can guarantee that we'll use compatible versions of the subprojects in Spring Cloud. It also means that we don't have to declare version numbers for our subdependencies.

> ### Come on, ride the train, the release train
>
> Spring Cloud uses a non-traditional mechanism for labeling Maven projects. Because Spring Cloud is a collection of independent subprojects, the Spring Cloud team releases updates to the projects through what they call the "release train." All the subprojects that make up Spring Cloud are packaged under one Maven BOM and released as a whole.
>
> The Spring Cloud team uses the names of London subway stops as the names of their releases, with each major release given a London subway stop that has the next highest letter. There have been several releases, from Angel, Brixton, Camden, Dalston, Edgware, Finchley, and Greenwich to Hoxton. Hoxton is the newest release, but it still has multiple release candidate branches for the subprojects within it.
>
> One thing to note is that Spring Boot is released independently of the Spring Cloud release train. Therefore, different versions of Spring Boot are incompatible with different releases of Spring Cloud. You can see the version dependences between Spring Boot and Spring Cloud, along with the different subproject versions contained within the release train, by referring to the Spring Cloud website (http://projects .spring.io/spring-cloud/).

The next step in creating our Spring Cloud Config Server is to set up one more file to define the core configuration of the server so that it can run. This can be one of the following: application.properties, application.yml, bootstrap.properties, or bootstrap.yml.

The bootstrap file is a specific Spring Cloud file type and is loaded before the application.properties or application.yml files. The bootstrap file is used for specifying the Spring application name, the Spring Cloud Configuration Git location, encryption/ decryption information, and so forth. Specifically, the bootstrap file is loaded by a parent Spring `ApplicationContext`, and that parent is loaded before the one that uses the application properties or YAML files.

As for the file extensions, .yml and .properties are just different data formats. You can choose the one you prefer. In this book, you'll see that we will use bootstrap.yml to define the configuration of the Config Server and the microservices.

Now, to continue, let's create our bootstrap.yml file in the /src/main/resources folder. This file tells the Spring Cloud Config service what port to listen in on, the application name, the application profiles, and the location where we will store the configuration data. Your bootstrap file should look like that shown in the following listing.

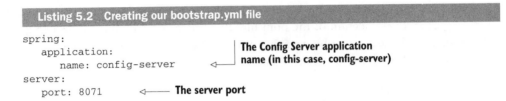

Listing 5.2   Creating our bootstrap.yml file

```
spring:
    application:
        name: config-server          The Config Server application
server:                               name (in this case, config-server)
    port: 8071          The server port
```

There are two important parts to highlight in listing 5.2. The first one is the application name. It is vital to name all of the services that we are going to create in our architecture for service discovery, which we will describe in the next chapter. The second point to note is the port the Spring Configuration Server is going to listen in on, in order to provide the requested configuration data.

5.2.1   Setting up the Spring Cloud Config bootstrap class

The next step in creating our Spring Cloud Config service is to set up the Spring Cloud Config bootstrap class. Every Spring Cloud service needs a bootstrap class that we can use to launch the service, as we explained in chapters 2 and 3 (where we created the licensing service).

Remember, this class contains several important parts: a Java `main()` method that acts as the entry point for the service to start in and a set of Spring annotations that tells the starting service what kind of behaviors Spring is going to launch for the service. The following listing shows the bootstrap class for our Spring Cloud Config Server.

Listing 5.3   Setting up the bootstrap class

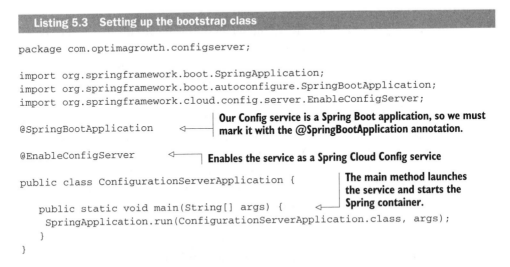

```
package com.optimagrowth.configserver;

import org.springframework.boot.SpringApplication;
import org.springframework.boot.autoconfigure.SpringBootApplication;
import org.springframework.cloud.config.server.EnableConfigServer;

@SpringBootApplication          Our Config service is a Spring Boot application, so we must
                                mark it with the @SpringBootApplication annotation.

@EnableConfigServer          Enables the service as a Spring Cloud Config service

public class ConfigurationServerApplication {          The main method launches
                                                       the service and starts the
                                                       Spring container.
    public static void main(String[] args) {
        SpringApplication.run(ConfigurationServerApplication.class, args);
    }
}
```

The next step is to define the search location for our configuration data. Let's start with the simplest example: the filesystem.

5.2.2 Using the Spring Cloud Config Server with a filesystem

The Spring Cloud Configuration Server uses an entry in the bootstrap.yml file to point to the repository that holds the application's configuration data. Setting up a filesystem-based repository is the easiest way to accomplish this. To do this, let's update our bootstrap file. The following listing shows the required contents for this file in order to set up a filesystem repository.

Listing 5.4 Our bootstrap.yml with a filesystem repository

```
spring:
    application:
        name: config-server        Sets the Spring profile
    profiles:                      associated with the backend
        active: native    ⊲──────┘ repository (filesystem)

    cloud:
        config:
            server:
            #Local configuration: This locations can either of
            classpath or locations in the filesystem.
                native:
                #Reads from a specific filesystem folder
                    search-locations:
                        file:///{FILE_PATH}   ⊲──┐ Sets the search location where the
    server:                                      │ configuration files are stored
        port: 8071
```

Because we will use the filesystem for storing application configuration information, we must tell the Spring Cloud Config Server to run with the native profile. Remember, a Spring profile is a core feature that the Spring framework offers. It allows us to map our beans to different environments, such as dev, test, staging, production, native, and others.

> **NOTE** Remember, native is just a profile created for the Spring Cloud Configuration Server, which indicates that the configuration files are going to be retrieved or read from the classpath or filesystem.

When we use a filesystem-based repository, we'll also use the native profile because it is a profile in the Config Server that doesn't use any Git or Vault configurations. Instead, it loads the configuration data directly from a local classpath or a filesystem. Finally, the last part of the bootstrap.yml shown in listing 5.4 provides the Spring Cloud configuration within the directory where the application data resides. For example:

```
server:
  native:
    search-locations: file:///Users/illary.huaylupo
```

The important parameter in the configuration entry is `search-locations`. This parameter provides a comma-separated list of the directories for each application that will have properties managed by the Config Server. In the previous example, we used a filesystem location (`file:///Users/illary.huaylupo`), but we can also indicate a specific classpath to look for our configuration data. This is set with the following code:

```
server:
  native:
    search-locations: classpath:/config
```

> **NOTE** The `classpath` attribute causes Spring Cloud Config Server to look in the src/main/resources/config folder.

Now that we have set up our Spring Configuration Server, let's create our licensing service properties files. In order to make this example simple, we'll use the classpath search location set in the preceding code snippet. Then, like the previous example, we'll create the licensing properties files in a /config folder.

5.2.3 *Setting up the configuration files for a service*

In this section, we will use the licensing service example that we began in the initial chapters of this book. It will serve as an example of how to use Spring Cloud Config.

> **NOTE** In case you didn't follow along in the previous chapter's code listings, you can download the code created in chapter 4 from the following link: https://github.com/ihuaylupo/manning-smia/tree/master/chapter4.

Again, to keep this example simple, we will set up application configuration data for three environments: a default environment for when we run the service locally, a dev environment, and a production environment.

With Spring Cloud Config, everything works off a hierarchy. Your application configuration is represented by the name of the application and then a property file for each environment you want to configure. In each of these environments, we'll set up the following configuration properties:

- An example property that will be used directly by our licensing service
- A Spring Actuator configuration that we will use in the licensing service
- A database configuration for the licensing service

Figure 5.5 illustrates how we will set up and use the Spring Cloud Config service. One important point to mention is that as you build your Config service, it will be another microservice running in your environment. Once it's set up, the contents of the service can be accessed via an HTTP-based REST endpoint.

The naming convention for the application configuration files are *appname-env*.properties or *appname-env*.yml. As you can see from figure 5.5, the environment names translate directly into the URLs that will be accessed to browse the configuration information. Later, when we start the licensing microservice example, the environment

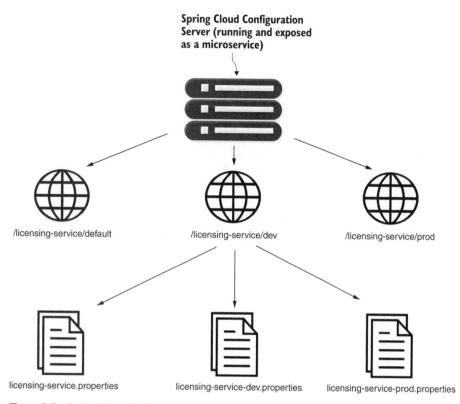

Figure 5.5 **Spring Cloud Config exposes environment-specific properties as HTTP-based endpoints.**

we want to run the service against is specified by the Spring Boot profile that you pass in on the command line at service startup. If a profile isn't passed in on the command line, Spring Boot defaults to the configuration data contained in the application.properties file packaged with the application.

Here is an example of some of the application configuration data we will serve up for the licensing service. This is the data that will be contained within the config-server/src/main/ resources/config/ licensing-service.properties file that was referred to in figure 5.5. Here is part of the contents of that file:

```
...
example.property= I AM THE DEFAULT
spring.jpa.hibernate.ddl-auto=none
spring.jpa.database=POSTGRESQL
spring.datasource.platform=postgres
spring.jpa.show-sql = true
spring.jpa.hibernate.naming-strategy =
     org.hibernate.cfg.ImprovedNamingStrategy
spring.jpa.properties.hibernate.dialect =
     org.hibernate.dialect.PostgreSQLDialect
spring.database.driverClassName= org.postgresql.Driver
```

```
spring.datasource.testWhileIdle = true
spring.datasource.validationQuery = SELECT 1
management.endpoints.web.exposure.include=*
management.endpoints.enabled-by-default=true
```

Think before you implement

We advise against using a filesystem-based solution for medium to large cloud applications. Using the filesystem approach means that you need to implement a shared file mount point for all Configuration Servers that want to access the application's configuration data. Setting up shared filesystem servers in the cloud is doable, but it puts the onus of maintaining this environment on you.

We're showing the filesystem approach as the easiest example to use when getting your feet wet with the Spring Cloud Configuration Server. In a later section, we'll show you how to configure the Config Server to use GitHub and HashiCorp Vault to store your application configuration.

To continue, let's create a licensing-service-dev.properties file that contains only the development data. The dev properties file should contain the following parameters:

```
example.property= I AM DEV
spring.datasource.url = jdbc:postgresql://localhost:5432/ostock_dev
spring.datasource.username = postgres
spring.datasource.password = postgres
```

Now that we have enough work done to start the Configuration Server, let's go ahead and do that by using the mvn spring-boot:run command or the docker-compose up command.

> **NOTE** From this point on, you will find a README file in the folder repository for each chapter. This file contains a section called "How to Use." This section describes how to run all the services together using the docker-compose command.

The server should now come up with the Spring Boot splash screen on the command line. If you point your browser to http://localhost:8071/licensing-service/default, you'll see a JSON payload returned with all of the properties contained within the licensing-service.properties file. Figure 5.6 shows the results of calling this endpoint.

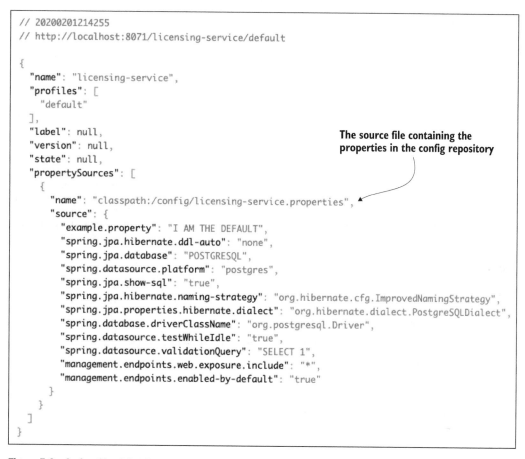

```
// 20200201214255
// http://localhost:8071/licensing-service/default

{
  "name": "licensing-service",
  "profiles": [
    "default"
  ],
  "label": null,
  "version": null,
  "state": null,
  "propertySources": [
    {
      "name": "classpath:/config/licensing-service.properties",
      "source": {
        "example.property": "I AM THE DEFAULT",
        "spring.jpa.hibernate.ddl-auto": "none",
        "spring.jpa.database": "POSTGRESQL",
        "spring.datasource.platform": "postgres",
        "spring.jpa.show-sql": "true",
        "spring.jpa.hibernate.naming-strategy": "org.hibernate.cfg.ImprovedNamingStrategy",
        "spring.jpa.properties.hibernate.dialect": "org.hibernate.dialect.PostgreSQLDialect",
        "spring.database.driverClassName": "org.postgresql.Driver",
        "spring.datasource.testWhileIdle": "true",
        "spring.datasource.validationQuery": "SELECT 1",
        "management.endpoints.web.exposure.include": "*",
        "management.endpoints.enabled-by-default": "true"
      }
    }
  ]
}
```

The source file containing the properties in the config repository

Figure 5.6 Spring Cloud Config exposes environment-specific properties as HTTP-based endpoints.

If you want to see the configuration information for the dev-based licensing service environment, select the GET `http://localhost:8071/licensing-service/dev` endpoint. Figure 5.7 shows the result of calling this endpoint.

NOTE The port is the one we set previously on the bootstrap.yml file.

If we look closely, we will see that when we selected the dev endpoint, the Spring Cloud Configuration Server returned both the default configuration properties and the dev licensing service configuration. The reason why Spring Cloud Config returns both sets

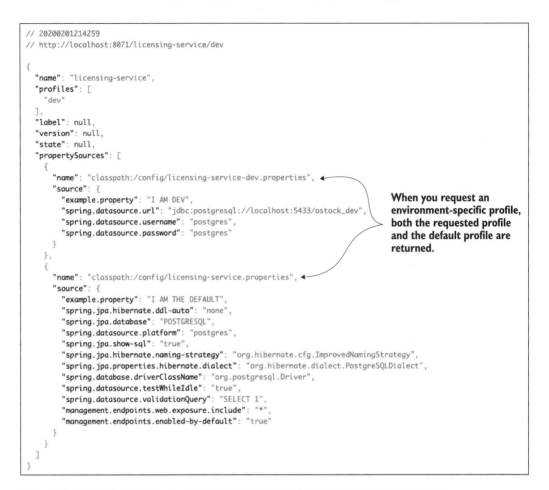

```
// 20200201214259
// http://localhost:8071/licensing-service/dev

{
  "name": "licensing-service",
  "profiles": [
    "dev"
  ],
  "label": null,
  "version": null,
  "state": null,
  "propertySources": [
    {
      "name": "classpath:/config/licensing-service-dev.properties",
      "source": {
        "example.property": "I AM DEV",
        "spring.datasource.url": "jdbc:postgresql://localhost:5433/ostock_dev",
        "spring.datasource.username": "postgres",
        "spring.datasource.password": "postgres"
      }
    },
    {
      "name": "classpath:/config/licensing-service.properties",
      "source": {
        "example.property": "I AM THE DEFAULT",
        "spring.jpa.hibernate.ddl-auto": "none",
        "spring.jpa.database": "POSTGRESQL",
        "spring.datasource.platform": "postgres",
        "spring.jpa.show-sql": "true",
        "spring.jpa.hibernate.naming-strategy": "org.hibernate.cfg.ImprovedNamingStrategy",
        "spring.jpa.properties.hibernate.dialect": "org.hibernate.dialect.PostgreSQLDialect",
        "spring.database.driverClassName": "org.postgresql.Driver",
        "spring.datasource.testWhileIdle": "true",
        "spring.datasource.validationQuery": "SELECT 1",
        "management.endpoints.web.exposure.include": "*",
        "management.endpoints.enabled-by-default": "true"
      }
    }
  ]
}
```

When you request an environment-specific profile, both the requested profile and the default profile are returned.

Figure 5.7   Retrieving configuration information for the licensing service using the dev profile

of configuration information is that the Spring framework implements a hierarchical mechanism for resolving problems. When the Spring framework does this, it looks for the property defined in the default properties file first and then overrides the default with an environment-specific value if one is present. In concrete terms, if you define a property in the licensing-service.properties file and don't define it in any of the other environment configurations (for example, licensing-service-dev.properties), the Spring framework will use the default value.

> **NOTE** This isn't the behavior you'll see by directly calling the Spring Cloud Config REST endpoint. The REST endpoint returns all configuration values for both the default and environment-specific value that was called.

Now that we finished configuring everything in our Spring Cloud Config service, let's move on to integrating Spring Cloud Config with our licensing microservice.

5.3 Integrating Spring Cloud Config with a Spring Boot client

In the previous chapters, we built a simple skeleton of our licensing service that did nothing more than to return a hardcoded Java object representing a single licensing record. In this section, we will build the licensing service with a PostgreSQL database to hold the licensing data.

Why use PostgreSQL?

PostgreSQL, also known as Postgres, is considered an enterprise system and one of the most interesting and advanced options for open source relational database management systems (RDBMSs). PostgreSQL has many advantages compared to other relational databases, but the main ones are that it offers a single license that is entirely free and open for anyone to use. The second advantage is that, in terms of its ability and functionality, it allows us to work with more significant amounts of data without increasing the complexity of the queries. Here are some of the main features of Postgres:

- Postgres uses a multiversion concurrency control that adds an image of the database status to each transaction, which produces consistent transactions with better performance advantages.
- Postgres doesn't use reading locks when it executes a transaction.
- Postgres has something called *hot standby*, which allows the client to search in the servers while the server is in recovery or standby mode. In other words, Postgres performs maintenance without completely locking down the database.

Some of the main characteristics of PostgreSQL are as follows:

- It is supported by languages such as C, C++, Java, PHP, Python, and more.
- It is capable of serving many clients while delivering the same information from its tables without blockages.
- It supports working with views so users can query the data differently from how it is stored.
- It is an object-relational database, allowing us to work with data as if it were objects, thus offering object-oriented mechanisms.
- It allows us to store and query JSON as a data type.

We are going to communicate with the database using Spring Data and map our data from the licensing table to a Plain Old Java Object (POJO) holding the data. We'll use the Spring Cloud Configuration Server to read the database connection and a simple property. Figure 5.8 shows what's going to happen between the licensing service and the Spring Cloud Config service.

When the licensing service is first started, we'll pass it three pieces of information: the Spring profile, the application name, and the endpoint the licensing service should use to communicate with the Spring Cloud Config service. The Spring profile maps to the environment of the properties being retrieved for the Spring service.

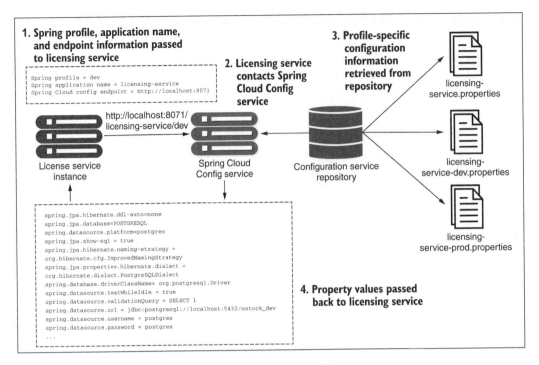

Figure 5.8   Retrieving configuration information using the `dev` profile

When the licensing service boots up, it will contact the Spring Cloud Config service via an endpoint built from the Spring profile passed into it. The Spring Cloud Config service will then use the configured backend repository (filesystem, Git, or Vault) to retrieve the configuration information specific to the Spring profile value passed in on the URI. The appropriate property values are then passed back to the licensing service. The Spring Boot framework will then inject these values into the appropriate parts of the application.

5.3.1   Setting up the licensing service Spring Cloud Config Service dependencies

Let's change our focus from the Spring Cloud Configuration Server to the licensing service. The first thing you need to do is to add a couple more entries to the Maven file in your licensing service. The following listing gives the entries that we need to add.

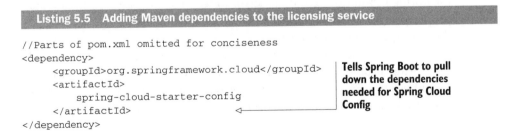

Listing 5.5   Adding Maven dependencies to the licensing service

```
//Parts of pom.xml omitted for conciseness
<dependency>
      <groupId>org.springframework.cloud</groupId>
      <artifactId>
          spring-cloud-starter-config
      </artifactId>
</dependency>
```

Tells Spring Boot to pull down the dependencies needed for Spring Cloud Config

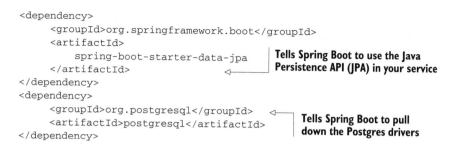

```
<dependency>
    <groupId>org.springframework.boot</groupId>
    <artifactId>
        spring-boot-starter-data-jpa
    </artifactId>
</dependency>
<dependency>
    <groupId>org.postgresql</groupId>
    <artifactId>postgresql</artifactId>
</dependency>
```

Tells Spring Boot to use the Java Persistence API (JPA) in your service

Tells Spring Boot to pull down the Postgres drivers

The first dependency's artifact ID, `spring-cloud-starter-config`, contains all the classes needed to interact with the Spring Cloud Config Server. The second and third dependencies, `spring-boot-starter-data-jpa` and `postgresql`, import the Spring Data Java Persistence API (JPA) and the Postgres JDBC drivers.

5.3.2 Configuring the licensing service to use Spring Cloud Config

After the Maven dependencies have been defined, we need to tell the licensing service where to contact the Spring Cloud Configuration Server. In a Spring Boot service that uses Spring Cloud Config, configuration information can be set in one of these files: bootstrap.yml, bootstrap.properties, application.yml, or application.properties.

As we mentioned previously, the bootstrap.yml file reads the application properties before any other configuration information. In general, the bootstrap.yml file contains the application name for the service, the application profile, and the URI to connect to a Configuration Server. Any other configuration information that you want to keep local to the service (and not stored in Spring Cloud Config) can be set in the services in the local application.yml file.

Usually, the information you store in the application.yml file is configuration data that you might want to have available to a service even if the Spring Cloud Config service is unavailable. Both the bootstrap.yml and application.yml files are stored in a project's src/main/resources directory.

To have the licensing service communicate with your Spring Cloud Config service, these parameters can be defined in the bootstrap.yml file, in the docker-compose.yml file of the licensing service, or via JVM arguments when you start the service. The following listing shows how bootstrap.yml should look in your application if you choose this option.

> **Listing 5.6 Configuring the licensing service's bootstrap.yml**

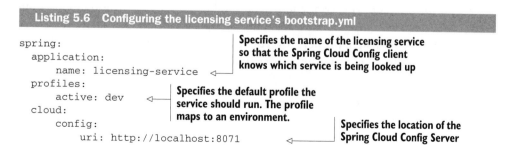

```
spring:
  application:
    name: licensing-service
  profiles:
    active: dev
  cloud:
    config:
      uri: http://localhost:8071
```

Specifies the name of the licensing service so that the Spring Cloud Config client knows which service is being looked up

Specifies the default profile the service should run. The profile maps to an environment.

Specifies the location of the Spring Cloud Config Server

> **NOTE** The Spring Boot application supports two mechanisms to define a property: YAML (YAML Ain't Markup Language) and a dot-separated property name. We will choose YAML as the means for configuring our application. The hierarchical format of YAML property values maps directly to these names: `spring.application.name`, `spring.profiles.active`, and `spring.cloud.config.uri`.

The `spring.application.name` is the name of your application (for example, licensing service) and *must* map directly to the name of the config directory within your Spring Cloud Configuration Server. The second property, `spring.profiles.active`, tells Spring Boot which profile the application should run as. Remember, a *profile* is a mechanism to differentiate the configuration data consumed by the Spring Boot application. For the licensing service's profile, you'll support the environment the service is going to map directly to in your cloud configuration environment. For instance, by passing in `dev` as your profile, the Config Server will use the `dev` properties. If you don't set a profile, the licensing service will use the default profile.

The third and last property, `spring.cloud.config.uri`, is the location where the licensing service will look for the Config Server endpoint. In this example, the licensing service looks for the configuration server at `http://localhost:8071`.

Later in this chapter, you'll see how to override the different properties defined in the bootstrap.yml and application.yml files on application startup. This allows you to tell the licensing microservice which environment it should be running in. Now, if you bring up the Spring Cloud Config service with the corresponding Postgres database running on your local machine, you can launch the licensing service using its `dev` profile. This is done by changing to the licensing service's directory and issuing the following command:

```
mvn spring-boot:run
```

> **NOTE** You first need to launch the Configuration Server to retrieve the configuration data for the licensing service.

By running this command without any properties set, the licensing server automatically attempts to connect to the Spring Cloud Configuration Server using the endpoint (in this case, our endpoint is `http://localhost:8071`) and the active profile (dev) defined previously in the bootstrap.yml file of the licensing service.

If you want to override these default values and point to another environment, you can do so by compiling the licensing service project down to a JAR file, and then run the JAR with a D system property override. The following command-line call demonstrates how to launch the licensing service, passing all the commands via JVM arguments:

```
java  -Dspring.cloud.config.uri=http://localhost:8071 \
      -Dspring.profiles.active=dev \
      -jar target/licensing-service-0.0.1-SNAPSHOT.jar
```

This example demonstrates how to override Spring properties via the command line. With this command line, we override these two parameters:

```
spring.cloud.config.uri
spring.profiles.active
```

> **NOTE** If you try to run the licensing service that you downloaded from the GitHub repository (https://github.com/ihuaylupo/manning-smia/tree/master/chapter5) from your desktop using the previous Java command, it will fail because of two reasons. The first one is that you don't have a desktop Postgres server running, and the second is because the source code in the GitHub repository uses encryption on the Config Server. We'll cover using encryption later in this chapter.

In the examples, we hardcoded the values to pass in to the -D parameter values. In the cloud, most of the application configuration data you'll need will be in your configuration server.

All the code examples for each chapter can be completely run from within Docker containers. With Docker, you simulate different environments through environment-specific Docker Compose files, which orchestrate the startup of all of your services. Environment-specific values needed by the containers are passed in as environment variables to the container. For example, to start your licensing service in a dev environment, the dev/docker-compose.yml file contains the entry displayed in the next listing for the licensing service.

Listing 5.7   Dev docker-compose.yml

```
licensingservice:
    image: ostock/licensing-service:0.0.1-SNAPSHOT
    ports:                        Specifies the start of the
      - "8080:8080"               environment variables for the
                                  licensing service container

    environment:  ◁──────┘
      SPRING_PROFILES_ACTIVE: "dev"    ◁─────

      SPRING_CLOUD_CONFIG_URI:
          http://configserver:8071  ◁──── The endpoint of the Config service
```

Passes the SPRING_PROFILES_ACTIVE environment variable to the Spring Boot service command line and tells Spring Boot what profile should be run

The environment entry in the YML file contains the values of two variables: SPRING_PROFILES_ACTIVE, which is the Spring Boot profile the licensing service will run under, and SPRING_CLOUD_CONFIG_URI, which is passed to your licensing service and defines the Spring Cloud Configuration Server instance where the service will read its configuration data. Once you have Docker Compose file set up, you can run the services just by executing the following command where the Docker Compose file is located:

```
docker-compose up
```

Because you enhance all your services with introspection capabilities via Spring Boot Actuator, you can confirm the environment you are running in by selecting the following endpoint: `http://localhost:8080/actuator/env`. The /env endpoint provides a complete list of the configuration information about the service, including the properties and endpoints the service is booted with (figure 5.9).

```
{
  "activeProfiles": [
    "dev"
  ],
  "propertySources": [
    {
      "name": "server.ports",
      "properties": {
        "local.server.port": {
          "value": 8080
        }
      }
    },
    {
      "name": "bootstrapProperties-classpath:/config/licensing-service-dev.properties",
      "properties": {
        "spring.datasource.username": {
          "value": "postgres"
        },
        "spring.datasource.url": {
          "value": "jdbc:postgresql://localhost:5433/ostock_dev"
        },
        "example.property": {
          "value": "I AM DEV"
        },
        "spring.datasource.password": {
          "value": "******"
        }
      }
    },
    {
      "name": "bootstrapProperties-classpath:/config/licensing-service.properties",
      "properties": {
        "management.endpoints.web.exposure.include": {
          "value": "*"
        },
        "spring.jpa.properties.hibernate.dialect": {
          "value": "org.hibernate.dialect.PostgreSQLDialect"
        },
```

Figure 5.9 You can check the licensing configuration service by calling the /actuator/env endpoint. In the code, you can see how both the licensing-service.properties and the licensing-service-dev.properties are displayed.

On exposing too much information

Every organization is going to have different rules about how to implement security around their services. Many organizations believe services shouldn't broadcast any information about themselves and won't allow things like a /env endpoint to be active on a service. Their belief (rightfully so) is that this provides too much information for a potential hacker.

Spring Boot provides a wealth of capabilities on how to configure what information is returned by the Spring Actuator endpoints. That's outside the scope of this book, however. Craig Walls' excellent book, *Spring Boot in Action* (Manning, 2016), covers this subject in detail. We highly recommend that you review your corporate security policies and Walls' book to provide the right level of information you want to expose through Spring Actuator.

5.3.3 *Wiring in a data source using Spring Cloud Config Server*

At this point, the database configuration information is directly injected into your microservice. With the database configuration set, configuring your licensing microservice becomes an exercise in using standard Spring components to build and retrieve the data from the Postgres database. In order to continue with the example, we need to refactor the licensing into different classes, where each class has separate responsibilities. These classes are shown in table 5.2.

Table 5.2 Licensing service classes and locations

Class name	Location
License	com.optimagrowth.license.model
LicenseRepository	com.optimagrowth.license.repository
LicenseService	com.optimagrowth.license.service

The License class is the model class that will hold the data retrieved from your licensing database. The following listing shows the code for this class.

Listing 5.8 The JPA model code for a single license record

```
package com.optimagrowth.license.model;

import javax.persistence.Column;
import javax.persistence.Entity;
import javax.persistence.Id;
import javax.persistence.Table;

import org.springframework.hateoas.RepresentationModel;

import lombok.Getter;
```

```
import lombok.Setter;
import lombok.ToString;

@Getter @Setter @ToString        | Tells Spring that this is a JPA class
@Entity                        ◁
@Table(name="licenses")          ◁──── Maps to the database table
public class License {
                                 | Marks this field as a primary key        Maps the field to a
    @Id                        ◁─────                                        specific database column
    @Column(name = "license_id", nullable = false)  ◁──┘
    private String licenseId;
    private String description;
    @Column(name = "organization_id", nullable = false)
    private String organizationId;
    @Column(name = "product_name", nullable = false)
    private String productName;
    @Column(name = "license_type", nullable = false)
    private String licenseType;
    @Column(name="comment")
    private String comment;

    public License withComment(String comment){
        this.setComment(comment);
        return this;
    }
}
```

In the listing, the `License` class uses several JPA annotations that will help the Spring Data framework map the data from the licenses table in the Postgres database to a Java object. The `@Entity` annotation lets Spring know that this Java POJO is going to be mapping objects that will hold data. The `@Table` annotation tells Spring/JPA what database table to map. The `@Id` annotation identifies the primary key for the database. Finally, each one of the columns from the database that will be mapped to individual properties is marked with a `@Column` attribute.

> **TIP** If your attribute has the same name as the database column, you don't need to add the `@Column` annotation.

The Spring Data and JPA framework provides your basic CRUD methods (Create, Replace, Update, Delete) for accessing a database. Table 5.3 shows some of these.

Table 5.3 CRUD methods for Spring Data and the JPA framework

Method	Description
count()	Returns the number of entities available
delete(entity)	Deletes a given entity
deleteAll()	Deletes all entities managed by the repository
deleteAll(entities)	Deletes the given entities

Table 5.3   CRUD methods for Spring Data and the JPA framework

Method	Description
deleteById(id)	Deletes the entity with the given ID
existsById(id)	Returns whether an entity with the given ID exists
findAll()	Returns all instances of the type
findAllById(ids)	Returns all instances of a given type T with the given IDs
findById(ID id)	Retrieves an entity by its ID
save(entity)	Saves a given entity
saveAll(entities)	Saves all given entities

If you want to build methods beyond this, you can use a Spring Data Repository interface and basic naming conventions to build those methods. At startup, Spring will parse the name of the methods from the Repository interface, convert them to an SQL statement based on the names, and then generate a dynamic proxy class (under the cover) to do the work. The repository for the licensing service is shown in the following listing.

Listing 5.9   The `LicenseRepository` interface defining the query methods

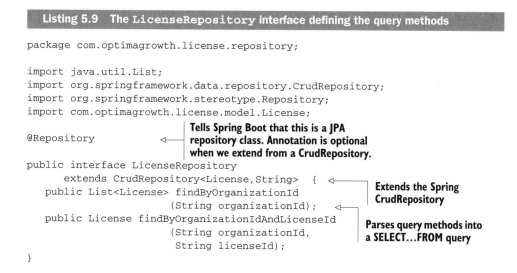

```
package com.optimagrowth.license.repository;

import java.util.List;
import org.springframework.data.repository.CrudRepository;
import org.springframework.stereotype.Repository;
import com.optimagrowth.license.model.License;
                                        Tells Spring Boot that this is a JPA
@Repository                     ◁─────  repository class. Annotation is optional
                                        when we extend from a CrudRepository.
public interface LicenseRepository
        extends CrudRepository<License,String>  {  ◁──── Extends the Spring
    public List<License> findByOrganizationId             CrudRepository
                    (String organizationId);  ◁─────┐
    public License findByOrganizationIdAndLicenseId     Parses query methods into
                    (String organizationId,             a SELECT...FROM query
                    String licenseId);
}
```

The repository interface, LicenseRepository, is marked with @Repository, which tells Spring that it should treat this interface as a repository and generate a dynamic proxy for it. The dynamic proxy, in this case, provides a set of fully featured, ready-to-use objects.

Spring offers different types of repositories for data access. In this example, we use the Spring CrudRepository base class to extend our LicenseRepository class. The CrudRepository base class contains basic CRUD methods. In addition to the CRUD methods extended from `CrudRepository`, we added two custom query methods to the `LicenseRepository` interface for retrieving data from the licensing table. The Spring Data framework pulls apart the name of the methods to build a query to access the underlying data.

NOTE The Spring Data framework provides an abstraction layer over various database platforms and isn't limited to relational databases. NoSQL databases, such as MongoDB and Cassandra, are also supported.

Unlike the previous incarnation of the licensing service in chapter 3, you've now separated the business and data access logic for the licensing service out of the `License-Controller` and into a standalone `Service` class called `LicenseService`. Listing 5.10 shows the license service. Between this `LicenseService` class and the versions seen in the previous chapters, there are a lot of changes because we added the database connection. Feel free to download the file from the following link:

https://github.com/ihuaylupo/manning-smia/tree/master/chapter5/licensing-service/
src/main/java/com/optimagrowth/license/service/LicenseService.java

Listing 5.10   A `LicenseService` class to execute database commands

```
@Service
public class LicenseService {

    @Autowired
    MessageSource messages;
    @Autowired
    private LicenseRepository licenseRepository;
    @Autowired
    ServiceConfig config;

    public License getLicense(String licenseId, String organizationId){
        License license = licenseRepository
            .findByOrganizationIdAndLicenseId(organizationId, licenseId);
        if (null == license) {
            throw new IllegalArgumentException(
                String.format(messages.getMessage(
                    "license.search.error.message", null, null),
                    licenseId, organizationId));
        }
        return license.withComment(config.getProperty());
    }

    public License createLicense(License license){
        license.setLicenseId(UUID.randomUUID().toString());
        licenseRepository.save(license);
        return license.withComment(config.getProperty());
    }

    public License updateLicense(License license){
        licenseRepository.save(license);
```

```
        return license.withComment(config.getProperty());
    }

    public String deleteLicense(String licenseId){
        String responseMessage = null;
        License license = new License();
        license.setLicenseId(licenseId);
        licenseRepository.delete(license);
        responseMessage = String.format(messages.getMessage(
                "license.delete.message", null, null),licenseId);
        return responseMessage;
    }
}
```

The controller, service, and repository classes are wired together using the standard Spring @Autowired annotation. Next, let's look at reading the configuration properties in the LicenseService class.

5.3.4 *Directly reading properties using @ConfigurationProperties*

In the LicenseService class, you might have noticed that we set the license .withComment() value in the getLicense() method with a value from the config .getProperty() class. The code referred to is shown here:

```
return license.withComment(config.getProperty());
```

If you look at the com.optimagrowth.license.config.ServiceConfig.java class, you'll see that the class is annotated with the following. (Listing 5.11 shows the @ConfigurationProperties annotation that we'll use.)

```
@ConfigurationProperties(prefix= "example")
```

Listing 5.11 Using `ServiceConfig` to centralize application properties

```
package com.optimagrowth.license.config;

import org.springframework.beans.factory.annotation.Value;
import org.springframework.stereotype.Component;

@ConfigurationProperties(prefix = "example")
public class ServiceConfig{

  private String property;

  public String getProperty(){
    return property;
  }
}
```

While Spring Data "auto-magically" injects the configuration data for the database into a database connection object, all other custom properties can be injected using the @ConfigurationProperties annotation. With the previous example,

```
@ConfigurationProperties(prefix= "example")
```

pulls all the example properties from the Spring Cloud Configuration Server and injects these into the property attribute on the ServiceConfig class.

> **TIP**   While it's possible to directly inject configuration values into properties in individual classes, we've found it useful to centralize all of the configuration information into a single configuration class and then inject the configuration class into where it's needed.

5.3.5   *Refreshing your properties using Spring Cloud Config Server*

One of the first questions that comes up from development teams when they want to use the Spring Cloud Configuration Server is how can they dynamically refresh their applications when a property changes. Rest assured. The Config Server always serves the latest version of a property. Changes made to a property via its underlying repository will be up to date!

Spring Boot applications, however, only read their properties at startup, so property changes made in the Config Server won't be automatically picked up by the Spring Boot application. But Spring Boot Actuator offers a @RefreshScope annotation that allows a development team to access a /refresh endpoint that will force the Spring Boot application to reread its application configuration. The following listing shows this annotation in action.

Listing 5.12   The @RefreshScope annotation

```
package com.optimagrowth.license;

import org.springframework.boot.SpringApplication;
import org.springframework.boot.autoconfigure.SpringBootApplication;
import org.springframework.cloud.context.config.annotation.RefreshScope;

@SpringBootApplication
@RefreshScope
public class LicenseServiceApplication {

    public static void main(String[] args) {
        SpringApplication.run(LicenseServiceApplication.class, args);
    }

}
```

Note a couple of things about the @RefreshScope annotation. This annotation only reloads the custom Spring properties you have in your application configuration.

Items like your database configuration used by Spring Data won't be reloaded by this annotation.

> **On refreshing microservices**
>
> When using Spring Cloud Config service with microservices, one thing you need to consider before you dynamically change properties is that you might have multiple instances of the same service running. You'll need to refresh all of those services with their new application configurations. There are several ways you can approach this problem.
>
> Spring Cloud Config service offers a push-based mechanism called Spring Cloud Bus that allows the Spring Cloud Configuration Server to publish to all the clients using the service where a change occurs. Spring Cloud Bus requires an extra piece of running middleware: RabbitMQ. This is an extremely useful means of detecting changes, but not all Spring Cloud Config backends support the push mechanism (the Consul server, for example). In the next chapter, you'll use Spring Cloud service discovery and Eureka to register all instances of a service.
>
> One technique that we've used to handle application configuration refresh events is to refresh the application properties in Spring Cloud Config. Then we write a simple script to query the service discovery engine to find all instances of a service and call the `/refresh` endpoint directly.
>
> You can also restart all the servers or containers to pick up the new property. This is a trivial exercise, especially if you're running your services in a container service such as Docker. Restarting Docker containers literally takes seconds and will force a reread of the application configuration.
>
> Remember that cloud-based servers are ephemeral. Don't be afraid to start new instances of a service with new configurations, then direct traffic to the new services and tear down the old ones.

5.3.6 *Using Spring Cloud Configuration Server with Git*

As mentioned earlier, using a filesystem as the backend repository for the Spring Cloud Configuration Server can be impractical for a cloud-based application. That's because the development team has to set up and manage a shared filesystem that's mounted on all instances of the Config Server, and the Config Server integrates with different backend repositories that can be used to host the application configuration properties.

One approach that we've used successfully is to employ a Spring Cloud Configuration Server with a Git source control repository. By using Git, you can get all the benefits of putting your configuration management properties under source control and provide an easy mechanism to integrate the deployment of your property configuration files in your build and deployment pipeline. To use Git, we need to add the configuration to the Spring Cloud Config service bootstrap.yml file. The next listing shows how.

Listing 5.13   Adding Git support to the Spring Cloud bootstrap.yml

```
spring:
    application:
        name: config-server
    profiles:
        active:                        Maps all the profiles (this is
        - native, git                  a comma-separated list)
    cloud:
        config:
            server:
                native:
                    search-locations: classpath:/config
                git:
                    uri: https://github.com/ihuaylupo/    Tells Spring Cloud Config the
                        config.git                         URL to the Git server and repo
                    searchPaths: licensingservice
server:                                    Tells Spring Cloud Config what path in
    port: 8071                             Git to use to look for the config files
```

Tells Spring Cloud Config to use Git as a backend repository

The four key pieces of configuration properties in the previous listing include the following:

- `spring.profiles.active`
- `spring.cloud.config.server.git`
- `spring.cloud.config.server.git.uri`
- `spring.cloud.config.server.git.searchPaths`

The `spring.profiles.active` property sets all the active profiles for the Spring Config service. This comma-separated list uses the same precedence rules as a Spring Boot application: active profiles have precedence over default profiles, and the last profile is the winner. The `spring.cloud.config.server.git` property tells the Spring Cloud Config Server to use a non-filesystem-based backend repository. In the previous listing, we connected to the cloud-based Git repository, GitHub.

> **NOTE**   If you're authorized to use GitHub, you need to set the username and password (personal token or SSH configuration) in the Git configuration on the bootstrap.yml of the configuration server.

The `spring.cloud.config.server.git.uri` property provides the URL of the repository you're connecting to. And finally, the `spring.cloud.config.server.git` `.searchPaths` property tells the Config Server the relative path on the Git repository that will be searched when the Cloud Config Server boots up. Like the filesystem version of the configuration, the value in the `spring.cloud.config.server.git.searchPaths` attribute will be a comma-separated list for each service hosted by the configuration service.

> **NOTE**   The default implementation of an environment repository in Spring Cloud Config is the Git backend.

5.3.7 *Integrating Vault with the Spring Cloud Config service*

As mentioned earlier, there is another backend repository that we will use: the HashiCorp Vault. Vault is a tool that allows us to securely access secrets. We can define secrets as any piece of information we want to restrict or control access to, such as passwords, certificates, API keys, and so forth.

To configure Vault in our Spring Config service, we must add a Vault profile. This profile enables integration with Vault and allows us to securely store the application properties of our microservices. To achieve this integration, we will use Docker to create a Vault container with the following command:

```
docker run -d -p 8200:8200 --name vault -e 'VAULT_DEV_ROOT_TOKEN_ID=myroot'
   -e 'VAULT_DEV_LISTEN_ADDRESS=0.0.0.0:8200' vault
```

The `docker run` command contains these parameters:

- `VAULT_DEV_ROOT_TOKEN_ID`—This parameter sets the ID of the generated root token. The *root token* is the initial access token to start configuring Vault. This sets the ID of the initial generated root token to a given value.
- `VAULT_DEV_LISTEN_ADDRESS`—This parameter sets the IP address and port of the development server listener; the default value is 0.0.0.0:8200.

> **NOTE** In this example, we will run Vault locally. If you need additional info on how to run Vault in server mode, we highly recommend that you visit the official Vault Docker image information at https://hub.docker.com/_/vault.

Once the latest Vault image is pulled into Docker, we can start creating our secrets. To make this example more straightforward, we will use the Vault UI, but if you prefer to move on with the CLI commands, go for it.

5.3.8 *Vault UI*

Vault offers a unified interface that facilitates the process of creating secrets. To access this UI, we need to enter the following URL: `http://0.0.0.0:8200/ui/vault/auth`. This URL was defined by the `VAULT_DEV_LISTEN_ADDRESS` parameter set with the `docker run` command. Figure 5.10 shows the login page for the Vault UI.

The next step is to create a secret. To create the secret after you've logged in, click the Secrets tab in the Vault UI dashboard. For this example, we will create a secret called `secret/licensingservice` with a property called `license.vault.property` and set its value to `Welcome to vault`. Remember, access to this piece of information will be restricted and will be encrypted. To achieve this, first we need to create a new secret engine and then add the specific secret to that engine. Figure 5.11 shows how to create this with the Vault UI.

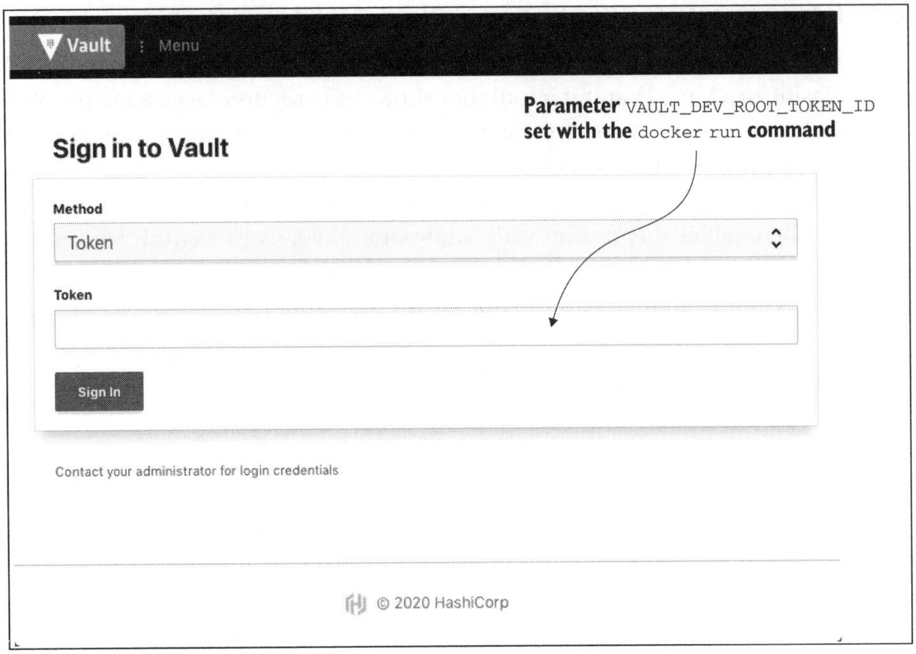

Figure 5.10   Login page in the Vault UI. Enter the following URL in the Token field to sign in:
`http://0.0.0.0:8200/ui/vault/auth`.

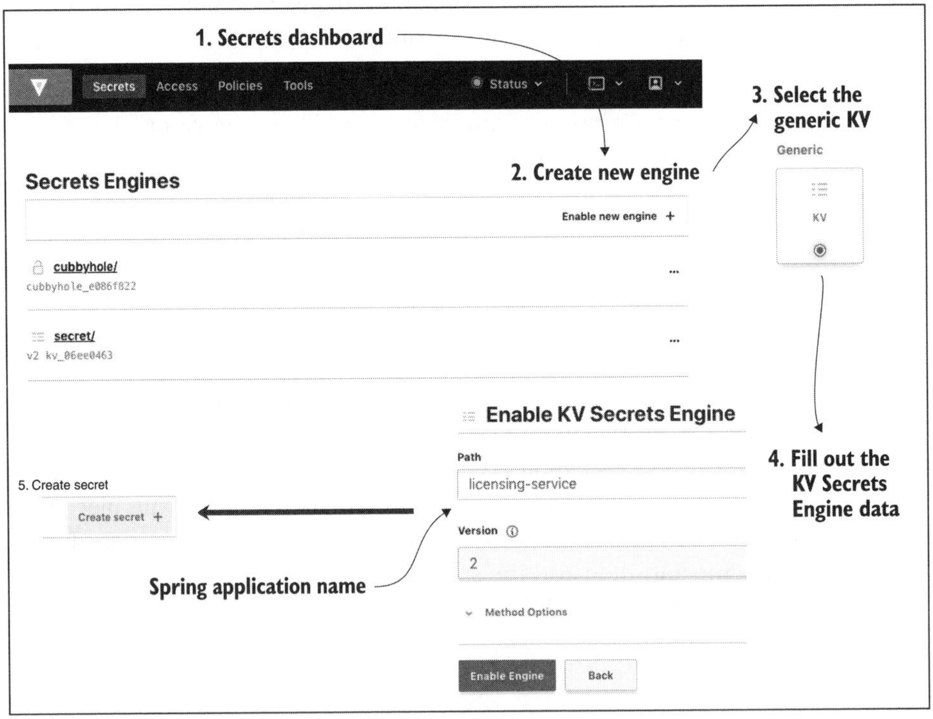

Figure 5.11   Creating a new secret engine in the Vault UI

Now, that we have our new secret engine, let's create our secret. Figure 5.12 shows you how.

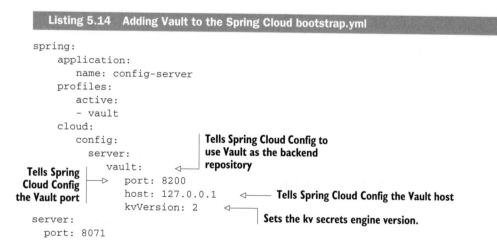

Figure 5.12 Creating a new secret in the Vault UI

Now that we have configured the Vault and a secret, let's configure our Spring Cloud Config Server to communicate with Vault. To do that, we'll add the Vault profile to our bootstrap.yml file for the Config Server. The next listing shows how your bootstrap file should look.

Listing 5.14 Adding Vault to the Spring Cloud bootstrap.yml

```
spring:
    application:
        name: config-server
    profiles:
        active:
        - vault
    cloud:
        config:
            server:
                vault:              ⟵  Tells Spring Cloud Config to
                    port: 8200           use Vault as the backend
                    host: 127.0.0.1      repository
                    kvVersion: 2
server:
    port: 8071
```

Tells Spring Cloud Config the Vault port

Tells Spring Cloud Config the Vault host

Sets the kv secrets engine version.

NOTE   An important point here is the kv secrets engine version. The default value for `spring.cloud.config.server.kv-version` is 1. But it is recommended to use version 2 when we use Vault 0.10.0 or later.

Now that we have everything set, let's test our Config Server via an HTTP request. Here you can use a cURL command or some REST client such as Postman:

```
$ curl -X "GET" "http://localhost:8071/licensing-service/default" -H
➥ "X-Config-Token: myroot"
```

If everything was configured successfully, the command should return a response like the following:

```
{
    "name": "licensing-service",
    "profiles": [
        "default"
    ],
    "label": null,
    "version": null,
    "state": null,
    "propertySources": [
        {
            "name": "vault:licensing-service",
            "source": {
                "license.vault.property": "Welcome to vault"
            }
        }
    ]
}
```

5.4   *Protecting sensitive configuration information*

By default, the Spring Cloud Configuration Server stores all properties in plain text within the application's configuration files. This includes sensitive information such as database credentials and so forth. It's extremely poor practice to keep sensitive credentials stored as plain text in your source code repository. Unfortunately, it happens far more often than you might think.

Spring Cloud Config gives you the ability to encrypt your sensitive properties easily. Spring Cloud Config supports using both symmetric (shared secret) and asymmetric encryption (public/private) keys. Asymmetric encryption is more secure than symmetric encryption because it uses modern and more complex algorithms. But sometimes it is more convenient to use the symmetric key because we only need to define a single property value in the bootstrap.yml file in the Config Server.

5.4.1   *Setting up a symmetric encryption key*

The symmetric encryption key is nothing more than a shared secret that's used by the encrypter to encrypt a value and by the decrypter to decrypt a value. With the Spring Cloud Configuration Server, the symmetric encryption key is a string of characters you select that can be either set in the bootstrap.yml file of your Config Server or passed to the service via an OS environment variable, ENCRYPT_KEY. You can select the option that best suits your needs.

NOTE Your symmetric key should be 12 or more characters long and, ideally, should be a random set of characters.

Let's start by looking at an example of how to configure the symmetric key on the bootstrap file for the Spring Cloud Configuration Server. The following listing shows how to do this.

Listing 5.15 Setting a symmetric key in the boostrap.yml file

```
cloud:
    config:
      server:
        native:
          search-locations: classpath:/config
        git:
            uri: https://github.com/ihuaylupo/config.git
            searchPaths: licensingservice

server:
  port: 8071

encrypt:
  key: secretkey
```

Tells the Config Server to use this value as the symmetric key

For the purposes of this book, we will always set the ENCRYPT_KEY environment variable to export ENCRYPT_KEY=IMSYMMETRIC. Feel free to use the bootstrap.yml file property if you need to locally test without using Docker.

Managing encryption keys

In this book, we did two things that we wouldn't normally recommend in a production deployment:

- We set the encryption key to a phrase. We wanted to keep the key simple so that we could remember it and so that it would fit nicely when reading the text. In a real-world deployment, we use a separate encryption key for each environment we deploy to, and we use random characters as a key.
- We've hardcoded the ENCRYPT_KEY environment variable directly in the Docker files used for the book. We did this so that you as the reader can download the files and start them without having to remember to set an environment variable.

In a real run-time environment, we would reference the ENCRYPT_KEY as an OS environment variable inside a Dockerfile. Be aware of this and don't hardcode your encryption key inside your Dockerfiles. Remember, your Dockerfiles are supposed to be kept under source control.

5.4.2   *Encrypting and decrypting a property*

We are now ready to begin encrypting properties for use with Spring Cloud Config. We will encrypt the licensing service Postgres database password you use to access the O-stock data. This property, called `spring.datasource.password`, is currently set as plain text with `postgres` as its value.

When you fire up your Spring Cloud Config instance, Spring Cloud Config detects that the `ENCRYPT_KEY` environment variable or the bootstrap file property is set, and automatically adds two new endpoints, `/encrypt` and `/decrypt` to the Spring Cloud Config service. We will use the `/encrypt` endpoint to encrypt the `postgres` value. Figure 5.13 shows how to encrypt the `postgres` value using the `/encrypt` endpoint and Postman.

NOTE   When you call the `/encrypt` or `/decrypt` endpoints, you need to make sure you do a POST to these endpoints.

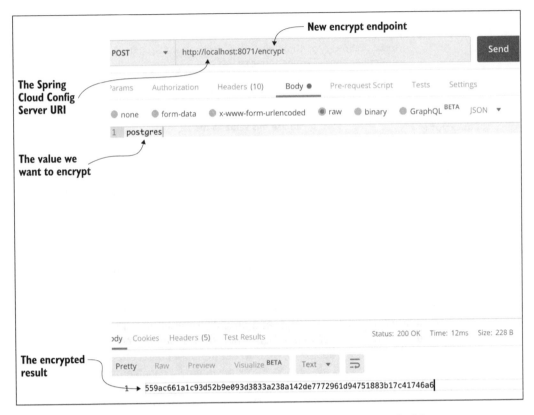

Figure 5.13   Encrypting the Spring data source password using the `/encrypt` endpoint

If we wanted to decrypt the value, we'd need to use the `/decrypt` endpoint, passing in the encrypted string. We can now add the encrypted property to our GitHub or filesystem-based configuration file for the licensing service using the syntax shown in the following listing.

> **Listing 5.16 Adding an encrypted value to the licensing service properties file**

```
spring.datasource.url = jdbc:postgresql://localhost:5432/ostock_dev
spring.datasource.username = postgres
spring.datasource.password = {cipher}
➥ 559ac661a1c93d52b9e093d3833a238a142de7772961d94751883b17c41746a6
```

The Spring Cloud Configuration Server requires all encrypted properties to be prepended with a value of {cipher}. This value tells the Config Server that it's dealing with an encrypted value.

5.5 *Closing thoughts*

Application configuration management might seem like a mundane topic, but it's of critical importance in a cloud-based environment. As we'll discuss in more detail in later chapters, it's vital that your applications and the servers these run on be immutable and that the entire server being promoted is never manually configured between environments. This flies in the face of traditional deployment models, where you deploy an application artifact (for example, a JAR or WAR file) along with its property files to a "fixed" environment.

With a cloud-based model, however, the application configuration data should be segregated completely from the application. The appropriate configuration data needs are then injected at run time so that the same server/application artifacts are consistently promoted throughout all environments.

Summary

- The Spring Cloud Configuration Server (aka Config Server) allows you to set up application properties with environment-specific values.
- Spring uses profiles to launch a service to determine what environment properties are to be retrieved from the Spring Cloud Config service.
- The Spring Cloud Config service can use a file-based, Git-based, or Vault-based application configuration repository to store application properties.
- The Spring Cloud Config service lets you encrypt sensitive property files using symmetric and asymmetric encryption.

On service discovery

6

This chapter covers

- Why service discovery is important to cloud-based applications
- The pros and cons of service discovery vs. the Load Balancer
- Setting up a Spring Netflix Eureka Server
- Registering a Spring Boot microservice with Eureka
- Using the Spring Cloud Load Balancer library for client-side load balancing

In any distributed architecture, we need to find the hostname or IP address of where a machine is located. This concept has been around since the beginning of distributed computing and is known formally as "service discovery." Service discovery can be something as simple as maintaining a property file with the addresses of all the remote services used by an application, or something as formalized as a Universal Description, Discovery, and Integration (UDDI) repository. Service discovery is critical to microservice, cloud-based applications for two key reasons:

- *Horizontal scaling or scale out*—This pattern usually requires adjustments in the application architecture, such as adding more instances of a service inside a cloud service and more containers.
- *Resiliency*—This pattern refers to the ability to absorb the impact of problems within an architecture or service without affecting the business. Microservice architectures need to be extremely sensitive to preventing a problem in a single service (or service instance) from cascading up and out to the consumers of the service.

First, service discovery allows the application team to quickly scale—horizontally—the number of service instances running in an environment. The service consumers are abstracted away from the physical location of the service. Because the service consumers don't know the physical location of the actual service instances, new service instances can be added or removed from the pool of available services.

This ability to quickly scale services without disrupting the service consumers is a compelling concept. It can move a development team that's used to building a monolithic, single-tenant (for example, one customer) application away from thinking about scaling only in terms of adding bigger and better hardware (vertical scaling) to the more robust approach to scaling by adding more servers with more services (horizontal scaling).

A monolithic approach usually drives development teams down the path of over-buying their capacity needs. Capacity increases come in clumps and spikes and are rarely a smooth, steady process. For example, consider the incremental number of requests made to e-commerce sites before some holidays. Microservices allow us to scale new service instances on demand. Service discovery helps abstract these deployments so that they occur away from the service consumer.

The second benefit of service discovery is that it helps increase application resiliency. When a microservice instance becomes unhealthy or unavailable, most service discovery engines remove that instance from their internal list of available services. The damage caused by a down service is minimized because the service discovery engine routes services around the unavailable service.

All of this may sound somewhat complicated, and you might be wondering why we can't use tried-and-true methods such as DNS (Domain Name Service) or a load balancer to help facilitate service discovery. Let's walk through why that won't work with a microservices-based application, particularly one that's running in the cloud. Then, we'll learn how to implement Eureka Discovery in our architecture.

6.1 Where's my service?

If you have an application that calls resources spread across multiple servers, it needs to find the physical location of those resources. In the non-cloud world, service location resolution was often solved through a combination of a DNS and a network load balancer (figure 6.1). In this traditional scenario, when an application needed to invoke a service located in another part of the organization, it attempted to invoke the service by using a generic DNS name along with a path that uniquely represented the service that the application wanted to invoke. The DNS name would resolve to a commercial load balancer such as the popular F5 load balancer (http://f5.com) or an open source load balancer such as HAProxy (http://haproxy.org).

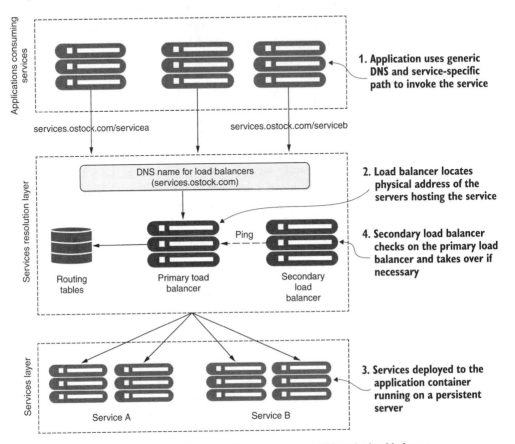

Figure 6.1   A traditional service location resolution model uses a DNS and a load balancer.

In the traditional scenario, the load balancer, upon receiving the request from the service consumer, located the physical address entry in a routing table based on the path the user was trying to access. This routing table entry contained a list of one or more servers hosting the service. The load balancer then picked one of the servers in the list and forwarded the request on to that server.

With this legacy model, each instance of a service was deployed in one or more application servers. The number of these application servers was often static (the number of application servers hosting a service didn't go up and down) and persistent (if a server running an application server crashed, it would be restored to the same state it was in at the time of the crash with the same IP address and configuration that it had previously). To achieve a form of high availability, a secondary idle load balancer pinged the primary load balancer to see if it was alive. If it wasn't alive, the secondary load balancer became active, taking over the IP address of the primary load balancer and began serving requests.

While this type of model works well with applications running inside the four walls of a corporate data center, and with a relatively small number of services running on a group of static servers, it doesn't work well for cloud-based microservice applications. The reasons for this include the following:

- *While the load balancer can be made highly available, it's a single point of failure for your entire infrastructure.* If the load balancer goes down, every application relying on it goes down too. While you can make a load balancer highly available, load balancers tend to be centralized chokepoints within your application infrastructure.

- *Centralizing your services into a single cluster of load balancers limits your ability to scale horizontally your load-balancing infrastructure across multiple servers.* Many commercial load balancers are constrained by two things: their redundancy model and their licensing costs.

  Most commercial load balancers use a hot-swap model for redundancy, so you only have a single server to handle the load, while the secondary load balancer is there only for failover in case the primary load balancer goes down. You are, in essence, constrained by your hardware. Commercial load balancers also have restrictive licensing models geared toward a fixed capacity rather than a more variable model.

- *Most traditional load balancers are statically managed.* They aren't designed for fast registration and deregistration of services. Traditional load balancers use a centralized database to store the routes for rules, and the only way to add new routes is often through the vendor's proprietary API.

- *Because a load balancer acts as a proxy to the services, service consumer requests need to have them mapped to the physical services.* This translation layer often adds another layer of complexity to your service infrastructure because the mapping rules for the service have to be defined and deployed by hand. Also, in a traditional load balancer scenario, the registration of new service instances is not done when a new service instance starts.

These four reasons aren't a general indictment of load balancers. A load balancer works well in a corporate environment where the size and scale of most applications can be handled through a centralized network infrastructure. But load balancers still have a role to play in centralizing SSL termination and managing service port security. A load balancer can lock down inbound (ingress) and outbound (egress) port access to all the servers sitting behind it. This concept of "least network access" is often a critical component when trying to meet industry-standard certification requirements such as PCI (Payment Card Industry) compliance.

However, in the cloud, where you have to deal with massive amounts of transactions and redundancy, a centralized piece of network infrastructure doesn't ultimately work as well. This is because it doesn't scale effectively and isn't cost effective. Let's now look at how you can implement a robust service discovery mechanism for your cloud-based applications.

6.2   Service discovery in the cloud

The solution for a cloud-based microservice environment is to use a service discovery mechanism that's

- *Highly available*—Service discovery needs to be able to support a "hot" clustering environment where service lookups can be shared across multiple nodes in a service discovery cluster. If a node becomes unavailable, other nodes in the cluster should be able to take over.

    A cluster can be defined as a group of multiple server instances. All instances of this environment have an identical configuration and work together to provide high availability, reliability, and scalability. A cluster combined with a load balancer can offer failover to prevent service interruptions and session replication to store session data.

- *Peer-to-peer*—Each node in the service discovery cluster shares the state of a service instance.

- *Load balanced*—Service discovery needs to dynamically load balance requests across all service instances. This ensures that the service invocations are spread across all the service instances managed by it. In many ways, service discovery replaces the more static, manually managed load balancers found in many early web application implementations.

- *Resilient*—The service discovery's client should cache service information locally. Local caching allows for gradual degradation of the service discovery feature so that if the service discovery service becomes unavailable, applications can still function and locate the services based on the information maintained in their local cache.

- *Fault tolerant*—Service discovery needs to detect when a service instance isn't healthy and remove that instance from the list of available services that can take client requests. It should detect these faults with services and take action without human intervention.

In the following sections, we're going to

- Walk you through the conceptual architecture of how a cloud-based service discovery agent works
- Show you how client-side caching and load balancing allows the service to continue to function even when the service discovery agent is unavailable
- Show you how to implement service discovery using Spring Cloud and Netflix's Eureka service discovery agents

6.2.1 *The architecture of service discovery*

To begin our discussion around service discovery, we need to understand four concepts. These general concepts are often shared across all service discovery implementations:

- *Service registration*—How a service registers with the service discovery agent
- *Client lookup of service address*—How a service client looks up service information
- *Information sharing*—How nodes share service information
- *Health monitoring*—How services communicate their health back to the service discovery agent

The principal objective of service discovery is to have an architecture where our services indicate where they are physically located instead of having to manually configure their location. Figure 6.2 shows how service instances are added and removed, and how they update the service discovery agent and become available to process user requests.

Figure 6.2 shows the flow of the previous four bulleted points (service registration, service discovery lookup, information sharing, and health monitoring) and what typically occurs when we implement a service discovery pattern. In the figure, one or

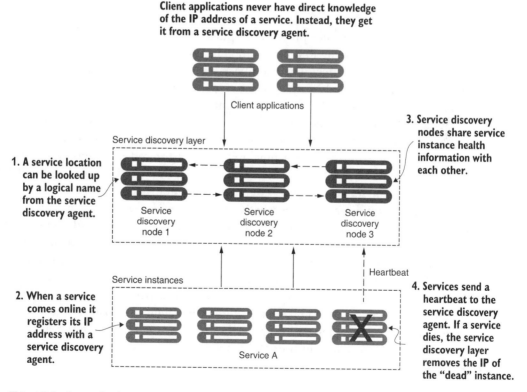

Client applications never have direct knowledge of the IP address of a service. Instead, they get it from a service discovery agent.

Client applications

Service discovery layer

3. Service discovery nodes share service instance health information with each other.

1. A service location can be looked up by a logical name from the service discovery agent.

Service discovery node 1

Service discovery node 2

Service discovery node 3

Service instances

Heartbeat

2. When a service comes online it registers its IP address with a service discovery agent.

Service A

4. Services send a heartbeat to the service discovery agent. If a service dies, the service discovery layer removes the IP of the "dead" instance.

Figure 6.2 As service instances are added or removed, the service discovery nodes are updated and made available to process user requests.

more service discovery nodes have started. These service discovery instances usually don't have a load balancer that sits in front of them.

As service instances start, they'll register their physical location, path, and port that one or more service discovery instances can use to access the instances. While each instance of a service has a unique IP address and port, each service instance that comes up registers under the same service ID. A service ID is nothing more than a key that uniquely identifies a group of the same service instances.

A service usually only registers with one service discovery service instance. Most service discovery implementations use a peer-to-peer model of data propagation, where the data around each service instance is communicated to all the other nodes in the cluster. Depending on the service discovery implementation, the propagation mechanism might use a hardcoded list of services to propagate to or use a multicasting protocol like the gossip or infection-style protocol to allow other nodes to "discover" changes in the cluster.

> **NOTE** If you are interested in knowing more about the gossip or infection-style protocols, we highly recommend you review the following: Consul's "Gossip Protocol" (https://www.consul.io/docs/internals/gossip.html) or Brian Storti's post, "SWIM: The scalable membership protocol" (https://www.brianstorti.com/swim/).

Finally, each service instance pushes to or pulls from its status by the service discovery service. Any services failing to return a good health check are removed from the pool of available service instances. Once a service is registered with a service discovery service, it's ready to be used by an application or service that needs to make use of its capabilities. Different models exist for a client to discover a service.

As a first approach, the client relies solely on the service discovery engine to resolve service locations each time a service is called. With this approach, the service discovery engine is invoked each time a call to a registered microservice instance is made. Unfortunately, this approach is brittle because the service client is completely dependent on the service discovery engine to find and invoke a service.

A more robust approach uses what's called *client-side load balancing*. This mechanism uses an algorithm like zone-specific or round-robin to invoke the instances of the calling services. When we say "round-robin algorithm load balancing," we are referring to a way of distributing client requests across several servers. This consists of forwarding a client request to each of the servers in turn. An advantage of using the client-side load balancer with Eureka is that when a service instance goes down, it is removed from the registry. Once that is done, the client-side load balancer updates itself without manual intervention by establishing constant communication with the registry service. Figure 6.3 illustrates this approach.

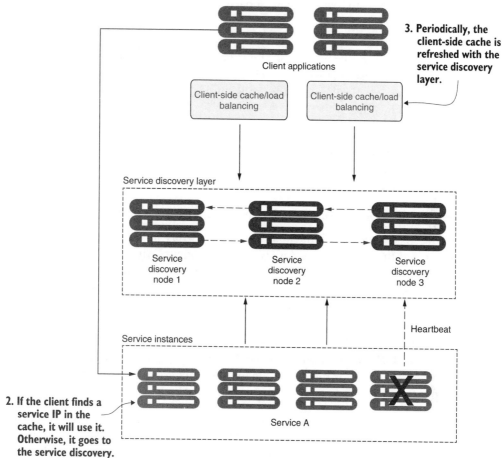

1. When a service client needs to call a service, it checks a local cache for the service instance IPs. Load balancing between service instances occurs on the service.

Client applications

3. Periodically, the client-side cache is refreshed with the service discovery layer.

Client-side cache/load balancing

Client-side cache/load balancing

Service discovery layer

Service discovery node 1

Service discovery node 2

Service discovery node 3

Heartbeat

Service instances

Service A

2. If the client finds a service IP in the cache, it will use it. Otherwise, it goes to the service discovery.

Figure 6.3 Client-side load balancing caches the location of the services so that the service client doesn't need to contact service discovery on every call.

In this model, when a consuming client needs to invoke a service

1 It contacts the discovery service for all the instances a service consumer (client) is asking for and then caches data locally on the service consumer's machine.

2 Each time a client wants to call the service, the service consumer looks up the location information for the service from the cache. Usually, client-side caching will use a simple load-balancing algorithm like the round-robin load-balancing algorithm to ensure that service calls are spread across multiple service instances.

3 The client then periodically contacts the discovery service and refreshes its cache of service instances. The client cache is eventually consistent, but there's always a risk that when the client contacts the service discovery instance for a refresh and calls are made, calls might be directed to a service instance that isn't healthy.

If during the course of calling a service, the service call fails, the local service discovery cache is invalidated and the service discovery client will attempt to refresh its entries from the service discovery agent. Let's now take the generic service discovery pattern and apply it to our O-stock problem domain.

6.2.2 Service discovery in action using Spring and Netflix Eureka

In this section, we will implement service discovery by setting up a service discovery agent and then register two services with the agent. With this implementation, we'll use the information retrieved by the service discovery to call a service from another service. Spring Cloud offers multiple methods for looking up information from a service discovery agent. We'll walk through the strengths and weaknesses of each approach.

Again, Spring Cloud makes this type of setup trivial to undertake. We'll use Spring Cloud and Netflix's Eureka Service Discovery engine to implement your service discovery pattern. For the client-side load balancing, we'll use the Spring Cloud Load Balancer.

> **NOTE** In this chapter, we are not going to use Ribbon. Ribbon was the de facto client-side load balancer for REST-based communications among applications using Spring Cloud. Although Netflix Ribbon client-side load balancing was a stable solution, it has now entered a maintenance mode, so unfortunately, it will not be developed anymore.

In this section, we will explain how to use the Spring Cloud Load Balancer, which is a replacement for Ribbon. Currently, the Spring Cloud Load Balancer is still under active development, so expect new functionalities soon. In the previous two chapters, we kept our licensing service simple and included the organization's name for the licenses with the license data. In this chapter, we'll break the organization information into its own service. Figure 6.4 shows the implementation of the client-side caching with Eureka for our O-stock microservices.

When the licensing service is invoked, it will call the organization service to retrieve the organization information associated with the designated organization ID.

**3. Periodically, Spring Cloud Load
Balancer refreshes its cache
of IP addresses.**

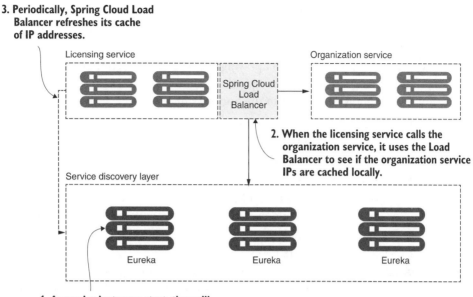

**2. When the licensing service calls the
organization service, it uses the Load
Balancer to see if the organization service
IPs are cached locally.**

**1. As service instances start, they will
register their IPs with Eureka.**

**Figure 6.4   By implementing client-side caching and Eureka with O-stock's licensing and organization
services, you can lessen the load on the Eureka Servers and improve client stability if Eureka becomes
unavailable.**

The actual resolution of the organization service's location is held in a service discovery registry. For this example, we'll register two instances of the organization service with a service discovery registry and then use client-side load balancing to look up and cache the registry in each service instance. Figure 6.4 shows this arrangement:

1   As the services are bootstrapped, the licensing and organization services register with the Eureka service. This registration process tells Eureka the physical location and port number of each service instance, along with a service ID for the service being started.

2   When the licensing service calls to the organization service, it uses the Spring Cloud Load Balancer to provide client-side load balancing. The Load Balancer contacts the Eureka service to retrieve service location information and then caches it locally.

3   Periodically, the Spring Cloud Load Balancer will ping the Eureka service and refresh its local cache of service locations.

Any new organization service instance is now visible to the licensing service locally, while any unhealthy instances are removed from the local cache. We'll implement this design by setting up our Spring Cloud Eureka service.

6.3   *Building our Spring Eureka service*

In this section, we'll set up our Eureka service using Spring Boot. Like the Spring Cloud Config service, setting up a Spring Cloud Eureka service starts with building a new Spring Boot project and applying annotations and configurations. Let's begin by creating this project with the Spring Initializr (https://start.spring.io/). To achieve this, we'll follow these steps in the Spring Initializr:

1   Select Maven as the project type.
2   Select Java as the language.
3   Select the 2.2.x latest or a more stable Spring version.
4   Write `com.optimagrowth` as the group and `eurekaserver` as the artifact.
5   Expand the options list and write `Eureka Server` as the name, `Eureka server` as the description, and `com.optimagrowth.eureka` as its package name.
6   Select JAR Packaging.
7   Select Java 11 as the Java version.
8   Add the Eureka Server, Config Client, and Spring Boot Actuator dependencies as shown in figure 6.5. Listing 6.1 shows the Eureka Server pom.xml file.

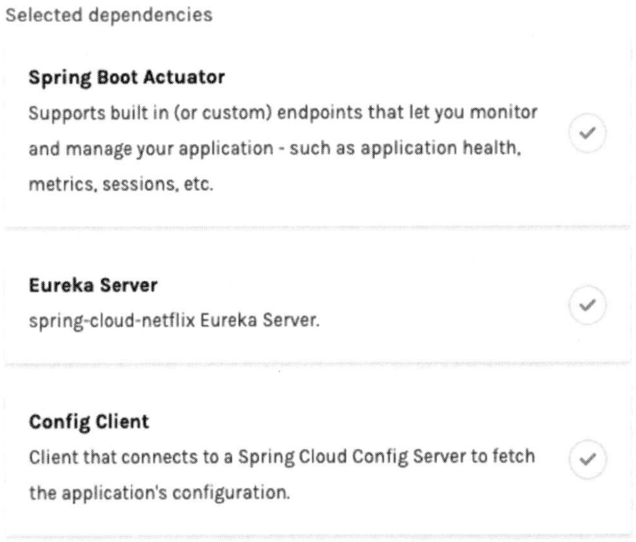

Selected dependencies

Spring Boot Actuator

Supports built in (or custom) endpoints that let you monitor
and manage your application - such as application health,
metrics, sessions, etc.

Eureka Server

spring-cloud-netflix Eureka Server.

Config Client

Client that connects to a Spring Cloud Config Server to fetch
the application's configuration.

**Figure 6.5   Eureka
Server dependencies
in Spring Initializr**

Listing 6.1   Maven pom file for the Eureka Server

```
<?xml version="1.0" encoding="UTF-8"?>
<project xmlns="http://maven.apache.org/POM/4.0.0"
  xmlns:xsi="http://www.w3.org/2001/XMLSchema-instance"
  xsi:schemaLocation="http://maven.apache.org/POM/4.0.0
  https://maven.apache.org/xsd/maven-4.0.0.xsd">
    <modelVersion>4.0.0</modelVersion>
    <parent>
```

```
        <groupId>org.springframework.boot</groupId>
        <artifactId>spring-boot-starter-parent</artifactId>
        <version>2.2.5.RELEASE</version>
        <relativePath/> <!-- lookup parent from repository -->
    </parent>
    <groupId>com.optimagrowth</groupId>
    <artifactId>eurekaserver</artifactId>
    <version>0.0.1-SNAPSHOT</version>
    <name>Eureka Server</name>
    <description>Eureka Server</description>

    <properties>
        <java.version>11</java.version>
        <spring-cloud.version>Hoxton.SR1</spring-cloud.version>
    </properties>

    <dependencies>
        <dependency>
            <groupId>org.springframework.boot</groupId>
            <artifactId>spring-boot-starter-actuator</artifactId>
        </dependency>
        <dependency>
            <groupId>org.springframework.cloud
            </groupId>
            <artifactId>spring-cloud-starter-config</artifactId>
        </dependency>
        <dependency>
            <groupId>org.springframework.cloud</groupId>
            <artifactId>spring-cloud-starter-netflix-eureka-server
            </artifactId>
            <exclusions>
                <exclusion>
                    <groupId>org.springframework.cloud</groupId>
                    <artifactId>spring-cloud-starter-ribbon</artifactId>
                </exclusion>
                <exclusion>
                    <groupId>com.netflix.ribbon</groupId>
                    <artifactId>ribbon-eureka</artifactId>
                </exclusion>
            </exclusions>
        </dependency>
        <dependency>
            <groupId>org.springframework.cloud</groupId>
            <artifactId>spring-cloud-starter-loadbalancer
            </artifactId>
        </dependency>
        <dependency>
            <groupId>org.springframework.boot</groupId>
            <artifactId>spring-boot-starter-test</artifactId>
            <scope>test</scope>
            <exclusions>
                <exclusion>
                    <groupId>org.junit.vintage</groupId>
                    <artifactId>junit-vintage-engine</artifactId>
                </exclusion>
```

Tells Maven to include the client that connects to a Spring ConfigServer to retrieve the application's configuration

Tells Maven to include the Eureka libraries

Excludes the Netflix Ribbon libraries

Tells Maven to include the Spring Cloud Load Balancer libraries

```
        </exclusions>
      </dependency>
    </dependencies>

<!--Rest of pom.xml omitted for conciseness
...
</project>
```

The next step is to set up the src/main/resources/bootstrap.yml file with the settings we need to retrieve the configuration from the Spring Config Server previously created in chapter 5. We also need to add the configuration to disable Ribbon as our default client-side load balancer. The following listing shows how your bootstrap.yml file should look.

Listing 6.2 Setting up the Eureka bootstrap.yml file

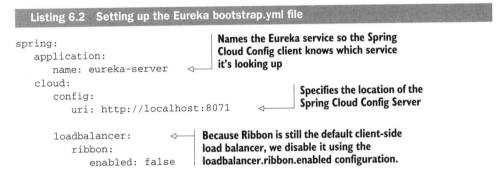

```
spring:
  application:
    name: eureka-server      ◁──┘ it's looking up
  cloud:
    config:
      uri: http://localhost:8071   ◁──┘

    loadbalancer:        ◁──┐
      ribbon:
        enabled: false
```

Names the Eureka service so the Spring Cloud Config client knows which service it's looking up

Specifies the location of the Spring Cloud Config Server

Because Ribbon is still the default client-side load balancer, we disable it using the loadbalancer.ribbon.enabled configuration.

Once we add the Spring Configuration Server information in the bootstrap file on the Eureka Server and we disable Ribbon as our load balancer, we can continue with the next step. That step adds the configuration needed to set up the Eureka service running in standalone mode (no other nodes in the cluster) in the Spring Configuration Server.

In order to achieve this, we must create the Eureka Server configuration file in the repository we set up in the Spring Config service. (Remember, we can specify a repository as a classpath, filesystem, GIT, or Vault.) The configuration file should be named as the spring.application.name property previously defined in the Eureka bootstrap.yml file of the Eureka service. For purposes of this example, we will create the eureka-server.yml file in classpath/configserver/src/main/resources/config/eureka-server.yml. Listing 6.3 shows the contents of this file.

> **NOTE** If you didn't follow the code listings in chapter 5, you can download the code from this link: https://github.com/ihuaylupo/manning-smia/tree/master/chapter5.

Listing 6.3 Setting up the Eureka configuration in the Spring Config Server

```
server:
  port: 8070    ◁──┘
eureka:
```

Sets the listening port for the Eureka Server

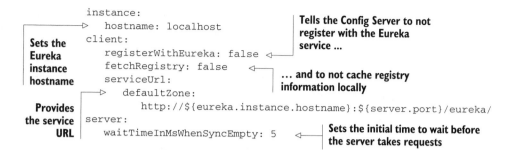

```
            instance:
               hostname: localhost
            client:
               registerWithEureka: false
               fetchRegistry: false
               serviceUrl:
                  defaultZone:
                     http://${eureka.instance.hostname}:${server.port}/eureka/
            server:
               waitTimeInMsWhenSyncEmpty: 5
```

The key properties set in listing 6.3 are as follows:

- `server.port`—Sets the default port.
- `eureka.instance.hostname`—Sets the Eureka instance hostname for the Eureka service.
- `eureka.client.registerWithEureka`—Tells the Config Server not to register with Eureka when the Spring Boot Eureka application starts.
- `eureka.client.fetchRegistry`—When set to false, tells the Eureka service that as it starts, it doesn't need to cache its registry information locally. When running a Eureka client, you'll want to change this value for the Spring Boot services that are going to register with Eureka.
- `eureka.client.serviceUrl.defaultZone`—Provides the service URL for any client. It is a combination of the `eureka.instance.hostname` and the `server.port` attributes.
- `eureka.server.waitTimeInMsWhenSyncEmpty`—Sets the time to wait before the server takes requests.

You'll notice that the last attribute in listing 6.3, `eureka.server.waitTimeInMsWhen-SyncEmpty`, indicates the time to wait in milliseconds before starting. When you're testing your service locally, you should use this line because Eureka won't immediately advertise any services that register with it. By default, it waits 5 minutes to give all of the services a chance to register with it before advertising them. Using this line for local testing helps to speed up the amount of time it takes for the Eureka service to start and to show the services registered with it.

> **NOTE** Individual services registering with Eureka take up to 30 seconds to show up in the Eureka service. That's because Eureka requires three consecutive heartbeat pings from the service, which are spaced 10 seconds apart, before it will say the service is ready for use. Keep this in mind as you're deploying and testing your own services.

The last piece of setup work you need to do for your Eureka service is to add an annotation to the application bootstrap class you use to start your Eureka service. For the Eureka service, you can find the application bootstrap class, `EurekaServerApplication`, in the

src/main/java/com/optimagrowth/eureka/EurekaServerApplication.java   class   file.
The following listing shows where to add the annotations.

> **Listing 6.4   Annotating the bootstrap class to enable the Eureka Server**

```
package com.optimagrowth.eureka;

import org.springframework.boot.SpringApplication;
import org.springframework.boot.autoconfigure.SpringBootApplication;
import org.springframework.cloud.netflix.eureka.server.EnableEurekaServer;

@SpringBootApplication
@EnableEurekaServer                        ⟵   Enables the Eureka Server
public class EurekaServerApplication {           in the Spring service

    public static void main(String[] args) {
      SpringApplication.run(EurekaServerApplication.class, args);
    }

}
```

At this point, we only use a new annotation, `@EnableEurekaServer`, to enable our service as an Eureka service. Now we can start the Eureka service by running the mvn
`spring-boot:run` or run `docker-compose` commands. Once the startup command is
executed, we should have a running Eureka service with no services registered in it.
We first need to run the Spring Config service because it contains the Eureka application configuration. If you don't run your configuration service first, you will get the
following error:

```
Connect Timeout Exception on Url - http://localhost:8071.
Will be trying the next url if available.
      com.sun.jersey.api.client.ClientHandlerException:
      java.net.ConnectException: Connection refused (Connection refused)
```

To avoid the previous issue, try running the services with Docker Compose. Remember, you can find the docker-compose.yml file updated in the chapter repository on
GitHub. Now, let's move on to building out the organization service. Then we will register the licensing and the organization services with our Eureka service.

6.4   *Registering services with Spring Eureka*

At this point, we have a Spring-based Eureka Server up and running. In this section,
we'll configure the organization and licensing services to register themselves with our
Eureka Server. This work is done in preparation for having a service client look up a
service from our Eureka registry. By the time we're done with this section, you should
have a firm understanding of how to register a Spring Boot microservice with Eureka.
    Registering a Spring Boot–based microservice with Eureka is a straightforward
exercise. For the purposes of this chapter, we're not going to walk through all of the
Java code involved with writing the service (we purposely kept that amount of code

small), but instead, focus on registering the service with the Eureka service registry you created in the previous section.

In this section, we introduce a new service that we'll call the *organization service*. This service will contain the CRUD endpoints. You can download the code for the licensing and organization services from this link:

https://github.com/ihuaylupo/manning-smia/tree/master/chapter6/Initial

> **NOTE** At this point, you can use other microservices you might have. Just pay attention to the service ID names as you register them with service discovery.

The first thing we need to do is to add the Spring Eureka dependency to our organization and licensing services' pom.xml files. The following listing shows how.

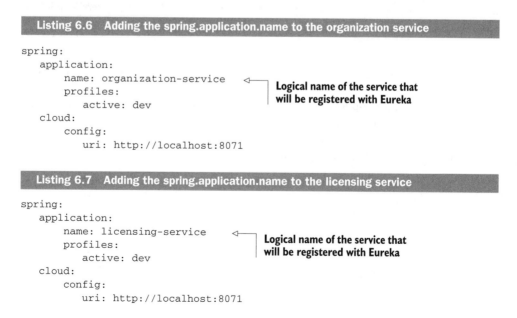

Listing 6.5 Adding the Spring Eureka dependency to the organization's service pom.xml

```
<dependency>
    <groupId>org.springframework.cloud</groupId>
    <artifactId>
        spring-cloud-starter-netflix-eureka-client
    </artifactId>
</dependency>
```

Includes the Eureka libraries so that the service can register with Eureka

The `spring-cloud-starter-netflix-eureka-client` artifact holds the JAR files that Spring Cloud uses to interact with your Eureka service. After we've set up the pom.xml file, we need to make sure we have set the `spring.application.name` in the bootstrap.yml file of the service we want to register. The following listings, 6.6 and 6.7, indicate how to do this.

Listing 6.6 Adding the spring.application.name to the organization service

```
spring:
    application:
        name: organization-service
        profiles:
            active: dev
    cloud:
        config:
            uri: http://localhost:8071
```

Logical name of the service that will be registered with Eureka

---

Listing 6.7 Adding the spring.application.name to the licensing service

```
spring:
    application:
        name: licensing-service
        profiles:
            active: dev
    cloud:
        config:
            uri: http://localhost:8071
```

Logical name of the service that will be registered with Eureka

Every service registered with Eureka will have two components associated with it: the application ID and the instance ID. The application ID represents a group service instance. In a Spring Boot microservice, the application ID is always the value set by the `spring.application.name` property. For our organization service, this property is creatively named `organization-service`, and for our licensing service, it's named `licensing-service`. The instance ID will be a randomly autogenerated number to represent a single service instance.

Next, we need to tell Spring Boot to register the organization and licensing services with Eureka. This registration is done via additional configuration in the service's configuration files managed by the Spring Config service. For this example, these files are located in the following two files for the Spring Configuration Server project. Listing 6.8 then shows how to register the services with Eureka.

- src/main/resources/config/organization-service.properties
- src/main/resources/config/licensing-service.properties

NOTE Remember, the configuration file can be either a YAML or a properties file and can be located in the classpath, filesystem, Git repository, or Vault. It depends on the configuration you've set in the Spring Config Server. For this example, we selected the classpath and properties file, but feel free to make the changes that best suit your needs.

Listing 6.8   Modifying the service application.properties files for Eureka

```
eureka.instance.preferIpAddress = true       ◁── Registers the IP address of the
                                                  service rather than the server name

eureka.client.registerWithEureka = true      ◁── Registers the service with Eureka

eureka.client.fetchRegistry = true           ◁── Pulls down a local copy of the registry

eureka.client.serviceUrl.defaultZone =
        http://localhost:8070/eureka/        ◁── Sets the location of the Eureka service
```

If you have an application.yml file, your file should look like that shown in the following code to register the services with Eureka. The `eureka.instance.preferIp-Address` property tells Eureka that you want to register the service's IP address with Eureka rather than its hostname.

```
eureka:
   instance:
      preferIpAddress: true
   client:
      registerWithEureka: true
      fetchRegistry: true
      serviceUrl: defaultZone: http://localhost:8070/eureka/
```

Why prefer an IP address?

By default, Eureka registers the services that contact it by hostname. This works well in a server-based environment, where a service is assigned a DNS-backed hostname. However, in a container-based deployment (for example, Docker), containers are started with randomly generated hostnames and no DNS entries for the containers. If you don't set the `eureka.instance.preferIpAddress` to true, your client applications won't correctly resolve the location of the hostnames; there will be no DNS entry for that container. Setting the `preferIpAddress` attribute informs the Eureka service that the client wants to be advertised by IP address.

Personally, we always set this attribute to `true`. Cloud-based microservices are supposed to be ephemeral and stateless. These can be started up and shut down at will, so IP addresses are more appropriate for these types of services.

The `eureka.client.registerWithEureka` attribute is the trigger to tell the organization and the licensing services to register with Eureka. The `eureka.client.fetchRegistry` attribute tells the Spring Eureka client to fetch a local copy of the registry. Setting this attribute to `true` caches the registry locally instead of calling the Eureka service with each lookup. Every 30 seconds, the client software recontacts the Eureka service for any changes to the registry.

> **NOTE** These two properties are set by default to `true`, but we've included the properties in the application configuration's file for illustrative purposes only. The code will work without setting those properties to `true`.

The last attribute, `eureka.serviceUrl.defaultZone`, holds a comma-separated list of Eureka services the client uses to resolve to service locations. For our purposes, we're only going to have one Eureka service. We can also declare all the key-value properties defined previously in the bootstrap file of each service. But the idea is to delegate the configuration to the Spring Config service. That's why we register all the configurations in the service configuration file in our Spring Config service repository. So far, the bootstrap file of these services should only contain the application name, a profile (if needed), and the Spring Cloud configuration URI.

Eureka and high availability

Setting up multiple URL services isn't enough for high availability. The `eureka.service-Url.defaultZone` attribute only provides a list of Eureka services for the client to communicate with. You also need to set up the Eureka services to replicate the contents of their registries with each other. A group of Eureka registries communicate with each other using a peer-to-peer communication model, where each Eureka service must be configured so that it knows about the other nodes in the cluster.

Setting up a Eureka cluster is outside of the scope of this book. If you're interested in setting up a Eureka cluster, visit the Spring Cloud project's website for further information:

https://projects.spring.io/spring-cloud/spring-cloud.html#spring-cloud-eureka-server

At this point, we have two services registered with our Eureka service. We can use Eureka's REST API or the Eureka dashboard to see the contents of the registry. We'll explain each in the following sections.

6.4.1   *Eureka's REST API*

To see all the instances of a service in the REST API, select the following GET endpoint:

```
http://<eureka service>:8070/eureka/apps/<APPID>
```

For instance, to see the organization service in the registry, you would call the following endpoint: `http://localhost:8070/eureka/apps/organization-service`. Figure 6.6 shows the response.

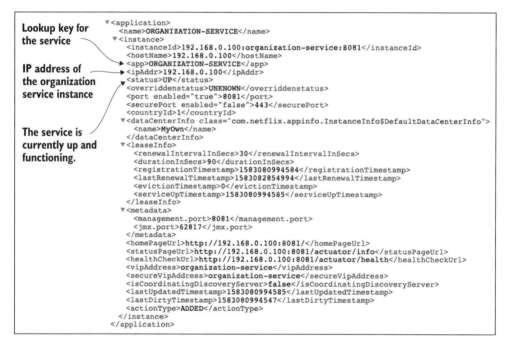

Figure 6.6   The Eureka REST API showing the organization service. The response shows the IP address of the service instances registered in Eureka, along with the service status.

The default format returned by the Eureka service is XML. Eureka can also return the data in figure 6.6 as a JSON payload, but you'll have to set the Accept HTTP header to `application/json`. An example of the JSON payload is shown in figure 6.7.

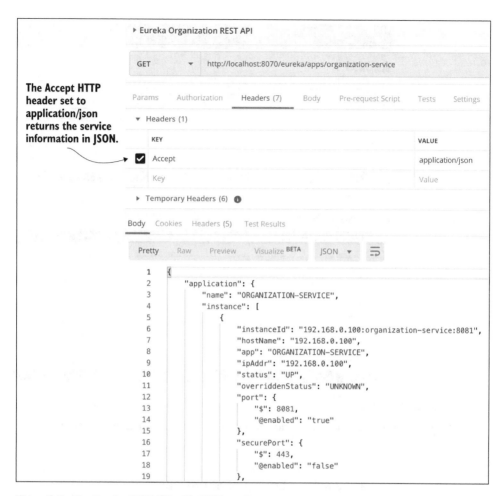

The Accept HTTP header set to application/json returns the service information in JSON.

Figure 6.7   The Eureka REST API with JSON results

6.4.2   *Eureka dashboard*

Once the Eureka service is up, we can point our browsers to http://localhost:8070 to view the Eureka dashboard. The Eureka dashboard allows us to see the registration status of our services. Figure 6.8 shows an example of the Eureka dashboard.

Now, that we've registered the organization and licensing services, let's see how we can use service discovery to look up a service.

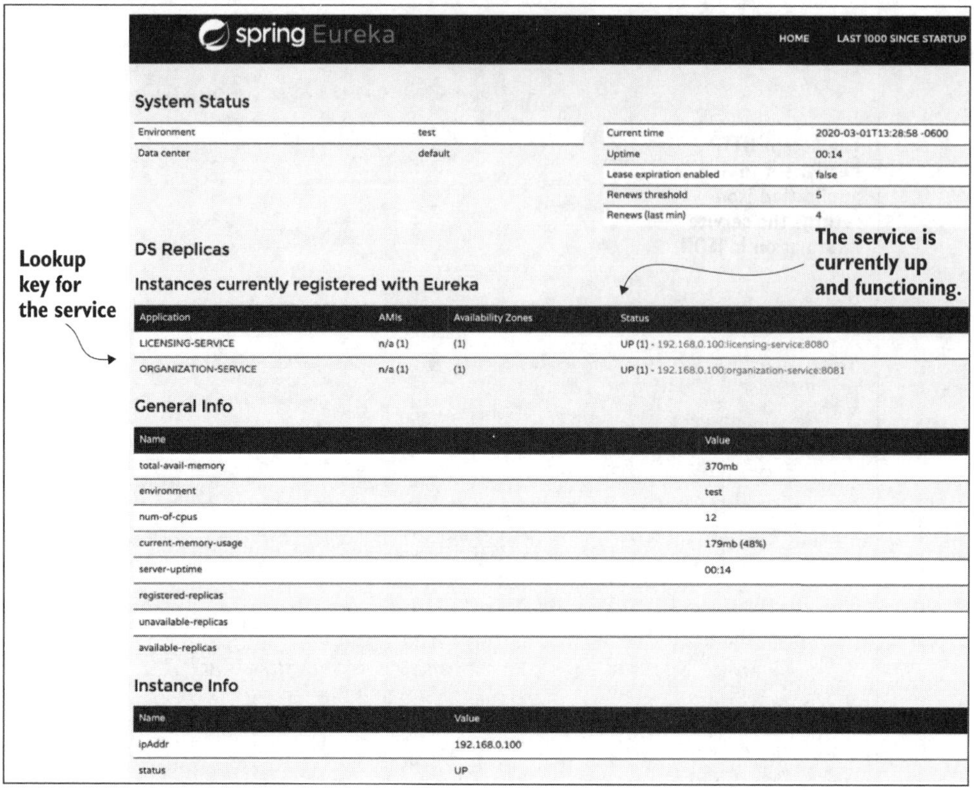

Figure 6.8   The Eureka dashboard with the registered organization and licensing instances

On Eureka and service startups: Don't be impatient

When a service registers with Eureka, Eureka waits for three successive health checks over the course of 30 seconds before the service becomes available. This warm-up period throws some developers off. They assume that Eureka hasn't registered their service if they try to call it immediately after the service is launched.

This is evident in our code examples running in the Docker environment because the Eureka service and the application services (licensing and organization) all start at the same time. Be aware that after starting an application, you might receive 404 errors about services not being found, even though the service itself has started. In that case, wait 30 seconds before trying to call your services.

In a production environment, your Eureka services will already be running. If you're deploying an existing service, the old services will still be in place to take requests.

6.5 *Using service discovery to look up a service*

In this section, we will explain how we can have the licensing service call the organization service without having direct knowledge of the location of any of the organization services. The licensing service will look up the physical location of the organization using Eureka.

For our purposes, we'll look at three different Spring/Netflix client libraries in which a service consumer can interact with the Spring Cloud Load Balancer. These libraries will move from the lowest level of abstraction for interacting with the Load Balancer to the highest. The libraries we'll explore include

- Spring Discovery Client
- Spring Discovery Client–enabled REST template
- Netflix Feign client

Let's walk through each of these clients and see their use in the context of the licensing service. Before we start into the specifics of the client, we wrote a few convenience classes and methods in the code. You can play with the different client types using the same service endpoint.

First, we've modified the src/main/java/com/optimagrowth/license/controller /LicenseController.java class to include a new route for the licensing services. This new route allows you to specify the type of client you want to use to invoke the service. This is a helper route so that as we explore each of the different methods for invoking the organization's service via the Load Balancer, you can try each mechanism through a single route. The following listing shows the code for the new route in the License-Controller class.

> **Listing 6.9 Calling the licensing service with different REST clients**

```
@RequestMapping(value="/{licenseId}/{clientType}",            The clientType parameter
           method = RequestMethod.GET)          ◁————         determines the type of
public License getLicensesWithClient(                          Spring REST client to use.
           @PathVariable("organizationId") String organizationId,
           @PathVariable("licenseId") String licenseId,
           @PathVariable("clientType") String clientType) {
        return licenseService.getLicense(organizationId,
                licenseId, clientType);
}
```

In listing 6.9, the clientType parameter passed on the route drives the type of client we're going to use in the code examples. The specific types we can pass in on this route include the following:

- *Discovery*—Uses the Discovery Client and a standard Spring RestTemplate class to invoke the organization service
- *Rest*—Uses an enhanced Spring RestTemplate to invoke the Load Balancer service
- *Feign*—Uses Netflix's Feign client library to invoke a service via the Load Balancer

NOTE Because we're using the same code for all three types of clients, you might see situations where you'll see annotations for specific clients even when they don't seem to be needed. For example, you'll see both the @EnableDiscoveryClient and @EnableFeignClients annotations in the code, even when the text is only explaining one of the client types. This is so that we can use one codebase for our examples. We'll call out these redundancies and code when these are encountered. The idea is that, as always, you choose the one that best suits your needs.

In the class src/main/java/com/optimagrowth/license/service/LicenseService .java, we added a simple retrieveOrganizationInfo() method that will resolve based on the clientType passed to the route. This client type is used to look up an organization service instance. The getLicense() method on the LicenseService class uses the retrieveOrganizationInfo() method to retrieve the organization data from a Postgres database. The following listing shows the code for the getLicense() service in the LicenseService class.

Listing 6.10   The getLicense() function using multiple methods for a REST call

```
public License getLicense(String licenseId, String organizationId, String
      clientType){
   License license = licenseRepository.findByOrganizationIdAndLicenseId
                     (organizationId, licenseId);
   if (null == license) {
      throw new IllegalArgumentException(String.format(
         messages.getMessage("license.search.error.message", null, null),
         licenseId, organizationId));
   }
   Organization organization = retrieveOrganizationInfo(organizationId,
                           clientType);
   if (null != organization) {
      license.setOrganizationName(organization.getName());
      license.setContactName(organization.getContactName());
      license.setContactEmail(organization.getContactEmail());
      license.setContactPhone(organization.getContactPhone());
   }
   return license.withComment(config.getExampleProperty());
}
```

You can find each of the clients we built using the Spring Discovery Client, the Spring RestTemplate class, or the Feign libraries in the src/main/java/com/optimagrowth/ license/service/client package of the licensing service. To call the getLicense() services with the different clients, you must call the following GET endpoint:

```
http://<licensing service Hostname/IP>:<licensing service Port>/v1/
organization/<organizationID>/license/<licenseID>/<client type( feign,
discovery, rest)>
```

6.5.1 Looking up service instances with Spring Discovery Client

The Spring Discovery Client offers the lowest level of access to the Load Balancer and the services registered within it. Using the Discovery Client, you can query for all the services registered with the Spring Cloud Load Balancer client and their corresponding URLs.

Next, we'll build a simple example of using the Discovery Client to retrieve one of the organization service URLs from the Load Balancer and then call the service using a standard `RestTemplate` class. To use the Discovery Client, we first need to annotate the src/main/java/com/optimagrowth/license/LicenseServiceApplication.java class with the `@EnableDiscoveryClient` annotation as shown in the following listing.

Listing 6.11 Setting up the bootstrap class to use the Eureka Discovery Client

```
package com.optimagrowth.license;
@SpringBootApplication
@RefreshScope                                      Activates the Eureka
@EnableDiscoveryClient          ◁─────────         Discovery Client
public class LicenseServiceApplication {

    public static void main(String[] args) {
        SpringApplication.run(LicenseServiceApplication.class, args);
    }
}
```

The `@EnableDiscoveryClient` is the trigger for Spring Cloud to enable the application to use the Discovery Client and the Spring Cloud Load Balancer libraries. Now, let's look at our implementation of the code that calls the organization service via the Spring Discovery Client. The following listing shows this implementation. You can find this code in the src/main/java/com/optimagrowth/license/service/client/OrganizationDiscoveryClient.java file.

Listing 6.12 Using the Discovery Client to look up information

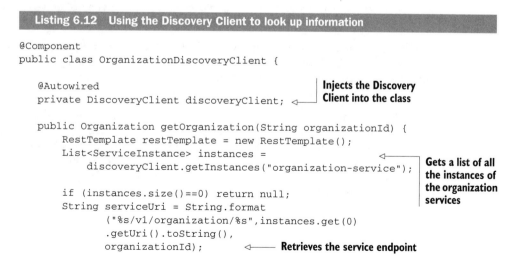

```
@Component
public class OrganizationDiscoveryClient {

    @Autowired                                          Injects the Discovery
    private DiscoveryClient discoveryClient;  ◁─────    Client into the class

    public Organization getOrganization(String organizationId) {
        RestTemplate restTemplate = new RestTemplate();
        List<ServiceInstance> instances =                    ◁─────       Gets a list of all
            discoveryClient.getInstances("organization-service");         the instances of
                                                                          the organization
        if (instances.size()==0) return null;                            services
        String serviceUri = String.format
            ("%s/v1/organization/%s",instances.get(0)
            .getUri().toString(),
            organizationId);          ◁────── Retrieves the service endpoint
```

```
ResponseEntity<Organization> restExchange =          ◁─┐ Uses a standard Spring
        restTemplate.exchange(                              RestTemplate class to
        serviceUri, HttpMethod.GET,                         call the service
        null, Organization.class, organizationId);

return restExchange.getBody();
    }
}
```

The first item of interest in the code is the `DiscoveryClient` class. You use this class to interact with the Spring Cloud Load Balancer. Then, to retrieve all instances of the organization services registered with Eureka, you use the `getInstances()` method, passing in the service key that you're looking for to retrieve a list of `ServiceInstance` objects. The `ServiceInstance` class holds information about a specific instance of a service, including its hostname, port, and URI.

In listing 6.12, you take the first `ServiceInstance` class in your list to build a target URL that can then be used to call your service. Once you have a target URL, you can use a standard Spring `RestTemplate` to call your organization service and retrieve the data.

The Discovery Client and real life

You should only use the Discovery Client when your service needs to query the Load Balancer to understand what services and service instances are registered with it. There are several problems with the code in listing 6.12, including these:

- *You aren't taking advantage of the Spring Cloud client-side Load Balancer.* By calling the Discovery Client directly, you get a list of services, but it becomes your responsibility to choose which returned service instance you're going to invoke.
- *You're doing too much work.* In the code, you have to build the URL that you'll use to call your service. It's a small thing, but every piece of code that you can avoid writing is one less piece of code that you have to debug.

Observant Spring developers might have also noticed that we directly instantiated the `RestTemplate` class in the code. This is antithetical to usual Spring REST invocations because you'll usually have the Spring framework inject the `RestTemplate` class via the `@Autowired` annotation.

We instantiated the `RestTemplate` class in listing 6.12. Once we've enabled the Spring Discovery Client in the application class via `@EnableDiscoveryClient`, all REST templates managed by the Spring framework will have a Load Balancer–enabled interceptor injected into those instances. This will change how URLs are created with the `RestTemplate` class. Directly instantiating `RestTemplate` allows you to avoid this behavior.

6.5.2 *Invoking services with a Load Balancer–aware Spring REST template*

Next, we'll see an example of how to use a REST template that's Load Balancer–aware. This is one of the more common mechanisms for interacting with the Load Balancer via Spring. To use a Load Balancer–aware `RestTemplate` class, we need to define a `RestTemplate` bean with a Spring Cloud `@LoadBalanced` annotation.

For the licensing service, the method that we'll use to create the `RestTemplate` bean can be found in the `LicenseServiceApplication` class in src/main/java/com/optimagrowth/license/LicenseServiceApplication.java. The following listing shows the `getRestTemplate()` method that will create the Load Balancer–backed Spring `RestTemplate` bean.

> **Listing 6.13 Annotating and defining a `RestTemplate` construction method**

```
//Most of the import statements have been removed for conciseness
import org.springframework.cloud.client.loadbalancer.LoadBalanced;
import org.springframework.context.annotation.Bean;
import org.springframework.web.client.RestTemplate;

@SpringBootApplication
@RefreshScope
public class LicenseServiceApplication {
    public static void main(String[] args) {
        SpringApplication.run(LicenseServiceApplication.class, args);
    }

    @LoadBalanced         ◁─┐ Gets a list of all the instances
    @Bean                    │ for the organization services
    public RestTemplate getRestTemplate(){
        return new RestTemplate();
    }
}
```

Now that the bean definition for the backed `RestTemplate` class is defined, any time you want to use the `RestTemplate` bean to call a service, you only need to autowire it to the class using it.

Using the backed `RestTemplate` class pretty much behaves like a standard Spring `RestTemplate` class, except for one small difference in how the URL for the target service is defined. Rather than using the physical location of the service in the `RestTemplate` call, you need to build the target URL using the Eureka service ID of the service you want to call. The following listing allows us to see this call. The code for this listing can be found in the src/main/java/com/optimagrowth/license/service/client/OrganizationRestTemplateClient.java class file.

> **Listing 6.14 Using a Load Balancer–backed `RestTemplate` to call a service**

```
//Package and import definitions left out for conciseness
@Component
public class OrganizationRestTemplateClient {
```

```
@Autowired
RestTemplate restTemplate;

public Organization getOrganization(String organizationId){
    ResponseEntity<Organization> restExchange =
        restTemplate.exchange(
            "http://organization-service/v1/
                organization/{organizationId}",
            HttpMethod.GET, null,
            Organization.class, organizationId);

    return restExchange.getBody();
    }
}
```

> When using a Load Balancer–backed RestTemplate, builds the target URL with the Eureka service ID

This code should look somewhat similar to the previous example except for two key differences. First, the Spring Cloud Discovery Client is nowhere in sight, and second, the URL used in the restTemplate.exchange() call should look odd to you. Here's that call:

```
restTemplate.exchange(
    "http://organization-service/v1/organization/{organizationId}",
    HttpMethod.GET, null, Organization.class, organizationId);
```

The server name in the URL matches the application ID of the organization service key that you used to register the organization service with Eureka:

```
http://{applicationid}/v1/organization/{organizationId}
```

The Load Balancer–enabled RestTemplate class parses the URL passed into it and uses whatever is passed in as the server name as the key to query the Load Balancer for an instance of a service. The actual service location and port are entirely abstracted from the developer. Also, by using the RestTemplate class, the Spring Cloud Load Balancer will round-robin load balance all requests among all the service instances.

6.5.3   *Invoking services with Netflix Feign client*

An alternative to the Spring Load Balancer–enabled RestTemplate class is Netflix's Feign client library. The Feign library takes a different approach to call a REST service. With this approach, the developer first defines a Java interface and then adds Spring Cloud annotations to map what Eureka-based service the Spring Cloud Load Balancer will invoke. The Spring Cloud framework will dynamically generate a proxy class to invoke the targeted REST service. There's no code written for calling the service other than an interface definition.

To enable the Feign client for use in our licensing service, we need to add a new annotation, @EnableFeignClients, to the licensing service's src/main/java/com/optimagrowth/license/LicenseServiceApplication.java class file. The following listing shows this code.

Listing 6.15 Enabling the Spring Cloud/Netflix Feign client in the licensing service

```
@SpringBootApplication
@EnableFeignClients
public class LicenseServiceApplication {          This annotation is needed to use
                                                  the Feign client in your code.
    public static void main(String[] args) {
        SpringApplication.run(LicenseServiceApplication.class, args);
    }
}
```

Now that we've enabled the Feign client for use in our licensing service, let's look at a Feign client interface definition that we can use to call an endpoint for the organization service. The following listing shows an example. You'll find the code in this listing in the src/main/java/com/optimagrowth/license/service/client/OrganizationFeignClient .java class file.

Listing 6.16 Defining a Feign interface for calling the organization service

```
//Package and import left out for conciseness      Identifies your
@FeignClient("organization-service")               service to Feign
public interface OrganizationFeignClient {
    @RequestMapping(                               Defines the path and
        method= RequestMethod.GET,                 action to your endpoint
        value="/v1/organization/{organizationId}",
        consumes="application/json")
    Organization getOrganization
        (@PathVariable("organizationId")           Defines the parameters
            String organizationId);                passed into the endpoint
}
```

In listing 6.16, we used the `@FeignClient` annotation, passing it the application ID of the service we want the interface to represent. Then we defined a method, `get-Organization()`, in our interface, which can be called by the client to invoke the organization service.

How we define the `getOrganization()` method looks exactly like how we would expose an endpoint in a Spring controller class. First, we define a `@RequestMapping` annotation for the `getOrganization()` method that maps the HTTP verb and end-point to be exposed to the organization service's invocation. Second, we map the organization ID passed in on the URL to an `organizationId` parameter on the method call using `@PathVariable`. The return value from the call to the organization service is automatically mapped to the `Organization` class that's defined as the return value for the `getOrganization()` method. To use the `OrganizationFeignClient` class, all we need to do is to autowire it and use it. The Feign client code takes care of all the coding for us.

On error handling

When you use the standard Spring `RestTemplate` class, all service call HTTP status codes are returned via the `ResponseEntity` class's `getStatusCode()` method. With the Feign client, any HTTP 4xx–5xx status codes returned by the service being called are mapped to a `FeignException`. The `FeignException` contains a JSON body that can be parsed for the specific error message.

Feign provides the ability to write an error decoder class that will map the error back to a custom `Exception` class. Writing this decoder is outside the scope of this book, but you can find examples of this in the Feign GitHub repository here:

https://github.com/Netflix/feign/wiki/Custom-error-handling

Summary

- We use a service discovery pattern to abstract away the physical location of our services.
- A service discovery engine like Eureka can seamlessly add and remove service instances from an environment without impacting the service clients.
- Client-side load balancing can provide an extra level of performance and resiliency by caching the physical location of a service on the client making the service call.
- Eureka is a Netflix project that, when used with Spring Cloud, is easy to set up and configure.
- You can use these three different mechanisms in Spring Cloud and Netflix Eureka to invoke a service: Spring Cloud Discovery Client, Spring Cloud Load Balancer–backed `RestTemplate`, and Netflix's Feign client.

When bad things happen: Resiliency patterns with Spring Cloud and Resilience4j

7

This chapter covers

- Implementing circuit breakers, fallbacks, and bulkheads
- Using the circuit breaker pattern to conserve client resources
- Using Resilience4j when a remote service fails
- Implementing Resilience4j's bulkhead pattern to segregate remote resource calls
- Tuning Resilience4j circuit breaker and bulkhead implementations
- Customizing Resilience4j's concurrency strategy

All systems, especially distributed systems, experience failure. How we build our applications to respond to that failure is a critical part of every software developer's job. However, when it comes to building resilient systems, most software engineers only take into account the complete failure of a piece of infrastructure or critical service. They focus on building redundancy into each layer of their application using techniques such as clustering key servers, load balancing between services, and segregating infrastructure into multiple locations.

While these approaches take into account the complete (and often spectacular) loss of a system component, they address only one small part of building resilient systems. When a service crashes, it's easy to detect that it's no longer there, and the application can route around it. However, when a service is running slow, detecting that poor performance and routing around it is extremely difficult. Let's look at some reasons why:

- *Service degradation can start out as intermittent and then build momentum.* Service degradation might also occur only in small bursts. The first signs of failure might be a small group of users complaining about a problem until suddenly, the application container exhausts its thread pool and collapses completely.

- *Calls to remote services are usually synchronous and don't cut short a long-running call.* The application developer normally calls a service to perform an action and waits for the service to return. The caller has no concept of a timeout to keep the service call from hanging.

- *Applications are often designed to deal with complete failures of remote resources, not partial degradations.* Often, as long as the service has not entirely failed, an application will continue to call a poorly behaving service and won't fail fast. In this case, the calling application or service can degrade gracefully or, more likely, crash because of resource exhaustion. *Resource exhaustion* is where a limited resource, such as a thread pool or database connection, maxes out, and the calling client must wait for that resource to become available again.

What's insidious about problems caused by poorly performing remote services is that they are not only difficult to detect but can trigger a cascading effect that can ripple throughout an entire application ecosystem. Without safeguards in place, a single, poorly performing service can quickly take down multiple applications. Cloud-based, microservice-based applications are particularly vulnerable to these types of outages because these applications are composed of a large number of fine-grained, distributed services with different pieces of infrastructure involved in completing a user's transaction.

Resiliency patterns are one of the most critical aspects of the microservices architecture. This chapter will explain four resiliency patterns and how to use Spring Cloud and Resilience4j to implement them in our licensing service so that it can fail fast when needed.

7.1   What are client-side resiliency patterns?

Client-side resiliency software patterns focus on protecting a client of a remote resource (another microservice call or database lookup) from crashing when the remote resource fails because of errors or poor performance. These patterns allow the client to fail fast and not consume valuable resources, such as database connections and thread pools. They also prevent the problem of the poorly performing remote service from spreading "upstream" to consumers of the client. In this chapter, we'll look at four client resiliency patterns. Figure 7.1 demonstrates how these patterns sit between the microservice service consumer and the microservice.

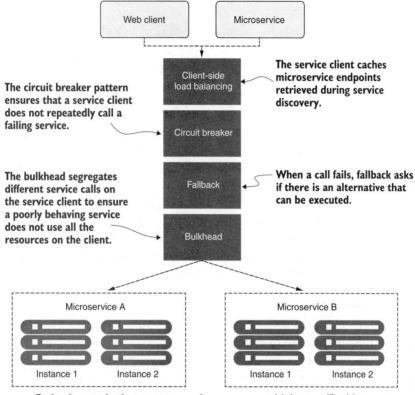

Each microservice instance runs on its own server with its own IP address.

Figure 7.1   The four client resiliency patterns act as a protective buffer between a service consumer and the service.

These patterns (client-side load balancing, circuit breaker, fallback, and bulkhead) are implemented in the client (microservice) calling the remote resource. The implementation of these patterns logically sits between the client consuming the remote resources and the resource itself. Let's spend some time with each of these patterns.

7.1.1   Client-side load balancing

We introduced the client-side load balancing pattern in the last chapter when we talked about service discovery. Client-side load balancing involves having the client look up all of a service's individual instances from a service discovery agent (like Netflix Eureka) and then caching the physical location of said service instances.

When a service consumer needs to call a service instance, the client-side load balancer returns a location from the pool of service locations it maintains. Because the client-side load balancer sits between the service client and the service consumer, the load balancer can detect if a service instance is throwing errors or behaving poorly. If the client-side load balancer detects a problem, it can remove that service instance from the pool of available service locations and prevent any future calls from hitting that service instance.

This is precisely the behavior that the Spring Cloud Load Balancer libraries provide out of the box (with no extra configuration). Because we've already covered client-side load balancing with Spring Cloud Load Balancer in chapter 6, we won't go into any more detail on that in this chapter.

7.1.2   Circuit breaker

The circuit breaker pattern is modeled after an electrical circuit breaker. In an electrical system, a circuit breaker detects if there's too much current flowing through the wire. If the circuit breaker detects a problem, it breaks the connection with the rest of the electrical system and keeps the system from frying the downstream components.

With a software circuit breaker, when a remote service is called, the circuit breaker monitors the call. If the calls take too long, the circuit breaker intercedes and kills the call. The circuit breaker pattern also monitors all calls to a remote resource, and if enough calls fail, the circuit breaker implementation will "pop," failing fast and preventing future calls to the failing remote resource.

7.1.3   Fallback processing

With the fallback pattern, when a remote service call fails, rather than generating an exception, the service consumer executes an alternative code path and tries to carry out the action through another means. This usually involves looking for data from another data source or queueing the user's request for future processing. The user's call is not shown an exception indicating a problem, but they can be notified that their request will have to be tried later.

For instance, let's suppose you have an e-commerce site that monitors your user's behavior and gives them recommendations for other items they might want to buy. Typically, you'd call a microservice to run an analysis of the user's past behavior and return a list of recommendations tailored to that specific user. However, if the preference service fails, your fallback might be to retrieve a more general list of preferences that are based on *all* user purchases, which is much more generalized. And, this data might come from a completely different service and data source.

7.1.4   Bulkheads

The bulkhead pattern is based on a concept from building ships. A ship is divided into compartments called bulkheads, which are entirely segregated and watertight. Even if the ship's hull is punctured, one bulkhead keeps the water confined to the area of the ship where the puncture occurred and prevents the entire ship from filling with water and sinking.

The same concept can be applied to a service that must interact with multiple remote resources. When using the bulkhead pattern, you break the calls to remote resources into their own thread pools and reduce the risk that a problem with one slow remote resource call will take down the entire application.

The thread pools act as the bulkheads for your service. Each remote resource is segregated and assigned to a thread pool. If one service is responding slowly, the thread pool for that type of service call can become saturated and stop processing requests. Assigning services to thread pools helps to bypass this type of bottleneck so that other services won't become saturated.

7.2 Why client resiliency matters

Although we've talked about these different patterns of client resiliency in the abstract, let's drill down to a more specific example of where these patterns can be applied. We'll walk through a typical scenario and see why client resiliency patterns are critical for implementing a microservice-based architecture running in the cloud.

Figure 7.2 shows a typical scenario involving the use of remote resources like a database and a remote service. This scenario doesn't contain any of the resiliency patterns that we have previously looked at, so it illustrates how an entire architecture (an ecosystem) can go down because of a single failing service. Let's take a look.

In the scenario in figure 7.2, three applications are communicating in one form or another with three different services. Applications A and B communicate directly with the licensing service. The licensing service retrieves data from a database and calls the organization service to do some work for it. The organization service retrieves data from a completely different database platform and calls out to another service, the inventory service, from a third-party cloud provider, whose service relies heavily on an internal Network Attached Storage (NAS) device to write data to a shared filesystem. Application C directly calls the inventory service.

Over the weekend, a network administrator made what they thought was a small tweak to the configuration on the NAS. This change appeared to work fine, but on Monday morning, reads to a particular disk subsystem began performing exceptionally slow.

The developers who wrote the organization service never anticipated slowdowns occurring with calls to the inventory service. They wrote their code so that the writes to their database and the reads from the service occur within the same transaction. When the inventory service starts running slowly, not only does the thread pool for requests to the inventory service start backing up, the number of database connections in the service container's connection pools becomes exhausted. These connections were held open because the calls to the inventory service never completed.

Now the licensing service starts running out of resources because it's calling the organization service, which is running slow because of the inventory service. Eventually, all three applications stop responding because they run out of resources while waiting for the requests to complete. This whole scenario could have been avoided if a

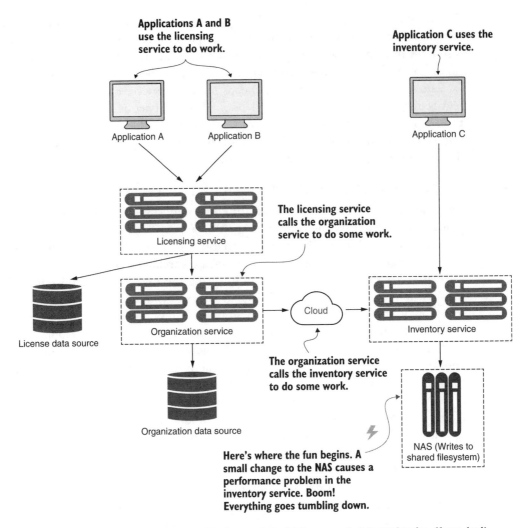

Applications A and B use the licensing service to do work.

Application C uses the inventory service.

Application A   Application B

Application C

Licensing service

The licensing service calls the organization service to do some work.

License data source

Organization service

Cloud

Inventory service

The organization service calls the inventory service to do some work.

Organization data source

NAS (Writes to shared filesystem)

Here's where the fun begins. A small change to the NAS causes a performance problem in the inventory service. Boom! Everything goes tumbling down.

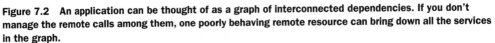

Figure 7.2   An application can be thought of as a graph of interconnected dependencies. If you don't manage the remote calls among them, one poorly behaving remote resource can bring down all the services in the graph.

circuit-breaker pattern had been implemented at each point where a distributed resource is called (either a call to the database or a call to the service).

In figure 7.2, if the call to the inventory service had been implemented with a circuit breaker, then when that service started performing poorly, the circuit breaker for that call would have tripped and failed fast without eating up a thread. If the organization service had multiple endpoints, only the endpoints that interacted with that specific call to the inventory service would be impacted. The rest of the organization service's functionality would still be intact and could fulfill user requests.

Remember, a circuit breaker acts as a middleman between the application and the remote service. In the scenario shown in figure 7.2, a circuit breaker implementation could have protected applications A, B, and C from completely crashing.

In figure 7.3, the licensing service never directly invokes the organization service. Instead, when the call is made, the licensing service delegates the actual invocation of the service to the circuit breaker, which takes the call and wraps it in a thread (usually managed in a thread pool) that's independent of the originating caller. By wrapping the call in a thread, the client is no longer directly waiting for the call to complete. Instead, the circuit breaker monitors the thread and can kill the call if the thread runs too long.

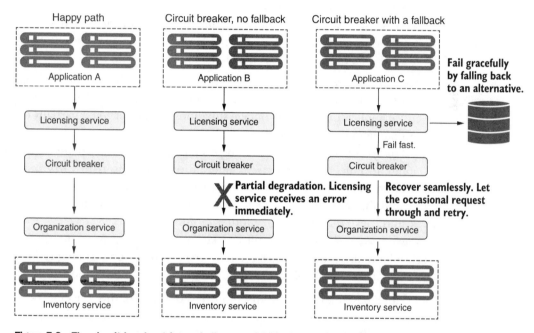

Figure 7.3 The circuit breaker trips and allows a misbehaving service call to fail quickly and gracefully.

Three scenarios are shown in figure 7.3. In the first scenario, "the happy path," the circuit breaker maintains a timer, and if the call to the remote service completes before the timer runs out, everything is good; the licensing service can continue its work.

In the second scenario, the partial degradation, the licensing service calls the organization service through the circuit breaker. This time, though, the organization service is running slow, so the circuit breaker kills the connection to the remote service if it doesn't complete before the timer on the thread maintained by the circuit breaker times out. The licensing service then returns an error from the call. The licensing service won't have its resources (its own thread or connection pool) tied up waiting for the organization service to complete.

If the call to the organization service times out, the circuit breaker starts tracking the number of failures that have occurred. If enough errors on the service occur within a specific time period, the circuit breaker now "trips" the circuit, and all calls to the organization service fail without making the call to it.

In the third scenario, the licensing service immediately knows there's a problem without having to wait for a timeout from the circuit breaker. It can then choose to either completely fail or to take action using an alternative set of code (a fallback). The organization service is given an opportunity to recover because the licensing service wasn't calling it when the circuit breaker tripped. This allows the organization service to have a bit of breathing room and helps to prevent the cascading shutdown that occurs when service degradation occurs.

The circuit breaker will occasionally let calls through to a degraded service. If those calls succeed enough times in a row, the circuit breaker resets itself. The key benefits a circuit break pattern offers is the ability for remote calls to

- *Fail fast*—When a remote service is experiencing a degradation, the application will fail fast and prevent resource-exhaustion issues that generally shut down the entire application. In most outage situations, it's better to be partially down rather than being entirely down.
- *Fail gracefully*—By timing out and failing fast, the circuit breaker pattern gives us the ability to fail gracefully or seek alternative mechanisms to carry out the user's intent. For instance, if a user is trying to retrieve data from one data source and that data source is experiencing service degradation, then our services can retrieve that data from another location.
- *Recover seamlessly*—With the circuit breaker pattern acting as an intermediary, the circuit breaker can periodically check to see if the resource being requested is back online and reenable access to it without human intervention.

In a sizeable cloud-based application with hundreds of services, this graceful recovery is critical because it can significantly cut down the amount of time needed to restore a service. It also significantly lessens the risk of a "tired" operator or application engineer causing more problems, allowing the circuit breaker to intervene directly (restarting a failed service) in the restoration of the service.

Before Resilience4j, we worked with Hystrix, one of the most common Java libraries to implement the resiliency patterns in microservices. Because Hystrix is now in maintenance mode, which means that new features are no longer included, one of the most recommended libraries to use as a substitute is Resilience4j. That's the main reason why we chose it for demonstration purposes in this chapter. With Resilience4j, we have similar (and some additional) benefits that we'll see throughout this chapter.

7.3 Implementing Resilience4j

Resilience4j is a fault tolerance library inspired by Hystrix. It offers the following patterns for increasing fault tolerance due to network problems or failure of any of our multiple services:

- *Circuit breaker*—Stops making requests when an invoked service is failing
- *Retry*—Retries a service when it temporarily fails
- *Bulkhead*—Limits the number of outgoing concurrent service requests to avoid overload
- *Rate limit*—Limits the number of calls that a service receives at a time
- *Fallback*—Sets alternative paths for failing requests

With Resilience4j, we can apply several patterns to the same method call by defining the annotations for that method. For example, if we want to limit the number of outgoing calls with the bulkhead and circuit breaker patterns, we can define the @CircuitBreaker and the @Bulkhead annotations for the method. It is important to note that Resilience4j's retry order is as follows:

```
Retry ( CircuitBreaker ( RateLimiter ( TimeLimiter ( Bulkhead ( Function ) )
➡ ) ) )
```

Retry is applied (if needed) at the end of the call. This is valuable to remember when trying to combine patterns, but we can also use the patterns as individual features.

Building implementations of the circuit breaker, retry, rate limit, fallback, and bulkhead patterns requires intimate knowledge of threads and thread management. To apply a high-quality set of implementations for these patterns requires a tremendous amount of work. Fortunately, we can use Spring Boot and the Resilience4j library to provide us with a battle-tested tool that's used daily in several microservice architectures. In the next several sections, we'll cover how to

- Configure the licensing service's Maven build file (pom.xml) to include the Spring Boot/Resilience4j wrappers
- Use Spring Boot/Resilience4j annotations to wrapper remote calls with the circuit breaker, retry, rate limit, and bulkhead patterns
- Customize the individual circuit breakers on a remote resource to use custom timeouts for each call
- Implement a fallback strategy in the event a circuit breaker has to interrupt a call or the call fails
- Use individual thread pools in our service to isolate service calls and build bulkheads between different remote resources

7.4   *Setting up the licensing service to use Spring Cloud and Resilience4j*

To begin our exploration of Resilience4j, we need to set up our project pom.xml to import the dependencies. To achieve that, we will take the licensing service that we are building and modify its pom.xml by adding the Maven dependencies for Resilience4j. The following listing indicates how to do this.

Listing 7.1   Adding Resilience4j dependency in pom.xml of the licensing service

```
<properties>
    ...
    <resilience4j.version>1.5.0</resilience4j.version>
</properties>
<dependencies>
    //Part of pom.xml omitted for conciseness
    ...
    <dependency>
        <groupId>io.github.resilience4j</groupId>
        <artifactId>resilience4j-spring-boot2</artifactId>
        <version>${resilience4j.version}</version>
    </dependency>

    <dependency>
        <groupId>io.github.resilience4j</groupId>
        <artifactId>resilience4j-circuitbreaker</artifactId>
        <version>${resilience4j.version}</version>
    </dependency>
    <dependency>
        <groupId>io.github.resilience4j</groupId>
        <artifactId>resilience4j-timelimiter</artifactId>
        <version>${resilience4j.version}</version>
    </dependency>
    <dependency>
        <groupId>org.springframework.boot</groupId>
        <artifactId>spring-boot-starter-aop</artifactId>
    </dependency>
//Rest of pom.xml omitted for conciseness
...
</dependencies>
```

The <dependency> tag with the resilience4j-spring-boot2 artifact tells Maven to pull down the Resilience4j Spring Boot library, which allows us to use custom pattern annotations. The dependencies with the resilience4j-circuitbreaker and resilience4j-timelimiter artifacts contain all the logic to implement the circuit breaker and rate limiter. The final dependency is the spring-boot-starter-aop. We need this library in our project because it allows Spring AOP aspects to run.

Aspect-oriented programming (AOP) is a programming paradigm that aims to increase modularity by allowing us to separate parts of the program that affect other parts of the system; in other words, cross-cutting concerns. AOP adds new behaviors to existing code without modifying the code itself. Now that we've added the Maven dependencies, we can go ahead and begin our Resilience4j implementation using the licensing and organization services we built in previous chapters.

> **NOTE** In case you didn't follow the previous chapter's code listings, you can download the code created in chapter 6 from the following link: https://github.com/ihuaylupo/manning-smia/tree/master/chapter6/Final.

7.5 Implementing a circuit breaker

To understand circuit breakers, we can think of electrical systems. What happens when there is too much current passing through a wire in an electrical system? As you'll recall, if the circuit breaker detects a problem, it breaks the connection with the rest of the system, avoiding further damage to other components. The same happens in our code architecture as well.

What we want to achieve with circuit breakers in our code is to monitor remote calls and avoid long waits on services. In these scenarios, the circuit breaker is in charge of killing those connections and monitoring if there are more failing or poorly behaving calls. This pattern then implements a fast fail and prevents future requests to a failing remote resource. In Resilience4j, the circuit breaker is implemented via a finite state machine with three normal states. Figure 7.4 shows the different states and the interaction between them.

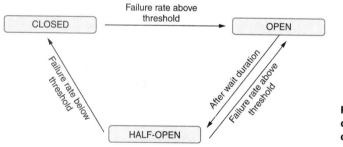

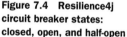

Figure 7.4 Resilience4j circuit breaker states: closed, open, and half-open

Initially, the Resilience4j circuit breaker starts in a closed state and waits for client requests. The closed state uses a ring bit buffer to store the success or failure status of the requests. When a successful request is made, the circuit breaker saves a 0 bit in the ring bit buffer. But if it fails to receive a response from the invoked service, it saves a 1 bit. Figure 7.5 shows a ring buffer with 12 results.

To calculate a failure rate, the ring must be full. For example, in the previous scenario, at least 12 calls must be evaluated before the failure rate can be calculated. If only 11 requests are evaluated, the circuit breaker will not change to an open state even if all 11 calls fail. Note that the circuit breaker only opens when the failure rate is above the configurable threshold.

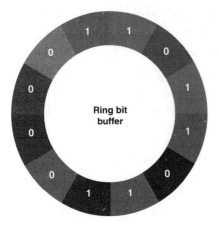

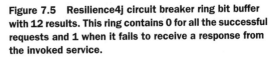

Figure 7.5   Resilience4j circuit breaker ring bit buffer with 12 results. This ring contains 0 for all the successful requests and 1 when it fails to receive a response from the invoked service.

When the circuit breaker is in the open state, all calls are rejected during a configurable time, and the circuit breaker throws a `CallNotPermittedException`. Once the configuration time expires, the circuit breaker changes to the half-open state and allows a number of requests to see if the service is still unavailable.

In the half-open state, the circuit breaker uses another configurable ring bit buffer to evaluate the failure rate. If this new failure rate is above the configured threshold, the circuit breaker changes back to open; if it is below or equal to the threshold, it changes back to closed. This might be somewhat confusing, but just remember, in the open state the circuit breaker rejects, and in the closed state, the circuit breaker accepts all the requests.

Also, in the Resilience4j circuit breaker pattern, you can define the following additional states. It is important to note that the only way to exit from the following states is to reset the circuit breaker or trigger a state transition:

- *DISABLED*—Always allow access
- *FORCED_OPEN*—Always deny access

NOTE   A detailed description of these two additional states is beyond the scope of this book. If you want to know more about these states, we recommend you read the official Resilience4j documentation at https://resilience4j .readme.io/v0.17.0/docs/circuitbreaker.

In this section, we'll look at implementing Resilience4j in two broad categories. In the first category, we'll wrap all calls to our database in the licensing and organization service with a Resilience4j circuit breaker. We will then wrap the interservice calls between the licensing and organization services using Resilience4j. While these are two different categories of calls, we'll see that, with the use of Resilience4j, these calls will be exactly the same. Figure 7.6 shows the remote resources that we're going to wrap within a Resilience4j circuit breaker.

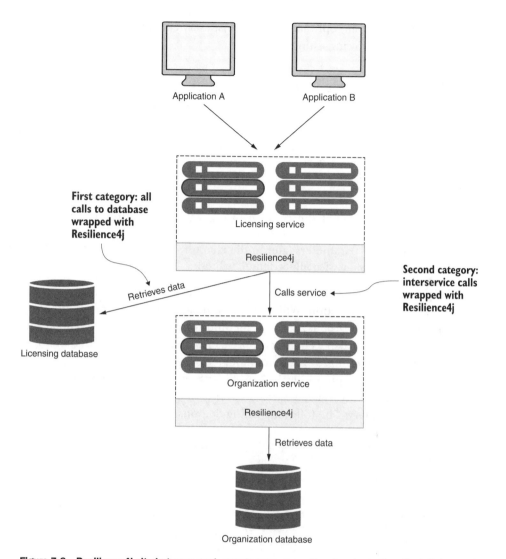

Figure 7.6 **Resilience4j sits between each remote resource call and protects the client. It doesn't matter if the remote resource calls a database or a REST-based service.**

Let's start our Resilience4j discussion by showing how to wrap the retrieval of licensing service data from the licensing database using a synchronous circuit breaker. With a synchronous call, the licensing service retrieves its data but waits for the SQL statement to complete or for a circuit breaker timeout before it continues processing.

Resilience4j and Spring Cloud use @CircuitBreaker to mark the Java class methods managed by a Resilience4j circuit breaker. When the Spring framework sees this annotation, it dynamically generates a proxy that wraps the method and manages all calls to that method through a thread pool specifically set aside to handle remote calls. Let's add @CircuitBreaker to the method getLicensesByOrganization in the src/main/java/com/optimagrowth/license/service/LicenseService.java class file as shown in the following listing.

Listing 7.2   Wrapping a remote resource call with a circuit breaker

```
//Part of LicenseService.java omitted for conciseness

@CircuitBreaker(name = "licenseService")          ◄─────

public List<License> getLicensesByOrganization(String organizationId) {
    return licenseRepository.findByOrganizationId(organizationId);
}
```
@CircuitBreaker wrapper for getLicensesByOrganization() with a Resilience4j circuit breaker

NOTE   If you look at the code in listing 7.2 in the source code repository, you'll see several more parameters on the @CircuitBreaker annotation. We'll get into those parameters later in the chapter, but the code in listing 7.2 uses @CircuitBreaker with all its default values.

This doesn't look like a lot of code, and it's not, but there is a lot of functionality inside this one annotation. With the use of the @CircuitBreaker annotation, any time the getLicensesByOrganization() method is called, the call is wrapped with a Resilience4j circuit breaker. The circuit breaker interrupts any failed attempt to call the getLicensesByOrganization() method.

This code example would be boring if the database was working correctly. Let's simulate the getLicensesByOrganization() method running into a slow or timed out database query. The following listing demonstrates this.

Listing 7.3   Purposely timing out a call to the licensing service database

```
//Part of LicenseService.java omitted for conciseness

private void randomlyRunLong(){          ◄─────
    Random rand = new Random();
    int randomNum = rand.nextInt(3) + 1;
    if (randomNum==3) sleep();
}

private void sleep(){
    try {
        Thread.sleep(5000);          ◄─────
        throw new java.util.concurrent.TimeoutException();
    } catch (InterruptedException e) {
        logger.error(e.getMessage());
    }
}

@CircuitBreaker(name = "licenseService")
public List<License> getLicensesByOrganization(String organizationId) {
    randomlyRunLong();
    return licenseRepository.findByOrganizationId(organizationId);
}
```
Gives us a one-in-three chance of a database call running long

Sleeps for 5000 ms (5 s) and then throws a TimeoutException

If you enter the `http://localhost:8080/v1/organization/e6a625cc-718b-48c2-ac76-1dfdff9a531e/license/` endpoint enough times in Postman, you'll see the following error message returned from the licensing service:

```
{
  "timestamp": 1595178498383,
  "status": 500,
  "error": "Internal Server Error",
  "message": "No message available",
  "path": "/v1/organization/e6a625cc-718b-48c2-ac76-1dfdff9a531e/
          license/"
}
```

If we keep executing the failing service, the ring bit buffer will eventually fill, and we should receive the error shown in figure 7.7.

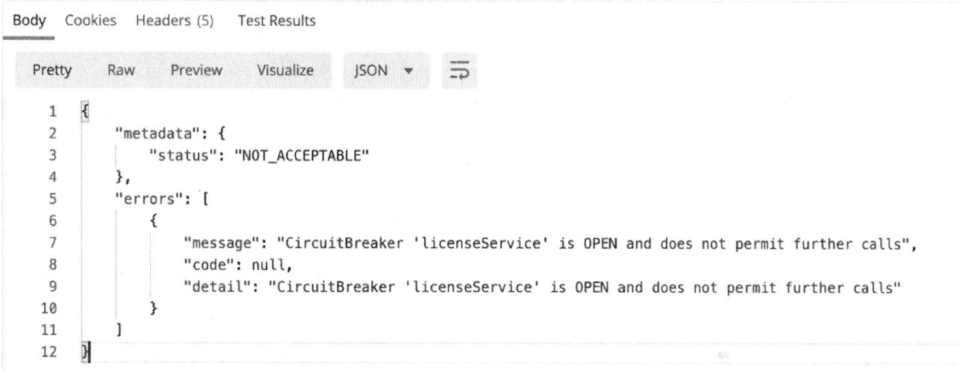

Figure 7.7 A circuit breaker error indicates the circuit breaker is now in the open state.

Now that we have our circuit breaker working for the licensing service, let's continue by setting up the circuit breaker for the organization microservice.

7.5.1 Adding the circuit breaker to the organization service

The beauty of using method-level annotations for tagging calls with the circuit breaker behavior is that it's the same annotation whether we're accessing a database or calling a microservice. For instance, in our licensing service, we need to look up the name of the organization associated with the license. If we want to wrap our call to the organization service with a circuit breaker, it's as simple as breaking down a `RestTemplate` call into a method and annotating it with `@CircuitBreaker` like this:

```
@CircuitBreaker(name = "organizationService")
private Organization getOrganization(String organizationId) {
    return organizationRestClient.getOrganization(organizationId);
}
```

NOTE Although using @CircuitBreaker is easy to implement, we do need to be careful about using the default values of this annotation. We highly recommend that you always analyze and set the configuration that best suits your needs.

To view the default values of your circuit breaker, you can select the following URL in Postman: http://localhost:<service_port>/actuator/health. By default, the circuit breaker exposes the configuration in the Spring Boot Actuator health service.

7.5.2 Customizing the circuit breaker

In this section, we will answer one of the most common questions developers ask when using Resilience4j: how do we customize the Resilience4j circuit breaker? This is easily accomplished by adding some parameters to the application.yml, boostrap.yml, or service configuration file located in the Spring Config Server repository. The following listing demonstrates how to customize the circuit breaker pattern in the boostrap.yml for both the licensing and the organization services.

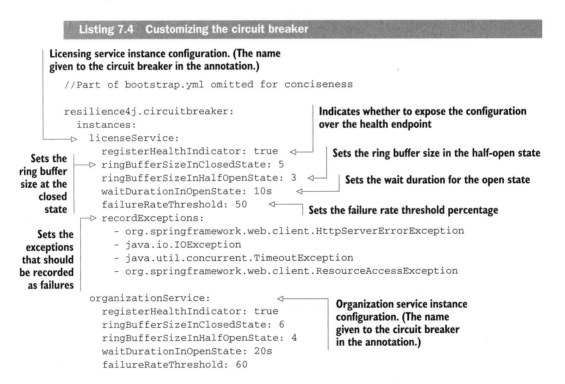

Listing 7.4   Customizing the circuit breaker

Licensing service instance configuration. (The name given to the circuit breaker in the annotation.)

```
//Part of bootstrap.yml omitted for conciseness

resilience4j.circuitbreaker:
  instances:
    licenseService:
      registerHealthIndicator: true
      ringBufferSizeInClosedState: 5
      ringBufferSizeInHalfOpenState: 3
      waitDurationInOpenState: 10s
      failureRateThreshold: 50
      recordExceptions:
        - org.springframework.web.client.HttpServerErrorException
        - java.io.IOException
        - java.util.concurrent.TimeoutException
        - org.springframework.web.client.ResourceAccessException
    organizationService:
      registerHealthIndicator: true
      ringBufferSizeInClosedState: 6
      ringBufferSizeInHalfOpenState: 4
      waitDurationInOpenState: 20s
      failureRateThreshold: 60
```

Indicates whether to expose the configuration over the health endpoint

Sets the ring buffer size in the half-open state

Sets the wait duration for the open state

Sets the failure rate threshold percentage

Sets the ring buffer size at the closed state

Sets the exceptions that should be recorded as failures

Organization service instance configuration. (The name given to the circuit breaker in the annotation.)

Resilience4j allows us to customize the behavior of the circuit breakers through the application's properties. We can configure as many instances as we want, and each instance can have a different configuration. Listing 7.4 contains the following configuration settings:

- ringBufferSizeInClosedState—Sets the size of the ring bit buffer when the circuit breaker is in the closed state. The default value is 100.

- ringBufferSizeInHalfOpenState—Sets the size of the ring bit buffer when the circuit breaker is in the half-open state. The default value is 10.

- waitDurationInOpenState—Sets the time the circuit breaker should wait before changing the status from open to half-open. The default value is 60,000 ms.

- failureRateThreshold—Configures the percentage of the failure rate threshold. Remember, when the failure rate is greater than or equal to this threshold, the circuit breaker changes to the open state and starts short-circuiting calls. The default value is 50.

- recordExceptions—Lists the exceptions that will be considered as failures. By default, all exceptions are recorded as failures.

In this book, we will not cover all of the Resilience4j circuit breaker parameters. If you want to know more about its possible configuration parameters, we recommend you visit the following link: https://resilience4j.readme.io/docs/circuitbreaker.

7.6 *Fallback processing*

Part of the beauty of the circuit breaker pattern is that because a "middleman" is between the consumer of a remote resource and the resource itself, we have the opportunity to intercept a service failure and choose an alternative course of action to take.

In Resilience4j, this is known as a fallback strategy and is easily implemented. Let's see how to build a simple fallback strategy for our licensing service that returns a licensing object that says no licensing information is currently available. The following listing demonstrates this.

> **Listing 7.5 Implementing a fallback in Resilience4j**

```
//Part of LicenseService.java omitted for conciseness

@CircuitBreaker(name= "licenseService",
        fallbackMethod= "buildFallbackLicenseList")      Defines a single function
public List<License> getLicensesByOrganization(         that's called if the calling
                    String organizationId) throws TimeoutException {   service fails

    logger.debug("getLicensesByOrganization Correlation id: {}",
        UserContextHolder.getContext().getCorrelationId());
    randomlyRunLong();
    return licenseRepository.findByOrganizationId(organizationId);
}

private List<License> buildFallbackLicenseList(String organizationId,
    Throwable t){
    List<License> fallbackList = new ArrayList<>();       Returns a hardcoded value
    License license = new License();                      in the fallback method
```

```
        license.setLicenseId("0000000-00-00000");
        license.setOrganizationId(organizationId);
        license.setProductName(
            "Sorry no licensing information currently available");
        fallbackList.add(license);
        return fallbackList;
    }
```

To implement a fallback strategy with Resilience4j, we need to do two things. First, we need to add a fallbackMethod attribute to @CircuitBreaker or any other annotation (we will explain this later on). This attribute must contain the name of the method that will be called when Resilience4j interrupts a call because of a failure.

The second thing we need to do is to define a fallback method. This method must reside in the same class as the original method that was protected by @Circuit-Breaker. To create the fallback method in Resilience4j, we need to create a method that contains the same signature as the originating function plus one extra parameter, which is the target exception parameter. With the same signature, we can pass all the parameters from the original method to the fallback method.

In the example in listing 7.5, the fallback method, buildFallbackLicenseList(), is simply constructing a single License object containing dummy information. We could have our fallback method read this data from an alternative data source, but for demonstration purposes, we're going to construct a list that can be returned by our original function call.

On fallbacks

Here are a few things to keep in mind as you determine whether you want to implement a fallback strategy:

- *Fallbacks provide a course of action when a resource has timed out or failed.* If you find yourself using fallbacks to catch a timeout exception and then doing nothing more than logging the error, you should use a standard try...catch block around your service invocation instead: catch the exception and put the logging logic in the try...catch block.
- *Be aware of the actions you take with your fallback functions.* If you call out to another distributed service in your fallback service, you may need to wrap the fallback with a @CircuitBreaker. Remember, the same failure that you're experiencing with your primary course of action might also impact your secondary fallback option. Code defensively.

Now that we have our fallback method in place, let's go ahead and call our endpoint again. This time when we select it in Postman and encounter a timeout error (remember we have a one-in-three chance), we shouldn't get an exception back from the service call. Instead, the dummy license values will return as in figure 7.8.

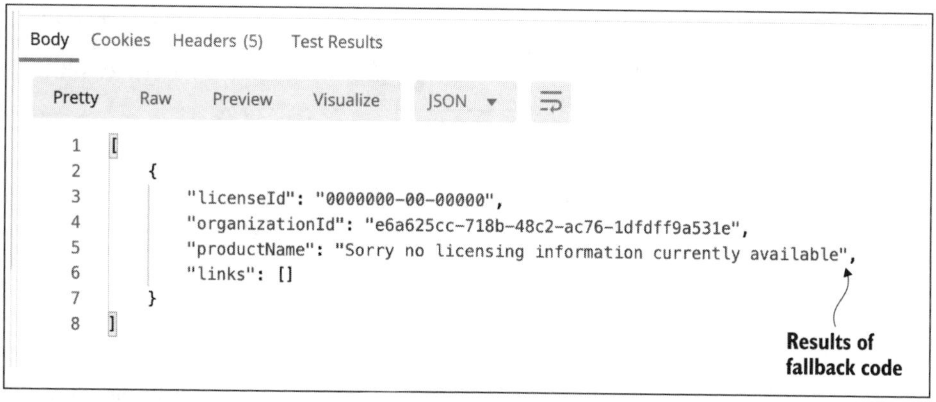

Body   Cookies   Headers (5)   Test Results

Pretty   Raw   Preview   Visualize   JSON   ▼   ⇥

```
1  [
2      {
3          "licenseId": "0000000-00-00000",
4          "organizationId": "e6a625cc-718b-48c2-ac76-1dfdff9a531e",
5          "productName": "Sorry no licensing information currently available",
6          "links": []
7      }
8  ]
```

**Results of
fallback code**

Figure 7.8   Your service invocation using a Resilience4j fallback

7.7   *Implementing the bulkhead pattern*

In a microservice-based application, we'll often need to call multiple microservices to complete a particular task. Without using a bulkhead pattern, the default behavior for these calls is that these are executed using the same threads that are reserved for handling requests for the entire Java container. In high volumes, performance problems with one service out of many can result in all of the threads for the Java container being maxed out and waiting to process work, while new requests for work back up. The Java container will eventually crash.

The bulkhead pattern segregates remote resource calls in their own thread pools so that a single misbehaving service can be contained and not crash the container. Resilience4j provides two different implementations of the bulkhead pattern. You can use these implementations to limit the number of concurrent executions:

- *Semaphore bulkhead*—Uses a semaphore isolation approach, limiting the number of concurrent requests to the service. Once the limit is reached, it starts rejecting requests.
- *Thread pool bulkhead*—Uses a bounded queue and a fixed thread pool. This approach only rejects a request when the pool and the queue are full.

Resilience4j, by default, uses the semaphore bulkhead type. Figure 7.9 illustrates this type.

This model works fine if we have a small number of remote resources being accessed within an application, and the call volumes for the individual services are (relatively) evenly distributed. The problem is that if we have services with far higher volumes or longer completion times than other services, we can end up introducing thread exhaustion into our thread pools because one service ends up dominating all of the threads in the default thread pool.

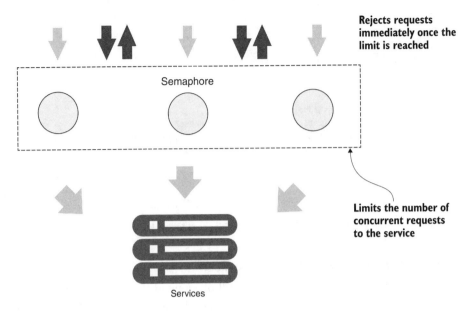

Figure 7.9   The default Resilience4j bulkhead type is the semaphore approach.

Fortunately, Resilience4j provides an easy-to-use mechanism for creating bulkheads between different remote resource calls. Figure 7.10 shows what managed resources look like when they're segregated into their own bulkheads.

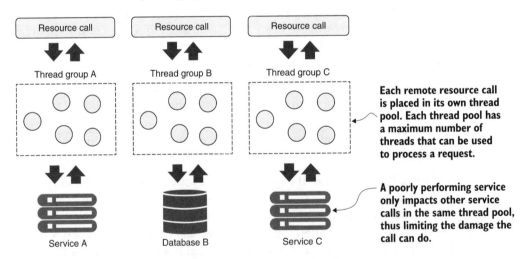

Figure 7.10   A Resilience4j command tied to segregated thread pools

To implement the bulkhead pattern in Resilience4j, we need to use an additional configuration to combine it with @CircuitBreaker. Let's look at some code that does this:

- Sets up a separate thread pool for the `getLicensesByOrganization()` call
- Creates the bulkhead configuration in the bootstrap.yml file
- With the semaphore approach, sets `maxConcurrentCalls` and `maxWaitDuration`
- With the thread pool approach, sets `maxThreadPoolSize`, `coreThreadPoolSize`, `queueCapacity`, and `keepAliveDuration`

The following listing shows the bootstrap.yml for the licensing service with these bulkhead configuration parameters.

> **Listing 7.6 Configuring the bulkhead pattern for the licensing service**

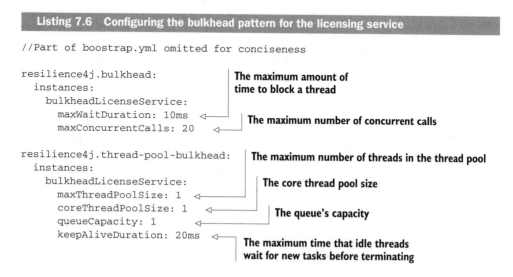

```
//Part of boostrap.yml omitted for conciseness

resilience4j.bulkhead:
  instances:
    bulkheadLicenseService:
      maxWaitDuration: 10ms          ◁        The maximum amount of
      maxConcurrentCalls: 20    ◁             time to block a thread
                                              The maximum number of concurrent calls

resilience4j.thread-pool-bulkhead:           The maximum number of threads in the thread pool
  instances:
    bulkheadLicenseService:                  The core thread pool size
      maxThreadPoolSize: 1   ◁
      coreThreadPoolSize: 1     ◁
      queueCapacity: 1       ◁               The queue's capacity
      keepAliveDuration: 20ms   ◁
                                             The maximum time that idle threads
                                             wait for new tasks before terminating
```

Resilience4j also lets us customize the behavior of the bulkhead patterns through the application's properties. Like the circuit breaker, we can create as many instances as we want, and each instance can have different configurations. Listing 7.6 contains the following properties:

- `maxWaitDuration`—Sets the maximum amount of time to block a thread when entering a bulkhead. The default value is 0.
- `maxConcurrentCalls`—Sets the maximum number of concurrent calls allowed by the bulkhead. The default value is 25.
- `maxThreadPoolSize`—Sets the maximum thread pool size. The default value is `Runtime.getRuntime().availableProcessors()`.
- `coreThreadPoolSize`—Sets the core thread pool size. The default value is `Runtime.getRuntime().availableProcessors()`.
- `queueCapacity`—Sets the capacity of the queue. The default value is 100.
- `KeepAliveDuration`—Sets the maximum time that idle threads will wait for new tasks before terminating. This happens when the number of threads is higher than the number of core threads. The default value is 20 ms.

What's the proper sizing for a custom thread pool? To answer that question, you can use the following formula:

(requests per second at peak when the service is healthy * 99th percentile latency in seconds) + small amount of extra threads for overhead

We often don't know the performance characteristics of a service until it functions under a load. A key indicator that the thread pool properties need to be adjusted is when a service call is in the process of timing out, even if the targeted remote resource is healthy. The following listing demonstrates how to set up a bulkhead around all calls surrounding the lookup of licensing data from our licensing service.

> **Listing 7.7 Creating a bulkhead around the getLicensesByOrganization() method**

```
//Part of LicenseService.java omitted for conciseness

@CircuitBreaker(name= "licenseService",
        fallbackMethod= "buildFallbackLicenseList")
@Bulkhead(name= "bulkheadLicenseService",
        fallbackMethod= "buildFallbackLicenseList")     ◁─┐

public List<License> getLicensesByOrganization(
                    String organizationId) throws TimeoutException {
   logger.debug("getLicensesByOrganization Correlation id: {}",
       UserContextHolder.getContext().getCorrelationId());
   randomlyRunLong();
   return licenseRepository.findByOrganizationId(organizationId);
}
```

Sets the instance name and fallback method for the bulkhead pattern

The first thing we should notice is that we've introduced a new annotation: @Bulkhead. This annotation indicates that we are setting up a bulkhead pattern. If we set no further values in the application properties, Resilience4j uses the default values previously mentioned for the semaphore bulkhead type.

The second thing to note in listing 7.7 is that we are not setting up the bulkhead type. In this case, the bulkhead pattern uses the semaphore approach. In order to change this to the thread pool approach, we need to add that type to the @Bulkhead annotation like so:

```
@Bulkhead(name = "bulkheadLicenseService", type = Bulkhead.Type.THREADPOOL,
➥ fallbackMethod = "buildFallbackLicenseList")
```

7.8   *Implementing the retry pattern*

As its name implies, the retry pattern is responsible for retrying attempts to communicate with a service when that service initially fails. The key concept behind this pattern is to provide a way to get the expected response by trying to invoke the same service one or more times despite the failure (for example, a network disruption). For this pattern, we must specify the number of retries for a given service instance and the interval we want to pass between each retry.

Like the circuit breaker, Resilience4j lets us specify which exceptions we want to retry and not to retry. The following listing shows the bootstrap.yml for the licensing service, where it contains the retry configuration parameters.

Listing 7.8　Configuring the retry pattern in the bootstrap.yml

```
//Part of boostrap.yml omitted for conciseness

resilience4j.retry:              The maximum number of retry attempts
  instances:
    retryLicenseService:         The wait duration between the retry attempts
      maxRetryAttempts: 5
      waitDuration: 10000        The list of exceptions you want to retry
      retry-exceptions:
        - java.util.concurrent.TimeoutException
```

The first parameter, maxRetryAttempts, allows us to define the maximum number of retry attempts for our service. The default value for this parameter is 3. The second parameter, waitDuration, allows us to define the wait duration between the retry attempts. The default value for this parameter is 500 ms. The third parameter, retry-exceptions, sets a list of error classes that will be retried. The default value is empty. For this book, we only use these three parameters, but you can also set the following:

- intervalFunction—Sets a function to update the waiting interval after a failure.
- retryOnResultPredicate—Configures a predicate that evaluates if a result should be retried. This predicate should return true if we want to retry.
- retryOnExceptionPredicate—Configures a predicate that evaluates if an exception should be retried. Same as the previous predicate; we must return true if we want to retry.
- ignoreExceptions—Sets a list of error classes that are ignored and will not be retried. The default value is empty.

The following listing demonstrates how to set up the retry pattern around all calls surrounding the lookup of licensing data from our licensing service.

Listing 7.9　Creating a bulkhead around the `getLicensesByOrganization()` method

```
//Part of LicenseService.java omitted for conciseness

@CircuitBreaker(name= "licenseService",
                fallbackMethod="buildFallbackLicenseList")
@Retry(name = "retryLicenseService",          Sets the instance name
                fallbackMethod=               and fallback method for
                    "buildFallbackLicenseList")   the retry pattern
@Bulkhead(name= "bulkheadLicenseService",
                fallbackMethod="buildFallbackLicenseList")

public List<License> getLicensesByOrganization(String organizationId)
        throws TimeoutException {
    logger.debug("getLicensesByOrganization Correlation id: {}",
```

```
        UserContextHolder.getContext().getCorrelationId());
                randomlyRunLong();
        return licenseRepository.findByOrganizationId(organizationId);
    }
```

Now that we know how to implement the circuit breaker and the retry pattern, let's continue with the rate limiter. Remember, Resilience4j allows us to combine different patterns in the same method calls.

7.9   *Implementing the rate limiter pattern*

This retry pattern stops overloading the service with more calls than it can consume in a given timeframe. This is an imperative technique to prepare our API for high availability and reliability.

> **NOTE**   In up-to-date cloud architectures, it is a good option to include auto-scaling, but we do not cover that topic in this book.

Resilience4j provides two implementations for the rate limiter pattern: `Atomic-RateLimiter` and `SemaphoreBasedRateLimiter`. The default implementation for the `RateLimiter` is the `AtomicRateLimiter`.

The `SemaphoreBasedRateLimiter` is the simplest. This implementation is based on having one `java.util.concurrent.Semaphore` store the current permissions. In this scenario, all the user threads will call the method `semaphore.tryAcquire` to trigger a call to an additional internal thread by executing `semaphore.release` when a new `limitRefreshPeriod` starts.

Unlike the `SemaphoreBasedRate`, the `AtomicRateLimiter` does not need thread management because the user threads themselves execute all the permissions logic. The `AtomicRateLimiter` splits all nanoseconds from the start into cycles, and each cycle duration is the refresh period (in nanoseconds). Then at the beginning of each cycle, we should set the active permissions to limit the period. To better understand this approach, let's look at the following settings:

- `ActiveCycle`—The cycle number used by the last call
- `ActivePermissions`—The count of available permissions after the last call
- `NanosToWait`—The count of nanoseconds to wait for permission for the last call

This implementation contains some tricky logic. To better understand it, we can consider the following Resilience4j statements for this pattern:

- Cycles are equal time pieces.
- If the available permissions are not enough, we can perform a permission reservation by decreasing the current permissions and calculating the time we need to wait for the permission to appear. Resilience4j allows this by defining the number of calls that are allowed during a time period (`limitForPeriod`); how often permissions are refreshed (`limitRefreshPeriod`); and how long a thread can wait to acquire permissions (`timeoutDuration`).

For this pattern, we must specify the timeout duration, the limit refresh, and the limit for the period. The following listing shows the bootstrap.yml for the licensing service, which contains the retry configuration parameters.

Listing 7.10 Configuring the retry pattern in the bootstrap.yml

```
//Part of boostrap.yml omitted for conciseness

resilience4j.ratelimiter:
    instances:
        licenseService:
            timeoutDuration: 1000ms
            limitRefreshPeriod: 5000
            limitForPeriod: 5
```

Defines the time a thread waits for permission

Defines the number of permissions available during a limit refresh period

Defines the period of a limit refresh

The first parameter, `timeoutDuration`, lets us define the time a thread waits for permission; the default value for this parameter is 5 s (seconds). The second parameter, `limitRefreshPeriod`, enables us to set the period that limits the refresh. After each period, the rate limiter resets the permissions count back to the `limitForPeriod` value. The default value for the `limitRefreshPeriod` is 500 ns (nanoseconds).

The final parameter, `limitForPeriod`, lets us set the number of permissions available during one refresh period. The default value for the `limitForPeriod` is 50. The following listing demonstrates how to set up the retry pattern around all calls surrounding the lookup of licensing data from our licensing service.

Listing 7.11 Creating a bulkhead around `getLicensesByOrganization()`

```
//Part of LicenseService.java omitted for conciseness

@CircuitBreaker(name= "licenseService",
        fallbackMethod= "buildFallbackLicenseList")
@RateLimiter(name = "licenseService",
        fallbackMethod = "buildFallbackLicenseList")
@Retry(name = "retryLicenseService",
        fallbackMethod = "buildFallbackLicenseList")
@Bulkhead(name= "bulkheadLicenseService",
        fallbackMethod= "buildFallbackLicenseList")
public List<License> getLicensesByOrganization(String organizationId)
        throws TimeoutException {
    logger.debug("getLicensesByOrganization Correlation id: {}",
    UserContextHolder.getContext().getCorrelationId());
    randomlyRunLong();
    return licenseRepository.findByOrganizationId(organizationId);
}
```

Sets the instance name and fallback method for the rate limiter pattern

The main difference between the bulkhead and the rate limiter pattern is that the bulkhead pattern is in charge of limiting the number of concurrent calls (for example, it only allows X concurrent calls at a time). With the rate limiter, we can limit the number of total calls in a given timeframe (for example, allow *X* number of calls every *Y* seconds).

In order to choose which pattern is right for you, double-check what your needs are. If you want to block concurrent times, your best choice is a bulkhead, but if you want to limit the total number of calls in a specific time period, your best option is the rate limiter. If you are looking at both scenarios, you can also combine them.

7.10 *ThreadLocal and Resilience4j*

In this section, we will define some values in `ThreadLocal` to see if they are propagated throughout the methods using Resilience4J annotations. Remember, Java `ThreadLocal` allows us to create variables that can be read and written to only by the same threads. When we work with threads, all the threads of a specific object share its variables, making these threads unsafe. The most common way to make them thread-safe in Java is to use synchronization. But if we want to avoid synchronization, we can also use `ThreadLocal` variables.

Let's look at a concrete example. Often in a REST-based environment, we want to pass contextual information to a service call that will help us operationally manage the service. For example, we might pass a correlation ID or authentication token in the HTTP header of the REST call that can then be propagated to any downstream service calls. The correlation ID allows us to have a unique identifier that can be traced across multiple service calls in a single transaction.

To make this value available anywhere within our service call, we might use a Spring `Filter` class to intercept every call in our REST service. It can then retrieve this information from the incoming HTTP request and store this contextual information in a custom `UserContext` object. Then, anytime our code needs to access this value in our REST service call, our code can retrieve the `UserContext` from the `ThreadLocal` storage variable and read the value. Listing 7.12 shows an example of a Spring filter that we can use in our licensing service.

> **NOTE** You can find this code at /licensing-service/src/main/java/com/ optimagrowth/license/utils/UserContextFilter.java in the source code for chapter 7. Here's the repository link: https://github.com/ihuaylupo/manning-smia/tree/master/chapter7.

Listing 7.12 The `UserContextFilter` parsing the HTTP header and retrieving data

```
package com.optimagrowth.license.utils;
...
//Imports removed for conciseness

@Component
public class UserContextFilter implements Filter {
    private static final Logger logger =
            LoggerFactory.getLogger(UserContextFilter.class);
```

```
@Override
public void doFilter(ServletRequest servletRequest, ServletResponse
        servletResponse, FilterChain filterChain) throws IOException,
        ServletException {

    HttpServletRequest httpServletRequest =
                        (HttpServletRequest) servletRequest;

    UserContextHolder.getContext().setCorrelationId(
            httpServletRequest.getHeader(
                    UserContext.CORRELATION_ID));
    UserContextHolder.getContext().setUserId(
            httpServletRequest.getHeader(
                    UserContext.USER_ID));
    UserContextHolder.getContext().setAuthToken(
            httpServletRequest.getHeader(
                    UserContext.AUTH_TOKEN));
    UserContextHolder.getContext().setOrganizationId(
            httpServletRequest.getHeader(
                    UserContext.ORGANIZATION_ID));

    filterChain.doFilter(httpServletRequest, servletResponse);
    }
    ...
    //Rest of UserContextFilter.java omitted for conciseness
}
```

> **Retrieves the values set in the HTTP header of the call to a UserContext. These are then stored in UserContextHolder.**

The UserContextHolder class stores the UserContext in a ThreadLocal class. Once it's stored in ThreadLocal, any code that's executed for a request will use the User-Context object stored in the UserContextHolder.

The following listing shows the UserContextHolder class. You can find this class in the /licensing-service/src/main/java/com/optimagrowth/license/utils/UserContext-Holder.java class file.

Listing 7.13 All `UserContext` data is managed by `UserContextHolder`

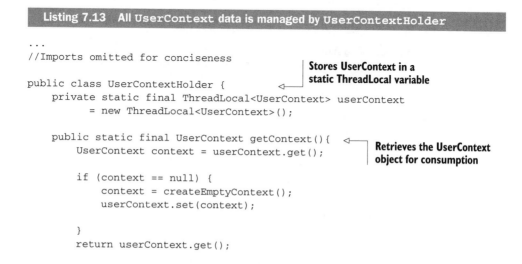

```
...
//Imports omitted for conciseness

public class UserContextHolder {
    private static final ThreadLocal<UserContext> userContext
        = new ThreadLocal<UserContext>();

    public static final UserContext getContext(){
        UserContext context = userContext.get();

        if (context == null) {
            context = createEmptyContext();
            userContext.set(context);

        }
        return userContext.get();
```

> **Stores UserContext in a static ThreadLocal variable**

> **Retrieves the UserContext object for consumption**

```
    }

    public static final void setContext(UserContext context) {
        userContext.set(context);
    }

    public static final UserContext createEmptyContext(){
        return new UserContext();
    }
}
```

NOTE We must be careful when we work directly with `ThreadLocal`. An incorrect development inside `ThreadLocal` can lead to memory leaks in our application.

The `UserContext` is a POJO class that contains all the specific data we want to store in the `UserContextHolder`. The following listing shows the content of this class. You can find this class in /licensing-service/src/main/java/com/optimagrowth/license/utils/UserContext.java.

Listing 7.14   Creating a `UserContext`

```
...
//Imports omitted for conciseness

@Component
public class UserContext {
    public static final String CORRELATION_ID = "tmx-correlation-id";
    public static final String AUTH_TOKEN    = "tmx-auth-token";
    public static final String USER_ID       = "tmx-user-id";
    public static final String ORGANIZATION_ID = "tmx-organization-id";

    private String correlationId= new String();
    private String authToken= new String();
    private String userId = new String();
    private String organizationId = new String();

    public String getCorrelationId() { return correlationId;}
    public void setCorrelationId(String correlationId) {
        this.correlationId = correlationId;
    }

    public String getAuthToken() {
        return authToken;
    }

    public void setAuthToken(String authToken) {
        this.authToken = authToken;
    }

    public String getUserId() {
        return userId;
    }
}
```

```
    public void setUserId(String userId) {
        this.userId = userId;
    }
    public String getOrganizationId() {
        return organizationId;
    }
    public void setOrganizationId(String organizationId) {
        this.organizationId = organizationId;
    }
}
```

The last step that we need to do to finish our example is to add the logging instruction to the `LicenseController.java` class, which is found in com/optimagrowth/license/controller/LicenseController.java. The following listing shows how.

Listing 7.15 Adding `logger` to the `LicenseController` `getLicenses()` method

```
//Some code omitted for conciseness
import org.slf4j.Logger;
import org.slf4j.LoggerFactory;

@RestController
@RequestMapping(value="v1/organization/{organizationId}/license")
public class LicenseController {
    private static final Logger logger =
                    LoggerFactory.getLogger(LicenseController.class);

    //Some code removed for conciseness
10

    @RequestMapping(value="/",method = RequestMethod.GET)
    public List<License> getLicenses( @PathVariable("organizationId")
                    String organizationId) {
        logger.debug("LicenseServiceController Correlation id: {}",
                UserContextHolder.getContext().getCorrelationId());
        return licenseService.getLicensesByOrganization(organizationId);
    }
}
```

At this point, we should have several log statements in our licensing service. We've already added logging to the following licensing service classes and methods:

- `doFilter()` in com/optimagrowth/license/utils/UserContextFilter.java.
- `getLicenses()` in com/optimagrowth/license/controller/LicenseController .java.
- `getLicensesByOrganization()` in com/optimagrowth/license/service/License-Service.java. This method is annotated with `@CircuitBreaker`, `@Retry`, `@Bulkhead`, and `@RateLimiter`.

To execute our example, we'll call our service, passing in a correlation ID using an HTTP header `tmx-correlation-id` and a value of `TEST-CORRELATION-ID`. Figure 7.11 shows an HTTP GET call in Postman.

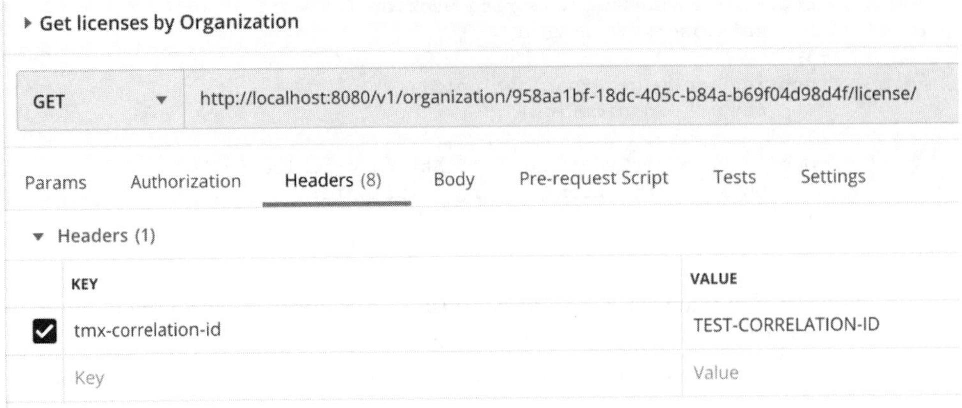

▸ Get licenses by Organization

| GET ▾ | http://localhost:8080/v1/organization/958aa1bf-18dc-405c-b84a-b69f04d98d4f/license/ |

Params   Authorization   **Headers** (8)   Body   Pre-request Script   Tests   Settings

▾ Headers (1)

	KEY	VALUE
☑	tmx-correlation-id	TEST-CORRELATION-ID
	Key	Value

Figure 7.11   Adding a correlation ID to the licensing service HTTP header

Once this call is submitted, we should see three log messages in the console, writing out the passed-in correlation ID as it flows through the `UserContext`, `License-Controller`, and `LicenseService` classes:

```
UserContextFilter Correlation id: TEST-CORRELATION-ID
LicenseServiceController Correlation id: TEST-CORRELATION-ID
LicenseService:getLicensesByOrganization Correlation id:
```

If you don't see the log messages on your console, add the code lines shown in the following listing to the application.yml or application.properties file of the licensing service.

Listing 7.16   Logger configuration on the licensing service application.yml file

```
//Some code omitted for conciseness
logging:
  level:
    org.springframework.web: WARN
    com.optimagrowth: DEBUG
```

Then build again and execute your microservices. If you are using Docker, you can execute the following commands in the root directory where the parent pom.xml is located:

```
mvn clean package dockerfile:build
docker-compose -f docker/docker-compose.yml up
```

You'll see that once the call hits the resiliency protected method, we still get the values written out for the correlation ID. This means that the parent thread values are available on the methods using the Resilience4j annotations.

Resilience4j is an excellent choice to implement a resilience pattern in our application. With Hystrix going into maintenance mode, Resilience4j has become the number-one choice in the Java ecosystem. Now that we have seen what can be achievable with Resilience4j, we can move on with our next subject, the Spring Cloud Gateway.

Summary

- When designing highly distributed applications like a microservice, client resiliency must be taken into account.
- Outright failures of a service (for example, the server crashes) are easy to detect and deal with.
- A single, poorly performing service can trigger a cascading effect of resource exhaustion as the threads in the calling client are blocked when waiting for a service to complete.
- Three core client resiliency patterns are the circuit-breaker pattern, the fallback pattern, and the bulkhead pattern.
- The circuit breaker pattern seeks to kill slow-running and degraded system calls so that these calls fail fast and prevent resource exhaustion.
- The fallback pattern allows you to define alternative code paths in the event that a remote service call fails or the circuit breaker for the call fails.
- The bulkhead pattern segregates remote resource calls away from each other, isolating calls to a remote service into their own thread pool. If one set of service calls fails, its failure shouldn't be allowed to "eat up" all the resources in the application container.
- The rate limiter pattern limits the number of total calls in a given time period.
- Resilience4j allows us to stack and use several patterns at the same time.
- The retry pattern is responsible for making attempts when a service has temporarily failed.
- The main difference between the bulkhead and the rate limiter patterns is that the bulkhead is in charge of limiting the number of concurrent calls at one time, and the rate limiter limits the number of total calls over a given time.
- Spring Cloud and the Resilince4j libraries provide implementations for the circuit breaker, fallback, retry, rate limiter, and bulkhead patterns.
- The Resilience4j libraries are highly configurable and can be set at global, class, and thread pool levels.

Service routing with Spring Cloud Gateway

In a distributed architecture like a microservice, there will come a point where we'll need to ensure that critical behaviors such as security, logging, and tracking users across multiple service calls occur. To implement this functionality, we'll want these attributes to be consistently enforced across all of our services without the need for each individual development team to build their own solution. While it's possible to use a common library or framework to assist with building these capabilities directly in an individual service, doing so has these implications:

- *It's challenging to implement these capabilities in each service consistently.* Developers are focused on delivering functionality, and in the whirlwind of day-to-day activity, they can easily forget to implement service logging or tracking unless they work in a regulated industry where it's required.

208

- *Pushing the responsibilities to implement cross-cutting concerns like security and logging down to the individual development teams greatly increases the odds that someone will not implement them properly or will forget to do them.* Cross-cutting concerns refer to parts or features of the program's design that are applicable throughout the application and may affect other parts of the application.

- *It's possible to create a hard dependency across all our services.* The more capabilities we build into a common framework shared across all our services, the more difficult it is to change or add behavior in our common code without having to recompile and redeploy all our services. Suddenly an upgrade of core capabilities built into a shared library becomes a long migration process.

To solve this problem, we need to abstract these cross-cutting concerns into a service that can sit independently and act as a filter and router for all the microservice calls in our architecture. We call this service a *gateway.* Our service clients no longer directly call a microservice. Instead, all calls are routed through the service gateway, which acts as a single Policy Enforcement Point (PEP), and are then routed to a final destination.

In this chapter, we'll see how to use Spring Cloud Gateway to implement a service gateway. Specifically, we'll look at how to use Spring Cloud Gateway to

- Put all service calls behind a single URL and map those calls using service discovery to their actual service instances
- Inject correlation IDs into every service call flowing through the service gateway
- Inject the correlation ID returned from the HTTP response and send it back to the client

Let's dive into more detail on how a service gateway fits into the overall microservices we're building in this book.

8.1 What is a service gateway?

Until now, with the microservices we built in earlier chapters, we've either directly called the individual services through a web client or called them programmatically via a service discovery engine such as Eureka. Figure 8.1 illustrates this approach.

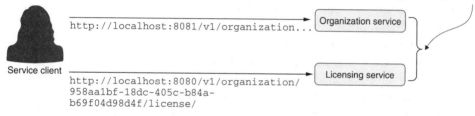

When a service client invokes a service directly, there's no way to quickly implement cross-cutting concerns like security or logging without having each service implement this logic directly in the service.

```
http://localhost:8081/v1/organization...
```
Organization service

Service client

```
http://localhost:8080/v1/organization/
958aa1bf-18dc-405c-b84a-
b69f04d98d4f/license/
```
Licensing service

Figure 8.1 Without a service gateway, the service client calls distinct endpoints for each service.

A service gateway acts as an intermediary between the service client and an invoked service. The service client talks only to a single URL managed by the service gateway. The service gateway pulls apart the path coming in from the service client call and determines what service the service client is trying to invoke. Figure 8.2 illustrates how the service gateway directs the user to a target microservice and corresponding instance, like a traffic cop directing traffic.

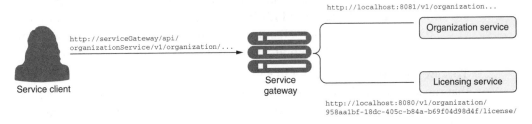

Figure 8.2   The service gateway sits between the service client and the corresponding service instances. All service calls (both internal-facing and external) should flow through the service gateway.

The service gateway sits as the gatekeeper for all inbound traffic to microservice calls within our application. With a service gateway in place, our service clients never directly call the URL of an individual service, but instead place all calls to the service gateway.

Because a service gateway sits between all calls from the client to the individual services, it also acts as a central PEP for service calls. The use of a centralized PEP means that cross-cutting service concerns can be carried out in a single place without the individual development teams having to implement those concerns. Examples of cross-cutting concerns that can be implemented in a service gateway include these:

- *Static routing*—A service gateway places all service calls behind a single URL and API route. This simplifies development as we only have to know about one service endpoint for all of our services.
- *Dynamic routing*—A service gateway can inspect incoming service requests and, based on the data from the incoming request, perform intelligent routing for the service caller. For instance, customers participating in a beta program might have all calls to a service routed to a specific cluster of services that are running a different version of code from what everyone else is using.
- *Authentication and authorization*—Because all service calls route through a service gateway, the service gateway is a natural place to check whether the callers of a service have authenticated themselves.
- *Metric collection and logging*—A service gateway can be used to collect metrics and log information as a service call passes through it. You can also use the service gateway to confirm that critical pieces of information are in place for user requests, thereby ensuring that logging is uniform. This doesn't mean that you shouldn't collect metrics from within your individual services. Rather, a service

gateway allows you to centralize the collection of many of your basic metrics, like the number of times the service is invoked and the service response times.

Wait—isn't a service gateway a single point of failure and a potential bottleneck?

Earlier in chapter 6, when we introduced Eureka, we talked about how centralized load balancers can be a single point of failure and a bottleneck for your services. A service gateway, if not implemented correctly, can carry the same risk. Keep the following in mind as you build your service gateway implementation:

- *Load balancers are useful when placed in front of individual groups of services.* In this case, a load balancer sitting in front of multiple service gateway instances is an appropriate design and ensures that your service gateway implementation can scale as needed. But having a load balancer sitting in front of all your service instances isn't a good idea because it becomes a bottleneck.

- *Keep any code you write for your service gateway stateless.* Don't store any information in memory for the service gateway. If you aren't careful, you can limit the scalability of the gateway. Then, you will need to ensure that the data gets replicated across all service gateway instances.

- *Keep the code you write for your service gateway light.* The service gateway is the "chokepoint" for your service invocation. Complex code with multiple database calls can be the source of difficult-to-track performance problems in the service gateway.

Let's now look at how to implement a service gateway using Spring Cloud Gateway. We'll use Spring Cloud Gateway because it is the preferred API gateway from the Spring Cloud team. This implementation is built on Spring 5 and is a nonblocking gateway that integrates much easier with the other Spring Cloud projects we've used throughout the book.

8.2   Introducing Spring Cloud Gateway

Spring Cloud Gateway is the API gateway implementation built on Spring framework 5, Project Reactor, and Spring Boot 2.0. This gateway is a nonblocking gateway. What does nonblocking mean? Nonblocking applications are written in such a way that the main threads are never blocked. Instead, these threads are always available to serve requests and to process them asynchronously in the background to return a response once processing is done. Spring Cloud Gateway offers several capabilities, including

- *Mapping the routes for all the services in your application to a single URL.* The Spring Cloud Gateway isn't limited to a single URL, however. Actually, with it, we can define multiple route entry points, making route mapping extremely fine-grained (each service endpoint gets its own route mapping). But the first and most common use case is to build a single entry point through which all service client calls will flow.

■ *Building filters that can inspect and act on the requests and responses coming through the gateway.* These filters allow us to inject policy enforcement points in our code and to perform a wide number of actions on all of our service calls in a consistent fashion. In other words, these filters allow us to modify the incoming and outgoing HTTP requests and responses.

■ *Building predicates, which are objects that allow us to check if the requests fulfill a set of given conditions before executing or processing a request.* The Spring Cloud Gateway includes a set of built-in Route Predicate Factories.

To get started with Spring Cloud Gateway, let's

1 Set up a Spring Boot project for Spring Cloud Gateway and configure the appropriate Maven dependencies
2 Configure the gateway to communicate with Eureka

8.2.1   *Setting up the Spring Boot gateway project*

In this section, we'll set up our Spring Cloud Gateway service using Spring Boot. Like the Spring Cloud Config service and the Eureka service that we already created in previous chapters, setting up a Spring Cloud Gateway service starts with building a new Spring Boot project and then applying annotations and configurations. Let's begin by creating that new project with the Spring Initializr (https://start.spring.io/) as shown in figure 8.3.

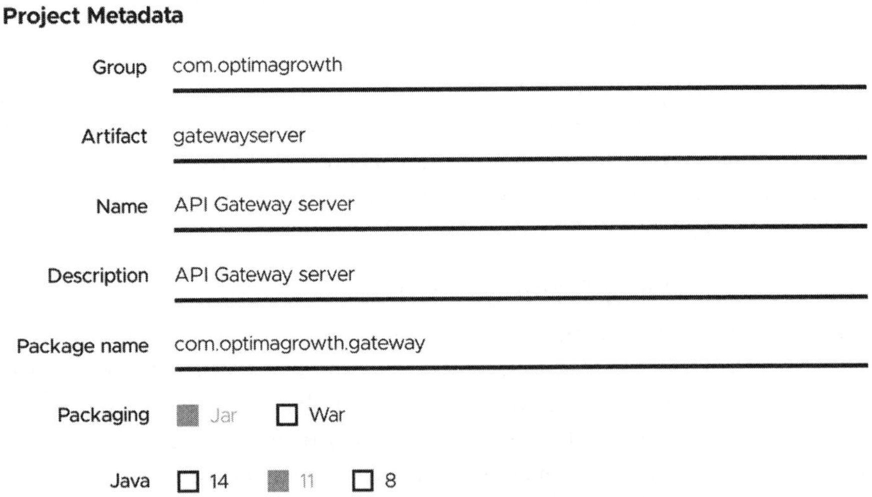

Project Metadata

Group	com.optimagrowth
Artifact	gatewayserver
Name	API Gateway server
Description	API Gateway server
Package name	com.optimagrowth.gateway
Packaging	■ Jar ☐ War
Java	☐ 14 ■ 11 ☐ 8

Figure 8.3   **Spring Initializr with our Spring Cloud Gateway information**

To achieve this setup, you'll need to follow these steps. Listing 8.1 then shows how the Gateway server pom.xml file should look.

1 Select Maven as the project type.
2 Select Java as the language.

3 Select the latest or more stable 2.x.x Spring version.

4 Write com.optimagrowth as the group and gatewayserver as the artifact.

5 Write API Gateway server as the name, API Gateway server as the description, and com.optimagrowth.gateway as the package name.

6 Select JAR Packaging.

7 Select Java 11 as the Java version.

8 Add the Eureka Client, Config Client, Gateway, and Spring Boot Actuator dependencies as shown in figure 8.4.

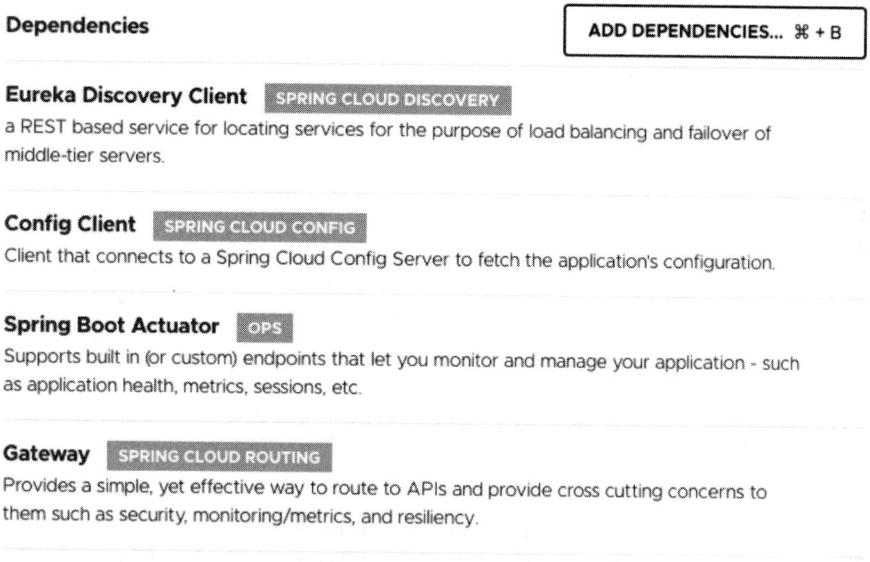

Dependencies

ADD DEPENDENCIES... ⌘ + B

Eureka Discovery Client SPRING CLOUD DISCOVERY

a REST based service for locating services for the purpose of load balancing and failover of middle-tier servers.

Config Client SPRING CLOUD CONFIG

Client that connects to a Spring Cloud Config Server to fetch the application's configuration.

Spring Boot Actuator OPS

Supports built in (or custom) endpoints that let you monitor and manage your application - such as application health, metrics, sessions, etc.

Gateway SPRING CLOUD ROUTING

Provides a simple, yet effective way to route to APIs and provide cross cutting concerns to them such as security, monitoring/metrics, and resiliency.

Figure 8.4 Our gateway server dependencies in Spring Initializr

Listing 8.1 Maven pom file for the Gateway server

```
//Part of pom.xml omitted for conciseness
...
<dependencies>
    <dependency>
        <groupId>org.springframework.boot</groupId>
        <artifactId>spring-boot-starter-actuator</artifactId>
    </dependency>
    <dependency>
        <groupId>org.springframework.cloud</groupId>
        <artifactId>spring-cloud-starter-config</artifactId>
    </dependency>
    <dependency>
        <groupId>
            org.springframework.cloud         ⟵ Tells Maven to include the
        </groupId>                              Spring Cloud Gateway libraries
        <artifactId>spring-cloud-starter-gateway</artifactId>
```

```
        </dependency>
        <dependency>
            <groupId>org.springframework.cloud</groupId>
            <artifactId>spring-cloud-starter-netflix-eureka-client</artifactId>
            <exclusions>
                <exclusion>
                    <groupId>org.springframework.cloud</groupId>
                    <artifactId>spring-cloud-starter-ribbon</artifactId>
                </exclusion>
                <exclusion>
                    <groupId>com.netflix.ribbon</groupId>
                    <artifactId>ribbon-eureka</artifactId>
                </exclusion>
            </exclusions>
        </dependency>
        <dependency>
            <groupId>org.springframework.boot</groupId>
            <artifactId>spring-boot-starter-test</artifactId>
            <scope>test</scope>
            <exclusions>
                <exclusion>
                    <groupId>org.junit.vintage</groupId>
                    <artifactId>junit-vintage-engine</artifactId>
                </exclusion>
            </exclusions>
        </dependency>
    </dependencies>
</dependencies>

//Rest of pom.xml removed for conciseness
...
```

The next step is to set up the src/main/resources/bootstrap.yml file with the configuration needed to retrieve the settings from the Spring Config Server that we previously created in chapter 5. The following listing shows how your bootstrap.yml file should look.

Listing 8.2 Setting up the Gateway bootstrap.yml file

```
spring:                              Names the gateway service so that
    application:                     the Spring Cloud Config client knows
        name: gateway-server   ◁─┘  which service is being looked up
    cloud:
        config:                               Specifies the location of the
            uri: http://localhost:8071  ◁─┘  Spring Cloud Config Server
```

NOTE In case you didn't follow the previous chapter's code listings, you can download the code created in chapter 7 from the following link: https://github.com/ihuaylupo/manning-smia/tree/master/chapter7.

8.2.2   *Configuring the Spring Cloud Gateway to communicate with Eureka*

The Spring Cloud Gateway can integrate with the Netflix Eureka Discovery service we created in chapter 6. To achieve this integration, we must add the Eureka configuration in the configuration server for the Gateway service we just created. This may sound somehow complicated, but don't worry. It is something that we already achieved in the previous chapter.

To add a new Gateway service, the first step is to create a configuration file for this service in the Spring Configuration Server repository. (Remember, this can be a Vault, Git, or filesystem or classpath.) For this example, we've created the gateway-server.yml file in the classpath of the project. You'll find it here: /configserver/src/main/resources/config/gateway-server.yml.

> **NOTE**   The filename is set with the `spring.application.name` property you defined in the bootstrap.yml for the service. For example, for the Gateway service, we defined the `spring.application.name` to be `gateway-server`, so the configuration file must be named gateway-server as well. As for the extension, you can choose between .properties or .yml.

Next, we will add the Eureka configuration data into the configuration file we just created. The following listing shows how.

Listing 8.3   Setting up the Eureka configuration in the Spring Configuration Server

```
server:
  port: 8072

eureka:
  instance:
    preferIpAddress: true
  client:
    registerWithEureka: true
    fetchRegistry: true
    serviceUrl:
      defaultZone: http://eurekaserver:8070/eureka/
```

And finally, we'll add the `@EnableEurekaClient` in the `ApiGatewayServerApplication` class. You'll find this class in the /gatewayserver/src/main/java/com/optimagrowth/gateway/ApiGatewayServerApplication.java class file. The following listing demonstrates this.

Listing 8.4   Adding `@EnableEurekaClient` to `ApiGatewayServerApplication`

```
package com.optimagrowth.gateway;

import org.springframework.boot.SpringApplication;
import org.springframework.boot.autoconfigure.SpringBootApplication;
import org.springframework.cloud.netflix.eureka.EnableEurekaClient;
```

```
@SpringBootApplication
@EnableEurekaClient
public class ApiGatewayServerApplication {

    public static void main(String[] args) {
        SpringApplication.run(ApiGatewayServerApplication.class, args);
    }
}
```

Now, that we've created the basic configuration for our Spring Cloud Gateway, let's start routing our services.

8.3 *Configuring routes in Spring Cloud Gateway*

At its heart, the Spring Cloud Gateway is a reverse proxy. A *reverse proxy* is an intermediate server that sits between the client trying to reach a resource and the resource itself. The client has no idea it's even communicating with a server. The reverse proxy takes care of capturing the client's request and then calls the remote resource on the client's behalf.

In the case of a microservice architecture, Spring Cloud Gateway (our reverse proxy) takes a microservice call from a client and forwards it to the upstream service. The service client thinks it's only communicating with the gateway. But it is not actually as simple as that. To communicate with the upstream services, the gateway has to know how to map the incoming call to the upstream route. The Spring Cloud Gateway has several mechanisms to do this, including

- Automated mapping of routes using service discovery
- Manual mapping of routes using service discovery

8.3.1 *Automated mapping of routes via service discovery*

All route mappings for the gateway are done by defining the routes in the /config-server/src/main/resources/config/gateway-server.yml file. However, the Spring Cloud Gateway can automatically route requests based on their service IDs by adding the following configurations to the gateway-server configuration file as shown in the following listing.

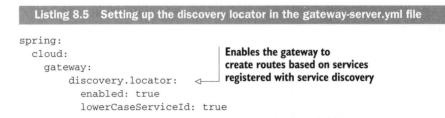

Listing 8.5 Setting up the discovery locator in the gateway-server.yml file

```
spring:
  cloud:
    gateway:                              Enables the gateway to
      discovery.locator:      ◁───┐       create routes based on services
        enabled: true                     registered with service discovery
        lowerCaseServiceId: true
```

By adding the lines in listing 8.5, the Spring Cloud Gateway automatically uses the Eureka service ID of the service being called and maps it to a downstream service instance. For instance, if we want to call our organization service and use automated routing via the Spring Cloud Gateway, we would have our client call the Gateway service instance using the following URL as the endpoint:

```
http://localhost:8072/organization-service/v1/organization/958aa1bf-18dc-
➥ 405c-b84a-b69f04d98d4f
```

The Gateway server is accessed via the `http://localhost:8072` endpoint. The service we want to invoke (the organization service) is represented by the first part of the endpoint path in the service. Figure 8.5 illustrates this mapping in action.

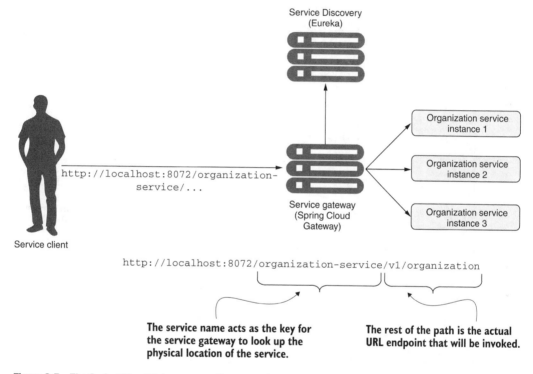

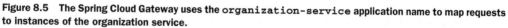

Figure 8.5 **The Spring Cloud Gateway uses the `organization-service` application name to map requests to instances of the organization service.**

The beauty of using Spring Cloud Gateway with Eureka is that not only do we now have a single endpoint through which we can make calls, but we can also add and remove instances of a service without ever having to modify the gateway. For instance, we can add a new service to Eureka, and the gateway automatically routes calls to it because it's communicating with Eureka about where the actual physical service endpoints are located.

If we want to see the routes managed by the Gateway server, we can list the routes via the `actuator/gateway/routes` endpoint on the Gateway server. This will return a listing of all the mappings on our service. Figure 8.6 shows the output from selecting http://localhost:8072/actuator/gateway/routes.

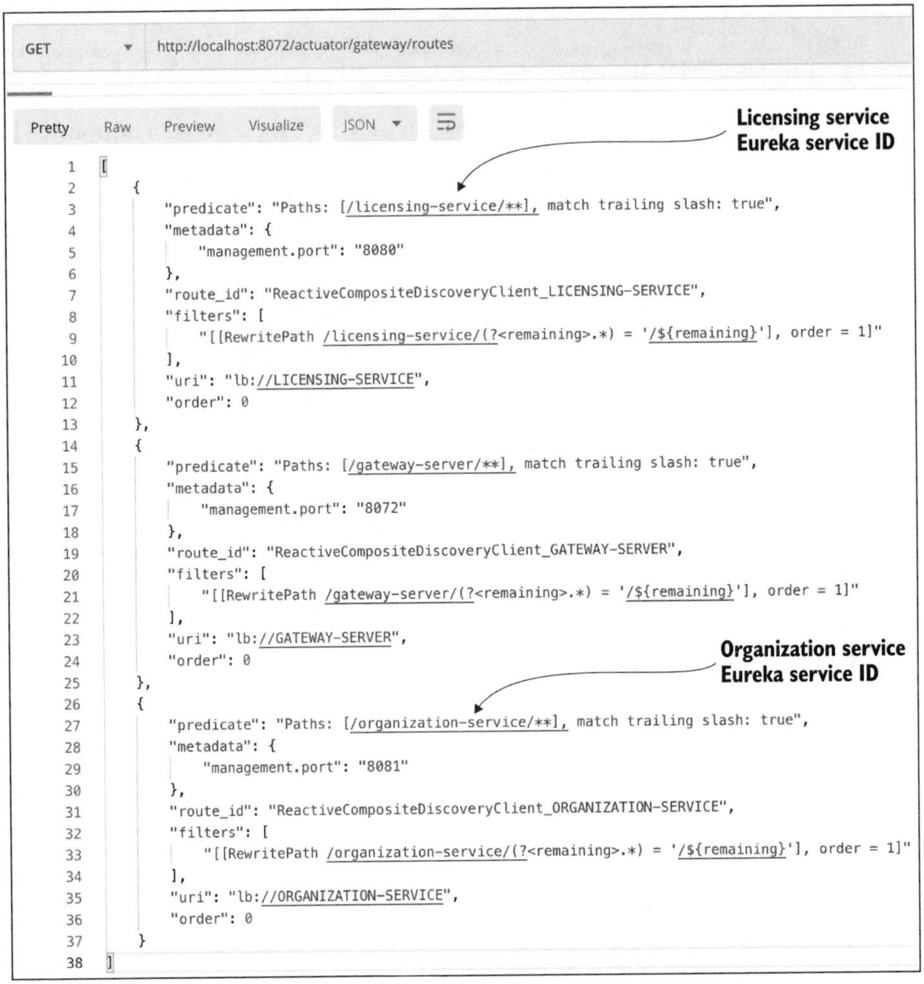

Figure 8.6   Each service that is mapped in Eureka is now mapped as a Spring Cloud Gateway route.

Figure 8.6 shows the mappings for the services registered with the Spring Cloud Gateway. You'll also notice additional data such as predicate, management port, route ID, filters, and others.

8.3.2   *Manually mapping routes using service discovery*

Spring Cloud Gateway allows our code to be more fine-grained by allowing us to explicitly define route mappings rather than relying solely on the automated routes created with the Eureka service ID. Suppose we want to simplify the route by shortening the organization name rather than having our organization service accessed in the gateway via the default route, /organization-service/v1/organization/{organization-id}. You can do this by manually defining the mapping for the route in the configuration file /configserver/src/main/resources/config/gateway-server.yml, which is located in the Spring Cloud Configuration Server repository. The following listing shows you how.

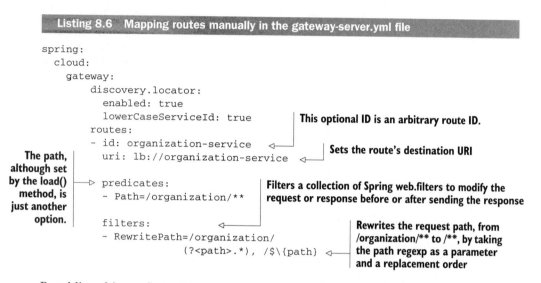

Listing 8.6 Mapping routes manually in the gateway-server.yml file

```
spring:
  cloud:
    gateway:
      discovery.locator:
        enabled: true
        lowerCaseServiceId: true
      routes:
      - id: organization-service
        uri: lb://organization-service
        predicates:
        - Path=/organization/**
        filters:
        - RewritePath=/organization/
            (?<path>.*), /$\{path}
```

This optional ID is an arbitrary route ID.

Sets the route's destination URI

The path, although set by the load() method, is just another option.

Filters a collection of Spring web.filters to modify the request or response before or after sending the response

Rewrites the request path, from /organization/** to /**, by taking the path regexp as a parameter and a replacement order

By adding this configuration, we can now access the organization service by entering the /organization/v1/organization/{organization-id} route. Now, if we recheck the Gateway server's endpoint, we should see the results shown in figure 8.7.

If you look carefully at figure 8.7, you'll notice that two entries are present for the organization service. One service entry is the mapping we defined in the gateway-server.yml file, which is organization/**: organization-service. The other service entry is the automatic mapping created by the gateway based on the Eureka ID for the organization service, which is /organization-service/**: organization-service.

> **NOTE** When we use automated route mapping where the gateway exposes the service based solely on the Eureka service ID, if no service instances are running, the gateway will not expose the route for the service. However, if we manually map a route to a service discovery ID and there are no instances registered with Eureka, the gateway will still show the route. If we try to call the route for the nonexistent service, it will return a 500 HTTP error.

If we want to exclude the automated mapping of the Eureka service ID route and only have the organization service route that we've defined, we can remove the spring .cloud.gateway.discovery.locator entries we added in the gateway-server.yml file, as shown in listing 8.7.

```
[
    {
        "predicate": "Paths: [/licensing-service/**], match trailing slash: true",
        "metadata": {
            "management.port": "8080"
        },
        "route_id": "ReactiveCompositeDiscoveryClient_LICENSING-SERVICE",
        "filters": [
            "[[RewritePath /licensing-service/(?<remaining>.*) = '/${remaining}'], order = 1]"
        ],
        "uri": "lb://LICENSING-SERVICE",
        "order": 0
    },
    {
        "predicate": "Paths: [/organization-service/**], match trailing slash: true",
        "metadata": {
            "management.port": "8081"
        },
        "route_id": "ReactiveCompositeDiscoveryClient_ORGANIZATION-SERVICE",
        "filters": [
            "[[RewritePath /organization-service/(?<remaining>.*) = '/${remaining}'], order = 1]"
        ],
        "uri": "lb://ORGANIZATION-SERVICE",
        "order": 0
    },
    {
        "predicate": "Paths: [/gateway-server/**], match trailing slash: true",
        "metadata": {
            "management.port": "8072"
        },
        "route_id": "ReactiveCompositeDiscoveryClient_GATEWAY-SERVER",
        "filters": [
            "[[RewritePath /gateway-server/(?<remaining>.*) = '/${remaining}'], order = 1]"
        ],
        "uri": "lb://GATEWAY-SERVER",
        "order": 0
    },
    {
        "predicate": "Paths: [/organization/**], match trailing slash: true",
        "route_id": "organization-service",
        "filters": [
            "[[RewritePath /organization/(?<path>.*) = '/${path}'], order = 1]"
        ],
        "uri": "lb://organization-service",
        "order": 0
    }
]
```

We still have the Eureka service ID–based route here.

Notice the custom route for the organization service.

Figure 8.7   The results of the gateway call to `/actuator/gateway/routes` **when manually mapping the organization service**

NOTE   The decision whether to use automated routing or not should be carefully thought out. In a stable environment where not many new services are added, having to add the route manually is a straightforward task. However, in a large environment with many new services, this is a bit tedious.

Listing 8.7   Removing the discovery locator entries in the gateway-server.yml file

```
spring:
  cloud:
    gateway:
```

```
routes:
- id: organization-service
  uri: lb://organization-service
  predicates:
  - Path=/organization/**
  filters:
  - RewritePath=/organization/
                (?<path>.*), /$\{path}
```

Now, when we call the `actuator/gateway/routes` endpoint on the Gateway server, we should only see the organization service mapping we've defined. Figure 8.8 shows the outcome of this mapping.

Figure 8.8 The result of the `gateway/actuator/gateway/routes` call with only a manual mapping of the organization service

8.3.3 Dynamically reloading route configuration

The next thing we'll look at when configuring routes in Spring Cloud Gateway is how to dynamically refresh routes. The ability to dynamically reload routes is useful because it allows us to change the mapping of routes without having to restart the Gateway server(s). Existing routes can be modified quickly, and new routes will have to go through the act of recycling each Gateway server in our environment.

If we enter the `actuator/gateway/routes` endpoint, we should see our organization service currently shown in the gateway. Now, if we want to add new route mappings on the fly, all we have to do is make the changes to the configuration file and commit those changes back to the Git repository where Spring Cloud Config pulls its configuration data. Then we can commit the changes to GitHub.

Spring Actuator exposes a POST-based endpoint route, `actuator/gateway/refresh`, that will cause it to reload its route configuration. Once this `actuator/gateway/refresh` is reached, if you then enter the `/routes` endpoint, you'll see that two new routes are exposed. The response of the `actuator/gateway/refresh` returns an HTTP 200 status code without a response body.

8.4   *The real power of Spring Cloud Gateway: Predicate and Filter Factories*

Because we can proxy all requests through the gateway, it allows us to simplify our service invocations. But the real power of the Spring Gateway comes into play when we want to write custom logic that will be applied against all the service calls flowing through the gateway. Most often, we'll use this custom logic to enforce a consistent set of application policies like security, logging, and tracking among all services.

These application policies are considered *cross-cutting concerns* because we want these strategies to be applied to all the services in our application without having to modify each one to implement them. In this fashion, the Spring Cloud Gateway Predicate and Filter Factories can be used similarly to Spring aspect classes. These can match or intercept a wide body of behaviors and decorate or change the behavior of the call without the original coder being aware of the change. While a servlet filter or Spring aspect is localized to a specific service, using the Gateway and its Predicate and Filter Factories allows us to implement cross-cutting concerns across all the services being routed through the gateway. Remember, predicates allow us to check if the requests fulfill a set of conditions before processing the request. Figure 8.9 shows the architecture that the Spring Cloud Gateway uses while applying predicates and filters when a request comes through the gateway.

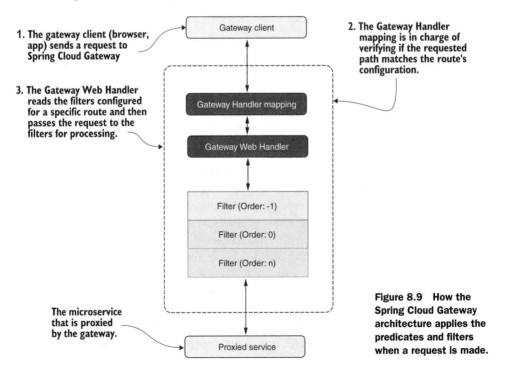

1. The gateway client (browser, app) sends a request to Spring Cloud Gateway

2. The Gateway Handler mapping is in charge of verifying if the requested path matches the route's configuration.

3. The Gateway Web Handler reads the filters configured for a specific route and then passes the request to the filters for processing.

Gateway client

Gateway Handler mapping

Gateway Web Handler

Filter (Order: -1)

Filter (Order: 0)

Filter (Order: n)

The microservice that is proxied by the gateway.

Proxied service

Figure 8.9   How the Spring Cloud Gateway architecture applies the predicates and filters when a request is made.

First, the gateway client (browsers, apps, and so forth) sends a request to Spring Cloud Gateway. Once that request is received, it goes directly to the Gateway Handler that is in charge of verifying that the requested path matches the configuration of the specific route it is trying to access. If everything matches, it enters the Gateway Web Handler that is in charge of reading the filters and sending the request to those filters for further processing. Once the request passes all the filters, it is forwarded to the routing configuration: a microservice.

8.4.1 Built-in Predicate Factories

Built-in predicates are objects that allow us to check if the requests fulfill a set of conditions before executing or processing the requests. For each route, we can set multiple Predicate Factories, which are used and combined via the logical AND. Table 8.1 lists all the built-in Predicate Factories in Spring Cloud Gateway.

These predicates can be applied in the code programmatically or via configurations, like the ones we created in the previous sections. In this book, we only use them via the configuration file under the `predicates` section, like this:

```
predicates:
    - Path=/organization/**
```

Table 8.1 Built-in predicates in Spring Cloud Gateway

Predicate	Description	Example
Before	Takes a date-time parameter and matches all the requests that happen before it.	Before=2020-03-11T...
After	Takes a date-time parameter and matches all the requests that happen after it.	After=2020-03-11T...
Between	Takes two date-time parameters and matches all the requests between them. The first date-time is inclusive, and the second one is exclusive.	Between=2020-03-11T..., 2020-04-11T...
Header	Receives two parameters, the name of the header, and a regular expression and then matches its value with the provided regular expression.	Header=X-Request-Id, \d+
Host	Receives an Ant-style pattern separated with the "." hostname pattern as a parameter. Then it matches the Host header with the given pattern.	Host=**.example.com
Method	Receives the HTTP method to match.	Method=GET
Path	Receives a Spring PathMatcher.	Path=/organization/{id}
Query	Receives two parameters, a required parameter and an optional regular expression, then matches these with the query parameters.	Query=id, 1

Table 8.1   Built-in predicates in Spring Cloud Gateway *(continued)*

Predicate	Description	Example
Cookie	Takes two parameters, a name for the cookie and a regular expression, and finds the cookies in the HTTP request header, then matches its value with the provided regular expression.	`Cookie=SessionID, abc`
RemoteAddr	Receives a list of IP addresses and matches these with the remote address of a request.	`RemoteAddr=192.168.3.5/24`

8.4.2   *Built-in Filter Factories*

The built-in Filter Factories allow us to inject policy enforcement points in our code and perform a wide number of actions on all service calls in a consistent fashion. In other words, these filters let us modify the incoming and outgoing HTTP requests and responses. Table 8.2 contains a list of all the built-in filters in Spring Cloud Gateway.

Table 8.2   Built-in filters in Spring Cloud Gateway

Predicate	Description	Example
AddRequestHeader	Adds an HTTP request header with the name and the value received as parameters.	`AddRequestHeader= X-Organization-ID, F39s2`
AddResponseHeader	Adds an HTTP response header with the name and the value received as parameters.	`AddResponseHeader= X-Organization-ID, F39s2`
AddRequestParameter	Adds an HTTP query parameter with the name and the value received as parameters.	`AddRequestParameter= Organizationid, F39s2`
PrefixPath	Adds a prefix to the HTTP request path.	`PrefixPath=/api`
RequestRateLimiter	Receives three parameters: `replenishRate`, which represents the requests per seconds that we want to allow the user to make; `capacity`, which defines how much bursting capacity is allowed; `keyResolverName`, which defines the name of a bean that implements the `KeyResolver` interface.	`RequestRateLimiter= 10, 20, #{@userKeyResolver}`
RedirectTo	Takes two parameters, a status and a URL. The status should be a 300 redirect HTTP code.	`RedirectTo=302, http://localhost:8072`
RemoveNonProxy	Removes some headers such as Keep-Alive, Proxy-Authenticate, or Proxy-Authorization.	NA

Table 8.2 Built-in filters in Spring Cloud Gateway

Predicate	Description	Example
RemoveRequestHeader	Removes a header that matches the name received as a parameter from the HTTP request.	`RemoveRequestHeader= X-Request-Foo`
RemoveResponseHeader	Removes a header that matches the name received as a parameter from the HTTP response.	`RemoveResponseHeader= X-Organization-ID`
RewritePath	Takes a path regexp parameter and a replacement parameter.	`RewritePath= /organization/ (?<path>.*), /$\{path}`
SecureHeaders	Adds secure headers to the response and receives a path template parameter, which changes the request path.	NA
SetPath	Receives the path template as a parameter. It manipulates the request path by allowing templated segments on the path. This uses the URI templates from the Spring framework. Multiple matching segments are permitted.	`SetPath= /{organization}`
SetStatus	Receives a valid HTTP status and changes the status of an HTTP response.	`SetStatus=500`
SetResponseHeader	Takes name and value parameters to set a header on the HTTP response.	`SetResponseHeader= X-Response-ID,123`

8.4.3 Custom filters

The ability to proxy all requests through the gateway lets us simplify our service invocations. But the real power of Spring Cloud Gateway comes into play when we want to write custom logic that can be applied against all the service calls flowing through the gateway. Most often, this custom logic is used to enforce a consistent set of application policies like security, logging, and tracking among all the services.

The Spring Cloud Gateway allows us to build custom logic using a filter within the gateway. Remember, a filter allows us to implement a chain of business logic that each service request passes through as it's implemented. Spring Cloud Gateway supports the following two types of filters. Figure 8.10 shows how the pre- and post-filters fit together when processing a service client's request.

- *Pre-filters*—A pre-filter is invoked before the actual request is sent to the target destination. A pre-filter usually carries out the task of making sure that the service has a consistent message format (key HTTP headers are in place, for example) or acts as a gatekeeper to ensure that the user calling the service is authenticated (they are whom they say they are).

- *Post-filters*—A post-filter is invoked after the target service, and a response is sent back to the client. Usually, we implement a post-filter to log the response back from the target service, handle errors, or audit the response for sensitive information.

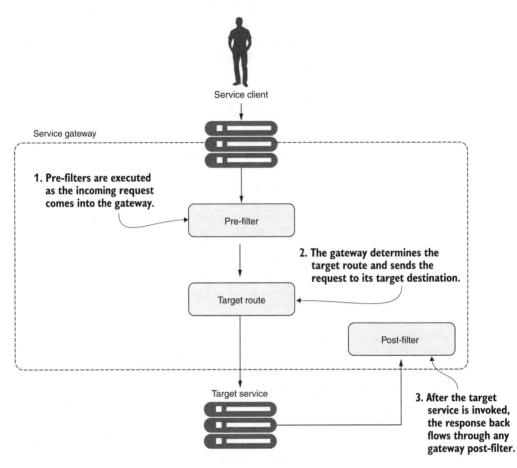

Figure 8.10   The pre-filters, target route, and post-filters form a pipeline in which a client request flows. As a request comes into the gateway, custom filters can manipulate the incoming request.

If we follow the flow laid out in figure 8.10, everything starts with a service client making a call to a service that's exposed through the service gateway. From there, the following takes place:

1 Any pre-filters defined in the gateway are invoked as a request enters the gateway. The pre-filters inspect and modify an HTTP request before it gets to the actual service. A pre-filter, however, cannot redirect the user to a different endpoint or service.

2 After the pre-filters are executed against the incoming request by the gateway, the gateway determines the destination (where the service is heading).

3 After the target service is invoked, the gateway post-filters are invoked. The post-filters inspect and modify the response from the invoked service.

The best way to understand how to implement the gateway filters is to see them in action. To this end, in the next several sections, we'll build pre- and post-filters and then run client requests through them. Figure 8.11 shows how these filters will fit together in processing requests for our O-stock services.

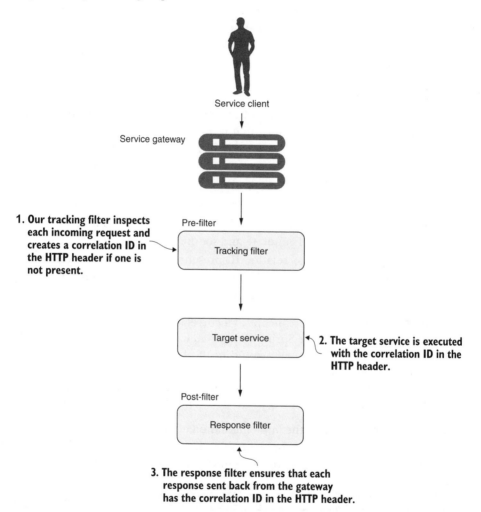

Figure 8.11 Gateway filters provide centralized tracking of service calls and logging. These filters allow us to enforce custom rules and policies against microservice calls.

Following the flow in figure 8.11, we can see the following custom filters in use:

- *Tracking filter*—The tracking filter is a pre-filter that ensures that every request flowing from the gateway has a correlation ID associated with it. A *correlation ID* is a unique ID that gets carried across all the microservices that are executed when carrying out a customer request. A correlation ID allows us to trace the chain of events that occur as a call goes through a series of microservice calls.
- *Target service*—The target service can either be an organization or the licensing service. Both services receive the correlation ID in the HTTP request header.
- *Response filter*—The response filter is a post-filter that injects the correlation ID associated with the service call into the HTTP response header sent to the client. This way, the client will have access to the correlation ID associated with the request.

8.5 *Building the pre-filter*

Building filters in the Spring Cloud Gateway is straightforward. To begin, we'll build a pre-filter, called `TrackingFilter`, that will inspect all incoming requests to the gateway and determine whether there's an HTTP header called `tmx-correlation-id` present in the request. The `tmx-correlation-id` header will contain a unique GUID (Globally Universal ID) that can be used to track a user's request across multiple microservices:

- If the `tmx-correlation-id` isn't present on the HTTP header, our gateway `TrackingFilter` will generate and set the correlation ID.
- If there's already a correlation ID present, the gateway won't do anything. (The presence of a correlation ID means that this particular service call is part of a chain of service calls carrying out the user's request.)

NOTE   We discussed the concept of a correlation ID in chapter 7. Here, we'll walk through how to use Spring Cloud Gateway to generate a correlation ID in more detail. If you skipped around in the book, we highly recommend you look at chapter 7 and read the section on thread context. Our implementation of correlation IDs will be implemented using `ThreadLocal` variables, and there's extra work to do in order to have your `ThreadLocal` variables work.

Let's go ahead and look at the implementation of the `TrackingFilter` in listing 8.8. You can also find this code in the book samples directories in the class file /gatewayserver/ src/main/java/com/optimagrowth/gateway/filters/TrackingFilter.java.

Listing 8.8   Pre-filter for generating correlation IDs

```
package com.optimagrowth.gateway.filters;
//Other imports omitted for conciseness

import org.springframework.http.HttpHeaders;
import reactor.core.publisher.Mono;
```

```
@Order(1)
@Component
public class TrackingFilter
            implements GlobalFilter {

    private static final Logger logger =
            LoggerFactory.getLogger(TrackingFilter.class);

    @Autowired
    FilterUtils filterUtils;

    @Override
    public Mono<Void> filter(ServerWebExchange exchange,
                    GatewayFilterChain chain) {

        HttpHeaders requestHeaders =
            exchange.getRequest().getHeaders();
        if (isCorrelationIdPresent(requestHeaders)) {
            logger.debug(
                "tmx-correlation-id found in tracking filter: {}. ",
                filterUtils.getCorrelationId(requestHeaders));
        } else {
            String correlationID = generateCorrelationId();
            exchange = filterUtils.setCorrelationId(exchange,
                    correlationID);
            logger.debug(
                "tmx-correlation-id generated in tracking filter: {}.",
                correlationID);
        }
        return chain.filter(exchange);
    }

    private boolean isCorrelationIdPresent(HttpHeaders
                    requestHeaders) {
        if (filterUtils.getCorrelationId(requestHeaders) != null) {
            return true;
        } else {
            return false;
        }
    }

    private String generateCorrelationId() {
        return java.util.UUID.randomUUID().toString();
    }
}
```

Global filters implement the GlobalFilter interface and must override the filter() method.

Commonly used functions across your filters are encapsulated in the FilterUtils class.

Extracts the HTTP header from the request using the ServerWebExchange object passed by parameters to the filter() method

Code that executes every time a request passes through the filter

A helper method that checks if there's a correlation ID in the request header

A helper method that checks if the tmx-correlation-id is present; it can also generate a correlation ID UUID value.

To create a global filter in the Spring Cloud Gateway, we need to implement the GlobalFilter class and then override the filter() method. This method contains the business logic that the filter implements. Another critical point to note from the previous code is the way that we obtain the HTTP headers from the ServerWeb-Exchange object:

```
HttpHeaders requestHeaders = exchange.getRequest().getHeaders();
```

We've implemented a class called `FilterUtils`, which encapsulates common functionality used by all the filters. It's located in the /gatewayserver/src/main/java/com/optimagrowth/gateway/filters/FilterUtils.java file. We're not going to walk through the entire `FilterUtils` class, but we'll discuss several key methods: `getCorrelationId()` and `setCorrelationId()`. The following listing shows the code for the `FilterUtils` `getCorrelationId()` method.

Listing 8.9   Retrieving the `tmx-correlation-id` with `getCorrelationId`

```
public String getCorrelationId(HttpHeaders requestHeaders){
   if (requestHeaders.get(CORRELATION_ID) !=null) {
      List<String> header = requestHeaders.get(CORRELATION_ID);
      return header.stream().findFirst().get();
   } else{
      return null;
   }
}
```

The key thing to notice in listing 8.9 is that we first check to see if `tmx-correlation-ID` is already set on the HTTP headers for the incoming request. If it isn't there, our code should return `null` to create one later on. You may remember that earlier, in the `filter()` method in our `TrackingFilter` class, we did exactly this with the following code:

```
} else {
  String correlationID = generateCorrelationId();
  exchange = filterUtils.setCorrelationId(exchange, correlationID);
  logger.debug("tmx-correlation-id generated in tracking filter: {}.",
            correlationID);
}
```

To set `tmx-correlation-id`, you'll use the `FilterUtils` `setCorrelationId()` method as shown in the following listing.

Listing 8.10   Setting the `tmx-correlation-id` in the HTTP headers

```
public ServerWebExchange setRequestHeader(ServerWebExchange exchange,
                                          String name, String value) {
   return exchange.mutate().request(
      exchange.getRequest().mutate()
      .header(name, value)
      .build())
      .build();
   }

public ServerWebExchange setCorrelationId(ServerWebExchange exchange,
         String correlationId) {
      return this.setRequestHeader(exchange,CORRELATION_ID,correlationId);
}
```

With the `FilterUtils setCorrelationId()` method, when we want to add a value to the HTTP request headers, we can use the `ServerWebExchange.Builder mutate()` method. This method returns a builder to mutate properties of the exchange object by wrapping it with `ServerWebExchangeDecorator` and either returning mutated values or delegating it back to this instance. To test this call, we can call our organization or licensing service. Once the call is submitted, we should see a log message in the console that writes out the passed-in correlation ID as it flows through the filter:

```
gatewayserver_1      | 2020-04-14 22:31:23.835 DEBUG 1 --- [or-http-epoll-3]
c.o.gateway.filters.TrackingFilter      : tmx-correlation-id generated in
tracking filter: 735d8a31-b4d1-4c13-816d-c31db20afb6a.
```

If you don't see the message on your console, just add the code lines shown in the following listing to the bootstrap.yml configuration file of the Gateway server. Then build again and execute your microservices.

> ### Listing 8.11 Logger configuration in the Gateway service bootstrap.yml file

```
//Some code removed for conciseness
logging:
  level:
    com.netflix: WARN
    org.springframework.web: WARN
    com.optimagrowth: DEBUG
```

If you are using Docker, you can execute the following commands in the root directory where the parent pom.xml is located:

```
mvn clean package dockerfile:build
docker-compose -f docker/docker-compose.yml up
```

8.6   *Using the correlation ID in the services*

Now that we've guaranteed that a correlation ID has been added to every microservice call flowing through the gateway, we want to ensure that

- The correlation ID is readily accessible to the microservice that's invoked.
- Any downstream service calls the microservice might make also propagate the correlation ID on to the downstream calls.

To implement this, we'll build a set of three classes for each of our microservices: `UserContextFilter`, `UserContext`, and `UserContextInterceptor`. These classes will work together to read the correlation ID (along with other information we'll add later) of the incoming HTTP request, map it to a class that's easily accessible and useable by the business logic in the application, and then ensure that the correlation ID is propagated to any downstream service calls. Figure 8.12 demonstrates how we will build these different pieces for our licensing service.

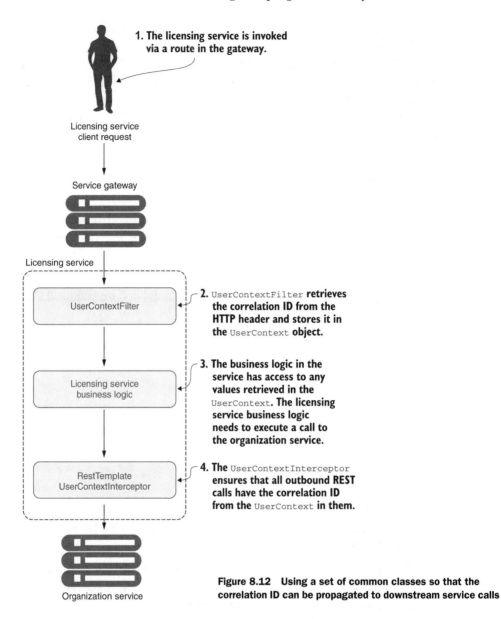

1. The licensing service is invoked via a route in the gateway.

Licensing service client request

Service gateway

Licensing service

UserContextFilter

2. `UserContextFilter` **retrieves the correlation ID from the HTTP header and stores it in the** `UserContext` **object.**

Licensing service business logic

3. The business logic in the service has access to any values retrieved in the `UserContext`. **The licensing service business logic needs to execute a call to the organization service.**

RestTemplate UserContextInterceptor

4. The `UserContextInterceptor` **ensures that all outbound REST calls have the correlation ID from the** `UserContext` **in them.**

Organization service

Figure 8.12   Using a set of common classes so that the correlation ID can be propagated to downstream service calls

Let's walk through what's happening in figure 8.12:

1 When a call is made to the licensing service through the gateway, the `Tracking-Filter` injects a correlation ID into the incoming HTTP header for any calls coming into the gateway.

2 The `UserContextFilter` class, a custom HTTP `ServletFilter`, maps a correlation ID to the `UserContext` class. The `UserContext` class stores the values in a thread for use later in the call.

3 The licensing service business logic executes a call to the organization service.

4 A `RestTemplate` invokes the organization service. The `RestTemplate` uses a custom Spring interceptor class, `UserContextInterceptor`, to inject the correlation ID into the outbound call as an HTTP header.

Repeated code vs. shared libraries

The subject of whether to use common libraries across your microservices is a gray area in microservice design. Microservice purists will tell you that you shouldn't use a custom framework across your services because it introduces artificial dependencies. Changes in business logic or a bug can introduce wide-scale refactoring of all your services. On the other hand, other microservice practitioners will say that a purist approach is impractical because certain situations exist (like the previous `UserContextFilter` example) where it makes sense to build a common library and share it across services.

We think there's a middle ground here. Common libraries are fine when dealing with infrastructure-style tasks. If you start sharing business-oriented classes, you're asking for trouble because you'll end up breaking down the boundaries between the services.

We seem to be breaking our own advice with the code examples in this chapter, however. If you look at all the services in the chapter, these have their own copies of the `UserContextFilter`, `UserContext`, and `UserContextInterceptor` classes.

8.6.1 *UserContextFilter: Intercepting the incoming HTTP request*

The first class we're going to build is the `UserContextFilter` class. This class is an HTTP servlet filter that will intercept all incoming HTTP requests coming into the service and map the correlation ID (and a few other values) from the HTTP request to the `UserContext` class. The following listing shows the code for the `UserContext` class in the licensing-service/src/main/java/com/optimagrowth/license/utils/UserContextFilter .java class file.

Listing 8.12   Mapping the correlation ID to the `UserContext` class

```
package com.optimagrowth.license.utils;
//Removed the imports for conciseness

@Component
public class UserContextFilter implements Filter {          ◄───┐
    private static final Logger logger =

    LoggerFactory.getLogger(UserContextFilter.class);

    @Override
    public void doFilter(ServletRequest servletRequest, ServletResponse
                    servletResponse, FilterChain filterChain)
```

Registers the filter that's picked up by Spring through @Component and a javax.servlet.Filter interface implementation

```
                               throws IOException, ServletException {

             HttpServletRequest httpServletRequest = (HttpServletRequest)
                                             servletRequest;

             UserContextHolder.getContext()
                 .setCorrelationId(
                   httpServletRequest.getHeader(UserContext.CORRELATION_ID) );
             UserContextHolder.getContext().setUserId(
                   httpServletRequest.getHeader(UserContext.USER_ID));
             UserContextHolder.getContext().setAuthToken(
                   httpServletRequest.getHeader(UserContext.AUTH_TOKEN));
             UserContextHolder.getContext().setOrganizationId(
                   httpServletRequest.getHeader(UserContext.ORGANIZATION_ID));

             logger.debug("UserContextFilter Correlation id: {}",
                          UserContextHolder.getContext().getCorrelationId());

             filterChain.doFilter(httpServletRequest, servletResponse);
         }
         // Not showing the empty init and destroy methods
     }
```

**Retrieves the correlation ID from the header
and sets the value in the UserContext class**

Ultimately, the UserContextFilter will map the HTTP header values you're interested in to a Java UserContext class.

8.6.2   *UserContext: Making the HTTP headers easily accessible to the service*

The UserContext class holds the HTTP header values for an individual service client request that is processed by our microservice. It consists of getter/setter methods that retrieve and store values from java.lang.ThreadLocal. The following listing shows the code from the UserContext class, which you'll find in /licensing-service/src/ main/java/com/optimagrowth/license/utils/UserContext.java.

Listing 8.13   Storing the HTTP header values inside the UserContext class

```
//Removed the imports for conciseness
@Component
public class UserContext {
    public static final String CORRELATION_ID = "tmx-correlation-id";
    public static final String AUTH_TOKEN     = "tmx-auth-token";
    public static final String USER_ID        = "tmx-user-id";
    public static final String ORGANIZATION_ID = "tmx-organization-id";

    private String correlationId= new String();
    private String authToken= new String();
    private String userId = new String();
    private String organizationId = new String();
}
```

Here the `UserContext` class is nothing more than a POJO holding the values scraped from the incoming HTTP request. Next, we'll use a `UserContextHolder` class found in /licensing-service/src/main/java/com/optimagrowth/license/utils/ UserContextHolder.java to store the `UserContext` in a `ThreadLocal` variable that is accessible by any method being invoked by the thread processing the user's request. The following listing shows the code for the `UserContextHolder` class.

Listing 8.14 The `UserContextHolder` stores the `UserContext` in a `ThreadLocal`

```
public class UserContextHolder {
    private static final ThreadLocal<UserContext> userContext =
                            new ThreadLocal<UserContext>();

    public static final UserContext getContext(){
        UserContext context = userContext.get();

        if (context == null) {
            context = createEmptyContext();
            userContext.set(context);

        }
        return userContext.get();
    }

    public static final void setContext(UserContext context) {
        Assert.notNull(context,
            "Only non-null UserContext instances are permitted");
        userContext.set(context);
    }

    public static final UserContext createEmptyContext(){
        return new UserContext();
    }
}
```

8.6.3 Custom RestTemplate and UserContextInterceptor: Ensuring that the correlation ID gets propagated

The last piece of code that we'll look at is the `UserContextInterceptor` class. This class injects the correlation ID into any outgoing HTTP-based service request that's executed from a `RestTemplate` instance. This is done to ensure that we can establish a link between service calls. To do this, we'll use a Spring interceptor that's injected into the `RestTemplate` class. Let's look at the `UserContextInterceptor` in the following listing.

Listing 8.15 Injecting the correlation ID into all outgoing microservice calls

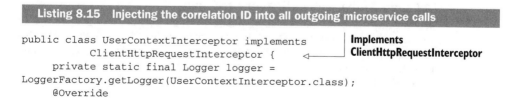

```
public class UserContextInterceptor implements
        ClientHttpRequestInterceptor {            ◁——— Implements ClientHttpRequestInterceptor
    private static final Logger logger =
LoggerFactory.getLogger(UserContextInterceptor.class);
    @Override
```

```
       public ClientHttpResponse intercept(
               HttpRequest request, byte[] body,
               ClientHttpRequestExecution execution)   throws IOException {
          HttpHeaders headers = request.getHeaders();
          headers.add(UserContext.CORRELATION_ID,
              UserContextHolder.getContext().
              getCorrelationId());
          headers.add(UserContext.AUTH_TOKEN,
              UserContextHolder.getContext().
              getAuthToken());

          return execution.execute(request, body);
       }
   }
```

Invokes intercept() before the actual HTTP service call occurs by the RestTemplate (annotation pointing to the `intercept(` method)

Takes the HTTP request header that's being prepared for the outgoing service call and adds the correlation ID stored in the UserContext (annotation pointing to `getCorrelationId());`)

To use `UserContextInterceptor`, we need to define a `RestTemplate` bean and then add `UserContextInterceptor` to it. To do this, we'll define our own `RestTemplate` bean in the `LicenseServiceApplication` class. You'll find the source for this class in /licensing-service/src/main/java/com/optimagrowth/license/. The following listing shows the method that's added to this `RestTemplate`.

Listing 8.16   Adding the `UserContextInterceptor` to the `RestTemplate` class

```
@LoadBalanced
@Bean
public RestTemplate getRestTemplate(){
   RestTemplate template = new RestTemplate();
   List interceptors = template.getInterceptors();
       if (interceptors==null){
           template.setInterceptors(Collections.singletonList(
                   new UserContextInterceptor()));
   }else{
       interceptors.add(new UserContextInterceptor());
       template.setInterceptors(interceptors);
   }

   return template;
}
```

Indicates that this RestTemplate object is going to use the load balancer (annotation pointing to `@LoadBalanced`/`@Bean`)

Adds UserContextInterceptor to the RestTemplate instance (annotation pointing to the if/else block)

With this bean definition in place, any time we use the `@Autowired` annotation and inject a `RestTemplate` into a class, we'll use the `RestTemplate` created in listing 8.16 with the `UserContextInterceptor` attached to it.

Log aggregation, authentication, and more

Now that we have correlation IDs passed to each service, it's possible to trace a transaction as it flows through all the services involved in the call. To do this, you need to ensure that each service logs to a central log aggregation point that captures log entries from all of your services into a single point. Each log entry captured in the log aggregation service will have a correlation ID associated with it.

Implementing a log aggregation solution is outside the scope of this chapter, but in chapter 10, we'll see how to use Spring Cloud Sleuth. Spring Cloud Sleuth won't use the `TrackingFilter` that we built here, but it will use the same concepts of tracking the correlation ID and ensuring that it's injected into every call.

8.7 *Building a post-filter receiving correlation ID*

Remember, Spring Gateway executes the actual HTTP call on behalf of the service client and inspects the response back from the target service call. It then alters the response or decorates it with additional information. When coupled with capturing data with the pre-filter, a gateway post-filter is an ideal location to collect metrics and complete any logging associated with the user's transaction. We'll want to take advantage of this by injecting the correlation ID that we've been passing around to our microservices back to the user. This way, we can pass the correlation ID back to the caller without ever having to touch the message body.

The following listing shows the code for building a post-filter. You can find this code in the /gatewayserver/src/main/java/com/optimagrowth/gateway/filters/ResponseFilter.java file.

Listing 8.17 Injecting the correlation ID into the HTTP response

```
@Configuration
public class ResponseFilter {

    final Logger logger =LoggerFactory.getLogger(ResponseFilter.class);

    @Autowired
    FilterUtils filterUtils;

    @Bean
    public GlobalFilter postGlobalFilter() {
        return (exchange, chain) -> {
            return chain.filter(exchange).then(Mono.fromRunnable(() -> {
                HttpHeaders requestHeaders = exchange.getRequest().getHeaders();
                String correlationId =
                    filterUtils.
                    getCorrelationId(requestHeaders);      ⬅ Grabs the correlation ID that
                logger.debug(                                  was passed in to the original
                    "Adding the correlation id to the outbound headers. {}",   HTTP request
                            correlationId);
                exchange.getResponse().getHeaders().
                add(FilterUtils.CORRELATION_ID,    ⬅ Injects the correlation
                correlationId);                        ID into the response
                logger.debug("Completing outgoing request
                        for {}.",
                        exchange.getRequest().getURI());
            }));
        };
    }
}
```

Logs the outgoing request URI so that you have "bookends" that show the incoming and outgoing entry of the user's request into the gateway

Once we've implemented the `ResponseFilter`, we can fire up our service and call the licensing or organization service with it. Once the service completes, you'll see a `tmx-correlation-id` on the HTTP response header from the call, as figure 8.13 shows.

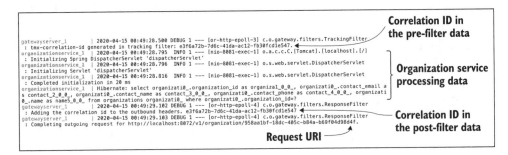

> ▸ Get Organization - Gateway
>
> GET ▾   http://localhost:8072/organization/v1/organization/958aa1bf-18dc-405c-b84a-b69f04d98d4f
>
> Params   Authorization   Headers (7)   **Body**   Pre-request Script   Tests   Settings
>
> ● none   ● form-data   ● x-www-form-urlencoded   ● raw   ● binary   ● GraphQL
>
> This request d⋯
>
> Body   Cookies   **Headers** (4)   Test Results
>
> | KEY | VALUE |
> |---|---|
> | transfer-encoding ⓘ | chunked |
> | Content-Type ⓘ | application/json |
> | Date ⓘ | Wed, 15 Apr 2020 00:49:29 GMT |
> | tmx-correlation-id ⓘ | e3f6a72b-7d6c-41da-ac12-fb30fcd1e547 ◀ |

The correlation ID returned in the HTTP response.

Figure 8.13 The `tmx-correlation-id` added to the response headers and sent back to the service client

You can also see the log messages in the console (figure 8.14), which write the passed-in correlation ID, `e3f6a72b-7d6c-41da-ac12-fb30fcd1e547,` as it flows through the pre- and post-filters.

Up to this point, all our filter examples have dealt with manipulating the service client calls before and after they were routed to a target destination. Now, that we know how to create a Spring Cloud Gateway, let's move on with our next chapter that describes how to secure our microservices using Keycloak and OAuth2.

```
gatewayserver_1      | 2020-04-15 00:49:28.500 DEBUG 1 --- [or-http-epoll-3] c.o.gateway.filters.TrackingFilter
: tmx-correlation-id generated in tracking filter: e3f6a72b-7d6c-41da-ac12-fb30fcd1e547. ◀
organizationservice_1 | 2020-04-15 00:49:28.795 INFO 1 --- [nio-8081-exec-1] o.a.c.c.C.[Tomcat].[localhost].[/]
: Initializing Spring DispatcherServlet 'dispatcherServlet'
organizationservice_1 | 2020-04-15 00:49:28.796 INFO 1 --- [nio-8081-exec-1] o.s.web.servlet.DispatcherServlet
: Initializing Servlet 'dispatcherServlet'
organizationservice_1 | 2020-04-15 00:49:28.816 INFO 1 --- [nio-8081-exec-1] o.s.web.servlet.DispatcherServlet
: Completed initialization in 20 ms
organizationservice_1 | Hibernate: select organizati0_.organization_id as organizat1_0_0_, organizati0_.contact_email a
s contact_2_0_0_, organizati0_.contact_name as contact_3_0_0_, organizati0_.contact_phone as contact_4_0_0_, organizati
0_.name as name5_0_0_ from organizations organizati0_ where organizati0_.organization_id=?
gatewayserver_1      | 2020-04-15 00:49:29.102 DEBUG 1 --- [or-http-epoll-4] c.o.gateway.filters.ResponseFilter
: Adding the correlation id to the outbound headers. e3f6a72b-7d6c-41da-ac12-fb30fcd1e547 ◀
gatewayserver_1      | 2020-04-15 00:49:29.103 DEBUG 1 --- [or-http-epoll-4] c.o.gateway.filters.ResponseFilter
: Completing outgoing request for http://localhost:8072/v1/organization/958aa1bf-18dc-405c-b84a-b69f04d98d4f.
```

Correlation ID in the pre-filter data

Organization service processing data

Correlation ID in the post-filter data

Request URI

Figure 8.14 Logger output that shows the pre-filter data, the organization service processing data, and the post-filter data

Summary

- Spring Cloud makes it trivial to build a service gateway.
- Spring Cloud Gateway contains a set of built-in Predicate and Filter Factories.
- Predicates are objects that allow us to check if the requests fulfill a set of given conditions before executing or processing a request.
- Filters allow us to modify the incoming and outgoing HTTP requests and responses.
- The Spring Cloud Gateway integrates with Netflix's Eureka Server and can automatically map services registered with Eureka to a route.
- Using the Spring Cloud Gateway, you can manually define route mappings in the application's configuration files.
- By using Spring Cloud Config Server, you can dynamically reload the route mappings without having to restart the Gateway server.
- Spring Cloud Gateway allows you to implement custom business logic through filters. With Spring Cloud Gateway, you can create pre- and post-filters.
- Pre-filters can be used to generate a correlation ID that can be injected into every service flowing through the gateway.
- Post-filters can be used to inject a correlation ID into every HTTP service response back to a service client.

9

Securing
your microservices

This chapter covers

- Learning why security matters in a microservice environment
- Understanding OAuth2 and OpenID
- Setting up and configuring Keycloak
- Performing authentication and authorization with Keycloak
- Protecting your Spring microservice with Keycloak
- Propagating access tokens between services

Now that we have a robust microservices architecture, the task of covering security vulnerabilities becomes more and more essential. In this chapter, security and vulnerability go hand in hand. We'll define vulnerability as a weakness or flaw presented in an application. Of course, all systems have vulnerabilities, but the big difference lies in whether these vulnerabilities are exploited and cause harm.

Mentioning security often causes an involuntary groan from developers. Among developers, we hear comments such as, "It's obtuse, hard to understand, and even harder to debug." Yet, we won't find any developer (except for maybe an inexperienced developer) who says that they don't worry about security. Securing a microservices architecture is a complex and laborious task that involves multiple layers of protection, including these:

- *The application layer*—Ensures that the proper user controls are in place so that we can validate that a user is who they say they are and that they have permission to do what they're trying to do
- *Infrastructure*—Keeps the service running, patched, and up to date to minimize the risk of vulnerabilities
- *A network layer*—Implements network access controls so that a service is only accessible through well-defined ports and only to a small number of authorized servers

This chapter only covers how to authenticate and authorize users in our application layer (the first bullet point in the list). The other two items are extremely broad security topics that are outside the scope of this book. As well, there are other tools, such as the OWASP Dependency-Check Project, that can help identify vulnerabilities.

> **NOTE** The OWASP Dependency-Check Project is an OWASP Software Composition Analysis (SCA) tool that allows us to identify publicly disclosed vulnerabilities. If you want to find out more, we highly recommend you look at https://owasp.org/www-project-dependency-check/.

To implement authorization and authentication controls, we'll use the Spring Cloud Security module and Keycloak to secure our Spring-based services. Keycloak is open source identity and access management software for modern applications and services. This open source software is written in Java, and it supports SAML (Security Assertion Markup Language) v2 and OpenID Connect (OIDC)/OAuth2-federated identity protocols.

9.1 What is OAuth2?

OAuth2 is a token-based security framework that describes patterns for granting authorization but does not define how to actually perform authentication. Instead, it allows users to authenticate themselves with a third-party authentication service, called an *identity provider* (IdP). If the user successfully authenticates, they are presented with a token that must be sent with every request. The token can then be validated back to the authentication service.

The main objective behind OAuth2 is that when multiple services are called to fulfill a user's request, the user can be authenticated by each service without having to present their credentials to each service processing their request. OAuth2 allows us to protect our REST-based services across different scenarios through authentication schemes called *grants*. The OAuth2 specification has four types of grants:

- Password
- Client credential
- Authorization code
- Implicit

We aren't going to walk through each of these grant types or provide code examples for each. That's too much material to cover in one chapter. Instead, we'll do the following:

- Discuss how our microservices can use OAuth2 through one of the simpler OAuth2 grant types, the password grant type
- Use JSON Web Tokens (JWTs) to provide a more robust OAuth2 solution and to establish a standard for encoding information in an OAuth2 token
- Walk through other security considerations that need to be taken into account when building microservices

NOTE   We provide an overview of the other OAuth2 grant types in appendix B. If you're interested in diving into more detail on the OAuth2 spec and how to implement all the grant types, we highly recommend Justin Richer and Antonio Sanso's book, *OAuth2 in Action* (Manning, 2017), which is a comprehensive explanation of OAuth2.

The real power behind OAuth2 is that it allows application developers to easily integrate with third-party cloud providers and authenticate and authorize users with those services without having to pass the user's credentials continually to the third-party service.

OpenID Connect (OIDC) is a layer on top of the OAuth2 framework that provides authentication and profile information about who is logged in to the application (the identity). When an authorization server supports OIDC, it is sometimes called an *identity provider*. Before we get into the technical details of protecting our services, let's walk through the Keycloak architecture.

9.2 *Introduction to Keycloak*

Keycloak is an open source identity and access management solution for our services and applications. The main objective of Keycloak is to facilitate the protection of the services and applications with little or no code. Some characteristics of Keycloak include the following:

- It centralizes authentication and enables single sign-on (SSO) authentication.
- It allows developers to focus on business functionality instead of worrying about security aspects like authorization and authentication.
- It allows two-factor authentication.
- It is LDAP compliant.
- It offers several adapters to secure applications and servers easily.
- It lets you customize password policies.

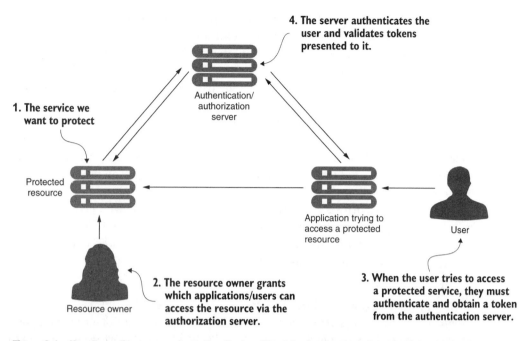

Figure 9.1 Keycloak allows a user to authenticate without having to present credentials constantly.

Keycloak security can be broken down into these four components: protected resource, resource owner, application, and authentication/authorization server. Figure 9.1 shows how the four components interact together.

- *A protected resource*—The resource (in our case, a microservice) you want to protect, ensuring that only authenticated users who have the proper authorization can access it.
- *A resource owner*—This owner defines which applications are allowed to call the service, which users are given access to the service, and what the users can do with the service. Each application registered by the resource owner is given an application name that identifies the application, along with a secret key. The combination of the application name and the secret key are part of the credentials that are passed when authenticating an access token.
- *An application*—This is the application that's going to call the service on behalf of a user. After all, users rarely invoke a service directly. Instead, they rely on an application to do the work for them.
- *Authentication/authorization server*—The authentication server is the intermediary between the application and the services being consumed. The authentication server allows the user to authenticate themselves without having to pass their user credentials to every service the application is going to call on their behalf.

As previously mentioned, the Keycloak security components interact together to authenticate the service users. Users authenticate with the Keycloak server by providing their credentials and the application/device they're using to access a protected resource (the microservice). If the users' credentials are valid, the Keycloak server provides an authentication token that can be passed from service to service each time a service is used by the users.

The protected resource can then contact the Keycloak server to determine the token's validity and to retrieve assigned roles for a user. Roles are used to group related users together and to define which resources they can access. For this chapter, we'll use Keycloak roles to determine what HTTP verbs a user can use to call on which authorized service endpoints.

Web service security is an extremely complicated subject. We need to understand who's going to call our services (internal users or external users), how they're going to call our service (internal web-based client, mobile device, or web application), and what actions they're going to take with our code.

On authentication vs. authorization

We've often found that developers "mix and match" the meaning of the terms authentication and authorization. *Authentication* is the act of a user proving who they are by providing credentials. *Authorization* determines whether a user is allowed to do what they want to do. For instance, user Illary could prove her identity by providing a user ID and password, but she may not be authorized to look at sensitive data (payroll data, for example). For our discussion, a user must be authenticated before authorization takes place.

9.3   *Starting small: Using Spring and Keycloak to protect a single endpoint*

To understand how to set up the authentication and authorization pieces, we'll do the following:

- Add a Keycloak service to Docker.
- Set up a Keycloak service and register the O-stock application as an authorized application that can authenticate and authorize user identities.
- Use Spring Security to protect our O-stock services. We're not going to build a UI for O-stock; instead, we'll simulate a user logging in to Postman to provide authentication for our Keycloak service.
- Protect the licensing and organization services so that they can only be called by an authenticated user.

9.3.1 Adding Keycloak to Docker

This section explains how to add the Keycloak service to our Docker environment. To achieve this, let's start by adding the code shown in the following listing to our docker-compose.yml file.

> **NOTE** In case you didn't follow the previous chapter's code listings, you can download the code created in chapter 8 from the following link: https://github.com/ihuaylupo/manning-smia/tree/master/chapter8.

Listing 9.1 Adding a Keycloack service in docker-compose.yml

```
//Part of docker-compose.yml omitted for conciseness
...

keycloak:                         ⟵—— Keycloak Docker service name
    image: jboss/keycloak
    restart: always
    environment:
      KEYCLOAK_USER: admin      ⟵—— Keycloak Admin Console's username
      KEYCLOAK_PASSWORD: admin  ⟵
    ports:                         | Keycloak Admin Console's password
      - "8080:8080"
    networks:
      backend:
        aliases:
          - "keycloak"
```

> **NOTE** You can use Keycloak with several databases like H2, PostgreSQL, MySQL, Microsoft SQL Server, Oracle, and MariaDB. For the examples in this chapter, we'll use the default embedded H2 database. We highly recommend visiting the following link if you want to use another database: https://github.com/keycloak/keycloak-containers/tree/master/docker-compose-examples.

Notice that in the code in listing 9.1, we used port 8080 for Keycloak. If we go back a few chapters, we also exposed the licensing service in that port. We will map the licensing service in the docker-compose.yml file to port 8180 instead of 8080 to make everything work, but in the meantime, the following code shows you how to change that port number:

```
licensingservice:
    image: ostock/licensing-service:0.0.3-SNAPSHOT
    ports:
      - "8180:8080"
```

> **NOTE** To make Keycloak work in our local environment, we need to add the host entry 127.0.0.1 Keycloak to our hosts file. If you are using Windows, you need to add the host entry at C:\Windows\System32\drivers\etc\hosts, and if you are using Linux, the host file is at /etc/hosts. Why do we need that entry? The containers can talk to each other using the network aliases or MAC addresses, but our Postman needs to use localhost to invoke the services.

9.3.2   Setting up Keycloak

Now that we have Keycloak in the docker-compose.yml, let's run the following command. We'll do this at the root folder of our code:

```
docker-compose -f docker/docker-compose.yml up
```

Once the services are up, let's visit the following link to open the Keycloak Administration Console: http://keycloak:8080/auth/. Configuring Keycloak is a straightforward process. The first time we access Keycloak, a Welcome page is displayed. This page shows different options, such as visiting the Administration Console, documentation, reporting issues, and more. In our case, we want to select Administration Console. Figure 9.2 shows the Welcome page.

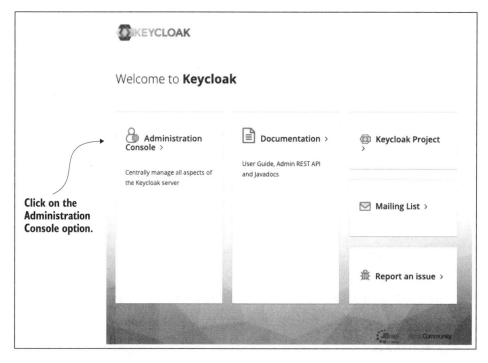

Figure 9.2   The Keycloak Welcome page

The next step is to enter the username and password that we previously defined in the docker-compose.yml file. Figure 9.3 shows this step.

To continue configuring our data, let's create our realm. A *realm* is a concept that Keycloak uses to refer to an object that manages a set of users, credentials, roles, and groups. To create our realm, click the Add Realm option that is shown in the Master drop-down menu after we log in to Keycloak. We'll call this realm spmia-realm.

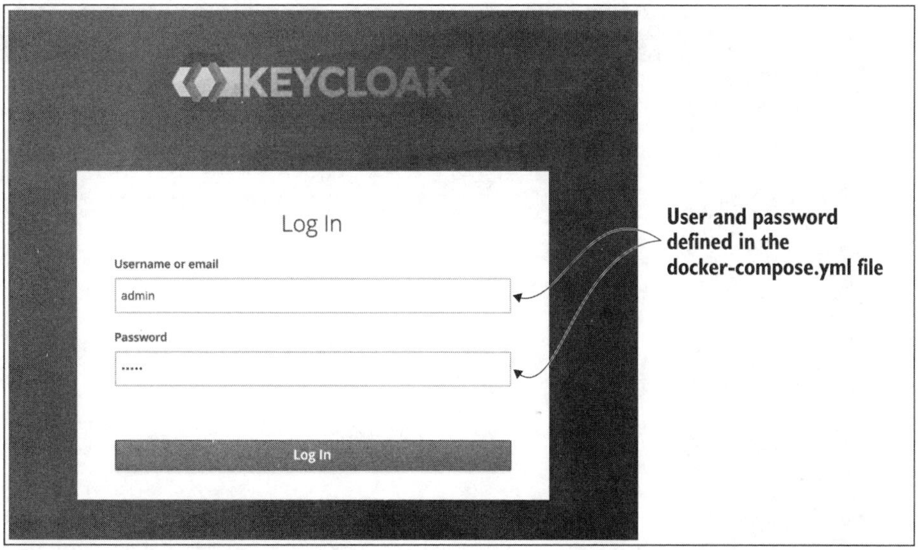

Figure 9.3 The Keycloak Log In page

Figure 9.4 shows how to create the spmia-realm in our Keycloak service.

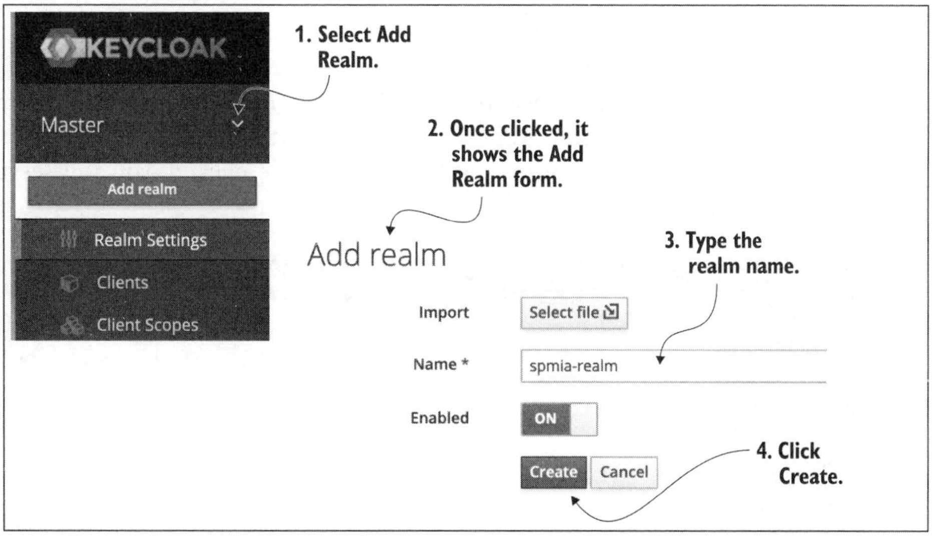

Figure 9.4 The Keycloak Add Realm page displays a form that allows the user to enter the realm name.

Once the realm is created, you will see the main page for spmia-realm with the configuration shown in figure 9.5.

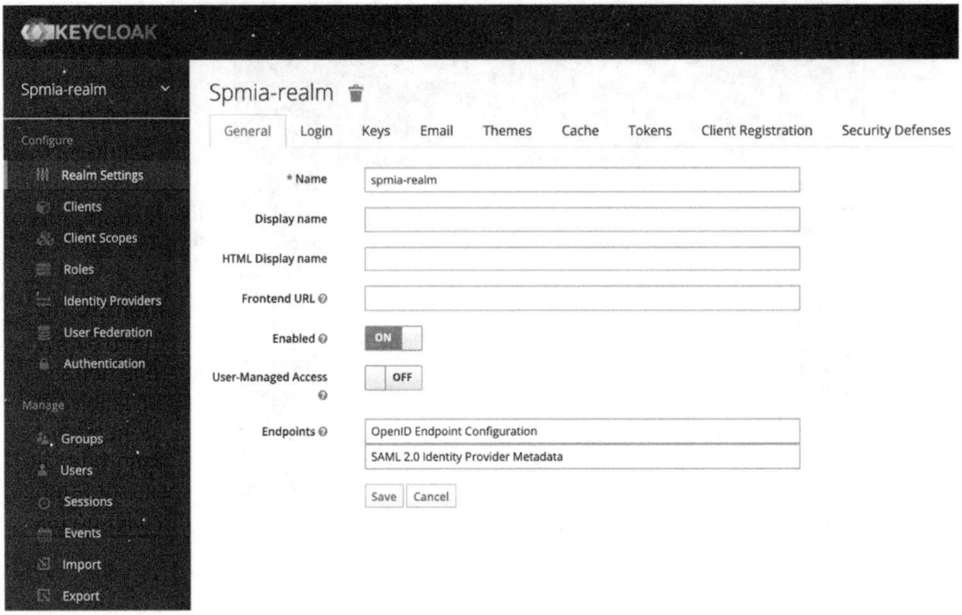

Figure 9.5   Our Keycloak Spmia-realm configuration page

9.3.3   *Registering a client application*

The next step in our configuration is to create a client. Clients in Keycloak are entities that can request user authentication. The clients are often the applications or services that we want to secure by providing a single sign-on (SSO) solution. To create a client, let's click the Clients option on the left menu. Once clicked, you will see the page shown in figure 9.6.

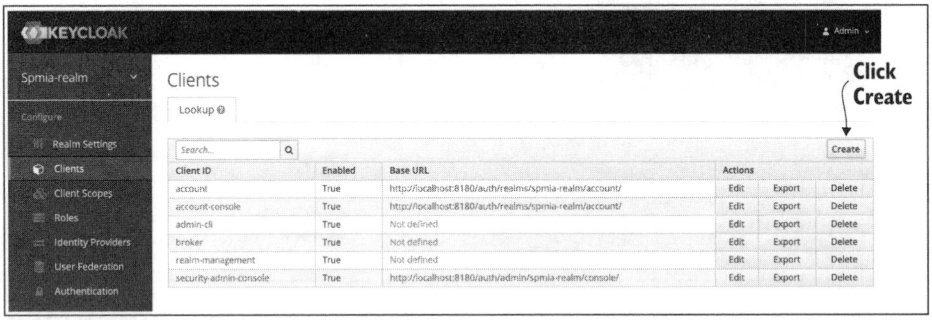

Figure 9.6   O-stock's Spmia-realm Clients page

Once the Client's list is shown, click the Create button (displayed in the table's top-right corner as shown in the previous figure). Once clicked, you will see an Add Client form that asks for the following information:

- Client ID
- Client Protocol
- Root URL

Enter the information as shown in figure 9.7.

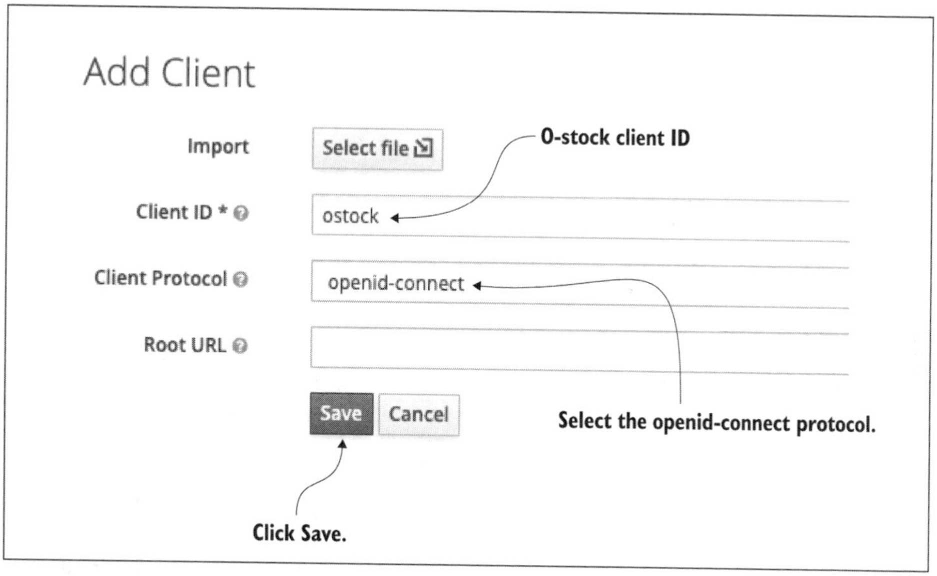

Figure 9.7　O-stock's Keycloak client information

After saving the client, you will be presented with the Client Configuration page shown in figure 9.8. On that page, we'll enter the following data:

- Access Type: Confidential
- Service Accounts Enabled: On
- Authorization Enabled: On
- Valid Redirect URLs: http://localhost:80*
- Web Origins: *

For this example, we only created a global client called ostock, but here's where you can configure as many clients as you want.

The next step is to set up the client roles, so let's click the Roles tab. To better understand client roles, let's imagine that our application will have two types of users: admins and regular users. The admin users can execute all of the application services, and the regular users are only going to be allowed to execute some of the services.

Once the Roles page is loaded, you will see a list of predefined client roles. Let's click the Add Role button displayed in the top-right corner of the Roles table. Once clicked, you will see the Add Role form shown in figure 9.9.

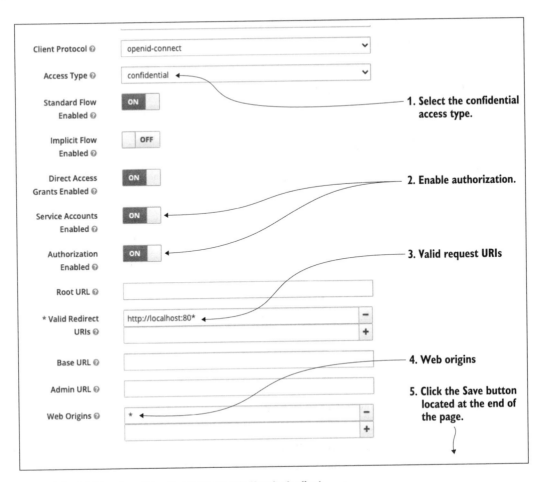

Figure 9.8   Additional configuration for O-stock's Keycloak client

Clients > ostock > Roles > Add Role

Add Role

Role Name *

Description

Save   Cancel

Figure 9.9   O-stock's Keycloak Add Role page

On the Add Role page, we need to create the following client roles. In the end, you will have a list similar to the one shown in figure 9.10.

- USER
- ADMIN

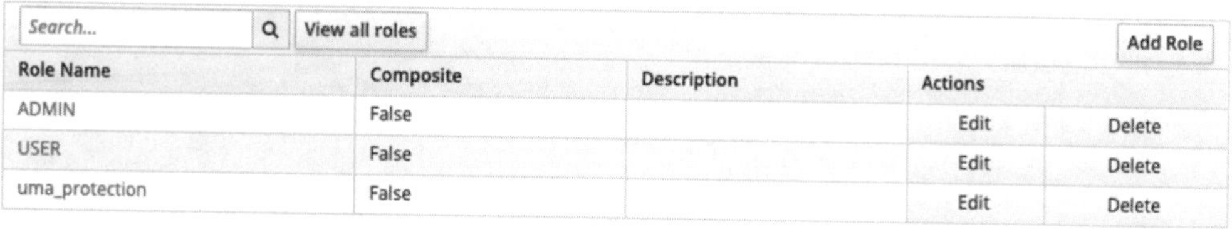

Search...	View all roles				Add Role
Role Name		**Composite**	**Description**	**Actions**	
ADMIN		False		Edit	Delete
USER		False		Edit	Delete
uma_protection		False		Edit	Delete

Figure 9.10   O-stock's Keycloak client roles: USER and ADMIN

Now that we have finished our basic client configuration, let's visit the Credentials page. The Credentials page will show the required client secret for the authentication process. Figure 9.11 shows how the Credentials page looks.

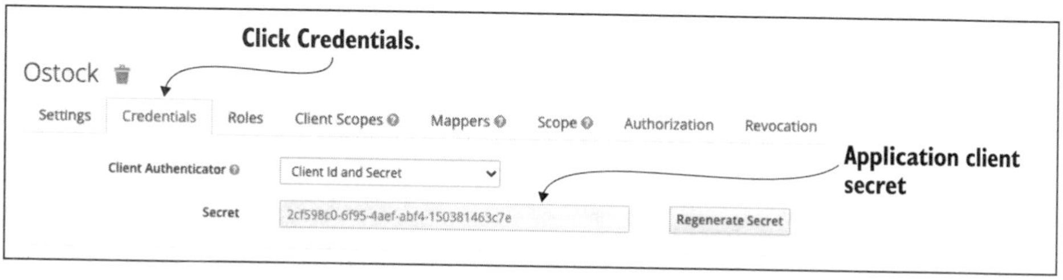

Click Credentials.

Ostock 🗑

| Settings | Credentials | Roles | Client Scopes ⊘ | Mappers ⊘ | Scope ⊘ | Authorization | Revocation |

Client Authenticator ⊘   Client Id and Secret ⌄

Secret   2cf598c0-6f95-4aef-abf4-150381463c7e   Regenerate Secret

Application client secret

Figure 9.11   O-stock's Keycloak client secret on the Credentials page

The next step in our configuration is to create realm roles. The realm roles will allow us to have better control of what roles are being set for each user. This is an optional step. If you don't want to create these roles, you can go ahead and create the users directly. But later on, it might be harder to identify and maintain the roles for each user.

To create the realm roles, let's click the Roles option shown in the left menu and then click the Add Role button at the table's top right. As with the client roles, we will create two types of realm roles: the ostock-user and the ostock-admin. Figures 9.12 and 9.13 show you how to create the ostock-admin realm role.

Roles > Add Role

Add Role

* Role Name

ostock-admin

Description

Save Cancel

Figure 9.12 Creating the ostock-admin realm role

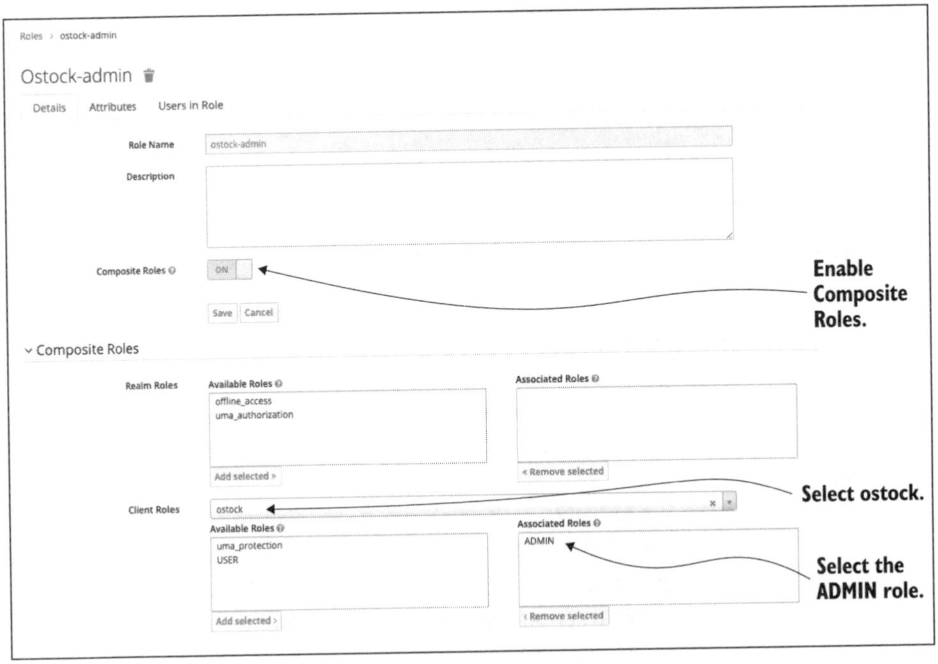

Figure 9.13 Specifying additional configurations for the ostock-admin realm role

Now that we have the ostock-admin realm role configured, let's repeat the same steps to create the ostock-user role. Once you are done, you should have a list similar to the one shown in figure 9.14.

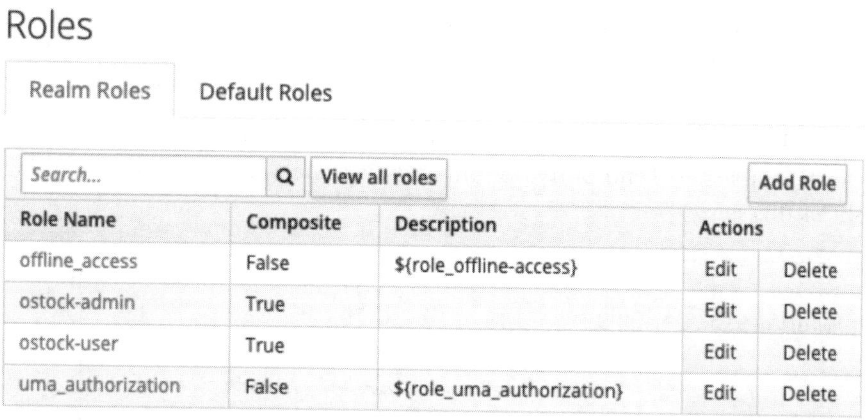

Roles

Realm Roles	Default Roles

Search... 🔍	View all roles			Add Role
Role Name	**Composite**	**Description**	**Actions**	
offline_access	False	${role_offline-access}	Edit	Delete
ostock-admin	True		Edit	Delete
ostock-user	True		Edit	Delete
uma_authorization	False	${role_uma_authorization}	Edit	Delete

Figure 9.14   A list of O-stock's spmia-realm roles

9.3.4 *Configuring O-stock users*

Now that we've defined application-level and realm-level roles, names, and secrets, we're ready to set up individual user credentials and the roles for the users. To create the users, let's click the Users option shown in the left menu in Keycloak's admin console.

For the examples in this chapter, we will define two user accounts: illary.huaylupo and john.carnell. The john.carnell account will have the role of ostock-user and the illary.huaylupo account will have the role of ostock-admin. Figure 9.15 shows the Add User page. On this page, let's type the username and enable the user and the email verified options as shown in the figure.

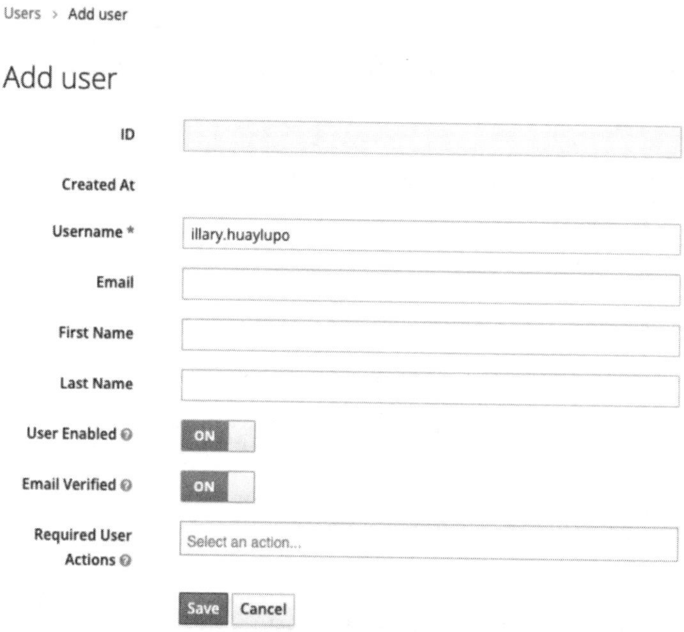

Users › Add user

Add user

ID	
Created At	
Username *	illary.huaylupo
Email	
First Name	
Last Name	
User Enabled ⓘ	`ON`
Email Verified ⓘ	`ON`
Required User Actions ⓘ	Select an action...

`Save` `Cancel`

Figure 9.15   Keycloak's Add User page for O-stock's spmia-realm

NOTE   Keycloak allows us to also add additional attributes to the users, such as first name, last name, email, address, birth date, phone number, and more. But, for this example, we will only set up the required attributes.

Once this form is saved, click the Credentials tab. You'll need to type the user's password, disable the Temporary option, and click the Set Password button. Figure 9.16 shows this step.

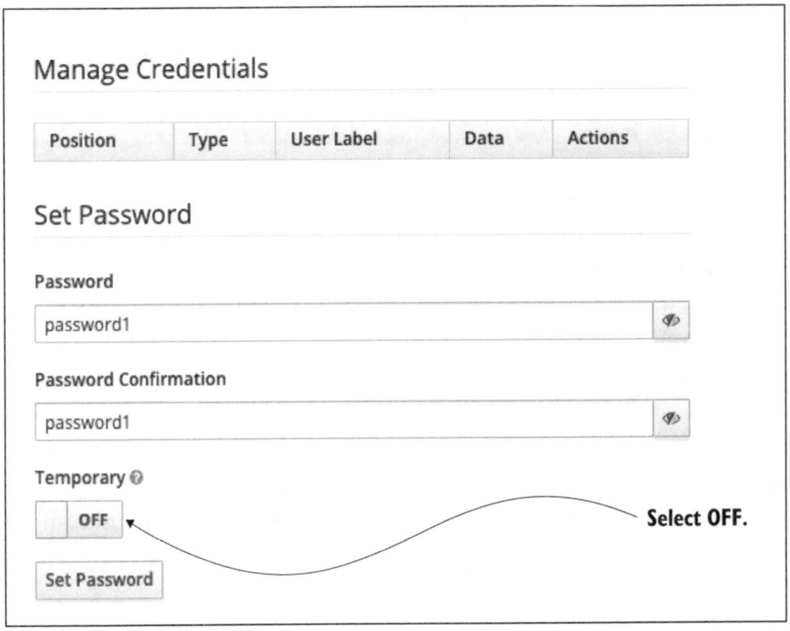

Figure 9.16   Setting the user's password and disabling the Temporary option for O-stock's user's credentials

Once the password is set, let's click the Role Mappings tab and assign the user a specific role. Figure 9.17 shows this step.

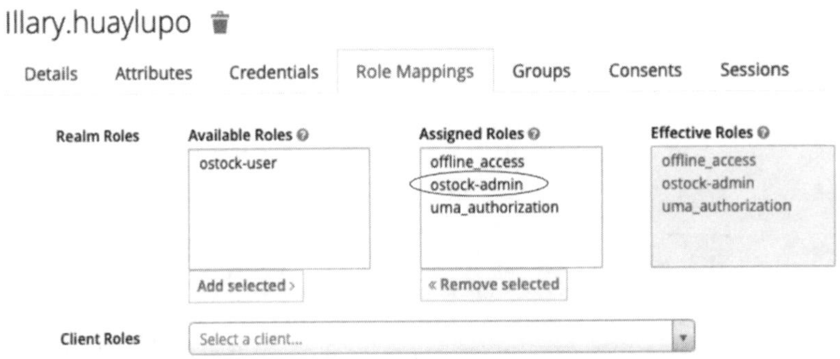

Figure 9.17   Mapping O-stock's realm roles to the created user

To finish our configuration, let's repeat the same steps for the other user, john.carnell in this example, assigning the ostock-user role to John.

9.3.5 *Authenticating our O-stock users*

At this point, we have enough of our base Keycloak server functionality in place to perform application and user authentication for the password grant flow. Let's start our authentication service. To do this, click the Realm Settings option in the left menu, and then click the OpenID Endpoint Configuration link to see a list of available endpoints for our realm. These steps are shown in figures 9.18 and 9.19.

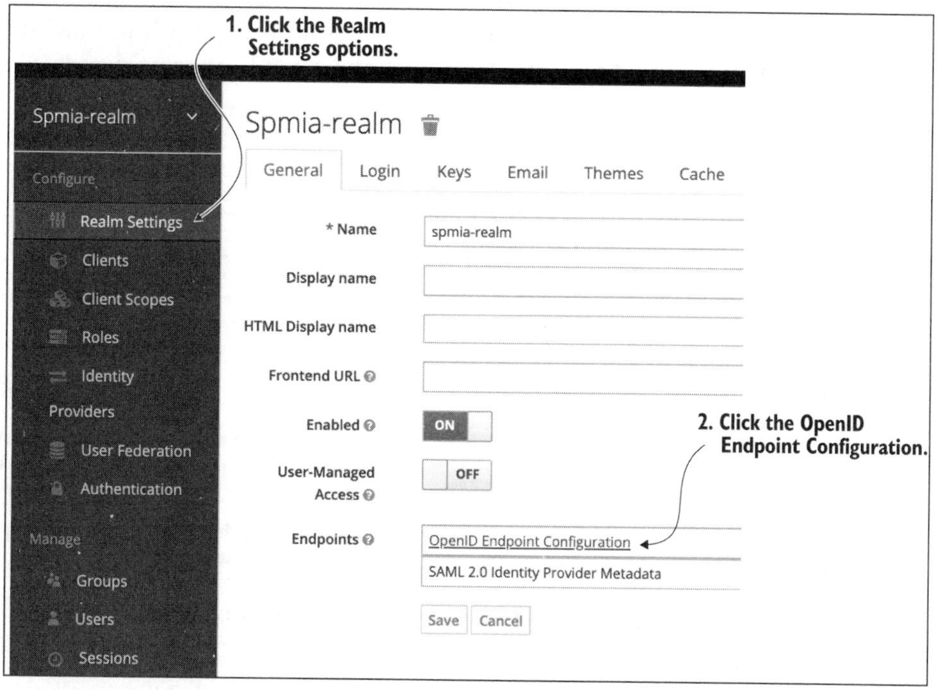

Figure 9.18   Selecting the OpenID Endpoint Configuration link for O-stock's Keycloak spmia-realm

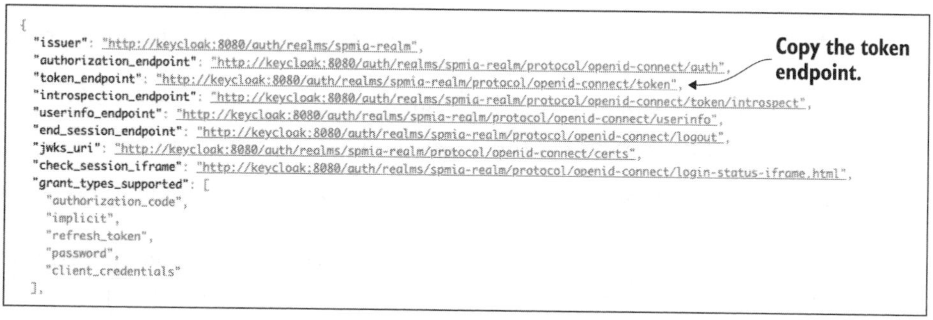

Figure 9.19   Mapping O-stock's realm roles to the created user

Now we'll simulate a user that wants to acquire an access token. We'll do this by using Postman to POST to the endpoint `http://keycloak:8080/auth/realms/spmia-realm/protocol/openid-connect/token` and then provide the application, secret key, user ID, and password.

> **NOTE** Remember, in this example, we use the 8080 port because it is the port we previously defined in the docker-compose.yml file for Keycloak.

To simulate a user acquiring an authentication token, we need to set up Postman with the application name and secret key. For this, we'll pass these elements to our authentication server endpoint using basic authentication. Figure 9.20 shows how Postman is set up to execute a basic authentication call. Note that we will use the application name we previously defined and the secret application key as a password:

```
Username: <CLIENT_APPLICATION_NAME>
Password: <CLIENT_APPLICATION_SECRET>
```

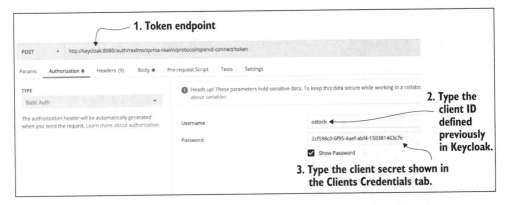

Figure 9.20 Setting up O-stock's basic authentication using the application key and secret

However, we're not ready to make the call to get the token just yet. Once the application name and secret key are configured, we need to pass in the following information to the service as HTTP form parameters:

- `grant_type`—The grant type to execute. In this example, we'll use a password grant.
- `username`—Name of the user logging in.
- `password`—Password of the user logging in.

Figure 9.21 shows how these HTTP form parameters are configured for our authentication call.

Unlike other REST calls in this book, this list's parameters will not be passed in as a JSON body. The authentication standard expects all parameters passed to the token

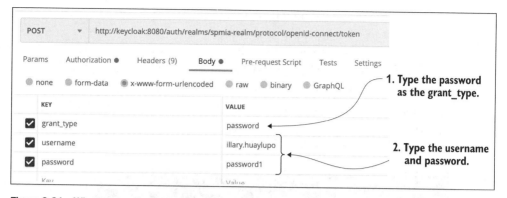

Figure 9.21 When requesting an access token, the user's credentials are passed in as HTTP form parameters to the `/openid-connect/token` endpoint.

generation endpoint to be HTTP form parameters. Figure 9.22 shows the JSON payload that's returned from the `/openid-connect/token` call.

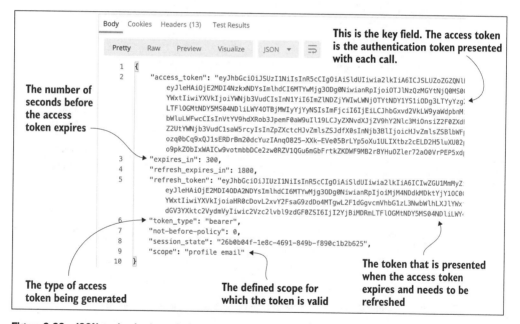

Figure 9.22 JSON payload returned after a successful client credential validation.

The JSON payload contains five attributes:

- `access_token`—The access token that will be presented with each service call the user makes to a protected resource.
- `token_type`—The authorization specification allows us to define multiple token types. The most common token type used is the Bearer Token. (We won't cover any of the other token types in this chapter.)

- refresh_token—The refresh token can be presented back to the authorization server to reissue a token after it expires.
- expires_in—This is the number of seconds before the access token expires. The default value for authorization token expiration in Spring is 12 hours.
- scope—This defines the scope for which this access token is valid.

Now that we have retrieved a valid access token from the authorization server, we can decode the JWT with https://jwt.io to retrieve all the access token information. Figure 9.23 shows the results of the decoded JWT.

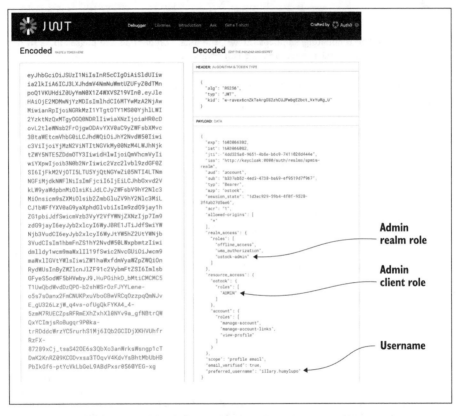

Figure 9.23   Looking up user information based on the issued access token

9.4   *Protecting the organization service using Keycloak*

Once we've registered a client in our Keycloak server and set up individual user accounts with roles, we can begin exploring how to protect a resource using Spring Security and the Keycloak Spring Boot Adapter. While the creation and management of access tokens is the Keycloak server's responsibility, in Spring, the definition of which user roles have permissions to do what actions occurs at the individual service level. To set up a protected resource, we need to take the following actions:

- Add the appropriate Spring Security and Keycloak JARs to the service we're protecting.
- Configure the service to point to our Keycloak server.
- Define what and who can access the service.

Let's start with one of the simplest examples of setting up a protected resource. For that, we'll take our organization service and ensure that it can only be called by an authenticated user.

9.4.1 Adding the Spring Security and Keycloak JARs to the individual services

As usual with Spring microservices, we have to add a couple of dependencies to the organization service's Maven configuration file: organization-service/pom.xml. The following listing shows the new dependencies.

Listing 9.2   Configuring Keycloak and Spring security dependencies

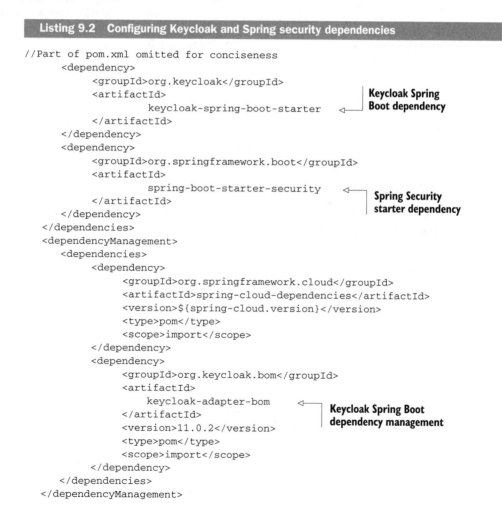

```
//Part of pom.xml omitted for conciseness
    <dependency>
        <groupId>org.keycloak</groupId>
        <artifactId>
            keycloak-spring-boot-starter          Keycloak Spring
        </artifactId>                              Boot dependency
    </dependency>
    <dependency>
        <groupId>org.springframework.boot</groupId>
        <artifactId>
            spring-boot-starter-security          Spring Security
        </artifactId>                             starter dependency
    </dependency>
</dependencies>
<dependencyManagement>
    <dependencies>
        <dependency>
            <groupId>org.springframework.cloud</groupId>
            <artifactId>spring-cloud-dependencies</artifactId>
            <version>${spring-cloud.version}</version>
            <type>pom</type>
            <scope>import</scope>
        </dependency>
        <dependency>
            <groupId>org.keycloak.bom</groupId>
            <artifactId>
                keycloak-adapter-bom              Keycloak Spring Boot
            </artifactId>                         dependency management
            <version>11.0.2</version>
            <type>pom</type>
            <scope>import</scope>
        </dependency>
    </dependencies>
</dependencyManagement>
```

9.4.2 *Configuring the service to point to our Keycloak server*

Once we set up the organization service as a protected resource, every time a call is made to the service, the caller must include the authentication HTTP header containing a Bearer access token to the service. Our protected resource then has to call back to the Keycloak server to see if the token is valid. Listing 9.3 shows the required Keycloak configuration. You need to add this configuration to the organization service's application properties file located in the configuration server repository.

> **Listing 9.3 Keycloak configuration in the organization-service.properties file**

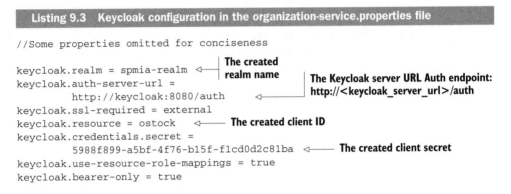

```
//Some properties omitted for conciseness

keycloak.realm = spmia-realm        ⟵──┤ The created
keycloak.auth-server-url =              │ realm name
        http://keycloak:8080/auth   ⟵──────┘ The Keycloak server URL Auth endpoint:
keycloak.ssl-required = external                 http://<keycloak_server_url>/auth
keycloak.resource = ostock          ⟵───── The created client ID
keycloak.credentials.secret =
        5988f899-a5bf-4f76-b15f-f1cd0d2c81ba  ⟵───── The created client secret
keycloak.use-resource-role-mappings = true
keycloak.bearer-only = true
```

> **NOTE** To make the examples more straightforward in this book, we use the classpath repository. You'll find the configuration file in this file: /configserver/src/main/resources/config/organization-service.properties.

9.4.3 *Defining who and what can access the service*

We're now ready to begin defining the access control rules around the service. To define access control rules, we need to extend a `KeycloakWebSecurityConfigurer-Adapter` class and override the following methods:

- `configure()`
- `configureGlobal()`
- `sessionAuthenticationStrategy()`
- `KeycloakConfigResolver()`

The organization service's `SecurityConfig` class is located in the /organizationservice/src/main/java/com/optimagrowth/organization/config/SecurityConfig.java file. The next listing shows the code for this class.

> **Listing 9.4 Extending `SecurityConfig`**

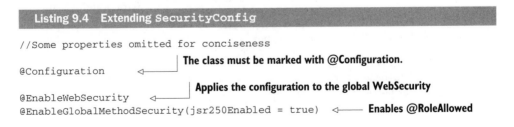

```
//Some properties omitted for conciseness
                                    The class must be marked with @Configuration.
@Configuration          ⟵────────┘
                                    Applies the configuration to the global WebSecurity
@EnableWebSecurity      ⟵────────┘
@EnableGlobalMethodSecurity(jsr250Enabled = true)  ⟵───── Enables @RoleAllowed
```

```
public class SecurityConfig extends
        KeycloakWebSecurityConfigurerAdapter {      Extends
                                                    KeycloakWebSecurityConfigurerAdapter

    @Override
    protected void configure(HttpSecurity http)
            throws Exception {
        super.configure(http);                      Registers the Keycloak
        http.authorizeRequests()                    authentication provider
            .anyRequest()
            .permitAll();
        http.csrf().disable();
    }

    @Autowired
    public void configureGlobal(
            AuthenticationManagerBuilder auth)       Defines the session
            throws Exception {                       authentication strategy
      KeycloakAuthenticationProvider keycloakAuthenticationProvider =
          keycloakAuthenticationProvider();
      keycloakAuthenticationProvider.setGrantedAuthoritiesMapper(
          new SimpleAuthorityMapper());
      auth.authenticationProvider(keycloakAuthenticationProvider);
    }

    @Bean
    @Override
    protected SessionAuthenticationStrategy         Defines the session
            sessionAuthenticationStrategy() {       authentication strategy
        return new RegisterSessionAuthenticationStrategy(
            new SessionRegistryImpl());
    }

    @Bean
    public KeycloakConfigResolver                   By default, the Spring Security Adapter
            KeycloakConfigResolver() {              looks for a keycloak.json file.
        return new KeycloakSpringBootConfigResolver();
    }
}
```

Access rules can range from coarse-grained (any authenticated user can access the entire service) to fine-grained (only the application with this role, but accessing this URL through a DELETE is allowed). We can't discuss every permutation of Spring Security's access control rules, but we can look at several of the more common examples. These examples include protecting a resource so that

- Only authenticated users can access a service URL.
- Only users with a specific role can access a service URL.

PROTECTING A SERVICE WITH AN AUTHENTICATED USER

The first thing we're going to do is to protect the organization service so that it can only be accessed by an authenticated user. The following listing shows how you can build this rule into the `SecurityConfig.java` class.

Listing 9.5   Restricting access to only authenticated users

```
package com.optimagrowth.organization.security;
import org.springframework.context.annotation.Configuration;
import org.springframework.http.HttpMethod;
import
➥ org.springframework.security.config.annotation.web.builders.HttpSecurity;

@Configuration
@EnableWebSecurity
@EnableGlobalMethodSecurity(jsr250Enabled = true)
public class SecurityConfig extends KeycloakWebSecurityConfigurerAdapter {

    @Override
    protected void configure(HttpSecurity http)
            throws Exception {
        super.configure(http);
        http.authorizeRequests()
            .anyRequest().authenticated();
    }
}
```

The HttpSecurity object passed into the method configures all access rules.

All access rules are defined inside the `configure()` method. We'll use the `HttpSecurity` class passed in by Spring to define our rules. In this example, we will restrict all access to any URL in the organization service to authenticated users only.

Suppose we were to access the organization service without an access token present in the HTTP header. In this case, we'd get a 401 HTTP response code and a message indicating that full authentication to the service is required. Figure 9.24 shows the output of a call to the organization service without the authentication HTTP header.

Figure 9.24   Calling the organization service without an access token results in a failed call.

Next, we'll call the organization service *with* an access token. (To generate an access token, see section 9.2.5.) We want to cut and paste the access_token value from the returned JSON call to the `/openid-connect/token` endpoint and use it in our call to the organization service. Remember, when we call the organization service, we need to set the authorization type to Bearer Token with the access_token value. Figure

9.25 shows the callout to the organization service, but this time with an access token passed to it.

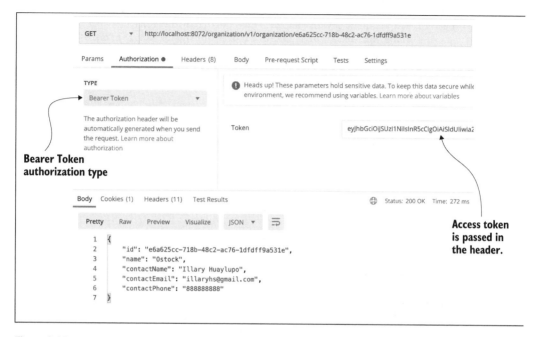

Figure 9.25   Passing in the access token on the call to the organization service

This is probably one of the most straightforward use cases for protecting an endpoint using JWTs. Next, we'll build on this example and restrict access to a specific endpoint for a specific role.

PROTECTING A SERVICE VIA A SPECIFIC ROLE

In the next example, we'll lock down the DELETE call on our organization service to only those users with ADMIN access. As you'll remember from section 9.2.4, we created two user accounts that can access O-stock services: illary.huaylupo and john.carnell. The john.carnell account had the role of USER assigned to it. The illary.huaylupo account had the USER role and the ADMIN role. We can permit specific roles to execute some methods by using @RolesAllowed in the controller. The following listing shows how.

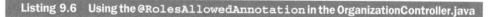

Listing 9.6   Using the @RolesAllowedAnnotation in the OrganizationController.java

```
package com.optimagrowth.organization.security;
//Imports removed for conciseness

@RestController
@RequestMapping(value="v1/organization")
public class OrganizationController {

    @Autowired
```

```
    private OrganizationService service;
```
Indicates that only users with the USER and ADMIN roles can execute this action
```
    @RolesAllowed({ "ADMIN", "USER" })
    @RequestMapping(value="/{organizationId}",method = RequestMethod.GET)
    public ResponseEntity<Organization> getOrganization(
            @PathVariable("organizationId") String organizationId) {
        return ResponseEntity.ok(service.findById(organizationId));
    }


    @RolesAllowed({ "ADMIN", "USER" })
    @RequestMapping(value="/{organizationId}",method = RequestMethod.PUT)
    public void updateOrganization( @PathVariable("organizationId")
                String id, @RequestBody Organization organization) {
        service.update(organization);
    }


    @RolesAllowed({ "ADMIN", "USER" })
    @PostMapping
    public ResponseEntity<Organization>  saveOrganization(
                @RequestBody Organization organization) {
        return ResponseEntity.ok(service.create(organization));
    }
```
Indicates that only users with the ADMIN role can execute this action
```
    @RolesAllowed("ADMIN")
    @DeleteMapping(value="/{organizationId}")
    @ResponseStatus(HttpStatus.NO_CONTENT)
    public void deleteLicense(@PathVariable("organizationId")
                                String organizationId) {
        service.delete(organizationId);
    }
}
```

Now, to obtain the token for john.carnell (password: password1), we need to execute the openid-connect/token POST request again. Once we have the new access token, we then need to call the DELETE endpoint for the organization service: http://localhost:8072/organization/v1/organization/dfd13002-57c5-47ce-a4c2-a1fda2f51513. We'll get a 403 Forbidden HTTP status code on the call and an error message indicating that access was denied for this service. The JSON text returned by our call is shown here:

```
{
    "timestamp": "2020-10-19T01:19:56.534+0000",
    "status": 403,
    "error": "Forbidden",
    "message": "Forbidden",
    "path": "/v1/organization/4d10ec24-141a-4980-be34-2ddb5e0458c7"
}
```

NOTE We use the 8072 port because it is the port we defined for the Spring Cloud Gateway in the previous chapter (specifically in the gateway-server.yml configuration file located in the Spring Cloud Configuration service repository).

If we tried the same call using the illary.huaylupo user account (password: password1) and its access token, we'd see a successful call that returns no content and the

HTTP status code 204, No Content. At this point, we've looked at how to call and protect a single service (the organization service) with Keycloak. However, often in a microservice environment, we will have multiple service calls to carry out a single transaction. In these types of situations, we need to ensure that the access token is propagated from service call to service call.

9.4.4 Propagating the access token

To demonstrate propagating a token between services, we'll protect our licensing service with Keycloak as well. Remember, the licensing service calls the organization service to look up information. The question becomes, how do we propagate the token from one service to another?

We're going to set up a simple example where we'll have the licensing service call the organization service. If you followed the examples we built in the previous chapters, you'd see that both services are running behind a gateway. Figure 9.26 shows how an authenticated user's token will flow through the gateway, the licensing service, and then down to the organization service.

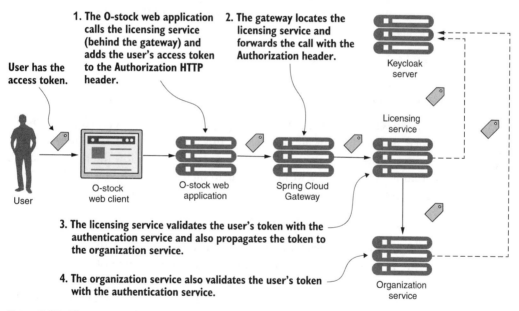

Figure 9.26   The access token must be carried throughout the entire call chain.

Here's what takes place in figure 9.26. Numbers corresponding to those in figure 9.26 are indicated in parentheses in the following.

- The user has already authenticated with the Keycloak server and places a call to the O-stock web application. The user's access token is stored in the user's session. The O-stock web application needs to retrieve some licensing data and call the licensing service REST endpoint (1). As part of the call to the licensing

REST endpoint, the O-stock web application adds the access token via the HTTP `Authorization` header. The licensing service is only accessible behind a Spring Cloud Gateway.

- The gateway looks up the licensing service endpoint and then forwards the call to one of the licensing service's servers (2). The services gateway copies the authorization HTTP header from the incoming call and ensures that the HTTP header is forwarded on to the new endpoint.
- The licensing service receives the incoming call. Because the licensing service is a protected resource, the licensing service will validate the token with the Keycloak server (3) and then check the user's roles for the appropriate permissions. As part of its work, the licensing service invokes the organization service. When doing this, the licensing service needs to propagate the user's access token to the organization service.
- When the organization service receives the call, it takes the HTTP `Authorization` header and validates the token with the Keycloak server (4).

To implement these steps, we need to make several changes to our code. If we don't do this, we will get the following error while retrieving the organization information from the licensing service:

```
message": "401 : {[status:401,
error: Unauthorized
message: Unauthorized,
path: /v1/organization/d898a142-de44-466c-8c88-9ceb2c2429d3}]
```

The first step is to modify the gateway so that it propagates the access token to the licensing service. By default, the gateway doesn't forward sensitive HTTP headers like cookie, set-cookie, and authorization to downstream services. To allow the propagation of the authorization HTTP header, we need to add to each route the following filter in the gateway-server.yml configuration file located in the Spring Cloud Config repository:

```
- RemoveRequestHeader= Cookie,Set-Cookie
```

This configuration is a blacklist of the sensitive headers that the gateway will keep from being propagated to a downstream service. The absence of the `Authorization` value in the `RemoveRequestHeader` list means that the gateway will allow that header through. If we don't set this configuration property, the gateway automatically blocks the propagation of all three values (`Cookie`, `Set-Cookie`, and `Authorization`).

Next, we need to configure our licensing service to include the Keycloak and Spring Security dependencies and set up any authorization rules we want for the service. Finally, we need to add the Keycloak properties to the application properties file in the configuration server.

CONFIGURING THE LICENSING SERVICE

When propagating access tokens, our first step is to add the Maven dependencies to our licensing service pom.xml file. The following listing shows the dependencies.

Listing 9.7 Configuring Keycloak and Spring Security dependencies

```
//Part of pom.xml omitted for conciseness
    <dependency>
        <groupId>org.keycloak</groupId>
        <artifactId>keycloak-spring-boot-starter</artifactId>
    </dependency>
    <dependency>
        <groupId>org.springframework.boot</groupId>
        <artifactId>spring-boot-starter-security</artifactId>
    </dependency>
</dependencies>
<dependencyManagement>
    <dependencies>
        <dependency>
            <groupId>org.springframework.cloud</groupId>
            <artifactId>spring-cloud-dependencies</artifactId>
            <version>${spring-cloud.version}</version>
            <type>pom</type>
            <scope>import</scope>
        </dependency>
        <dependency>
            <groupId>org.keycloak.bom</groupId>
            <artifactId>keycloak-adapter-bom</artifactId>
            <version>11.0.2</version>
            <type>pom</type>
            <scope>import</scope>
        </dependency>
    </dependencies>
</dependencyManagement>
```

The next step is to protect the licensing service so that it can only be accessed by an authenticated user. The following listing shows the `SecurityConfig` class. You'll find the source code for this class in /licensing-service/src/main/java/com/optimagrowth/ license/config/SecurityConfig.java.

Listing 9.8 Restricting access to authenticated users only

```
//Part of class declaration omitted for conciseness

@Configuration
@EnableWebSecurity
public class SecurityConfig extends KeycloakWebSecurityConfigurerAdapter {

  @Override
  protected void configure(HttpSecurity http) throws Exception {
      super.configure(http);
      http.authorizeRequests()
            .anyRequest().authenticated();
            http.csrf().disable();
  }
  @Override
  protected void configure(HttpSecurity http) throws Exception {
      super.configure(http);
      http.authorizeRequests()
```

```
            .anyRequest().authenticated();
        http.csrf().disable();
    }

    @Autowired
    public void configureGlobal(AuthenticationManagerBuilder auth)
                                              throws Exception {
        KeycloakAuthenticationProvider keycloakAuthenticationProvider =
                                  keycloakAuthenticationProvider();
        keycloakAuthenticationProvider.setGrantedAuthoritiesMapper(new
                                  SimpleAuthorityMapper());
        auth.authenticationProvider(keycloakAuthenticationProvider);
    }

    @Bean
    @Override
    protected SessionAuthenticationStrategy sessionAuthenticationStrategy() {
        return new RegisterSessionAuthenticationStrategy(
                new SessionRegistryImpl());
    }

    @Bean
    public KeycloakConfigResolver KeycloakConfigResolver() {
        return new KeycloakSpringBootConfigResolver();
    }
}
```

The final step in configuring the licensing service is to add the Keycloak configuration to our licensing-service.properties file. The following listing shows how this file should look.

Listing 9.9 Configuring Keycloak in licensing-service.properties

```
//Some properties omitted for conciseness

keycloak.realm = spmia-realm
keycloak.auth-server-url = http://keycloak:8080/auth
keycloak.ssl-required = external
keycloak.resource = ostock
keycloak.credentials.secret = 5988f899-a5bf-4f76-b15f-f1cd0d2c81ba
keycloak.use-resource-role-mappings = true
keycloak.bearer-only = true
```

Now that we have the gateway changes to propagate the authorization header and the licensing service set up, we can move on to our final step, which is to propagate the access token. All we need to do for this step is to modify how the code in the licensing service calls the organization service. For that, we need to ensure that the HTTP `Authorization` header is injected into the application call to the organization service.

Without Spring Security, we'd have to write a servlet filter to grab the HTTP header of the incoming licensing service call and then manually add it to every outbound service call in the licensing service. Keycloak provides a new REST template class that supports these calls. The class is called `KeycloakRestTemplate`. To use this class, we first need to expose it as a bean that can be autowired into a service calling another protected service. We'll do this in the /licensing-service/src/main/java/com/optimagrowth/license/config/SecurityConfig.java file by adding the code in the following listing.

Listing 9.10   Exposing `KeycloakRestTemplate` in `SecurityConfig`

```
package com.optimagrowth.license.service.client;
//Part of class definition omitted for conciseness

@ComponentScan(basePackageClasses = KeycloakSecurityComponents.class)
public class SecurityConfig extends KeycloakWebSecurityConfigurerAdapter {

    ...

    @Autowired
    public KeycloakClientRequestFactory keycloakClientRequestFactory;

    @Bean      #A
    @Scope(ConfigurableBeanFactory.SCOPE_PROTOTYPE)
    public KeycloakRestTemplate keycloakRestTemplate() {
        return new KeycloakRestTemplate(keycloakClientRequestFactory);
    }

    ...

}
```

To see the KeycloakRestTemplate class in action, we can look in the Organization-RestTemplateClient class found in /licensing-service/src/main/java/com/optimagrowth/license/service/client/OrganizationRestTemplateClient.java.   The following listing shows how KeycloakRestTemplate is autowired to this class.

Listing 9.11   Using `KeycloakRestTemplate` to propagate the access token

```
package com.optimagrowth.license.service.client;
//Imports removed for conciseness

@Component
public class OrganizationRestTemplateClient {
    @Autowired
    KeycloakRestTemplate restTemplate;       ⟵──  KeycloakRestTemplate is a drop-in
                                                  replacement for the standard
                                                  RestTemplate. It handles the
                                                  propagation of the access token.

    public Organization getOrganization(String organizationId){
        ResponseEntity<Organization> restExchange =          ⟵─────────
            restTemplate.exchange("http://gateway:8072/organization/
                            v1/organization/{organizationId}",
                        HttpMethod.GET,
                        null, Organization.class, organizationId);

        return restExchange.getBody();      The invocation of the organization service is done in
    }                                       the exact same manner as a standard RestTemplate.
}                                           Here, we point to the gateway server.
```

To test this code, you can request a service in the licensing service that calls the organization service to retrieve the data. For example, the following service retrieves the data of a specific license and then gets the associated information for the organization. Figure 9.27 shows the output of this call:

```
http://localhost:8072/license/v1/organization/d898a142-de44-466c-8c88-
    9ceb2c2429d3/license/f2a9c9d4-d2c0-44fa-97fe-724d77173c62
```

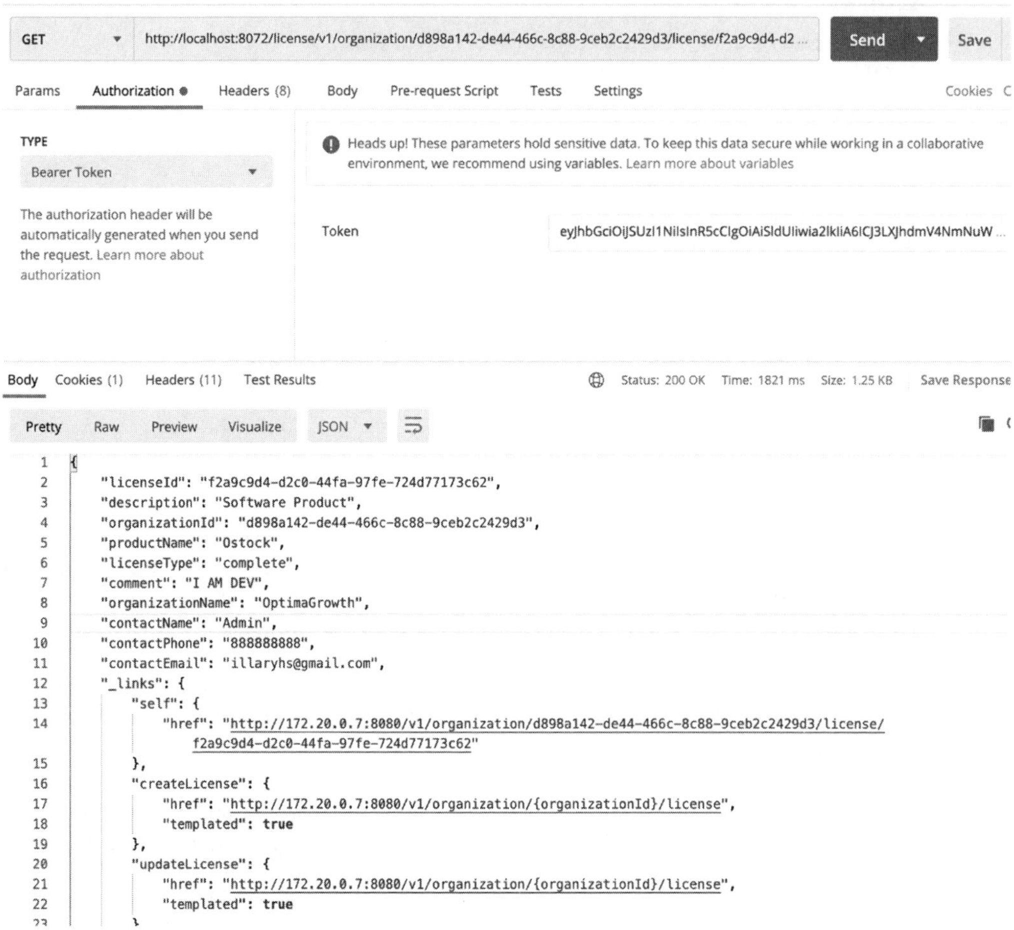

Figure 9.27   Passing the access token from the licensing service to the organization service

9.4.5   *Parsing a custom field in a JWT*

We're going to turn to our gateway for an example of how to parse a custom field in a JWT. Specifically, we'll modify the `TrackingFilter` class that we introduced in chapter 8 to decode the `preferred_username` field from the JWT flowing through the gateway. To do this, we'll pull in a JWT parser library and add it to the Gateway server's pom.xml file. Multiple token parsers are available, but we chose the Apache Commons Codec and the org.json package to parse the JSON body.

```
<dependency>
     <groupId>commons-codec</groupId>
     <artifactId>commons-codec</artifactId>
</dependency>
<dependency>
     <groupId>org.json</groupId>
     <artifactId>json</artifactId>
     <version>20190722</version>
</dependency>
```

Once the libraries are added, we can then add a new method called getUsername() to the tracking filter. The following listing shows this new method. You'll find the source code for this method in the class file at /gatewayserver/src/main/java/com/optimagrowth/gateway/filters/TrackingFilter.java.

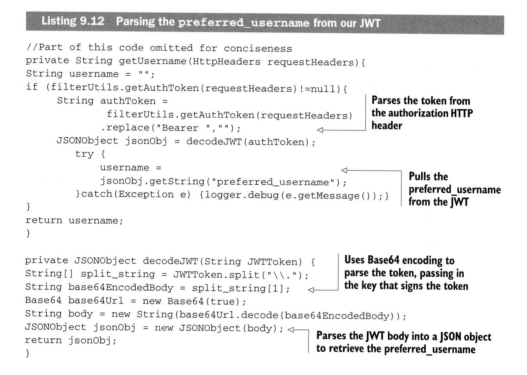

> **Listing 9.12 Parsing the `preferred_username` from our JWT**

```
//Part of this code omitted for conciseness
private String getUsername(HttpHeaders requestHeaders){
String username = "";
if (filterUtils.getAuthToken(requestHeaders)!=null){
    String authToken =
            filterUtils.getAuthToken(requestHeaders)        ⟵ Parses the token from
            .replace("Bearer ","");                            the authorization HTTP
    JSONObject jsonObj = decodeJWT(authToken);                 header
        try {
            username =                                   ⟵
            jsonObj.getString("preferred_username");          Pulls the
        }catch(Exception e) {logger.debug(e.getMessage());}   preferred_username
}                                                             from the JWT
return username;
}

private JSONObject decodeJWT(String JWTToken) {      Uses Base64 encoding to
String[] split_string = JWTToken.split("\\.");      parse the token, passing in
String base64EncodedBody = split_string[1];      ⟵ the key that signs the token
Base64 base64Url = new Base64(true);
String body = new String(base64Url.decode(base64EncodedBody));
JSONObject jsonObj = new JSONObject(body);  ⟵
return jsonObj;                                Parses the JWT body into a JSON object
}                                              to retrieve the preferred_username
```

To make this example work, we need to make sure the AUTH_TOKEN variable in Filter-Utils is set to Authorization as in the following code snippet. (You'll find the source for this in /gatewayserver/src/main/java/com/optimagrowth/gateway/filters/Filter-Utils.java.)

```
public static final String AUTH_TOKEN = "Authorization";
```

Once we implement the getUsername() function, we can add a System.out.println to the filter() method on the tracking filter to print the preferred_username parsed from our JWT that's flowing through the gateway. Now when we make a call to the gateway, we'll see the `preferred_username` in the console output.

> **NOTE** When you make this call, you still need to set up all the HTTP form parameters, including the HTTP `Authorization` header and the JWT.

If everything was successful, you should see the following `System.out.println` in your console log:

```
tmx-correlation-id found in tracking filter:
        26f2b2b7-51f0-4574-9d84-07e563577641.
The authentication name from the token is : illary.huaylupo
```

9.5 *Some closing thoughts on microservice security*

While this chapter has introduced you to OpenID, OAuth2, and the Keycloak specification and how you can use Spring Cloud security with Keycloak to implement an authentication and authorization service, Keycloak is only one piece of the microservice security puzzle. As you shape your microservices for production use, you should also build your microservice security around the following practices:

- Use HTTPS/Secure Sockets Layer (SSL) for all service communications.
- Use an API gateway for all service calls.
- Provide zones for your services (for example, a public API and private API).
- Limit the attack surface of your microservices by locking down unneeded network ports.

Figure 9.28 shows how these different pieces fit together. Each of the bulleted items in the list maps to the numbers in figure 9.28. We'll examine each of the topic areas enumerated in the previous list and in the figure in more detail throughout the next sections.

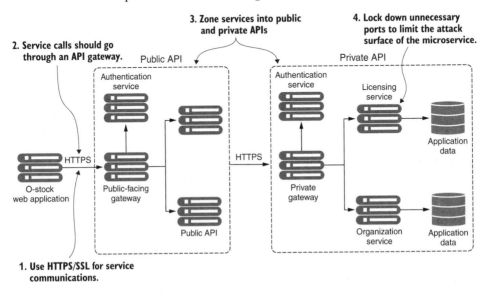

Figure 9.28 A microservice security architecture is more than implementing authentication and authorization.

9.5.1 Use HTTPS secure sockets layer (SSL) for all service communication

In all the code examples in this book, we've used HTTP because HTTP is a simple protocol and doesn't require setting up on every service before you start using the service. In a production environment, however, your microservices should communicate only through the encrypted channels provided through HTTPS and SSL. Note that the configuration and setup of HTTPS can be automated through your DevOps scripts.

9.5.2 Use a service gateway to access your microservices

The individual servers, service endpoints, and ports your services are running on should never be directly accessible to the client. Instead, use a service gateway to act as an entry point and gatekeeper for your service calls. Configure the network layer on the operating system or container that your microservices are running in to only accept traffic from the service gateway. Remember, the service gateway can act as a Policy Enforcement Point (PEP), which can be enforced in all services.

Putting service calls through a service gateway allows you to be consistent in how you're securing and auditing your services. A service gateway also allows you to lock down what port and endpoints you're going to expose to the outside world.

9.5.3 Zone your services into a public API and private API

Security, in general, is all about building layers of access and enforcing the concept of *least privilege.* Least privilege implies that a user should have only the bare minimum network access and privileges to do their day-to-day job. To this end, you should implement least privilege by separating your services into two distinct zones: public and private.

The public zone contains all the public APIs that will be consumed by your clients (in this book's examples, the O-stock application). Public API microservices should carry out narrow tasks that are workflow oriented. These microservices tend to be service aggregators, pulling data and carrying out tasks across multiple services. Public microservices should also be behind their own service gateway and have their own authentication service for performing authentication and authorization. Access to public services by client applications should go through a single route protected by the service gateway. Also, the public zone should have its own authentication service.

The private zone acts as a wall to protect your core application functionality and data. It should only be accessible through a single, well-known port and should be locked down to only accept network traffic from the network subnet where the private services are running. The private zone should have its own gateway and authentication service. Public API services should authenticate against the private zone's authentication service. All application data should at least be in the private zone's network subnet and only accessible by microservices residing in the private zone.

9.5.4 *Limit the attack surface of your microservices by locking down unneeded network ports*

Many developers don't take a hard look at the absolute minimum number of ports they need to open for their services to function. Configure the operating system your service is running on to only allow inbound and outbound access to the ports or a piece of infrastructure needed by your service (monitoring, log aggregation).

Don't focus only on inbound access ports. Many developers forget to lock down their outbound ports. Locking down your outbound ports can prevent data from being leaked out of your service if an attacker has compromised the service itself. Also, make sure you look at network port access in both your public and private API zones.

Summary

- OAuth2 is a token-based authorization framework that provides different mechanisms for protecting web service calls. These mechanisms are called *grants*.
- OpenID Connect (OIDC) is a layer on top of the OAuth2 framework that provides authentication and profile information about who is logged in to the application (identity).
- Keycloak is an open source identity and access management solution for microservices and applications. The main objective of Keycloak is to facilitate the protection of the services and applications with little or no code.
- Each application can have its own Keycloak application name and secret key.
- Each service must define what actions a role can take.
- Spring Cloud Security supports the JSON Web Token (JWT) specification. With JWT, we can inject custom fields into the specification.
- Securing our microservices involves more than just using authentication and authorization.
- In a production environment, we should use HTTPS to encrypt all calls between services.
- Use a service gateway to narrow the number of access points through which a service can be reached.
- Limit the attack surface for a service by limiting the number of inbound and outbound ports on the operating system that the service is running on.

Event-driven architecture
with Spring Cloud Stream

10

This chapter covers

- Understanding event-driven architecture processing and its relevance
- Using Spring Cloud Stream to simplify event processing
- Configuring Spring Cloud Stream
- Publishing messages with Spring Cloud Stream and Kafka
- Consuming messages with Spring Cloud Stream and Kafka
- Implementing distributed caching with Spring Cloud Stream, Kafka, and Redis

Human beings are always in a state of motion as they interact with their environment. Typically, their conversations aren't synchronous, linear, or as narrowly defined as a request-response model. It's something more like message-driven, where we're constantly sending and receiving messages from the things around us. As we receive messages, we react to those messages, often interrupting the primary task that we're working on.

This chapter is about how to design and implement our Spring-based microservices to communicate with other microservices using asynchronous messages. Using asynchronous messages to communicate between applications isn't new. What's new is the concept of using messages to communicate events representing changes in state. This concept is called event-driven architecture (EDA). It's also known as message-driven architecture (MDA). What an EDA-based approach allows us to do is to build highly decoupled systems that can react to changes without being tightly coupled to specific libraries or services. When combined with microservices, EDA allows us to quickly add new functionality to our application by merely having the service listen to the stream of events (messages) being emitted by our application.

The Spring Cloud project makes it trivial to build message-based solutions through the Spring Cloud Stream subproject. Spring Cloud Stream allows us to easily implement message publication and consumption while shielding our services from the implementation details associated with the underlying messaging platform.

10.1   *The case for messaging, EDA, and microservices*

Why is messaging important in building microservice-based applications? To answer that question, let's start with an example. For this, we'll use the two services that we've used throughout the book: our licensing and organization services.

Let's imagine that after these services are deployed to production, we find that the licensing service calls are taking an exceedingly long time when looking up information from the organization service. When we look at the usage patterns of the organization data, we find that the organization data rarely changes and that most of the data reads from the organization service are done by the primary key of the organization record. If we could cache the reads for the organization data without having to incur the cost of accessing a database, we could significantly improve the response time of the licensing service calls. To implement a caching solution, we need to consider the following three core requirements:

1   *Cached data needs to be consistent across all instances of the licensing service.* This means that we can't cache the data locally within the licensing service because we want to guarantee that the same organization data is read regardless of the service instance hitting it.

2   *We cannot cache the organization data within the memory of the container hosting the licensing service.* The run-time container hosting our service is often restricted in size and can obtain data using different access patterns. A local cache can introduce complexity because we have to guarantee our local cache is in sync with all of the other services in the cluster.

3   *When an organization record changes via an update or delete, we want the licensing service to recognize that there has been a state change in the organization service.* The licensing service should then invalidate any cached data it has for that specific organization and evict it from the cache.

Let's look at two approaches to implement these requirements. The first approach will implement the previously stated requirements using a synchronous request-response model. When the organization state changes, the licensing and organization services will communicate back and forth via their REST endpoints.

For the second approach, the organization service will emit an asynchronous event (message) to communicate that its organization data has changed. The organization service will then publish a message to a queue, which will indicate that an organization record was updated or deleted—a change in state. The licensing service will listen with an intermediary (message broker or queue) to determine if an organization event occurred, and if so, clear the organization data from its cache.

10.1.1 *Using a synchronous request-response approach to communicate state change*

For our organization data cache, we're going to use Redis (https://redis.io/), a distributed key-value store used as a database, cache, or message broker. Figure 10.1 provides a high-level overview of how to build a caching solution using a traditional synchronous request-response programming model such as Redis.

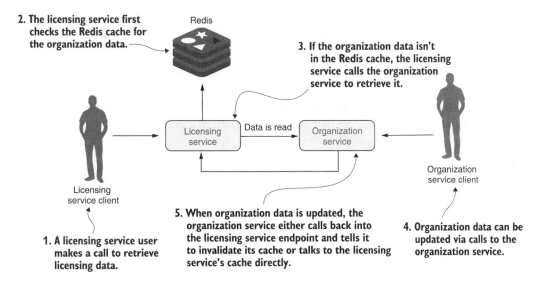

2. The licensing service first checks the Redis cache for the organization data.

Redis

3. If the organization data isn't in the Redis cache, the licensing service calls the organization service to retrieve it.

Licensing service — Data is read → Organization service

Organization service client

Licensing service client

1. A licensing service user makes a call to retrieve licensing data.

5. When organization data is updated, the organization service either calls back into the licensing service endpoint and tells it to invalidate its cache or talks to the licensing service's cache directly.

4. Organization data can be updated via calls to the organization service.

Figure 10.1 In a synchronous request-response model, tightly coupled services introduce complexity and brittleness.

In figure 10.1, when a user calls the licensing service, the licensing service will need to look up the organization data. To do so, the licensing service will first retrieve the desired organization by its ID from a Redis cluster. If the licensing service can't find the organization data, it will then call the organization service using a REST-based endpoint, storing the data returned in Redis before returning the organization data back to the user.

If someone updates or deletes the organization record using the organization service's REST endpoint, the organization service will need to call an endpoint exposed on the licensing service and tell it to invalidate the organization data in its cache. In figure 10.1, if we look at where the organization service calls back into the licensing service to tell it to invalidate the Redis cache, we can see at least three problems:

- The organization and licensing services are tightly coupled. This coupling introduces brittleness between the services.
- If the licensing service endpoint for invalidating the cache changes, the organization service has to change. This approach is inflexible.
- We can't add new consumers of the organization data without modifying the code on the organization service to verify that it calls the licensing service to let it know about any changes.

TIGHT COUPLING BETWEEN SERVICES

To retrieve data, the licensing service is dependent on the organization service. However, by having the organization service directly communicate back to the licensing service when an organization record is updated or deleted, we've introduced coupling from the organization service back to the licensing service (figure 10.1). For the data in the Redis cache to be invalidated, the organization service either needs an exposed endpoint on the licensing service that can be called to invalidate its Redis cache, or the organization service needs to talk directly to the Redis server owned by the licensing service to clear the data in it.

Having the organization service talk to Redis has its own problems because we're talking to a data store owned directly by another service. In a microservice environment, this a big no-no. While one can argue that the organization data rightly belongs to the organization service, the licensing service uses it in a specific context and could potentially transform the data or build business rules around it. If the organization service talks directly to the Redis service, it can accidentally break rules implemented by the team owning the licensing service.

BRITTLENESS BETWEEN THE SERVICES

The tight coupling between the licensing service and the organization service also introduced brittleness between the two services. If the licensing service is down or running slowly, the organization service can be impacted since the organization service is now communicating directly with the licensing service. Again, if the organization service talks directly to the licensing service's Redis data store, we create a dependency between the organization service and Redis. In this scenario, any problem with the shared Redis server now has the potential to take down both services.

INFLEXIBILITY IN ADDING NEW CONSUMERS TO CHANGES IN THE ORGANIZATION SERVICE

With the model in figure 10.1, if we had another service that was interested in the organization data changes, we'd need to add another call from the organization service to the other service. This means a code change and redeployment of the organization service, which can introduce a state of inflexibility in our code.

If we use the synchronous, request-response model for communicating state change, we start to see a web-like pattern of dependency between our core services in our application and other services. The centers of these webs become our major points of failure within our application.

> **Another kind of coupling**
>
> While messaging adds a layer of indirection between our services, we can introduce tight coupling between two services. Later in this chapter, we'll send messages between the organization and licensing services. These messages are going to be serialized and deserialized to a Java object using JSON formatting for the message. Changes to the structure of the JSON message can cause problems when converting back and forth to Java if the two services don't gracefully handle different versions of the same message type.
>
> JSON doesn't natively support versioning. However, we can use Apache Avro (https://avro.apache.org/) if we need that. Avro is a binary protocol that has versioning built into it. Spring Cloud Stream supports Apache Avro as a messaging protocol. Unfortunately, using Avro is outside the scope of this book, but we did want to make you aware that it helps if you truly need to consider message versioning.

10.1.2 *Using messaging to communicate state changes between services*

We're going to inject a topic between the licensing and organization service with a messaging approach. The messaging system won't be used to read data from the organization service but will instead be used by the organization service to publish any state changes within the data managed by the organization service when these occur. Figure 10.2 demonstrates this approach.

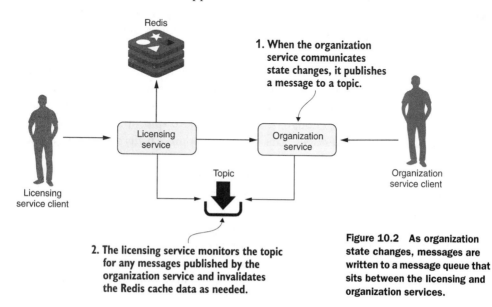

Redis

1. When the organization service communicates state changes, it publishes a message to a topic.

Licensing service

Organization service

Topic

Licensing service client

Organization service client

2. The licensing service monitors the topic for any messages published by the organization service and invalidates the Redis cache data as needed.

Figure 10.2 As organization state changes, messages are written to a message queue that sits between the licensing and organization services.

In the model in figure 10.2, when organization data changes, the organization service publishes a message to a topic. The licensing service monitors the topic for messages, and when a message arrives, it clears the appropriate organization record from the Redis cache. When it comes to communicating state, the message queue acts as an intermediary between the licensing and organization services. This approach offers four benefits: loose coupling, durability, scalability, and flexibility. We'll look at each in the following sections.

LOOSE COUPLING

A microservices application can be composed of dozens of small and distributed services that interact with each other and the data managed by one another. As we saw with the synchronous design proposed earlier, a synchronous HTTP response creates a hard dependency between the licensing and organization services. We can't eliminate these dependencies completely, but we can try to minimize dependencies by only exposing endpoints that directly manage the data owned by the service.

A messaging approach allows us to decouple the two services because, when it comes to communicating state changes, neither service knows about each other. When the organization service needs to publish a state change, it writes a message to a queue. The licensing service only knows that it gets a message; it has no idea who has published the message.

DURABILITY

The presence of the queue allows us to guarantee that a message will be delivered even if the consumer of the service is down. For example, the organization service can keep publishing messages even if the licensing service is unavailable. The messages are stored in the queue and stay there until the licensing service becomes available. Conversely, with the combination of a cache and the queue approach, if the organization service is down, the licensing service can degrade gracefully because at least part of the organization data will be in its cache. Sometimes old data is better than no data.

SCALABILITY

Because messages are stored in a queue, the sender of the message doesn't have to wait for a response from the message consumer. The sender can go on its way and continue working. Likewise, if a consumer reading a message from the queue isn't processing messages fast enough, it's a trivial task to spin up more consumers and have them process the messages. This scalability approach fits well within a microservices model.

One of the things we've emphasized throughout this book is that it should be trivial to spin up new instances of a microservice. The additional microservice can then become another service to process the message queue. This is an example of scaling horizontally.

Traditional scaling mechanisms for reading messages in a queue involved increasing the number of threads that a message consumer could process at one time. Unfortunately, with this approach, we were ultimately limited by the number of CPUs available to the message consumer. A microservice model doesn't have this limitation because we can scale by increasing the number of machines hosting the service consuming the messages.

FLEXIBILITY

The sender of a message has no idea who is going to consume it. This means we can easily add new message consumers (and new functionality) without impacting the original sending service. This is an extremely powerful concept because new functionality can be added to an application without having to touch existing services. Instead, the new code can listen for events being published and react to them accordingly.

10.1.3 Downsides of a messaging architecture

Like any architectural model, a message-based architecture has trade-offs. A message-based architecture can be complicated and requires the development team to pay close attention to several key things, including message-handling semantics, message visibility, and message choreography. Let's look at these in more detail.

MESSAGE-HANDLING SEMANTICS

Using messages in a microservice-based application requires more than understanding how to publish and consume messages. It requires that we understand how our application will behave based on the order in which messages are consumed and what happens if a message is processed out of order. For example, if we have strict requirements that all orders from a single customer must be processed in the order they are received, we'll need to set up and structure our message handling differently than if every message can be consumed independently of one another.

It also means that if we're using messaging to enforce strict state transitions of our data, we need to think about designing our applications to take into consideration scenarios where a message throws an exception or an error is processed out of order. If a message fails, do we retry processing the error or do we let it fail? How do we handle future messages related to that customer if one of the customer's messages fails? These are important questions to think through.

MESSAGE VISIBILITY

Using messages in our microservices often means a mix of synchronous service calls and asynchronous service processing. The asynchronous nature of messages means they might not be received or processed in close proximity to when the message is published or consumed. Also, having things like correlation IDs for tracking a user's transactions across web service invocations and messages is critical to understanding and debugging what's going on in our application. As you may remember from chapter 8, a correlation ID is a unique number that's generated at the start of a user's transaction and passed along with every service call. It should also be passed along with every message that's published and consumed.

MESSAGE CHOREOGRAPHY

As alluded to in the section on message visibility, a message-based application makes it more difficult to reason through its business logic because its code is no longer processed in a linear fashion with a simple block request-response model. Instead, debugging message-based applications can involve wading through the logs of several different services, where user transactions can be executed out of order and at different times.

> **NOTE** Messaging can be complicated but powerful. In the previous sections, we didn't mean to scare you away from using messaging in your applications. Instead, our goal was to highlight that using messaging in your services requires forethought. A positive side of messaging is that businesses themselves work asynchronously, so in the end, we are modeling our business more closely.

10.2 Introducing Spring Cloud Stream

Spring Cloud makes it easy to integrate messaging into our Spring-based microservices. It does this through the Spring Cloud Stream project (https://spring.io/projects/spring-cloud-stream), which is an annotation-driven framework that allows us to easily build message publishers and consumers in our Spring applications.

Spring Cloud Stream also allows us to abstract away the implementation details of the messaging platform that we're using. We can use multiple message platforms with Spring Cloud Stream, including the Apache Kafka project and RabbitMQ, and the platform's implementation-specific details are kept out of the application code. The implementation of message publication and consumption in your application is done through platform-neutral Spring interfaces.

> **NOTE** For this chapter, we'll use a message bus called Kafka (https://kafka.apache.org/). Kafka is a highly performant message bus that allows us to asynchronously send streams of messages from one application to one or more other applications. Written in Java, Kafka is the de facto message bus for many cloud-based applications because it's highly reliable and scalable. Spring Cloud Stream also supports the use of RabbitMQ as a message bus.

To understand Spring Cloud Stream, let's begin with a discussion of its architecture and familiarize ourselves with some terminology. The new terminology can be somewhat overwhelming if you've never worked with a message-based platform before, so let's begin our discussion by looking at the Spring Cloud Stream architecture through the lens of two services communicating via messaging. One service is the message publisher, and one service is the message consumer. Figure 10.3 shows how Spring Cloud Stream is used to facilitate this message passing.

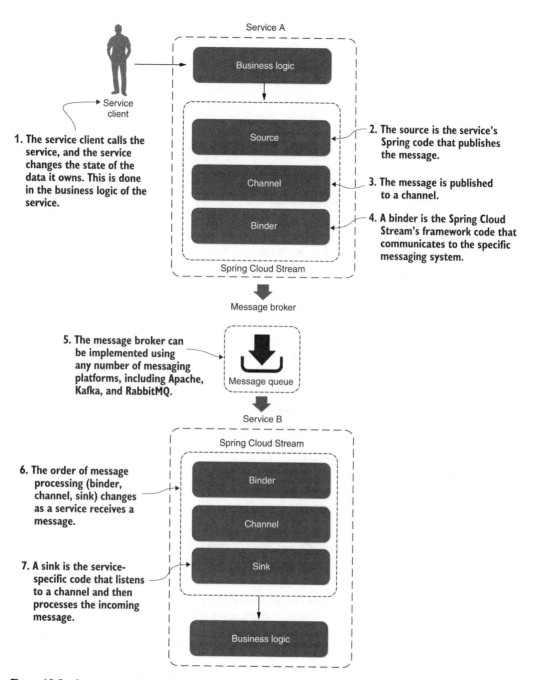

Figure 10.3 As a message is published and consumed, it flows through a series of Spring Cloud Stream components that abstract away the underlying messaging platform.

With Spring Cloud, four components are involved in publishing and consuming a message:

- Source
- Channel
- Binder
- Sink

When a service gets ready to publish a message, it will publish the message using a *source*. A source is a Spring-annotated interface that takes a Plain Old Java Object (POJO), which represents the message to be published. The source takes the message, serializes it (the default serialization is JSON), and publishes the message to a channel.

A *channel* is an abstraction over the queue that's going to hold the message after it's published by a message producer or consumed by a message consumer. In other words, we can describe a channel as a queue that sends and receives messages. A channel name is always associated with a target queue name, but that queue name is never directly exposed to the code. Instead, the channel name is used in the code, which means that we can switch the queues the channel reads or writes from by changing the application's configuration, not the application's code.

The *binder* is part of the Spring Cloud Stream framework. It's the Spring code that talks to a specific message platform. The binder part of the Spring Cloud Stream framework allows us to work with messages without having to be exposed to platform-specific libraries and APIs for publishing and consuming messages.

In Spring Cloud Stream, when a service receives a message from a queue, it does it through a *sink*. A sink listens to a channel for incoming messages and deserializes the message back into a POJO object. From there, the message can be processed by the business logic of the Spring service.

10.3 *Writing a simple message producer and consumer*

Now that we've walked through the essential components in Spring Cloud Stream, let's look at a simple Spring Cloud Stream example. For the first example, we'll pass a message from our organization service to our licensing service, which prints a log message to the console. In addition, because we'll only have one Spring Cloud Stream source (the message producer) and a sink (message consumer) in this example, we'll start the example with a few simple Spring Cloud shortcuts. This will make setting up the source in the organization service and in a sink in the licensing service trivial. Figure 10.4 highlights the message producer and builds on the general Spring Cloud Stream architecture from figure 10.3.

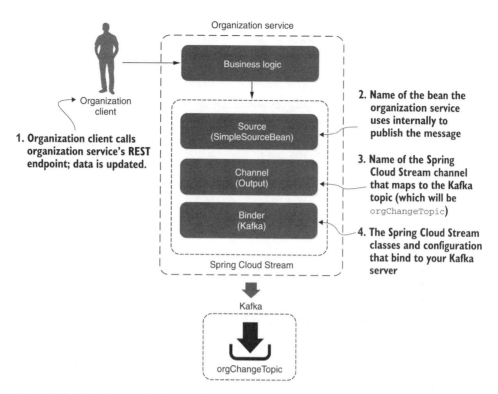

Figure 10.4 When the organization service data changes, it publishes a message to `orgChangeTopic`.

10.3.1 *Configuring Apache Kafka and Redis in Docker*

In this section, we'll explain how to add the Kafka and Redis services to our Docker environment for our message producer. To achieve this, let's start by adding the code shown in the following listing to our docker-compose.yml file.

Listing 10.1 Adding Kafka and Redis services to docker-compose.yml

```
//Parts of docker-compose.yml removed for conciseness
...

zookeeper:
    image: wurstmeister/zookeeper:latest
    ports:
      - 2181:2181
    networks:
      backend:
        aliases:
          - "zookeeper"
  kafkaserver:
    image: wurstmeister/kafka:latest
    ports:
      - 9092:9092
```

```
   environment:
     - KAFKA_ADVERTISED_HOST_NAME=kafka
     - KAFKA_ADVERTISED_PORT=9092
     - KAFKA_ZOOKEEPER_CONNECT=zookeeper:2181
     - KAFKA_CREATE_TOPICS=dresses:1:1,ratings:1:1
   volumes:
     - "/var/run/docker.sock:/var/run/docker.sock"
   depends_on:
     - zookeeper
   networks:
     backend:
       aliases:
         - "kafka"
redisserver:
  image: redis:alpine
  ports:
    - 6379:6379
  networks:
    backend:
      aliases:
        - "redis"
```

10.3.2 *Writing the message producer in the organization service*

To focus on how to use topics in our architecture, we'll begin by modifying the organization service so that every time organization data is added, updated, or deleted, the organization service will publish a message to a Kafka topic, indicating that an organization change event has occurred. The published message will include the organization ID associated with the change event and what action occurred (add, update, or delete).

The first thing we need to do is set up our Maven dependencies in the organization service's Maven pom.xml file. You'll find the pom.xml file in the root directory for the organization service. In the pom.xml, we need to add two dependencies, one for the core Spring Cloud Stream libraries and the other for the Spring Cloud Stream Kafka libraries:

```xml
<dependency>
    <groupId>org.springframework.cloud</groupId>
    <artifactId>spring-cloud-stream</artifactId>
</dependency>

<dependency>
    <groupId>org.springframework.cloud</groupId>
    <artifactId>spring-cloud-starter-stream-kafka</artifactId>
</dependency>
```

> **NOTE** We're using Docker to run all the examples. If you want to run this locally, you need to have Apache Kafka installed on your computer. If you are using Docker, you can find the up-to-date docker-compose.yml file with the Kafka and Zookeeper containers here: https://github.com/ihuaylupo/manning-smia/tree/master/chapter10/docker.

Remember to execute the services by executing the following commands in the root directory where the parent pom.xml is located:

```
mvn clean package dockerfile:build && docker-compose
          -f docker/docker-compose.yml up
```

Once we've defined the Maven dependencies, we need to tell our application that it's going to bind to a Spring Cloud Stream message broker. We can do this by annotating the organization service's bootstrap class, OrganizationServiceApplication, with @EnableBinding. You'll find the code for this class in /organization-service/src/main/java/com/optimagrowth/organization/OrganizationServiceApplication.java. For your convenience, the following listing shows the OrganizationServiceApplication.java source code.

Listing 10.2 The annotated `OrganizationServiceApplication.java` class

```java
package com.optimagrowth.organization;

import org.springframework.boot.SpringApplication;
import org.springframework.boot.autoconfigure.SpringBootApplication;
import org.springframework.cloud.context.config.annotation.RefreshScope;
import org.springframework.cloud.stream.annotation.EnableBinding;
import org.springframework.cloud.stream.messaging.Source;
import
    org.springframework.security.oauth2.config.annotation.web.configuration.
    EnableResourceServer;

@SpringBootApplication
@RefreshScope
@EnableResourceServer
@EnableBinding(Source.class)       ◁──────  Tells Spring Cloud Stream
public class OrganizationServiceApplication {    to bind the application to
                                                 a message broker
    public static void main(String[] args) {
        SpringApplication.run(OrganizationServiceApplication.class, args);
    }
}
```

In listing 10.2, the @EnableBinding annotation tells Spring Cloud Stream that we want to bind the service to a message broker. The use of Source.class in @EnableBinding tells Spring Cloud Stream that this service will communicate with the message broker via a set of channels defined in the Source class. Remember, channels sit above a message queue. Spring Cloud Stream has a default set of channels that can be configured to speak to a message broker.

At this point, we haven't told Spring Cloud Stream what message broker we want the organization service to bind to. We'll get to that shortly. Now, we can go ahead and implement the code that publishes a message. The first step is to change the UserContext

class in /organization-service/src/main/java/com/optimagrowth/organization/utils/
UserContext.java. This change will make our variables thread local. The following listing shows the code for the ThreadLocal class.

Listing 10.3 Making our UserContext variables ThreadLocal

```
package com.optimagrowth.organization.utils;
//Imports removed for conciseness

@Component
public class UserContext {
    public static final String CORRELATION_ID = "tmx-correlation-id";
    public static final String AUTH_TOKEN     = "Authorization";
    public static final String USER_ID        = "tmx-user-id";
    public static final String ORG_ID         = "tmx-org-id";

    private static final ThreadLocal<String> correlationId =
            new ThreadLocal<String>();
    private static final ThreadLocal<String> authToken =
            new ThreadLocal<String>();
    private static final ThreadLocal<String> userId =
            new ThreadLocal<String>();
    private static final ThreadLocal<String> orgId =
            new ThreadLocal<String>();          ◁——

    public static HttpHeaders getHttpHeaders(){
        HttpHeaders httpHeaders = new HttpHeaders();
        httpHeaders.set(CORRELATION_ID, getCorrelationId());

        return httpHeaders;
    }
}
```

> **Defining our variables as ThreadLocal lets us store data individually for the current thread. The information set here can only be read by the thread that set the value.**

The next step is to create the logic to publish the message. You'll find the code to publish
our message in the /organization-service/src/main/java/com/optimagrowth/
organization/events/source/SimpleSourceBean.java class file. The following listing
shows the code for this class.

Listing 10.4 Publishing a message to the message broker

```
package com.optimagrowth.organization.events.source;

import org.slf4j.Logger;
import org.slf4j.LoggerFactory;
import org.springframework.beans.factory.annotation.Autowired;
import org.springframework.cloud.stream.messaging.Source;
import org.springframework.messaging.support.MessageBuilder;
import org.springframework.stereotype.Component;

import com.optimagrowth.organization.events.model.OrganizationChangeModel;
import com.optimagrowth.organization.utils.UserContext;
```

```
@Component
public class SimpleSourceBean {
    private Source source;

    private static final Logger logger =
        LoggerFactory.getLogger(SimpleSourceBean.class);

    public SimpleSourceBean(Source source){           ⟵──┐  Injects a Source interface
        this.source = source;                               │  implementation for use
    }                                                       │  by the service

    public void publishOrganizationChange(ActionEnum action,
                                String organizationId){
        logger.debug("Sending Kafka message {} for Organization Id: {}",
                action, organizationId);
        OrganizationChangeModel change =  new OrganizationChangeModel(
                OrganizationChangeModel.class.getTypeName(),
                action.toString(),
                organizationId,                       ──┐  Publishes a Java
                UserContext.getCorrelationId());     ⟵──┘  POJO message

        source.output().send(MessageBuilder         ⟵──┐  Sends the message from
                    .withPayload(change)                  │  a channel defined in the
                    .build());                            │  Source class
    }
}
```

In listing 10.4, we injected the Spring Cloud `Source` class into our code. Remember, all communication to a specific message topic occurs through a Spring Cloud Stream construct called a *channel*, which is represented by a Java interface class. In the listing, we used the `Source` interface, which exposes a single method called `output()`.

The `Source` interface is convenient to use when our service only needs to publish to a single channel. The `output()` method returns a class of type `MessageChannel`. With this type, we'll send messages to the message broker. (Later in this chapter, we'll show you how to expose multiple messaging channels using a custom interface.) The `ActionEnum` passed by the parameters in the `output()` method contains the following actions:

```
public enum ActionEnum {
    GET,
    CREATED,
    UPDATED,
    DELETED
}
```

The actual publication of the message occurs in the `publishOrganizationChange()` method. This method builds a Java POJO called `OrganizationChangeModel`. The following listing shows the code for this POJO.

Listing 10.5 Publishing the `OrganizationChangeModel` object

```
package com.optimagrowth.organization.events.model;

import lombok.Getter;
import lombok.Setter;
import lombok.ToString;

@Getter @Setter @ToString
public class OrganizationChangeModel {
    private String type;
    private String action;
    private String organizationId;
    private String correlationId;

    public OrganizationChangeModel(String type,
            String action, String organizationId,
            String correlationId) {
        this.type = type;
        this.action = action;
        this.organizationId = organizationId;
        this.correlationId = correlationId;
    }
}
```

The `OrganizationChangeModel` class declares three data elements:

- `action`—This is the action that triggered the event. We've included the `action` element in the message to give the message consumer more context on how it should process an event.
- `organizationId`—This is the organization ID associated with the event.
- `correlationId`—This is the correlation ID of the service call that triggered the event. We should always include a correlation ID in our events as it helps greatly with tracking and debugging the flow of messages through our services.

If we go back to the `SimpleSourceBean` class, we can see that when we're ready to publish the message, we can use the `send()` method on the `MessageChannel` class returned from the `source.output()` method like this:

```
source.output().send(MessageBuilder.withPayload(change).build());
```

The `send()` method takes a Spring `Message` class. We use a Spring helper class, called `MessageBuilder`, to take the contents of the `OrganizationChangeModel` class and convert it to a Spring `Message` class. This is all the code we need to send a message. However, at this point, everything should feel a little bit like magic because we haven't seen how to bind our organization service to a specific message queue, let alone the actual message broker. This is all done through configuration.

Listing 10.6 shows the configuration that maps our service's Spring Cloud Stream `Source` to a Kafka message broker and a message topic. This configuration information can be localized in our Spring Cloud Config entry for the organization service.

NOTE For this example, we use the classpath repository on the Spring Cloud Config. The configuration for the organization service is found in /configserver/ src/main/resources/config/organization-service.properties.

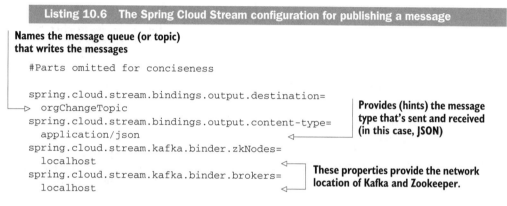

Listing 10.6 The Spring Cloud Stream configuration for publishing a message

Names the message queue (or topic)
that writes the messages

```
#Parts omitted for conciseness

spring.cloud.stream.bindings.output.destination=
    orgChangeTopic
spring.cloud.stream.bindings.output.content-type=
    application/json
spring.cloud.stream.kafka.binder.zkNodes=
    localhost
spring.cloud.stream.kafka.binder.brokers=
    localhost
```

Provides (hints) the message
type that's sent and received
(in this case, JSON)

These properties provide the network
location of Kafka and Zookeeper.

NOTE Apache Zookeeper is used to maintain configuration and name data. It also provides flexible synchronization in distributed systems. Apache Kafka acts like a centralized service that keeps track of the Kafka cluster nodes and topics configuration.

The configuration in code listing 10.6 looks dense, but it's quite straightforward. The `spring.cloud.stream.bindings` is the start of the configuration needed for our service to publish to a Spring Cloud Stream message broker. The configuration property `spring.cloud.stream.bindings.output` in the listing maps the `source.output()` channel in listing 10.4 to the `orgChangeTopic` on the message broker we're going to communicate with. It also tells Spring Cloud Stream that messages sent to this topic should be serialized as JSON. Spring Cloud Stream can serialize messages in multiple formats including JSON, XML, and the Apache Foundation's Avro format (https://avro.apache.org/).

Now that we have the code that will publish a message via Spring Cloud Stream and the configuration to tell Spring Cloud Stream to use Kafka as a message broker, let's look at where the publication of the message in our organization service actually occurs. The class `OrganizationService` will do this for us. You'll find the code for this class in /organization-service/src/main/java/com/optimagrowth/organization/ service/OrganizationService.java. The following listing shows the code for this class.

Listing 10.7   Publishing a message in the organization service

```
package com.optimagrowth.organization.service;
//Imports removed for conciseness
@Service
public class OrganizationService {

    private static final Logger logger =
     LoggerFactory.getLogger(OrganizationService.class);

    @Autowired
    private OrganizationRepository repository;

    @Autowired
    SimpleSourceBean simpleSourceBean;

    public Organization create(Organization organization){
        organization.setId( UUID.randomUUID().toString());
        organization = repository.save(organization);
        simpleSourceBean.publishOrganizationChange(
            ActionEnum.CREATED,
            organization.getId());
        return organization;

    }

    //Rest of the code removed for conciseness
}
```

Uses autowiring to inject the SimpleSourceBean into the organization service

For each method in the service that changes organization data, calls simpleSourceBean.publishOrgChange()

What data should I put in the message?

One of the most common questions we get from teams when they're first embarking on their message journey is, exactly how much data should I put in the message? Our answer is, it depends on your application.

As you may have noticed, in all our examples, we only return the organization ID of the organization record that's changed. We never put a copy of the data changes in the message. Also, we use messages based on system events to tell other services that the data state has changed, and we always force the other services to go back to the master (the service that owns the data) to retrieve a new copy of the data. This approach is costlier in terms of execution time, but it guarantees we always have the latest copy of the data. But a slight chance exists that the data we work with could change right after we've read it from the source system. That's much less likely to occur, however, than if we blindly consume the information right off the queue.

Our advice is to think carefully about how much data you're passing around. Sooner or later, you'll run into a situation where the data passed is "stale." It could be because a problem caused it to sit in the message queue too long, or a previous message containing data failed and the data you're passing in the message now represents data in an inconsistent state. This might be because your application relied on the message's state rather than on the actual state in the underlying data store. If you're going to pass state in your message, make sure to include a date-time stamp or version number so that the service that's consuming the data can inspect the data passed to it and ensure that it's not older than the copy of the data it already has.

10.3.3 *Writing the message consumer in the licensing service*

At this point, we've modified the organization service to publish a message to Kafka every time the organization service changes data. Any interested service can react without having to be explicitly called by the organization service. It also means we can easily add new functionality that can react to the changes in the organization service by listening to messages coming into the message queue.

Let's now switch directions and look at how a service can consume a message using Spring Cloud Stream. For this example, the licensing service will consume the message published by the organization service. To begin, we need to add our Spring Cloud Stream dependencies to the licensing services pom.xml file. You'll find this file in the licensing-service root directory of the source code for the book. Figure 10.5 shows where the licensing service fits into the Spring Cloud architecture, first shown in figure 10.3. Similar to the organization-service pom.xml file that you saw earlier, we'll add the following two dependency entries to the .pom file:

```
<dependency>
    <groupId>org.springframework.cloud</groupId>
    <artifactId>spring-cloud-stream</artifactId>
</dependency>

<dependency>
    <groupId>org.springframework.cloud</groupId>
    <artifactId>spring-cloud-starter-stream-kafka</artifactId>
</dependency>
```

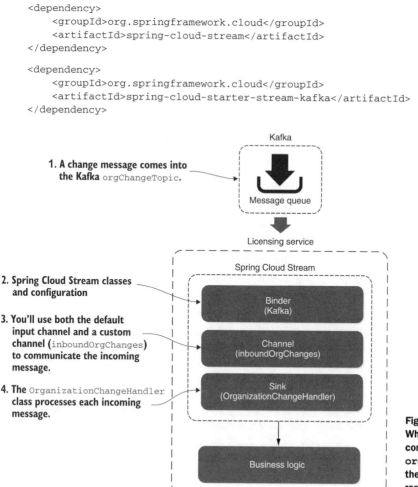

1. A change message comes into the Kafka orgChangeTopic.

2. Spring Cloud Stream classes and configuration

3. You'll use both the default input channel and a custom channel (inboundOrgChanges**) to communicate the incoming message.**

4. The OrganizationChangeHandler **class processes each incoming message.**

Figure 10.5 When a message comes into the Kafka orgChangeTopic, **the licensing service responds.**

Next, we'll tell the licensing service that it needs to use Spring Cloud Stream to bind to a message broker. Like the organization service, we'll annotate the licensing service's bootstrap class, `LicenseServiceApplication`, with the `@EnableBinding` annotation. You can find the code for this class in the /licensing-service/src/main/java/com/optimagrowth/license/LicenseServiceApplication.java file. The difference between the licensing service and the organization service is the value we'll pass to `@EnableBinding`, which the following listing shows.

Listing 10.8   Consuming a message using Spring Cloud Stream

Tells the service to the use the channels defined in the Sink interface to listen for incoming messages

```
package com.optimagrowth.license;
//Imports and some annotations removed for conciseness

@EnableBinding(Sink.class)
public class LicenseServiceApplication {

    @StreamListener(Sink.INPUT)
    public void loggerSink(OrganizationChangeModel orgChange) {
        logger.debug("Received an {} event for organization id {}",
          orgChange.getAction(), orgChange.getOrganizationId());
    }

    //Rest of the code omitted for conciseness
}
```

Executes this method each time a message is received from the input channel

Because the licensing service is the message consumer, we'll pass `@EnableBinding` the value `Sink.class`. This tells Spring Cloud Stream to bind to a message broker using the default Spring `Sink` interface. Similar to the `Source` interface (described in section 10.3.1), Spring Cloud Stream exposes a default channel on the `Sink` interface. This `Sink` interface channel is called `input` and is used to listen for incoming messages.

Once we've defined that we want to listen for messages via the `@EnableBinding` annotation, we can write the code to process a message coming from the `Sink` input channel. To do this, we'll use the Spring Cloud Stream `@StreamListener` annotation. This annotation tells Spring Cloud Stream to execute the `loggerSink()` method when receiving a message from the input channel. Spring Cloud Stream automatically deserializes the incoming message to a Java POJO called `OrganizationChangeModel`.

Again, the licensing service's configuration implements the mapping of the message broker's topic to the input channel. Its configuration is shown in listing 10.9 and can be found in the Spring Cloud config repository for this example in the /configserver/src/main/resources/config/licensing-service.properties file.

Listing 10.9   Mapping the licensing service to a message topic in Kafka

```
#Some properties removed for conciseness

spring.cloud.stream.bindings.input.destination=
  orgChangeTopic
```

Maps the input channel to the orgChangeTopic queue

```
spring.cloud.stream.bindings.input.content-type=
  application/json
spring.cloud.stream.bindings.input.group=          Process semantics
  licensingGroup                                    once per service
spring.cloud.stream.kafka.binder.zkNodes=
  localhost
spring.cloud.stream.kafka.binder.brokers=
  localhost
```

The configuration in this listing looks like the configuration for the organization service. It has, however, two key differences. First, we now have an input channel defined with the `spring.cloud.stream.bindings` property. This value maps to the `Sink.INPUT` channel defined in the code from listing 10.8. This property maps the input channel to the `orgChangeTopic`. Second, we see the introduction of a new property called `spring.cloud.stream.bindings.input.group`. The `group` property defines the name of the consumer group that will consume the message.

The concept of a consumer group is this: we can have multiple services with each service having multiple instances listening to the same message queue. We want each unique service to process a copy of a message, but we only want one service instance within a group of service instances to consume and process a message. The `group` property identifies the consumer group that the service belongs to.

As long as all the service instances have the same group name, Spring Cloud Stream and the underlying message broker will guarantee that only one copy of the message will be consumed by a service instance belonging to that group. In the case of our licensing service, we'll call the `group` property value `licensingGroup`. Figure 10.6 illustrates how this consumer group helps to enforce consumption once the semantics for a consumed message across multiple services is satisfied.

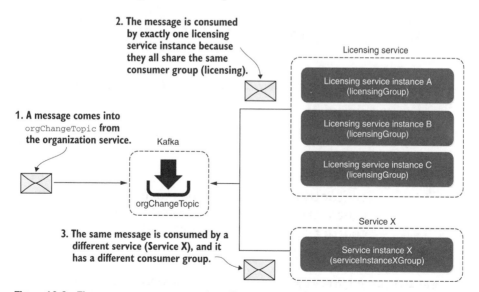

Figure 10.6 The consumer group guarantees that a message is only processed once by a group of service instances.

10.3.4   *Seeing the message service in action*

At this point, the organization service publishes a message to the `orgChangeTopic` each time a record is added, updated, or deleted, and the licensing service receives the message with the same topic. Next, we'll see this code in action by creating an organization service record and watching the console to see the corresponding log message from the licensing service.

To create the organization service record, we're going to issue a POST on the organization service. We'll use the `http://localhost:8072/organization/v1/organization/` endpoint and send the following body on the POST call to the endpoint. Figure 10.7 shows the returned output from this POST call:

```
{
    "name":"Ostock",
    "contactName":"Illary Huaylupo",
    "contactEmail":"illaryhs@gmail.com",
    "contactPhone":"888888888"
}
```

NOTE Remember that we first needed to implement the authentication to retrieve the tokens and pass the access token via the authorization header as a Bearer Token. We discussed this in the previous chapter. If you didn't follow the code samples there, download the code from http://github.com/ihuaylupo/manning-smia/tree/master/chapter9. We then pointed our code to the Spring Cloud Gateway. That's why the endpoint has the 8072 port and the /organization/v1/organization path instead of just /v1/organization.

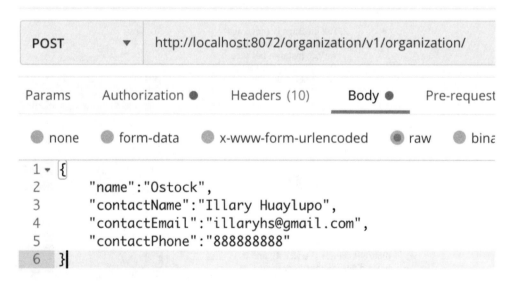

Figure 10.7   Creating a new organization service record using the organization service

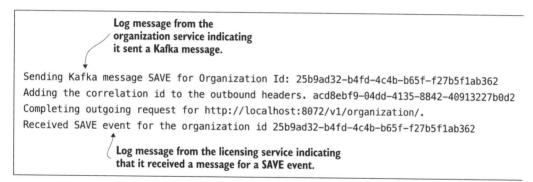

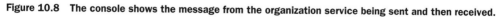

Figure 10.8 **The console shows the message from the organization service being sent and then received.**

Once we make the organization service call, we should see the output shown in figure 10.8 in the console window running the services.

Now we have two services communicating with each other using messages. Spring Cloud Stream acts as the middleman for these services. From a messaging perspective, the services know nothing about each other. They're using a messaging broker to communicate as an intermediary and Spring Cloud Stream as an abstraction layer over the messaging broker.

10.4 *A Spring Cloud Stream use case: Distributed caching*

We now have two services communicating with messaging, but we're not really doing anything with the messages. Next, we'll build the distributed caching example we discussed earlier in the chapter. For that, the licensing service will always check a distributed Redis cache for the organization data associated with a particular license. If the organization data exists in the cache, we'll return the data from the cache. If it doesn't, we'll call the organization service and cache the results of the call in a Redis hash.

When the data is updated in the organization service, the organization service will issue a message to Kafka. The licensing service will pick up the message and issue a DELETE against Redis to clear the cache.

Cloud caching and messaging

Using Redis as a distributed cache is relevant to microservices development in the cloud. You can use Redis to

- *Improve performance when looking up commonly held data.* Using a cache, you can significantly improve the performance of several key services by avoiding reads to the database.
- *Reduce the load (and cost) on the database tables holding your data.* Accessing data in a database can be a costly undertaking. With every read, you make a chargeable event. Using a Redis server, you can implement reads by a primary key rather than by accessing a database, which is significantly more cost effective.

(continued)

- *Increase resiliency so your services can degrade gracefully if your primary data store or database is having performance problems.* Depending on how much data you keep in your cache, a caching solution can help reduce the number of errors you might get from accessing your data store.

Redis is far more than a caching solution. It can, however, fill that role if you need a distributed cache.

10.4.1 Using Redis to cache lookups

In this section, we'll begin by setting up the licensing service to use Redis. Fortunately, Spring Data makes it simple to introduce Redis into our licensing service. To use Redis in the licensing service, we need to do the following:

1. Configure the licensing service to include the Spring Data Redis dependencies.
2. Construct a database connection to Redis.
3. Define the Spring Data Redis repositories that our code will use to interact with a Redis hash.
4. Use Redis and the licensing service to store and read organization data.

CONFIGURING THE LICENSING SERVICE WITH SPRING DATA REDIS DEPENDENCIES

The first thing we need to do is include the `spring-data-redis` dependencies, along with `jedis` into the licensing service's pom.xml file. The next listing shows these dependencies.

Listing 10.10   Adding the Spring Redis dependencies

```
//Some code removed for conciseness
<dependency>
    <groupId>org.springframework.data</groupId>
    <artifactId>spring-data-redis</artifactId>
</dependency>

<dependency>
    <groupId>redis.clients</groupId>
    <artifactId>jedis</artifactId>
    <type>jar</type>
</dependency>
```

CONSTRUCTING THE DATABASE CONNECTION TO A REDIS SERVER

Now that we have the dependencies in Maven, we need to establish a connection to our Redis server. Spring uses the Jedis open source project (https://github.com/xetorthio/jedis) to communicate with a Redis server. To communicate with a specific Redis instance, we'll expose a `JedisConnectionFactory` class as a Spring bean. You'll find the source for this class in /licensing-service/src/main/java/com/optimagrowth/license/LicenseServiceApplication.java.

Once we have a connection to Redis, we'll use that connection to create a Spring `RedisTemplate` object. The Spring Data repository classes that we'll implement shortly use the `RedisTemplate` object to execute the queries and saves of organization service data to our Redis service. The following listing shows this code.

Listing 10.11 Establishing how our licensing service communicates with Redis

```
package com.optimagrowth.license;

import org.springframework.data.redis.connection.RedisPassword;
import org.springframework.data.redis.connection.
    RedisStandaloneConfiguration;
import org.springframework.data.redis.connection.jedis.
    JedisConnectionFactory;
import org.springframework.data.redis.core.RedisTemplate;

//Most of the imports and annotations removed for conciseness

@SpringBootApplication
@EnableBinding(Sink.class)
public class LicenseServiceApplication {

    @Autowired
    private ServiceConfig serviceConfig;                    Sets up the database
                                                      connection to the Redis server

    //All other methods in the class have been removed for conciseness

    @Bean
    JedisConnectionFactory jedisConnectionFactory() {    ◁──
        String hostname = serviceConfig.getRedisServer();
        int port = Integer.parseInt(serviceConfig.getRedisPort());
        RedisStandaloneConfiguration redisStandaloneConfiguration
            = new RedisStandaloneConfiguration(hostname, port);
     return new JedisConnectionFactory(redisStandaloneConfiguration);
    }

    @Bean
    public RedisTemplate<String, Object> redisTemplate() {    ◁──
        RedisTemplate<String, Object> template = new RedisTemplate<>();
        template.setConnectionFactory(jedisConnectionFactory());
        return template;
                                                  Creates a RedisTemplate to carry
    }                                             out actions for our Redis server

    //Rest of the code removed for conciseness
}
```

The foundational work for setting up the licensing service to communicate with Redis is complete. Let's now move on to writing the logic that will get, add, update, and delete data.

`ServiceConfig` is a simple class that contains the logic to retrieve the custom parameters that we'll define in the configuration file for the licensing service; in this particular scenario, the Redis host and port. The following listing shows the code for this class.

Listing 10.12　Setting up the `ServiceConfig` class with Redis data

```
package com.optimagrowth.license.config;
//Imports removed for conciseness

@Component @Getter
public class ServiceConfig{

//Some code removed for conciseness

   @Value("${redis.server}")
      private String redisServer="";

   @Value("${redis.port}")
      private String redisPort="";
}
```

The Spring Cloud Config service repository defines the following host and port for the Redis server in the /configserver/src/main/resources/config/licensing-service .properties file:

```
redis.server = localhost
redis.port = 6379
```

> **NOTE**　We use Docker to run all the examples. If you want to run this example locally, you need to install Redis on your computer. But if you use Docker, you'll find the docker-compose.yml file up to date with the Redis container at the following link: https://github.com/ihuaylupo/manning-smia/tree/master/ chapter10/docker.

DEFINING THE SPRING DATA REDIS REPOSITORIES

Redis is a key-value data store that acts like a big, distributed, in-memory HashMap. In the simplest case, it stores and looks up data with a key. It doesn't have any sophisticated query language to retrieve data. Its simplicity is its strength, and one of the reasons why so many developers have adopted it for use in their projects.

Because we're using Spring Data to access our Redis store, we need to define a repository class. As may you remember from early on in the first chapters, Spring Data uses user-defined repository classes to provide a simple mechanism for a Java class to access our Postgres database without having to write low-level SQL queries. For the licensing service, we'll define two files for our Redis repository. The first file is a Java interface that will be injected into any of the licensing service classes that need to access Redis. The following listing shows the /licensing-service/src/main/java/com/ optimagrowth/license/repository/OrganizationRedis-Repository.java interface.

> **Listing 10.13** `OrganizationRedisRepository` **defines methods used to call Redis**

```
package com.optimagrowth.license.repository;

import org.springframework.data.repository.CrudRepository;
import org.springframework.stereotype.Repository;
import com.optimagrowth.license.model.Organization;

@Repository
public interface OrganizationRedisRepository extends
    CrudRepository<Organization,String>{
}
```

By extending from `CrudRepository`, `OrganizationRedisRepository` contains all the CRUD (Create, Read, Update, Delete) logic used for storing and retrieving data from Redis (in this case). The second file is the model we'll use for our repository. This class is a POJO containing the data that we'll store in our Redis cache. The /licensing-service/src/main/java/com/optimagrowth/license/model/Organization.java class is shown in the following listing.

> **Listing 10.14** **Organization model for Redis hash**

```
package com.optimagrowth.license.model;

import org.springframework.data.redis.core.RedisHash;
import org.springframework.hateoas.RepresentationModel;
import javax.persistence.Id;

import lombok.Getter;
import lombok.Setter;
import lombok.ToString;
                                            Sets the name of the hash in
                                            the Redis server where the
@Getter @Setter @ToString                   organization data is stored
@RedisHash("organization")          ⟵───────┘
public class Organization extends RepresentationModel<Organization> {

    @Id
    String id;
    String name;
    String contactName;
    String contactEmail;
    String contactPhone;
}
```

One important thing to note from the code in listing 10.14 is that a Redis server can contain multiple hashes and data structures within it. We therefore need to tell Redis the name of the data structure we want to perform the operation against in every interaction with Redis.

USING REDIS AND THE LICENSING SERVICE TO STORE AND READ ORGANIZATION DATA

Now that we have the code in place to perform operations with Redis, we can modify our licensing service so that every time the licensing service needs the organization data, it checks the Redis cache before calling the organization service. You'll find the logic for doing this in the `OrganizationRestTemplateClient` class in the class file /service/src/ main/java/com/optimagrowth/license/service/client/OrganizationRestTemplateClient .java. The next listing shows this class.

> **Listing 10.15   Implementing cache logic with `OrganizationRestTemplateClient`**

```
package com.optimagrowth.license.service.client;
//Imports removed for conciseness

@Component
public class OrganizationRestTemplateClient {
@Autowired
RestTemplate restTemplate;                          Autowires
@Autowired                                          OrganizationRedisRepository in
OrganizationRedisRepository redisRepository;    ◁── OrganizationRestTemplateClient
private static final Logger logger =
    LoggerFactory.getLogger(OrganizationRestTemplateClient.class);

private Organization checkRedisCache(String organizationId) {
    try {
        return redisRepository              Tries to retrieve an
                .findById(organizationId)   Organization class with its
                .orElse(null);          ◁── organization ID from Redis
    }catch (Exception ex){
        logger.error("Error encountered while trying to retrieve
        organization{} check Redis Cache.  Exception {}",
        organizationId, ex);
        return null;
    }
}
private void cacheOrganizationObject(Organization organization) {
    try {
        redisRepository.save(organization);   ◁── Saves the organization in Redis
    }catch (Exception ex){
        logger.error("Unable to cache organization {} in
        Redis. Exception {}",                 If you can't retrieve data from Redis, calls the
        organization.getId(), ex);            organization service to retrieve the data from
    }                                         the source database to later save it in Redis
}
public Organization getOrganization(String organizationId){
    logger.debug("In Licensing Service.getOrganization: {}",
        UserContext.getCorrelationId());

    Organization organization = checkRedisCache(organizationId);
    if (organization != null){                         ◁─────────────────
        logger.debug("I have successfully retrieved an organization
        {} from the redis cache: {}", organizationId,
        organization);
```

```
        return organization;
    }
    logger.debug("Unable to locate organization from the
        redis cache: {}.",organizationId);
    ResponseEntity<Organization> restExchange =
        restTemplate.exchange(
          "http://gateway:8072/organization/v1/organization/
          {organizationId}",HttpMethod.GET,
          null, Organization.class, organizationId);

    organization = restExchange.getBody();
    if (organization != null) {
      cacheOrganizationObject(organization);
    }
      return restExchange.getBody();
    }
}
```

The getOrganization() method is where the call to the organization service takes place. Before we make the actual REST call, we need to retrieve the Organization object associated with the call from Redis using the checkRedisCache() method.

If the organization object in question is not in Redis, the code returns a null value. If a null value is returned from the checkRedisCache() method, the code invokes the organization service's REST endpoint to retrieve the desired organization record. If the organization service returns an organization, the returned organization object is cached using the cacheOrganizationObject() method.

> **NOTE** Pay close attention to exception handling when interacting with the cache. To increase resiliency, we never let the entire call fail if we cannot communicate with the Redis server. Instead, we log the exception and let the call through to the organization service. In this particular case, caching is meant to help improve performance, and the absence of the caching server shouldn't impact the success of the call.

With the Redis caching code in place, using Postman, we can select the licensing service to view the logging messages. If we make two back-to-back GET requests on the licensing service endpoint, http://localhost:8072/license/v1/organization e839ee96-28de-4f67-bb79-870ca89743a0/license/279709ff-e6d5-4a54-8b55-a5c37542025b, we'll see the following two output statements in our log:

```
licensingservice_1        | DEBUG 1 --- [nio-8080-exec-4]
c.o.l.s.c.OrganizationRestTemplateClient : Unable to locate organization from
the redis cache: e839ee96-28de-4f67-bb79-870ca89743a0.

licensingservice_1        | DEBUG 1 --- [nio-8080-exec-7]
c.o.l.s.c.OrganizationRestTemplateClient : I have successfully retrieved an
organization e839ee96-28de-4f67-bb79-870ca89743a0 from the redis cache:
Organization(id=e839ee96-28de-4f67-bb79-870ca89743a0, name=Ostock,
contactName=Illary Huaylupo, contactEmail=illaryhs@gmail.com,
contactPhone=888888888)
```

The first output from the console shows the first time we tried to access the licensing service endpoint for the organization e839ee96-28de-4f67-bb79-870ca89743a0. The licensing service checked the Redis cache and couldn't find the organization record it was looking for. The code then called the organization service to retrieve the data. The next output shows that when you entered the licensing service endpoint a second time, the organization record is now cached.

10.4.2 *Defining custom channels*

Previously we built our messaging integration between the licensing and organization services to use the default output and input channels that are packaged with the Source and Sink interfaces in Spring Cloud Stream. However, if we want to define more than one channel for our application, or we want to customize the names of our channels, we can define our own interface and expose as many input and output channels as our application needs.

To create a custom channel, we'll call inboundOrgChanges in the licensing service. You can define the channel with the CustomChannels interface found in /licensing-service/src/main/java/com/optimagrowth/license/events/CustomChannels.java, as shown in the following listing.

> **Listing 10.16 Defining a custom input channel for the licensing service**

```
package com.optimagrowth.license.service.client;
//Imports removed for conciseness
package com.optimagrowth.license.events;

import org.springframework.cloud.stream.annotation.Input;
import org.springframework.messaging.SubscribableChannel;

public interface CustomChannels {

    @Input("inboundOrgChanges")
    SubscribableChannel orgs();

}
```

Names the channel → @Input("inboundOrgChanges")
SubscribableChannel orgs(); ← **Returns a SubscribableChannel class for each channel exposed by @Input**

The key takeaway from listing 10.16 is that for each custom input channel we want to expose, we define a method with @Input that returns a SubscribableChannel class. We then use @OutputChannel before the method that will be called if we want to define output channels for publishing messages. In the case of an output channel, the defined method returns a MessageChannel class instead of the SubscribableChannel class used with the input channel. Here's the call to @OutputChannel:

```
@OutputChannel("outboundOrg")
MessageChannel outboundOrg();
```

Now that we have a custom input channel, we need to modify two more things to use it in the licensing service. First, we need to modify the licensing service to map the Kafka topic's custom input channel name in the licensing configuration file. The following listing shows this change.

Listing 10.17 Modifying the licensing service to use our custom input channel

```
//Parts removed for conciseness
spring.cloud.stream.bindings.inboundOrgChanges.destination=
    orgChangeTopic
spring.cloud.stream.bindings.inboundOrgChanges.content-type=
    application/json
spring.cloud.stream.bindings.inboundOrgChanges.group=
    licensingGroup
spring.cloud.stream.kafka.binder.zkNodes=
    localhost
spring.cloud.stream.kafka.binder.brokers=
    localhost
```

Next, we need to inject the CustomChannels interface previously defined into a class that's going to use it to process messages. For the distributed caching example, we've moved the code for handling an incoming message to the OrganizationChangeHandler licensing service class. You'll find the source for this class in /licensing-service/src/main/java/com/optima-growth/license/events/handler/OrganizationChangeHandler.java.

The following listing shows the message handling code that we'll use with the inboundOrgChanges channel we just defined.

Listing 10.18 Processing an organization change with the new custom channel

```
package com.optimagrowth.license.events.handler;
//Imports removed for conciseness

@EnableBinding(CustomChannels.class)          ◁── Moves the @EnableBindings out of
public class OrganizationChangeHandler {           Application.java and into
                                                   OrganizationChangeHandler. This time
                                                   instead of using the Sink class, we use
                                                   CustomChannels as the parameter to pass.
private static final Logger logger =
    LoggerFactory.getLogger(OrganizationChangeHandler.class);

private OrganizationRedisRepository          Injects OrganizationRedisRepository
        organizationRedisRepository;  ◁──    into OrganizationChangeHandler to
                                             allow for CRUD operations

@StreamListener("inboundOrgChanges")
public void loggerSink(
        OrganizationChangeModel organization) {  ◁──  Inspects the action that
                                                       the data undertakes and
                                                       then reacts accordingly
    logger.debug("Received a message of type " +
            organization.getType());
    logger.debug("Received a message with an event {} from the
            organization service for the organization id {} ",
            organization.getType(), organization.getType());
    }
}
```

The utility class doing all the metadata extraction work (annotation pointing to `@StreamListener("inboundOrgChanges")`)

Now, let's create an organization and then find it. We can do this using the following two endpoints. (Figure 10.9 shows the console output of these calls with the `Organization-ChangeHandler` class.)

```
http://localhost:8072/organization/v1/organization/
http://localhost:8072/organization/v1/organization/d989f37d-9a59-4b59-b276-
    2c79005ea0d9
```

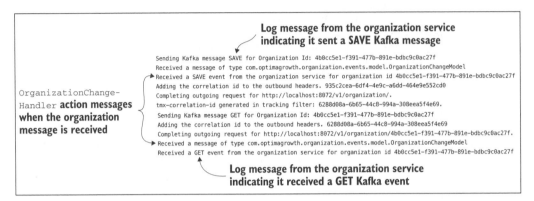

Figure 10.9   The console shows the message from the organization service that was sent and then received.

Now that we know how to use Spring Cloud Stream and Redis, let's continue with the next chapter, where we will see several techniques and technologies to create a distributed tracing using Spring Cloud.

Summary

- Asynchronous communication with messaging is a critical part of microservices architecture.
- Using messaging within our applications allows our services to scale and become more fault tolerant.
- Spring Cloud Stream simplifies the production and consumption of messages by using simple annotations and abstracting away platform-specific details of the underlying message platform.
- A Spring Cloud Stream message source is an annotated Java method that's used to publish messages to a message broker's queue.
- A Spring Cloud Stream message sink is an annotated Java method that receives messages from a message broker's queue.
- Redis is a key-value store that you can use as both a database and a cache.

Distributed tracing with Spring Cloud Sleuth and Zipkin

11

This chapter covers

- Using Spring Cloud Sleuth to inject tracing information into service calls
- Using log aggregation to see logs for distributed transactions
- Transforming, searching, analyzing, and visualizing log data in real time
- Understanding a user transaction as it flows across multiple service classes
- Customizing tracing information with Spring Cloud Sleuth and Zipkin

The microservices architecture is a powerful design paradigm for breaking down complex monolithic software systems into smaller, more manageable pieces. These pieces can be built and deployed independently of each other; however, this flexibility comes at a price—complexity.

Because microservices are distributed by nature, trying to debug where a problem occurs can be maddening. The distributed nature of the services means that we need to trace one or more transactions across multiple services, physical machines, and different data stores, and then try to piece together what exactly is going on. This chapter lays out several techniques and technologies for using distributed debugging. In this chapter, we look at the following:

- Using correlation IDs to link together transactions across multiple services
- Aggregating log data from various services into a single searchable source
- Visualizing the flow of a user transaction across multiple services to understand each part of the transaction's performance characteristics
- Analyzing, searching, and visualizing log data in real time using the ELK stack

To accomplish this, we will use the following technologies:

- *Spring Cloud Sleuth* (https://cloud.spring.io/spring-cloud-sleuth/reference/html/)—The Spring Cloud Sleuth project instruments our incoming HTTP requests with trace IDs (aka correlation IDs). It does this by adding filters and interacting with other Spring components to let the generated correlation IDs pass through to all the system calls.
- *Zipkin* (https://zipkin.io/)—Zipkin is an open source data-visualization tool that shows the flow of a transaction across multiple services. Zipkin allows us to break a transaction down into its component pieces and visually identify where there might be performance hotspots.
- *ELK stack* (https://www.elastic.co/what-is/elk-stack)—The ELK stack combines three open source tools—Elasticsearch, Logstash, and Kibana—that allow us to analyze, search, and visualize logs in real time.
  - Elasticsearch is a distributed analytics engine for all types of data (structured and non-structured, numeric, text-based, and so on).
  - Logstash is a server-side data processing pipeline that allows us to add and ingest data from multiple sources simultaneously and transform it before it is indexed in Elasticsearch.
  - Kibana is the visualization and data management tool for Elasticsearch. It provides charts, maps, and real-time histograms.

To begin this chapter, we'll start with the simplest of tracing tools: the correlation ID. We'll cover this in the following section.

NOTE Parts of this chapter rely on material covered in chapter 8 (mainly the material on the Spring Gateway response, pre-, and post-filters). If you haven't read chapter 8 yet, we recommend that you do so before you read this chapter.

11.1 *Spring Cloud Sleuth and the correlation ID*

We first introduced the concept of correlation IDs in chapters 7 and 8. A *correlation ID* is a randomly generated unique number or string assigned to a transaction as the transaction is initiated. As the transaction flows across multiple services, the correlation ID is propagated from one service call to another.

In the context of chapter 8, we used a Spring Cloud Gateway filter to inspect all incoming HTTP requests and inject a correlation ID into the request if one wasn't present. Once the correlation ID was present, we used a custom Spring HTTP filter on each one of our services to map the incoming variable to a custom `UserContext` object. With this object in place, we manually added the correlation ID to our log statements by appending the correlation ID to a log statement or, with a little work, adding the correlation ID directly to Spring's Mapped Diagnostic Context (MDC). MDC is a map that stores a set of key-value pairs provided by the application that's inserted in the log messages.

In that chapter, we also wrote a Spring interceptor to ensure that all HTTP calls from a service would propagate the correlation ID by adding the correlation ID to the HTTP headers of outbound calls. Fortunately, Spring Cloud Sleuth manages all this code infrastructure and complexity for us. Let's go ahead and add Spring Cloud Sleuth to our licensing and organization services. We'll see that by adding Spring Cloud Sleuth to our microservices, we can

- Transparently create and inject a correlation ID into our service calls if one doesn't exist
- Manage the propagation of correlation IDs to outbound service calls so that the correlation ID for a transaction is automatically added
- Add the correlation information to Spring's MDC logging so that the generated correlation ID is automatically logged by Spring Boot's default SL4J and Logback implementation
- Optionally, publish the tracing information in the service call to the Zipkin distributed tracing platform

NOTE With Spring Cloud Sleuth, if we use Spring Boot's logging implementation, we'll automatically get correlation IDs added to the log statements we put in our microservices.

11.1.1 *Adding Spring Cloud Sleuth to licensing and organization*

To start using Spring Cloud Sleuth in our two services (licensing and organization), we need to add a single Maven dependency to the pom.xml files in both services. The following shows you how to do this:

```
<dependency>
    <groupId>org.springframework.cloud</groupId>
    <artifactId>spring-cloud-starter-sleuth</artifactId>
</dependency>
```

These dependencies pull in all the core libraries needed for Spring Cloud Sleuth. That's it. Once they are pulled in, our service will now

- Inspect every incoming HTTP service and determine whether Spring Cloud Sleuth tracing information exists in the incoming call. If the Spring Cloud Sleuth tracing data is present, the tracing information passed into our microservice will be captured and made available to our service for logging and processing.
- Add Spring Cloud Sleuth tracing information to the Spring MDC so that every log statement created by our microservice will be added to the log.
- Inject Spring Cloud tracing information into every outbound HTTP call and Spring messaging channel message our service makes.

11.1.2 Anatomy of a Spring Cloud Sleuth trace

If everything is set up correctly, any log statements written in our service application code will now include Spring Cloud Sleuth trace information. For example, figure 11.1 shows what the service's output would look like if we were to issue an HTTP GET on the following endpoint in the organization service:

```
http://localhost:8072/organization/v1/organization/95c0dab4-0a7e-48f8-805a-
➥ 0ba31c3687b8
```

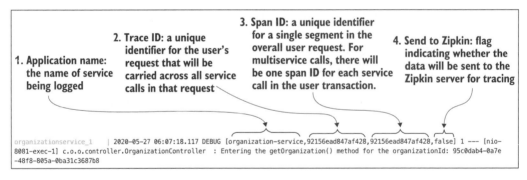

Figure 11.1   Spring Cloud Sleuth adds tracing information to each log entry written by our organization service. This data helps tie together service calls for a user's request.

Spring Cloud Sleuth adds four pieces of information to each log entry. These four pieces (numbered to correspond with the numbers in figure 11.1) are as follows:

1. *The application name of the service where the log entry is entered.* By default, Spring Cloud Sleuth uses the application name (`spring.application.name`) as the name that gets written in the trace.
2. *The trace ID, which is the equivalent term for correlation ID.* This is a unique number that represents an entire transaction.

3 *The span ID, which is a unique ID that represents part of the overall transaction.* Each service participating within the transaction will have its own span ID. Span IDs are particularly relevant if you integrate with Zipkin to visualize your transactions.

4 *Export, a true/false indicator that determines whether trace data is sent to Zipkin.* In high-volume services, the amount of trace data generated can be overwhelming and not add a significant amount of value. Spring Cloud Sleuth lets us determine when and how to send a transaction to Zipkin.

NOTE By default, any application flow starts with the same trace and span IDs.

Up to now, we've only looked at the logging data produced by a single service call. Let's look at what happens when you also make a call to the licensing service. Figure 11.2 shows the logging output from the two service calls.

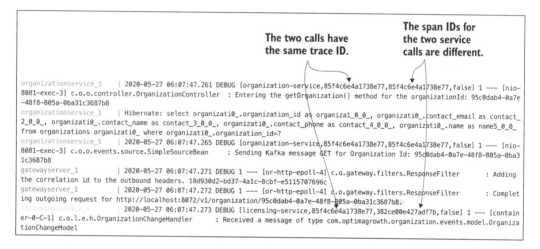

Figure 11.2 With multiple services involved in a transaction, we see that they share the same trace ID.

In figure 11.2, we can see that both the licensing and organization services have the same trace ID, `85f4c6e4a1738e77`. However, the organization service has a span ID of `85f4c6e4a1738e77` (the same value as the transaction ID). The licensing service has a span ID of `382ce00e427adf7b`. By adding nothing more than a few .pom dependencies, we've replaced all the correlation ID infrastructure that you built in chapters 7 and 8.

11.2 Log aggregation and Spring Cloud Sleuth

In a large-scale microservice environment (especially in the cloud), logging data is a critical tool for debugging. However, because the functionality of a microservice-based application is decomposed into small, granular services, and we can have multiple service instances for a single service type, trying to tie debugging to log data from multiple services to resolve a user's problem can be extremely difficult. Developers wanting to debug a problem across multiple servers often have to try the following:

- *Log into multiple servers to inspect the logs present on each server.* This is an extremely laborious task, especially if the services in question have different transaction volumes that cause logs to roll over at different rates.
- *Write home-grown query scripts that will attempt to parse the logs and identify the relevant log entries.* Because every query might be different, we often end up with a large proliferation of custom scripts for querying data from our logs.
- *Prolong the recovery of a downgraded service process to back up the logs residing on a server.* If a server hosting a service crashes completely, the logs are usually lost.

Each of the problems listed are real concerns that we often run into. Debugging a problem across distributed servers is ugly work and often significantly increases the amount of time it takes to identify and resolve an issue. A much better approach is to stream, real time, all the logs from all of our service instances to a centralized aggregation point, where the log data can be indexed and made searchable. Figure 11.3 shows at a conceptual level how this "unified" logging architecture would work.

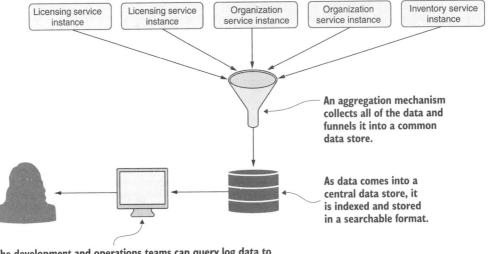

An aggregation mechanism collects all of the data and funnels it into a common data store.

As data comes into a central data store, it is indexed and stored in a searchable format.

The development and operations teams can query log data to find individual transactions. The trace IDs from Spring Cloud Sleuth log entries allow us to tie log entries across services.

Figure 11.3   The combination of aggregated logs and a unique transaction ID across service log entries makes debugging distributed transactions more manageable.

Fortunately, there are multiple open source and commercial products that can help us implement the logging architecture in figure 11.3. Also, multiple implementation models exist that allow us to choose between an on-premises, locally managed solution or a cloud-based solution. Table 11.1 summarizes several of the choices available for logging infrastructure.

With all these choices, it might be challenging to choose which one is the best. Every organization is going to be different and have different needs. For this chapter,

Table 11.1 Log aggregation solutions for use with Spring Boot

Product name	Implementation models	Notes
Elasticsearch, Logstash, Kibana (the ELK Stack)	Commercial Open source	https://www.elastic.co/what-is/elk-stack General-purpose search engine Log aggregation through the ELK stack Typically implemented on premises
Graylog	Commercial Open source	https://www.graylog.org/ Designed to be installed on premises
Splunk	Commercial	https://www.splunk.com/ Oldest and most comprehensive of the log management and aggregation tools Initially an on-premises solution, now with a cloud offering
Sumo Logic	Commercial Freemium/tiered	https://www.sumologic.com/ Runs only as a cloud service Requires a corporate work account to sign up (no Gmail or Yahoo accounts)
Papertrail	Commercial Freemium/tiered	https://www.papertrail.com/ Runs only as a cloud service

we'll look at ELK as an example of how to integrate Spring Cloud Sleuth-backed logs into a unified logging platform. We've chosen the ELK Stack because:

- ELK is open source.
- It's straightforward to set up, simple to use, and user friendly.
- It's a complete tool that allows us to search, analyze, and visualize real-time logs generated from different services.
- It allows us to centralize all the logging to identify server and application issues.

11.2.1 A Spring Cloud Sleuth/ELK Stack implementation in action

In figure 11.3, we saw a general unified logging architecture. Let's now see how we can implement the same architecture with Spring Cloud Sleuth and the ELK Stack. To set up ELK to work with our environment, we need to take the following actions:

1 Configure Logback in our services
2 Define and run the ELK Stack applications in Docker containers
3 Configure Kibana
4 Test the implementation by issuing queries based on the correlation IDs from Spring Cloud Sleuth

Figure 11.4 shows the end state for our implementation. In the figure, we can see how Spring Cloud Sleuth and ELK fit together for our solution.

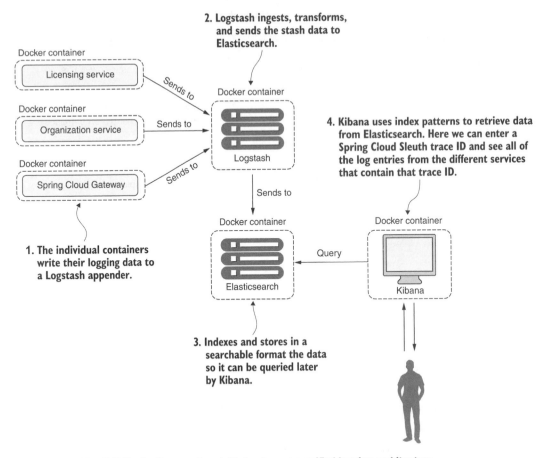

Figure 11.4   The ELK Stack allows us to quickly implement a unified logging architecture.

In figure 11.4, the licensing, organization, and gateway services communicate via TCP with Logstash to send the log data. Logstash filters, transforms, and passes the data to a central data store (in this case, Elasticsearch). Elasticsearch indexes and stores the data in a searchable format so it can be queried later by Kibana. Once the data is stored, Kibana uses the index patterns from Elasticsearch to retrieve the data.

At this point, we can create a specific query index and enter a Spring Cloud Sleuth trace ID to see all of the log entries from the different services that contain it. Once the data is stored, we can look for the real-time logs by just accessing Kibana.

11.2.2   *Configuring Logback in our services*

Now that we've seen the logging architecture with ELK, let's start configuring Logback for our services. In order to do this, we need to do the following:

1 Add the `logstash-logback-encoder` dependency in the pom.xml of our services
2 Create the Logstash TCP appender in a Logback configuration file

ADDING THE LOGSTASH ENCODER

To begin, we need to add the `logstash-logback-encoder` dependency to the pom.xml file of our licensing, organization, and gateway services. Remember, the pom.xml file can be found in the root directory of the source code. Here's the code to add the dependency:

```xml
<dependency>
    <groupId>net.logstash.logback</groupId>
    <artifactId>logstash-logback-encoder</artifactId>
    <version>6.3</version>
</dependency>
```

CREATING THE LOGSTASH TCP APPENDER

Once the dependency is added to each service, we need to tell the licensing service that it needs to communicate with Logstash to send the applications logs, formatted as JSON. (Logback, by default, produces the application logs in plain text, but to use Elasticsearch indexes, we need to make sure we send the log data in a JSON format.) There are three ways to accomplish this:

- Using the `net.logstash.logback.encoder.LogstashEncoder` class
- Using the `net.logstash.logback.encoder.LoggingEventCompositeJson-Encoder` class
- Parsing the plain-text log data with Logstash

For this example, we will use `LogstashEncoder`. We've chosen this class because it is the easiest and fastest to implement and because, in this example, we don't need to add additional fields to the logger. With `LoggingEventCompositeJsonEncoder`, we can add new patterns or fields, disable default providers, and more. If we choose one of these two classes, the one in charge of parsing the log files into a Logstash format is the Logback. With the third option, we can delegate parsing entirely to the Logstash using a JSON filter. All three options are good, but we suggest using the `LoggingEventCompositeJson-Encoder` when you have to add or remove default configurations. The other two options will depend entirely on your business needs.

> **NOTE** You can choose whether to handle the log info in the application or in Logstash.

To configure this encoder, we'll create a Logback configuration file called logback-spring.xml. This configuration file should be located in the service resources folder. For the licensing service, the Logback configuration is shown in listing 11.1 and can be found in the licensing service's /licensing-service/src/main/resources/logback-spring.xml file. Figure 11.5 shows the log output that this configuration produces.

Listing 11.1 Configuring Logback with Logstash for the licensing service

```xml
<?xml version="1.0" encoding="UTF-8"?>
<configuration>
    <include resource="org/springframework/boot/logging/logback/base.xml"/>
```

```
<springProperty scope="context" name="application_name"
        source="spring.application.name"/>

<appender name="logstash" class="net.logstash.logback.appender.
        LogstashTcpSocketAppender">
    <destination>logstash:5000</destination>
    <encoder class="net.logstash.logback.encoder.LogstashEncoder"/>
</appender>

<root level="INFO">
    <appender-ref ref="logstash"/>
    <appender-ref ref="CONSOLE"/>
</root>
<logger name="org.springframework" level="INFO"/>
<logger name="com.optimagrowth" level="DEBUG"/>
</configuration>
```

Logstash hostname and port to establish the TCP communication

Indicates that we use TcpSocketAppender to communicate with Logstash

```
{
  "_index": "logstash-2020.05.30-000001",
  "_type": "_doc",
  "_id": "NwhPY3IBRu5zD4iyn8zO",
  "_version": 1,
  "_score": null,
  "_source": {
    "X-Span-Export": "false",
    "level_value": 10000,
    "@version": "1",
    "thread_name": "http-nio-8080-exec-9",
    "host": "licensing-service.docker_backend",
    "spanId": "6e761268be8708ed",
    "X-B3-TraceId": "6e761268be8708ed",
    "logger_name": "com.optimagrowth.license.service.client.OrganizationRestTemplateClient",
    "X-B3-SpanId": "6e761268be8708ed",
    "port": 51522,
    "spanExportable": "false",
    "message": "I have successfully retrieved an organization f31ced82-53e6-48d3-8969-0095ec7cdaf5 from the redis cache
    "@timestamp": "2020-05-30T02:01:02.043Z",
    "traceId": "6e761268be8708ed",
    "application_name": "licensing-service",
    "level": "DEBUG"
  },
  "fields": {
    "@timestamp": [
      "2020-05-30T02:01:02.043Z"
    ]
  },
  "sort": [
    1590804062043
  ]
}
```

Figure 11.5   Application log formatted with the LogstashEncoder

In figure 11.5, we can see two important aspects. The first is that LogstashEncoder includes all the values stored in Spring's MDC logger by default, and the second is that because we added the Spring Cloud Sleuth dependency to our service, we can see the TraceId, X-B3-TraceId, SpanId, X-B3-SpanId, and spanExportable fields in our log data. Note that the prefix *X-B3* propagates the default header that Spring Cloud Sleuth uses from service to service. This name consists of *X*, which is used for custom headers that are not part of the HTTP specification and *B3*, which stands for "Big-BrotherBird," Zipkin's previous name.

> **NOTE** If you want to know more about the MDC fields, we highly recommend that you read the SL4J logger documentation at http://www.slf4j.org/manual .html#mdc and the Spring Cloud Sleuth documentation at https://cloud .spring.io/spring-cloud-static/spring-cloud-sleuth/2.1.0.RELEASE/single/ spring-cloud-sleuth.html.

You can also configure the log data shown in figure 11.5 by using the `Logging-EventCompositeJsonEncoder`. Using this composite encoder, we can disable all the providers that were added by default to our configuration, add new patterns to display custom or existent MDC fields, and more. The following listing shows a brief example of the logback-spring.xml configuration that deletes some output fields and creates a new pattern with a custom field and other existent fields.

Listing 11.2 Customizing the Logback configuration for the licensing service

```
<encoder class="net.logstash.logback.encoder
            .LoggingEventCompositeJsonEncoder">
    <providers>
        <mdc>
            <excludeMdcKeyName>X-B3-TraceId</excludeMdcKeyName>
            <excludeMdcKeyName>X-B3-SpanId</excludeMdcKeyName>
            <excludeMdcKeyName>X-B3-ParentSpanId</excludeMdcKeyName>
        </mdc>
        <context/>
        <version/>
        <logLevel/>
        <loggerName/>
        <pattern>
            <pattern>
                <omitEmptyFields>true</omitEmptyFields>
                {
                    "application": {
                        version: "1.0"
                    },
                    "trace": {
                        "trace_id": "%mdc{traceId}",
                        "span_id": "%mdc{spanId}",
                        "parent_span_id": "%mdc{X-B3-ParentSpanId}",
                        "exportable": "%mdc{spanExportable}"
                    }
                }
            </pattern>
        </pattern>
        <threadName/>
        <message/>
        <logstashMarkers/>
        <arguments/>
        <stackTrace/>
    </providers>
</encoder>
```

Although we chose the `LogstashEncoder` option for this example, you should select the option that best fits your needs. Now that we have our Logback configuration in the licensing service, let's add the same configuration to our other services: configuration and gateway. We'll define and run the ELK Stack applications in Docker containers.

11.2.3 *Defining and running ELK Stack applications in Docker*

To set up our ELK Stack containers, we need to follow two simple steps. The first is to create the Logstash configuration file, and the second is to define the ELK Stack applications in our Docker configuration. Before we start creating our configuration, though, it's important to note that the Logstash pipeline has two required and one optional element. The required elements are the inputs and outputs:

- *The input enables a specific source of events to be read by Logstash.* Logstash supports a variety of input plugins such as GitHub, Http, TCP, Kafka, and others.
- *The output is in charge of sending the event data to a particular destination.* Elastic supports a variety of plugins such as CSV, Elasticsearch, email, file, MongoDB, Redis, stdout, and others.

The optional element in the Logstash configuration is the filter plugins. These filters are in charge of performing intermediary processing on an event such as translations, adding new information, parsing dates, truncating fields, and so forth. Remember, Logstash ingests and transforms the log data received. Figure 11.6 describes the Logstash process.

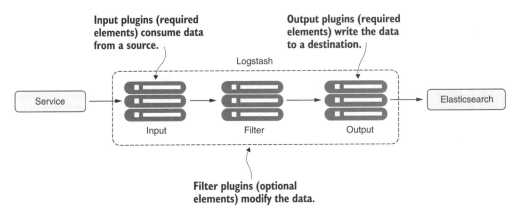

Figure 11.6   The Logstash configuration process contains two required (input and output) and one optional element (filter).

For this example, we'll use as the input plugin the Logback TCP appender that we previously configured and as the output plugin the Elasticsearch engine. The following listing shows the /docker/config/logstash.conf file.

Listing 11.3 Adding the Logstash configuration file

```
input {
  tcp {
    port => 5000
    codec => json_lines
  }
}

filter {
  mutate {
    add_tag => [ "manningPublications" ]
  }
}

output {
  elasticsearch {
    hosts => "elasticsearch:9200"
  }
}
```

TCP input plugin that reads events from a TCP socket

Logstash port

Mutate filter that adds a specific tag to the events

Elasticsearch output plugin that sends the log data to the Elasticsearch engine

Elasticsearch port

In listing 11.3, we can see five essential elements. The first is the `input` section. In this section, we specify the `tcp` plugin for consuming the log data. Next is the port number 5000; this is the port that we'll specify for Logstash later in the docker-compose.yml file. (If you take another look at figure 11.4, you'll notice that we are going to send the applications logs directly to Logstash.)

The third element is optional and corresponds to the filters; for this particular scenario, we added a mutate filter. This filter adds a `manningPublications` tag to the events. A real-world scenario of a possible tag for your services might be the environment where the application runs. Finally, the fourth and fifth elements specify the output plugin for our Logstash service and send the processed data to the Elasticsearch service running on port 9200. If you are interested in knowing more about all the input, output, and filter plugins Elastic offers, we highly recommend you visit the following pages:

- https://www.elastic.co/guide/en/logstash/current/input-plugins.html
- https://www.elastic.co/guide/en/logstash/current/output-plugins.html
- https://www.elastic.co/guide/en/logstash/current/filter-plugins.html

Now that we have the Logstash configuration, let's add the three ELK Docker entries to the docker-compose.yml file. Remember, we are using this file to fire up all of the Docker containers used for the code examples in this and the previous chapters. The following listing shows the docker/docker-compose.yml file with the new entries.

Listing 11.4 Configuring ELK Stack/Docker Compose

```
#Part of the docker-compose.yml removed for conciseness
#Some additional configuration also removed for conciseness

elasticsearch:
```

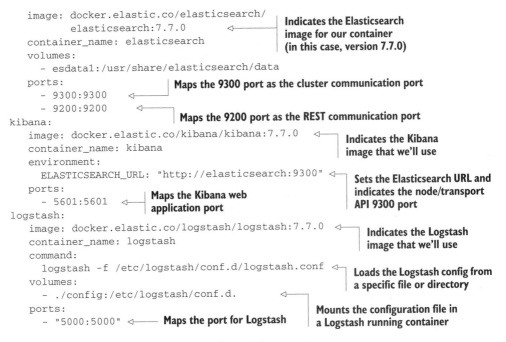

```
#Rest of the docker-compose.yml omitted for conciseness
```

NOTE   Listing 11.4 contains a small part of the docker-compose.yml file for this chapter. In case you want to see the complete file, you can visit the following link: https://github.com/ihuaylupo/manning-smia/tree/master/chapter11/docker.

To run the Docker environment, we need to execute the following commands in the root directory where the parent pom.xml is located. The `mvn` command creates a new image with the changes we made for the organization, licensing, and gateway services:

```
mvn clean package dockerfile:build
docker-compose -f docker/docker-compose.yml up
```

NOTE If you see an error 137 exit code with `<container_name>` container on your console while executing the `docker-compose` command, visit the following link to increase the memory for Docker: https://www.petefreitag.com/item/848.cfm.

Now that we have our Docker environment set up and running, let's move on with the next step.

11.2.4 Configuring Kibana

Configuring Kibana is a straightforward process, and we only need to configure it once. To access Kibana, open a web browser to the following link: http://localhost:5601/. The first time we access Kibana, a Welcome page is displayed. This page shows two options.

The first allows us to play with some sample data, and the second lets us explore the generated data from our services. Figure 11.7 shows Kibana's Welcome page.

Figure 11.7   The Kibana Welcome page with two options: trying out the application with sample data or exploring it on your own.

To explore our data, let's click the Explore on My Own link. Once clicked, we will see an Add Data page like the one shown in figure 11.8. On this page, we need to click the Discover icon on the left side of the page.

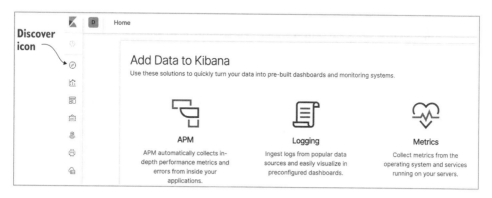

Figure 11.8   The Kibana setup page. Here we will see a set of options we can use to configure our Kibana application. Notice the icon menu on the left.

In order to continue, we must create an index pattern. Kibana uses a set of index patterns to retrieve the data from an Elasticsearch engine. The index pattern is in charge of telling Kibana which Elasticsearch indexes we want to explore. For example, in our case, we will create an index pattern indicating that we want to retrieve all of

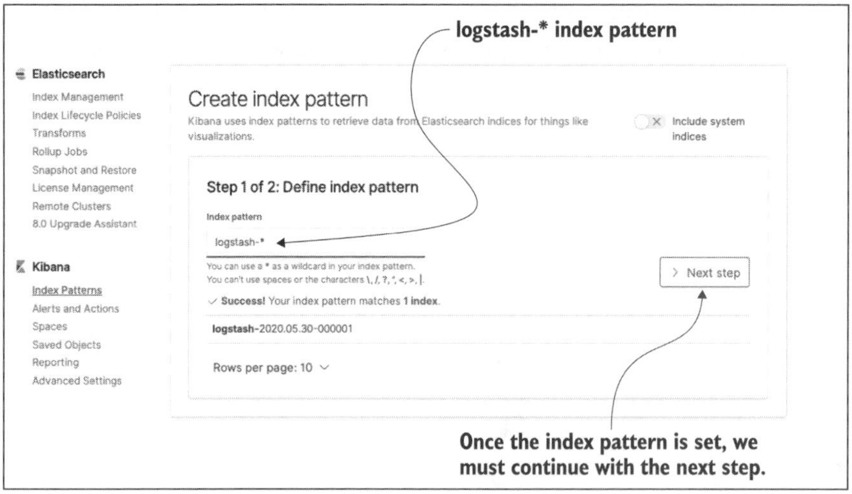

Figure 11.9   Configuring the index pattern for the Elasticsearch engine

the Logstash information from Elasticsearch. To create our index pattern, click the Index Patterns link under the Kibana section at the left of the page. Figure 11.9 shows step 1 of this process.

On the Create Index Pattern page in figure 11.9, we can see that Logstash has already created an index as a first step. However, this index is not ready to use yet. To finish setting up the index, we must specify an index pattern for that index. To create it, we need to write the index pattern, `logstash-*`, and click the Next Step button.

For step 2, we'll specify a time filter. To do this, we need to select the @timestamp option under the Time Filter Field Name drop-down list and then click the Create Index Pattern button. Figure 11.10 shows this process.

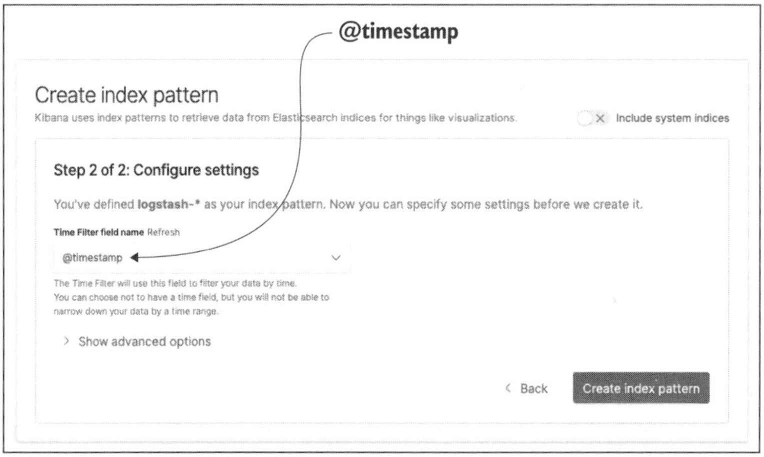

Figure 11.10   Configuring the timestamp filter for our index pattern. This pattern allows us to filter events within a time range.

We can now start making requests to our services to see the real-time logs in Kibana. Figure 11.11 shows an example of what the data sent to ELK should look like. If you don't see the page displayed in the figure, click the Discover icon again.

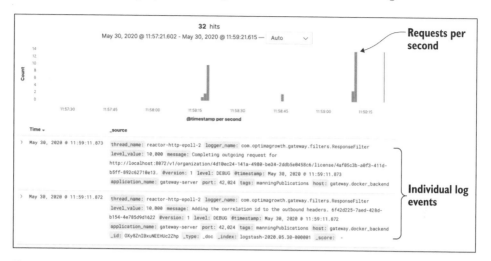

Figure 11.11 Individual service log events are stored, analyzed, and displayed by the ELK Stack.

At this point, we're all set up with Kibana. Let's continue with our final step.

11.2.5 Searching for Spring Cloud Sleuth trace IDs in Kibana

Now that our logs are flowing to ELK, we can start to appreciate how Spring Cloud Sleuth adds trace IDs to our log entries. To query for all the log entries related to a single transaction, we need to take a trace ID and query it on Kibana's Discover screen (figure 11.12). By default, Kibana uses the Kibana Query Language (KQL), which is a simplified query syntax. When writing our query, you'll see that Kibana also provides a guide and autocomplete option to simplify the process of creating custom queries.

> **NOTE** In order to apply the next filter, you need to select a valid trace ID. The trace ID used in the next example is not going to work in your Kibana instance.

Figure 11.12 shows how to execute a query with the Spring Cloud Sleuth trace ID. Here we use the trace ID `3ff985508b1b9365`.

We can expand each log event if we want to see more details. By doing this, all the fields associated with a particular event will be displayed in a table or in JSON format. We will also be able to see all the additional information we added or transformed during the Logstash processing. For example, we added a tag with the mutate filter in Logstash in listing 11.3. Figure 11.13 shows all the fields for this event.

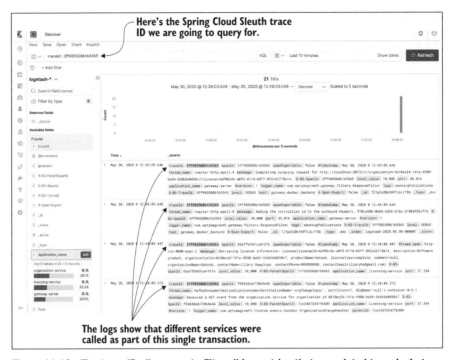

Figure 11.12   **The trace ID allows you to filter all log entries that are related to a single transaction.**

@timestamp	May 30, 2020 @ 12:48:09.487	
@version	1	
X-B3-ParentSpanId	3ff985508b1b9365	
X-B3-SpanId	05effb9d1ca4137e	
X-B3-TraceId	3ff985508b1b9365	
X-Span-Export	false	
_id	SS7pZnIBcvXP7L6LrD-B	
_index	logstash-2020.05.30-000001	**Index pattern with timestamp**
_score	-	
_type	_doc	
application_name	licensing-service	**Spring application name**
host	licensing-service.docker_backend	
level	DEBUG	
level_value	10,000	
logger_name	com.optimagrowth.license.service.LicenseService	**Logger class**
message	Retrieving license information: License(licenseId=4af05c3b-a0f3-411d-b5ff-892c62710e14, description=Software product, organizationId=4d10ec24-141a-4980-be34-2ddb5e0458c7, productName=Ostock, licenseType=complete, comment=null, organizationName=Ostock, contactName=Illary Huaylupo, contactPhone=888888888, contactEmail=illaryhs@gmail.com)	
parentId	3ff985508b1b9365	
port	37,394	
spanExportable	false	
spanId	05effb9d1ca4137e	**Spring Cloud Sleuth span ID**
tags	manningPublications	**Tag added with Logstash**
thread_name	http-nio-8080-exec-2	
traceId	3ff985508b1b9365	**Spring Cloud Sleuth trace ID**

Figure 11.13   **Detailed view of all the fields of a log event in Kibana**

11.2.6 *Adding the correlation ID to the HTTP response with Spring Cloud Gateway*

If we inspect the HTTP response from any service call made with Spring Cloud Sleuth, we'll see that the trace ID used in the call is never returned in the HTTP response headers. If we inspect the documentation for Spring Cloud Sleuth, we'll see that the Spring Cloud Sleuth team believes that returning any of the tracing data can be a potential security issue (though they don't explicitly list their reasons why they believe this). But we've found that returning a correlation or tracing ID in the HTTP response is invaluable when debugging a problem.

Spring Cloud Sleuth lets us "decorate" the HTTP response information with its tracing and span IDs. The process to do this, however, involves writing three classes and injecting two custom Spring beans. If you'd like to take this approach, you can see it in the Spring Cloud Sleuth documentation here:

- https://cloud.spring.io/spring-cloud-static/spring-cloud-sleuth/1.0.12.RELEASE/

A much simpler solution is to write a Spring Cloud Gateway filter that injects the trace ID into the HTTP response. In chapter 8, where we introduced the Spring Cloud Gateway, we saw how to build a gateway response filter, adding the generated correlation ID to the HTTP response returned by the caller for use in our services. Now we'll modify that filter to add a Spring Cloud Sleuth header. To set up our gateway response filter, we need to make sure that we have the Spring Cloud Sleuth dependencies in our pom.xml file like this:

```
<dependency>
    <groupId>org.springframework.cloud</groupId>
    <artifactId>spring-cloud-starter-sleuth</artifactId>
</dependency>
```

We'll use the `spring-cloud-starter-sleuth` dependency to tell Spring Cloud Sleuth that we want the gateway to participate in a Spring Cloud trace. Later in this chapter, when we introduce Zipkin, we'll see that the gateway service will be the first call in any service invocation. Once the dependency is in place, the actual response filter is trivial to implement.

The following listing shows the source code used to build the filter. The file is located in /gatewayserver/src/main/java/com/optimagrowth/gateway/filters/ResponseFilter.java.

> **Listing 11.5** **Adding the Spring Cloud Sleuth trace ID via a response filter**

```
package com.optimagrowth.gateway.filters;
//Imports removed for conciseness.
import brave.Tracer;
import reactor.core.publisher.Mono;

@Configuration
public class ResponseFilter {
```

```
final Logger logger =LoggerFactory.getLogger(ResponseFilter.class);

@Autowired
Tracer tracer;                      Sets the entry point to access
                                    trace and span ID information
@Autowired
FilterUtils filterUtils;

@Bean
public GlobalFilter postGlobalFilter() {
    return (exchange, chain) -> {
        return chain.filter(exchange)
            .then(Mono.fromRunnable(() -> {
                String traceId =                    Adds a span to the HTTP response
                    Tracer.currentSpan()            header tmx-correlation-ID in the
                    .context()                      Spring Cloud Sleuth trace ID
                    .traceIdString();
                logger.debug("Adding the correlation id to the outbound
                    headers. {}",traceId);
                exchange.getResponse().getHeaders()
                    .add(FilterUtils.CORRELATION_ID,traceId);
                logger.debug("Completing outgoing request for {}.",
                    exchange.getRequest().getURI());
            }));
    };
}
}
```

Because the gateway is now Spring Cloud Sleuth–enabled, we can access tracing information from within our ResponseFilter by autowiring in the Tracer class. This class lets us access information about the currently executed trace. The tracer.currentSpan() .context().traceIdString() method enables us to retrieve the current trace ID as a String for the transaction underway. It's trivial to add the trace ID to the outgoing HTTP response passing back through the gateway. This is done with the following method call:

```
exchange.getResponse().getHeaders()
        .add(FilterUtils.CORRELATION_ID, traceId);
```

With this code in place, if we invoke an O-stock microservice through our gateway, we should get an HTTP response called tmx-correlation-id with a Spring Cloud Sleuth trace ID. Figure 11.14 shows the results of a call to the following endpoint to GET the licenses of an organization:

```
http://localhost:8072/license/v1/organization/4d10ec24-141a-4980-be34-
➥ 2ddb5e0458c7/license/4af05c3b-a0f3-411d-b5ff-892c62710e14
```

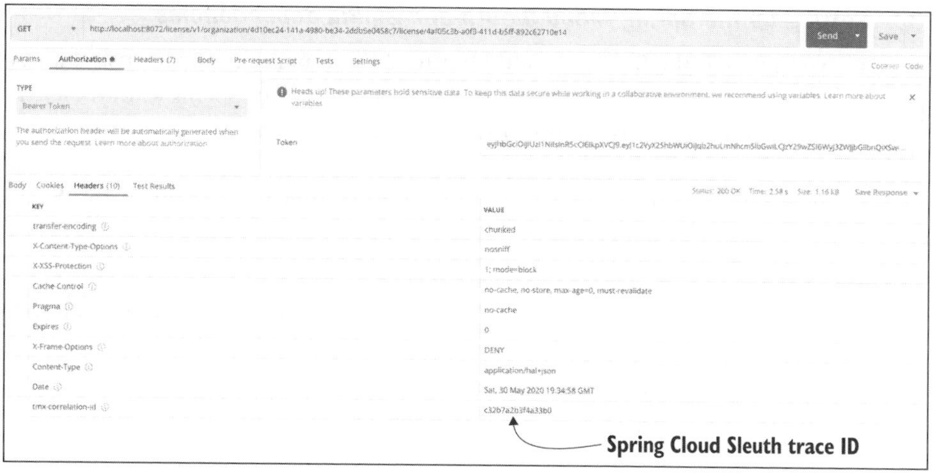

Figure 11.14 With the Spring Cloud Sleuth trace ID returned, we can easily query Kibana for the logs.

11.3 *Distributed tracing with Zipkin*

Having a unified logging platform with correlation IDs is a powerful debugging tool. However, for the rest of the chapter, we'll move away from tracing log entries and look at how to visualize the flow of transactions as they move across different microservices instead. A bright, concise picture is worth more than a million log entries.

Distributed tracing involves providing a visual picture of how a transaction flows across our different microservices. Distributed tracing tools also give a rough approximation of individual microservice response times. However, distributed tracing tools shouldn't be confused with full-blown Application Performance Management (APM) packages. APM packages offer out-of-the-box, low-level performance data on the actual service code, as well as performance data such as memory, CPU utilization, and I/O utilization beyond the response time.

This is where the Spring Cloud Sleuth and Zipkin (also referred to as OpenZipkin) projects shine. Zipkin (http://zipkin.io/) is a distributed tracing platform that allows us to trace transactions across multiple service invocations. It lets us graphically see the amount of time a transaction takes and breaks down the time spent in each microservice involved in the call. Zipkin is an invaluable tool for identifying performance issues in a microservices architecture. Setting up Spring Cloud Sleuth and Zipkin involves

- Adding Spring Cloud Sleuth and Zipkin JAR files to the services that capture trace data
- Configuring a Spring property in each service to point to the Zipkin server that will collect the trace data
- Installing and configuring a Zipkin server to collect the data
- Defining the sampling strategy each client will use to send tracing information to Zipkin

11.3.1 Setting up the Spring Cloud Sleuth and Zipkin dependencies

We've included the Spring Cloud Sleuth dependencies in our licensing and organization services. These JAR files now include the necessary Spring Cloud Sleuth libraries to enable Spring Cloud Sleuth within a service. We next need to include a new dependency, the `spring-cloud-sleuth-zipkin` dependency, to integrate with Zipkin. The following listing shows the Maven entry that should be present in the Spring Cloud Gateway, licensing, and organization services.

> **Listing 11.6   Client-side Spring Cloud Sleuth and Zipkin dependencies**

```
<dependency>
    <groupId>org.springframework.cloud</groupId>
    <artifactId>spring-cloud-sleuth-zipkin</artifactId>
</dependency>
```

11.3.2 Configuring the services to point to Zipkin

With the JAR files in place, we need to configure each service that wants to communicate with Zipkin. We'll do this by setting a Spring property that defines the URL used to communicate with Zipkin. The property that needs to be set is the `spring.zipkin.baseUrl` property. This property is set in each service's configuration file located in the repository of the Spring Cloud Config Server (for example, the /configserver/src/main/resources/config/licensing-service.properties file for the licensing service). To run it locally, set the value of the `baseUrl` property to `localhost:9411`. However, if you want to run it with Docker, you need to override that value with `zipkin:9411` like this:

```
zipkin.baseUrl: zipkin:9411
```

> **Zipkin, RabbitMQ, and Kafka**
>
> Zipkin has the ability to send its tracing data to a Zipkin server via RabbitMQ or Kafka. From a functionality perspective, there's no difference in Zipkin's behavior if we use HTTP, RabbitMQ, or Kafka. With HTTP tracing, Zipkin uses an asynchronous thread to send performance data. The main advantage of using RabbitMQ or Kafka to collect tracing data is that if our Zipkin server is down, tracing messages sent to Zipkin are "enqueued" until Zipkin can pick up the data. Configuring Spring Cloud Sleuth to send data to Zipkin via RabbitMQ and Kafka is covered in the Spring Cloud Sleuth documentation, so we won't cover it here in further detail.

11.3.3 Configuring a Zipkin server

There are several ways to set up Zipkin, but we'll use a Docker container with the Zipkin server. This option will allow us to avoid the creation of a new project in our architecture. To set up Zipkin, we'll add the following registry entry to our docker-compose.yml file located in the Docker folder for the project:

```
zipkin:
    image: openzipkin/zipkin
    container_name: zipkin
    ports:
      - 9411: 9411
    networks:
      backend:
        aliases:
          - "zipkin"
```

To run a Zipkin server, little configuration is needed. One of the few things we need to configure when we run Zipkin is the backend data store that Zipkin uses to store the tracing data. Zipkin supports four different backend data stores:

- In-memory data
- MySQL (http://mysql.com/)
- Cassandra (https://cassandra.apache.org/)
- Elasticsearch (http://elastic.co/)

By default, Zipkin uses an in-memory data store for storage. The Zipkin team, however, advises against using the in-memory database in a production environment. The in-memory database holds a limited amount of data, and the data is lost when the Zipkin server is shut down or fails.

For this example, we'll show you how to use Elasticsearch as a data store because we've already configured Elasticsearch. The only additional settings we need to add are the STORAGE_TYPE and ES_HOSTS variables in the environment section of our configuration file. The following code shows the complete Docker Compose registry:

```
zipkin:
    image: openzipkin/zipkin
    container_name: zipkin
    depends_on:
      - elasticsearch
    environment:
      - STORAGE_TYPE=elasticsearch
      - "ES_HOSTS=elasticsearch:9300"
    ports:
      - "9411:9411"
    networks:
      backend:
        aliases:
          - "zipkin"
```

11.3.4 Setting tracing levels

Now we have the clients configured to talk to a Zipkin server, and we have the server configured and ready to run. But we need to do one more step before we can start using Zipkin and that is to define how often each service should write data to Zipkin.

By default, Zipkin only writes 10% of all transactions to the Zipkin server. The default value ensures that Zipkin will not overwhelm our logging and analysis infrastructure.

The transaction sampling can be controlled by setting a Spring property on each of the services sending data to Zipkin: the `spring.sleuth.sampler.percentage` property. This property takes a value between 0 and 1 as follows:

- A value of 0 means Spring Cloud Sleuth doesn't send Zipkin any transactions.
- A value of .5 means Spring Cloud Sleuth sends 50% of all transactions.
- A value of 1 means Spring Cloud Sleuth sends all transactions (100%).

For our purposes, we'll send all trace information (100%) for our services and all transactions. To do this, we can set the value of `spring.sleuth.sampler.percentage`, or we can replace the default `Sampler` class used in Spring Cloud Sleuth with `Always-Sampler`. The class `AlwaysSampler` can be injected as a Spring bean into an application. But for this example, we will use the `spring.sleuth.sampler.percentage` in the configuration file of the licensing, organization, and gateway services as follows:

```
zipkin.baseUrl: zipkin:9411
spring.sleuth.sampler.percentage: 1
```

11.3.5 Using Zipkin to trace transactions

Let's start this section with a scenario. Imagine you're one of the developers on the O-stock application, and you're on call this week. You get a support ticket from a customer who's complaining that one of the screens in the application is running slow. You have a suspicion that the licensing service being used by the screen is the culprit. But why and where?

In our scenario, the licensing service relies on the organization service, and both services make calls to different databases. Which service is the poor performer? Also, you know that these services are continually being modified, so someone might have added a new service call to the mix.

> **NOTE** Understanding all the services that participate in the user's transaction and their individual performance times is critical in supporting a distributed architecture such as a microservices architecture.

To solve this dilemma, we'll use Zipkin to watch two transactions from our organization service as the Zipkin service traces them. The organization service is a simple service that only makes a call to a single database. What we're going to do is to use Postman to send two calls to the organization service with the following endpoint. The organization service calls will flow through the gateway before the calls get directed downstream to an organization service instance:

```
GET http://localhost:8072/organization/v1/organization/4d10ec24-141a-4980-
➥ be34-2ddb5e0458c6
```

If we look at the screenshot in figure 11.15, we'll see that Zipkin captured two transactions and that each transaction is broken down into one or more spans. In Zipkin, a *span* represents a specific service or call in which timing information is captured. Each of the transactions in figure 11.15 has five spans: two spans in the gateway, two for the organization, and one for the licensing service.

Remember, the gateway doesn't blindly forward an HTTP call. It receives the incoming HTTP call, terminates it, and then builds a new call to send to the targeted service (in this case, the organization service). The termination of the original call is how the gateway can add response, pre-, and post-filters to each call entering the gateway. It's also why we see two spans in the gateway service in figure 11.15.

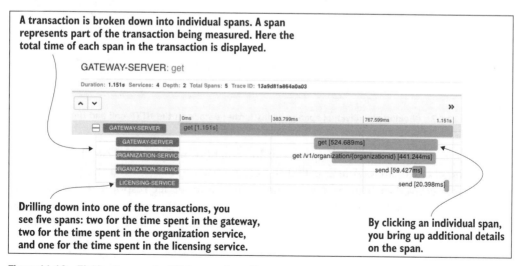

Figure 11.15 The Zipkin query screen, where we can select the service we want to trace, along with some basic query filters

The two calls to the organization service through the gateway took 1.151 seconds and 39.152 ms, respectively. Let's dig into the details of the longest-running call (1.151 seconds). We can see more detail by clicking the transaction and drilling down. Figure 11.16 shows the details for our calls to the organization service.

A transaction is broken down into individual spans. A span represents part of the transaction being measured. Here the total time of each span in the transaction is displayed.

GATEWAY-SERVER: get

Duration: **1.151s** Services: **4** Depth: **2** Total Spans: **5** Trace ID: **13a9d81a864a0a03**

	0ms	383.799ms	767.599ms	1.151s
GATEWAY-SERVER	get [1.151s]			
GATEWAY-SERVER			get [524.689ms]	
ORGANIZATION-SERVICE			get /v1/organization/{organizationid} [441.244ms]	
ORGANIZATION-SERVICE				send [59.427ms]
LICENSING-SERVICE				send [20.398ms]

Drilling down into one of the transactions, you see five spans: two for the time spent in the gateway, two for the time spent in the organization service, and one for the time spent in the licensing service.

By clicking an individual span, you bring up additional details on the span.

Figure 11.16 Zipkin allows us to drill down and see the amount of time each span takes with a transaction.

In figure 11.16, we can see that the entire transaction from a gateway perspective took approximately 1.151 seconds. However, the organization service call made by the gateway took 524.689 ms of the 1.151 seconds involved in the overall call. Let's drill down in each span for even more detail. Click the organization-service span and notice the additional details from the call (figure 11.17).

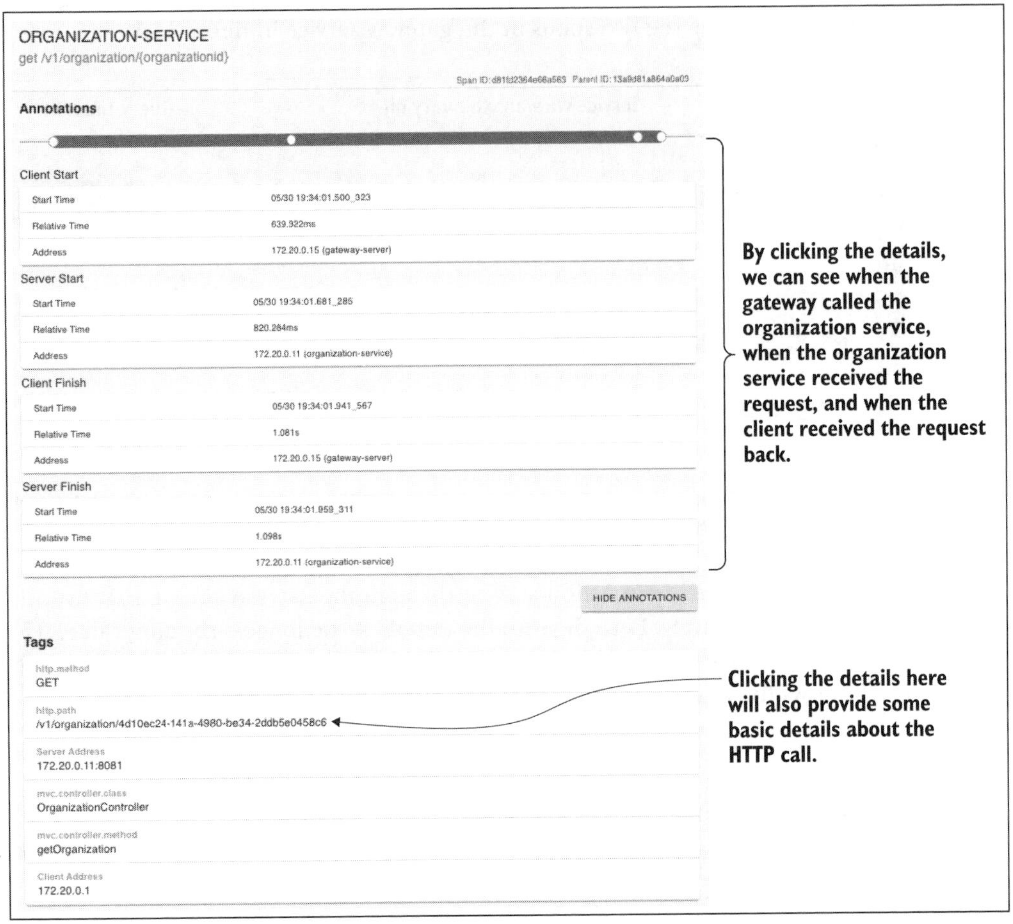

Figure 11.17   Clicking an individual span provides further details on the HTTP call and timing.

One of the most valuable pieces of information in figure 11.17 is the breakdown of the client (Gateway) as it called the organization service, when the organization service received the call, and when the organization service responded. This type of timing information is invaluable in detecting and identifying network latency issues. To add a custom span to the licensing service's call to Redis, we'll use the following class:

```
/licensing-service/src/main/java/com/optimagrowth/license/service/client/
    OrganizationRestTemplateClient.java
```

With the `OrganizationRestTemplateClient`, we'll implement the `checkRedisCache()` method. The following listing shows this code.

Listing 11.7 Adding `checkRedisCache()` to `OrganizationRestTemplate`

```
package com.optimagrowth.license.service.client;
//Rest of imports omitted for conciseness

@Component
public class OrganizationRestTemplateClient {
    @Autowired
    RestTemplate restTemplate;

    @Autowired
    Tracer tracer;                          ◁── Tracer accesses the Spring Cloud
                                               Sleuth trace information.
    @Autowired
    OrganizationRedisRepository redisRepository;

    private static final Logger logger =
        LoggerFactory.getLogger(OrganizationRestTemplateClient.class);

    private Organization checkRedisCache       ◁── Implements the
            (String organizationId) {              CheckRedisCache method
      try {
        return redisRepository.findById(organizationId).orElse(null);
      } catch (Exception ex){
          logger.error("Error encountered while trying to retrieve
              organization {} check Redis Cache. Exception {}",
              organizationId, ex);
          return null;
      }
    }

    //Rest of class omitted for conciseness
}
```

11.3.6 *Visualizing a more complex transaction*

What if we want to understand precisely which service dependencies exist between service calls? We can call the licensing service through the gateway and then query Zipkin for licensing service traces with a GET call to the licensing services using the following endpoint. Figure 11.18 shows the detailed trace of this call.

```
http://localhost:8072/license/v1/organization/4d10ec24-141a-4980-be34-
➥ 2ddb5e0458c8/license/4af05c3b-a0f3-411d-b5ff-892c62710e15
```

In figure 11.18, we can see that the call to the licensing service involves eight HTTP calls. We see the call to the gateway and then from the gateway to the licensing service; the licensing service to the gateway and the gateway to the organization; and finally, the organization to the licensing service using Apache Kafka to update the Redis cache.

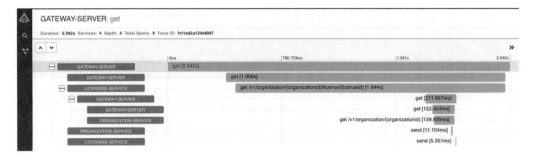

Figure 11.18 Viewing the details of a trace that shows how a licensing service call flows from the gateway to the licensing service and then to the organization service.

11.3.7 *Capturing messaging traces*

Messaging can introduce its own performance and latency issues inside an application. A service might not be processing a message from a queue quickly enough. Or there could be a network latency problem. We've encountered these scenarios while building microservice-based applications.

Spring Cloud Sleuth sends Zipkin trace data on any inbound or outbound message channel registered in the service. Using Spring Cloud Sleuth and Zipkin, we can identify when a message is published from a queue and when it's received. We can also see what behavior takes place when the message is received on a queue and processed. And, you'll remember from chapter 10, when an organization record is added, updated, or deleted, a Kafka message is produced and published via Spring Cloud Stream. The licensing service receives the message and updates a Redis key-value store that it uses to cache the data.

Next we'll delete an organization record and watch Spring Cloud Sleuth and Zipkin trace the transaction. We'll issue a DELETE to the following endpoint for the organization service via Postman:

```
http://localhost:8072/organization/v1/organization/4d10ec24-141a-4980-be34-
2ddb5e0458c7
```

Earlier in the chapter, we saw how to add the trace ID as an HTTP response header, adding a new HTTP response header called `tmx-correlation-id`. We had the `tmx-correlation-id` returned on our call with a value of `054accff01c9ba6b`. We can search Zipkin for this specific trace by entering the trace ID returned by our call into the search box in the upper-right corner of the Zipkin query screen. Figure 11.19 shows where we can enter the trace ID.

With the specific trace in hand, we can query Zipkin for the transaction and view the publication of the DELETE message. The second span in figure 11.20 is the output message from the channel output, which is used to publish to a Kafka topic called `orgChangeTopic`. Figure 11.20 shows the output message channel and how it appears in the Zipkin trace.

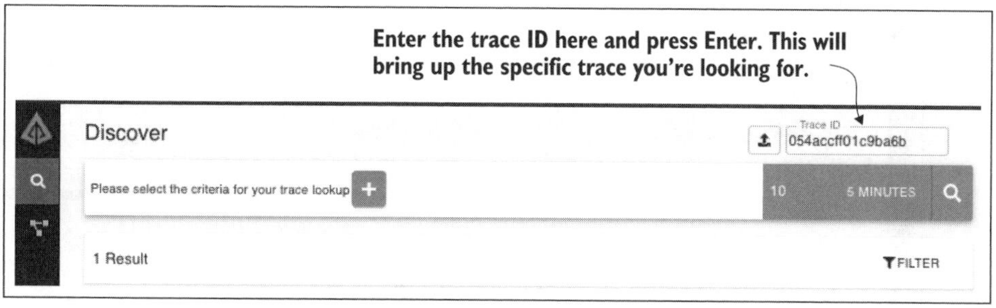

Enter the trace ID here and press Enter. This will
bring up the specific trace you're looking for.

**Figure 11.19   With the trace ID returned in the HTTP `tmx-correlation-id` response header, we
can easily find the transaction by searching on the specific trace ID.**

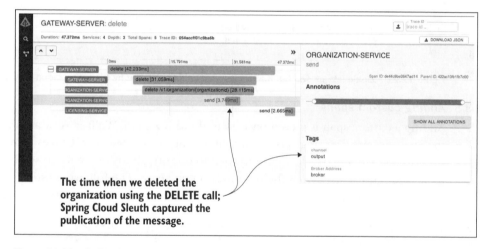

The time when we deleted the
organization using the DELETE call;
Spring Cloud Sleuth captured the
publication of the message.

**Figure 11.20   Spring Cloud Sleuth automatically traces the publication and receipt of messages on
the Spring message channels. We can view the details of the trace with Zipkin.**

You can see the licensing service receive the message by clicking the licensing service
span. Figure 11.21 shows this data.

Until now, we've used Zipkin to trace our HTTP and messaging calls from within
our services. However, what if we want to perform traces out to third-party services
that aren't monitored by Zipkin? For example, what if we want to get tracing and timing information for a specific Redis or Postgres SQL call? Fortunately, Spring Cloud
Sleuth and Zipkin allow us to add custom spans to our transactions so that we can
trace the execution time associated with third-party calls.

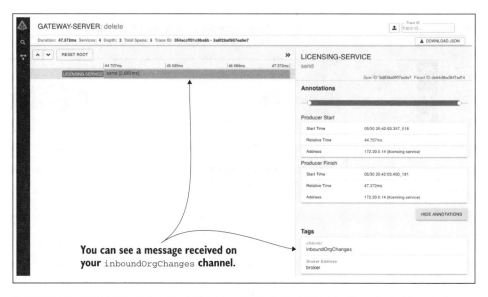

Figure 11.21   Zipkin lets us see the Kafka message being published by the organization service.

11.3.8   Adding custom spans

Adding a custom span is incredibly easy to do with Zipkin. We'll start by adding a custom span to our licensing service so that we can trace how long it takes to pull data from Redis. Then we'll add a custom span to our organization service to see how long it takes to retrieve data from the organization database. The following listing creates a custom span for the licensing service that's called `readLicensingDataFromRedis`.

Listing 11.8   Adding the Spring Cloud Sleuth trace ID via a response filter

```
package com.optimagrowth.license.service.client;
//Rest of code removed for conciseness

    private Organization checkRedisCache(String organizationId) {
        ScopedSpan newSpan =
            tracer.startScopedSpan                          Creates a custom span called
            ("readLicensingDataFromRedis");          ◁──┘  readLicensingDataFromRedis
        try {
          return redisRepository.findById(organizationId).orElse(null);
        } catch (Exception ex){
            logger.error("Error encountered while trying to retrieve
                organization {} check Redis Cache.  Exception {}",
                organizationId, ex);                          Adds tag information to the
            return null;                                      span and names the service
        } finally {                                           that Zipkin will capture
            newSpan.tag("peer.service", "redis");      ◁──┘
            newSpan.annotate("Client received");
            newSpan.finish();        ◁──┐
        }                                Closes and finishes the span. If this is not
    }                                    done, we'll get an error message in the
}                                        log saying that a span was left open.
```

Next we'll add a custom span, called `getOrgDbCall`, to the organization service to monitor how long it takes to retrieve organization data from the Postgres database. The trace for the organization service database calls can be seen in the `Organization-Service` class, which you'll find in the file /organization-service/src/main/java/com/optimagrowth/organization/service/OrganizationService.java. The `findById()` method call contains the custom trace. The following listing shows the source code for this method.

Listing 11.9   Implementing the `findById()` method

```
package com.optimagrowth.organization.service;
//Some imports omitted for conciseness
import brave.ScopedSpan;
import brave.Tracer;

@Service
public class OrganizationService {
    //Some code omitted for conciseness
    @Autowired
    Tracer tracer;

    public Organization findById(String organizationId) {
        Optional<Organization> opt = null;
        ScopedSpan newSpan = tracer.startScopedSpan("getOrgDBCall");
        try {
          opt = repository.findById(organizationId);
          simpleSourceBean.publishOrganizationChange("GET", organizationId);
          if (!opt.isPresent()) {
            String message = String.format("Unable to find an
                organization with theOrganization id %s",
              organizationId);
            logger.error(message);
            throw new IllegalArgumentException(message);
          }
          logger.debug("Retrieving Organization Info: " +
          opt.get().toString());

        } finally {
            newSpan.tag("peer.service", "postgres");
            newSpan.annotate("Client received");
            newSpan.finish();
        }

        return opt.get();
    }
    //Rest of class removed for conciseness
}
```

With these two custom spans in place, restart the services. Then select the following GET endpoint:

```
http://localhost:8072/license/v1/organization/4d10ec24-141a-4980-be34-
    2ddb5e0458c9/license/4af05c3b-a0f3-411d-b5ff-892c62710e16
```

If we look at the transaction in Zipkin, we should see the addition of two new spans when we call the licensing service endpoint to retrieve licensing information. Figure 11.22 shows the custom spans.

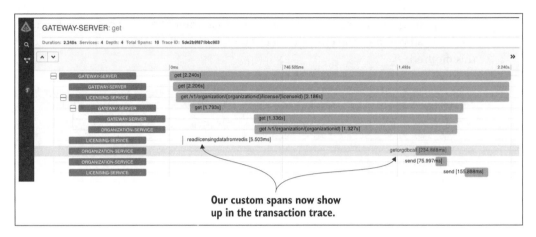

Figure 11.22   The custom spans for our services show up in the transaction trace.

Figure 11.22 also shows additional tracing and timing information related to our Redis and database lookups. Drilling down, we can see that the read call to Redis took 5.503 ms. Because the call didn't find an item in the Redis cache, the SQL call to the Postgres database took 234.888 ms.

Now that we know how to set up a distributed tracing, API gateway, discovery service, and custom spans, let's continue with the next chapter. In the next chapter, we will explain how to deploy everything that we've built throughout the book.

Summary

- Spring Cloud Sleuth allows us to seamlessly add tracing information (correlation IDs) to our microservice calls.
- Correlation IDs can be used to link log entries across multiple services. This lets us observe the behavior of a transaction across all the services involved in a single transaction.
- While correlation IDs are powerful, we need to partner this concept with a log aggregation platform that will allow us to ingest logs from multiple sources and then search and query their contents.
- We can integrate Docker containers with a log aggregation platform to capture all the application logging data.
- We integrate our Docker containers with the ELK (Elasticsearch, Logstash, Kibana) Stack. This lets us transform, store, visualize, and query the logging data from our services.

- While a unified logging platform is essential, the ability to visually trace a transaction through its microservices is also a valuable tool.
- Zipkin allows us to see the dependencies that exist between services and the flow of our transactions, and understand the performance characteristics of each microservice involved in a user's transaction.
- Spring Cloud Sleuth integrates with Zipkin easily. Zipkin automatically captures trace data from an HTTP call, which becomes an inbound/outbound message channel used within a Spring Cloud Sleuth–enabled service.
- Spring Cloud Sleuth maps each service call to the concept of a span. Zipkin then allows us to see the performance of a span.
- Spring Cloud Sleuth and Zipkin also let us define our own custom spans so that we can understand the performance of non-Spring-based resources (a database server such as Postgres or Redis).

12

Deploying your microservices

This chapter covers

- Understanding why DevOps is critical to microservices
- Configuring the core Amazon infrastructure for O-stock services
- Manually deploying O-stock services to Amazon
- Designing a build/deployment pipeline for your services
- Treating your infrastructure as code
- Deploying your application to the cloud

We're almost at the end of the book, but not the end of our microservices journey. While most of this book has focused on designing, building, and putting Spring-based microservices into operation using the Spring Cloud technology, we haven't touched on how to build and deploy microservices. Creating a build/deployment pipeline might seem like a mundane task, but in reality, it's one of the most critical pieces of our microservices architecture.

340

Why? Remember, one of the key advantages of a microservices architecture is that microservices are small units of code that can be quickly built, modified, and deployed to a production environment independently of one another. The small size of the service means that new features (and critical bug fixes) can be delivered with a high degree of *velocity*. Velocity is the keyword here because velocity implies that little to no friction exists between creating a new feature or fixing a bug and getting our service redeployed. Lead times for deployment should be minutes, not days. To accomplish this, the mechanism that you use to build and deploy your code needs to be

- *Automated*—When we build our code, there should be no human intervention in the build/deployment process. The process of building the software, provisioning a machine image, and deploying the service should be automated and initiated by the act of committing code to the source repository.
- *Repeatable*—The process that we use to build and deploy our software should be repeatable; the same thing happens every time a build and deploy kicks off. Variability in our process is often the source of subtle bugs that are difficult to track down and resolve.
- *Complete*—The outcome of our deployed artifact should be an entire virtual machine or container image (Docker, for example) that contains the "complete" run-time environment for the service. This is an important shift in the way we think about our infrastructure.

  The provisioning of our machine images needs to be completely automated via scripts and kept under source control along with the service source code. In a microservice environment, this responsibility usually shifts from an operations team to the development team owning the service. One of the core tenets of microservice development is pushing the developers to complete operational responsibility for the service.
- *Immutable*—Once the machine image containing our service is built, the image's run-time configuration should not be touched or changed after deploying the image. If changes need to be made, they need to happen in the scripts kept under source control, and the service and infrastructure must go through the build process again.

  Run-time configuration changes (garbage collection settings, Spring profile used, and so forth) should be passed as environment variables to the image, while application configuration should be kept separate from the container (Spring Cloud Config).

Building a robust and generalized build deployment pipeline is a significant amount of work and is often explicitly designed toward the run-time environment. It usually involves a specialized team of DevOps (developer/operations) engineers, whose sole job is to generalize the build process so that each team can build their microservices without having to reinvent the entire build process. Unfortunately, Spring is a development framework and doesn't offer a significant number of capabilities to implement a build/deployment pipeline. But that doesn't mean that such a pipeline can't be built.

12.1   *The architecture of a build/deployment pipeline*

The goal of this chapter is to provide you with the working pieces of a build/deployment pipeline so that you can take these pieces and tailor to your own environment. Let's start our discussion by looking at the general architecture of our build/deployment pipeline and several of the general patterns and themes that it represents. To keep the examples flowing, we've done a few things that we wouldn't normally do in our own environment, and we'll call those pieces out accordingly.

Our discussion on deploying microservices begins with a picture you saw way back in chapter 1. Figure 12.1 is a duplicate of the diagram you saw in chapter 1, showing the pieces and steps involved in creating a microservices build/deployment pipeline.

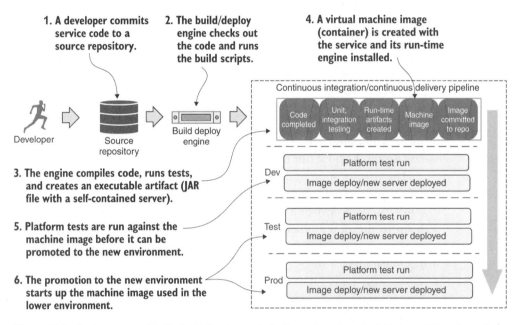

Figure 12.1   Each component in the build/deployment pipeline automates a task that would have been done manually.

Figure 12.1 should look somewhat familiar because it's based on the general build/deployment pattern used for implementing continuous integration (CI):

1. A developer commits their code to the source code repository.

2. A build tool monitors the source control repository for changes and kicks off a build when a change is detected.

3. During the build, the application's unit and integration tests are run, and if everything passes, a deployable software artifact is created (a JAR, WAR, or EAR).

4. This JAR, WAR, or EAR might then be deployed to an application server running on another server (usually a development server).

A similar process is followed by the build/deployment pipeline until the code is ready to be deployed. We're going to tack continuous delivery (CD) onto the build/deployment process shown in figure 12.1 with the following steps:

1 A developer commits their service code to a source repository.

2 A build/deploy engine monitors the source code repository for changes. If code is committed, the build/deploy engine checks out the code and runs the build scripts.

3 After the build scripts compile the code and run its unit and integration tests, the service is then compiled to an executable artifact. Because our microservices were built using Spring Boot, our build process creates an executable JAR file that contains both the service code and a self-contained Tomcat server.

Note that the next step is where our build/deploy pipeline begins to deviate from a traditional Java CI build process.

4 After the executable JAR is built, we "bake" a machine image with our microservice deployed to it. This baking process creates a virtual machine image or container (Docker) and installs our service onto it.

When the virtual machine image starts, our service also starts and is ready to begin taking requests. Unlike a traditional CI build process, where you might deploy the compiled JAR or WAR to an application server that's independently (and often with a separate team) managed from the application, with the CI/CD process, we deploy the microservice, the run-time engine for the service, and the machine image all as one codependent unit managed by the development team that wrote the software.

5 Before we officially deploy to a new environment, the machine image starts, and a series of platform tests are run against the image for the environment to determine if everything is proceeding correctly. If the platform tests pass, the machine image is promoted to the new environment and made available for use.

6 The promotion of the service to the new environment involves starting up the exact machine image that was used in the lower environment. This is the secret sauce of the whole process. The entire machine image is deployed.

With CD, no changes are made to any installed software (including the operating system) after the server is created. By promoting and using the same machine image, you guarantee the immutability of the server as it moves from one environment to the next.

Unit tests vs. integration tests vs. platform tests
Figure 12.1 exposes several types of testing (unit, integration, and platform) during the building and deployment of a service. Three types of testing are typical in this type of a pipeline:

(continued)

- *Unit tests*—These are run immediately before the compilation of the service code, but before deployment to an environment. The tests are designed to run in complete isolation, with each unit test being small and narrow in focus. A unit test should have no dependencies on third-party infrastructure databases, services, and so on. Usually, a unit test scope encompasses the testing of a single method or function.

- *Integration tests*—These are run immediately after packaging the service code. They are designed to test an entire workflow, code path, and stub or to mock primary services or components that would need to be called with third-party services. During integration testing, you might be running an in-memory database to hold data, mocking out third-party service calls, and so on. With integration tests, third-party dependencies are mocked or stubbed so that any requests that would invoke a remote service are also mocked or stubbed. The calls never leave the build server.

- *Platform tests*—These are run right before a service is deployed to an environment. These tests typically test an entire business flow and also call all the third-party dependencies that would normally be called in a production system. Platform tests are running live in a particular environment and don't involve any mocked-out services. This type of test is run to determine integration problems with third-party services that would typically not be detected when a third-party service is stubbed out during an integration test.

If you are interested in diving into more detail on how to create unit, integration, and platform tests, we highly recommend *Testing Java Microservices* (Manning, 2018) by Alex Soto Bueno, Andy Gumbrecht, and Jason Porter.

The build/deploy process is built on four core patterns. These patterns have emerged from the collective experience of development teams building microservice and cloud-based applications. These patterns include

- *Continuous integration/continuous delivery (CI/CD)*—With CI/CD, your application code isn't only built and tested when it is committed and deployed. The deployment of your code should go something like this: if the code passes its unit, integration, and platform tests, it's immediately promoted to the next environment. The only stopping point in most organizations is the push to production.

- *Infrastructure as code*—The final software artifact that's pushed to development and beyond is a machine image. The machine image with your microservice installed in it is provisioned immediately after your microservice's source code is compiled and tested. The provisioning of the machine image occurs through a series of scripts that run with each build. No human hands should ever touch the server after it's built. The provisioning scripts should be kept under source control and managed like any other piece of code.

■ *Immutable server*—Once a server image is built, the server's configuration and microservice are never touched after the provisioning process. This guarantees that your environment won't suffer from "configuration drift," where a developer or system administrator made "one small change" that later caused an outage. If a change needs to be made, change the provisioning scripts for the server and kick off a new build.

On immutability and the rise of the Phoenix Server

With the concept of immutable servers, we should always be guaranteed that a server's configuration matches precisely with what the machine image for the server says it does. A server should have the option to be killed and restarted from the machine image without any changes in the service or microservice behavior. This killing and resurrection of a new server was termed "Phoenix Server" by Martin Fowler because, when the old server is killed, the new server should rise from the ashes. For more information, see the following link:

■ http://martinfowler.com/bliki/PhoenixServer.html

The Phoenix Server pattern has two fundamental benefits. First, it exposes and drives configuration drift from your environment. If you're constantly tearing down and setting up new servers, you're more likely to expose configuration drift early. This is a tremendous help in ensuring consistency.

Second, the Phoenix Server pattern helps to improve resiliency by allowing you to find situations where a server or service isn't cleanly recoverable after it's killed and restarted. Remember, in a microservices architecture, your services should be stateless, and the death of a server should be a minor blip. Randomly killing and restarting servers quickly exposes situations where you have a state in your services or infrastructure. It's better to find these situations and dependencies early in your deployment pipeline than when you're on the phone with an angry customer or company.

For this chapter, we'll see how to implement a build/deployment pipeline using several non-Spring tools. We're going to take the suite of microservices we've built for this book and do the following:

1 Integrate our Maven build scripts into a CI/deployment cloud-based tool called Jenkins
2 Build immutable Docker images for each service and push those images to a centralized repository
3 Deploy the entire suite of microservices to Amazon's cloud using Amazon's container service called the Elastic Kubernetes Service (EKS)

NOTE In this book, we won't explain in detail how Kubernetes works. In case you are new or want to learn more about how it works, we highly recommend you read Marko Lukša's excellent book, *Kubernetes in Action* (Manning, 2017), which covers the subject in detail.

Before we start with our pipeline, let's begin by setting up the core infrastructure in the cloud.

12.2 Setting up O-stock's core infrastructure in the cloud

Throughout all the code examples in this book, we've run our applications inside a single virtual machine image with each individual service running as a Docker container. We're going to change that now by separating our database server (PostgreSQL) and caching server (Redis) away from Docker into the Amazon cloud. All the other services will remain running as Docker containers inside a single-node Amazon EKS cluster. Figure 12.2 shows the deployment of the O-stock services to the Amazon cloud.

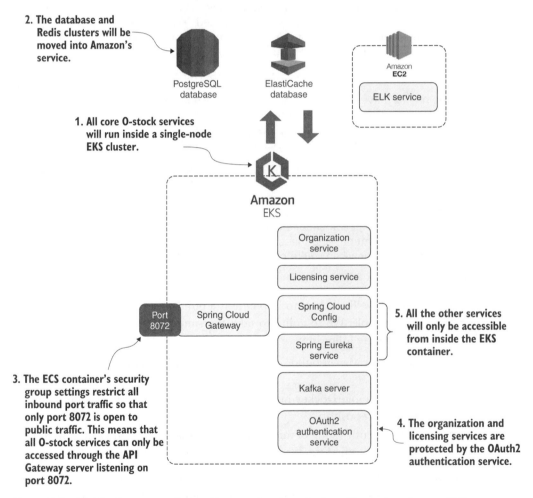

Figure 12.2   With Docker, we can deploy all our services to a cloud provider such as Amazon EKS.

Let's walk through the details in figure 12.2. Note that the numbers correspond to those in the figure:

1 All our O-stock services (minus the database and the Redis cluster) will be deployed as Docker containers running inside a single-node EKS cluster. EKS configures and sets up the servers needed to run a Docker cluster. EKS can also monitor the health of containers running in Docker and restart our service if it crashes.

2 With the deployment to the Amazon cloud, we'll move away from using our PostgreSQL database and Redis server and instead use the Amazon Relational Database Service (Amazon RDS) and Amazon ElastiCache services. We could continue to run the Postgres and Redis data stores in Docker, but we wanted to highlight how easy it is to move from one infrastructure to another that's managed completely by a cloud provider.

3 Unlike our desktop deployment, we want all traffic for the server to go through our API gateway. We're going to use an Amazon security group to only allow port 8072 on the deployed EKS cluster to be accessible to the world.

4 We'll still use Spring's OAuth2 server to protect our services. Before the organization and licensing services can be accessed, the user needs to authenticate with our authentication services (see chapter 9 for details on this) and present a valid OAuth2 token on every service call.

5 All our servers, including our Kafka server, won't be publicly accessible to the outside world via their exposed Docker ports. They will only be available from inside an EKS container.

Some prerequisites for working with AWS

To set up your Amazon infrastructure, you'll need the following:

- *Your own Amazon Web Services (AWS) account*—You should have a basic understanding of the AWS console and the concepts behind working in this environment.
- *A web browser*
- *The AWS CLI (command-line interface)*—This unified tool manages AWS Services. See https://docs.aws.amazon.com/cli/latest/userguide/install-cliv2 .html.
- *Kubectl*—This tool allow us to communicate and interact with our Kubernetes cluster. See https://kubernetes.io/docs/tasks/tools/install-kubectl/#install-kubectl.
- *IAM Authenticator*—This tool provides authentication to our Kubernetes cluster. See https://docs.aws.amazon.com/eks/latest/userguide/install-aws-iam-authenticator.html.
- *Eksctl*—A simple command-line utility for managing and creating AWS EKS clusters in our AWS account. See https://docs.aws.amazon.com/eks/latest/userguide/getting-started-eksctl.html.

(continued)

If you're entirely new to AWS, we highly recommend you pick up a copy of Michael and Andreas Wittig's book, *Amazon Web Services in Action* (Manning, 2018). The first chapter in this book includes a well-written tutorial at the end of the chapter on how to sign up and configure your AWS account. That chapter is available for download here:

https://www.manning.com/books/amazon-web-services-in-action-second-edition

In this chapter, we've tried as much as possible to use the free-tier services offered by Amazon. The only place where we couldn't do this was when setting up the EKS cluster. We used an M4 large server that costs approximately $0.10 per hour to run. If you don't want to incur high costs running this server, ensure that you shut down your services after you're done. If you want to know more about AWS EC2 instance pricing, visit the official Amazon documentation at the following link: https://aws.amazon.com/ec2/pricing/on-demand/.

And finally, there's no guarantee that the Amazon resources (Postgres, Redis, and EKS) that we use in this chapter will be available if you want to run this code yourself. If you're going to run the code from this chapter, you need to set up your own GitHub repository (for your application configuration), your own Jenkins environment, Docker Hub (for your Docker images), and Amazon account. You'll then need to modify your application configuration to point to your account and credentials.

12.2.1 Creating the PostgreSQL database using Amazon RDS

To begin, we need to set up and configure our Amazon AWS account. Once this is done, we'll create the PostgreSQL database that we'll use for our O-stock services. To do this, we first need to log in to the Amazon AWS Management Console (https://aws.amazon.com/console/). You'll be presented with a list of Amazon web services when you first log into the console.

1 Locate the link called RDS. Click the link, which takes you to the RDS dashboard.
2 On the RDS dashboard, click the big Create Database button.
3 You should see a list of databases. Although Amazon RDS supports different database engines, select PostgreSQL and click Option. This displays the database fields.

You should now see a screen with three template options: a production database, a dev/test database, and a free tier. Select the Free Tier option. Next, under Settings, add the necessary information about our PostgreSQL database, setting the master user ID and password that we'll use to log in to the database. Figure 12.3 shows this screen.

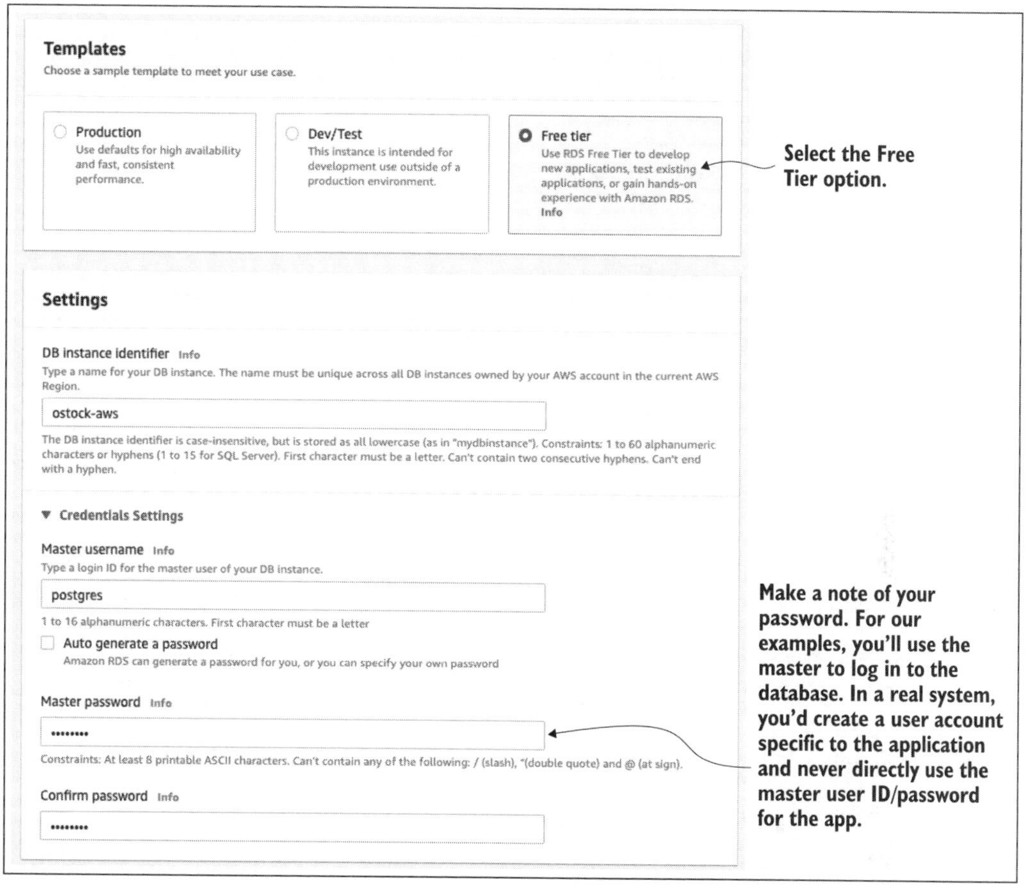

Templates

Choose a sample template to meet your use case.

○ **Production**
Use defaults for high availability and fast, consistent performance.

○ **Dev/Test**
This instance is intended for development use outside of a production environment.

● **Free tier**
Use RDS Free Tier to develop new applications, test existing applications, or gain hands-on experience with Amazon RDS. Info

Select the Free Tier option.

Settings

DB instance identifier Info

Type a name for your DB instance. The name must be unique across all DB instances owned by your AWS account in the current AWS Region.

ostock-aws

The DB instance identifier is case-insensitive, but is stored as all lowercase (as in "mydbinstance"). Constraints: 1 to 60 alphanumeric characters or hyphens (1 to 15 for SQL Server). First character must be a letter. Can't contain two consecutive hyphens. Can't end with a hyphen.

▼ **Credentials Settings**

Master username Info

Type a login ID for the master user of your DB instance.

postgres

1 to 16 alphanumeric characters. First character must be a letter

☐ **Auto generate a password**
Amazon RDS can generate a password for you, or you can specify your own password

Master password Info

••••••••

Constraints: At least 8 printable ASCII characters. Can't contain any of the following: / (slash), "(double quote) and @ (at sign).

Confirm password Info

••••••••

Make a note of your password. For our examples, you'll use the master to log in to the database. In a real system, you'd create a user account specific to the application and never directly use the master user ID/password for the app.

Figure 12.3   Selecting whether our database is going to use a production, test, or free tier template and setting up the basic database configuration in Amazon's AWS Management Console

Next, we'll leave the default configurations for these sections: DB Instance Size, Storage, Availability & Durability, and Database Authentication. The final step is to set the following options. At any time you can click Info to get help about your selection. Figure 12.4 shows this screen.

- *Virtual Private Cloud (VPC)*—Choose Default VPC.
- *Publicly Accessible*—Select Yes.
- *VPC Security Group*—Select Create New, and add a name for the group. For this example, we named the security group ostock-sg.
- *Database Port*—Enter 5432 for the TCP/IP port.

At this point, our database creation process begins (it can take several minutes). Once it's done, we'll need to configure the O-stock service properties to use the database in

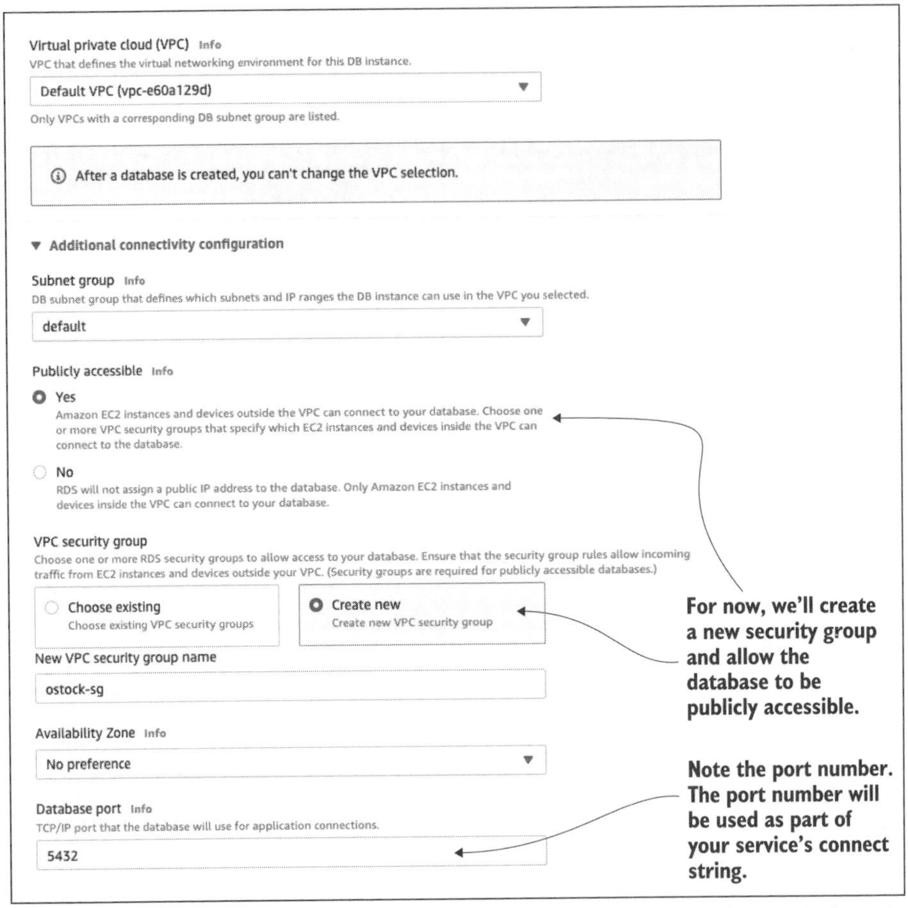

Virtual private cloud (VPC) Info
VPC that defines the virtual networking environment for this DB instance.

> Default VPC (vpc-e60a129d)   ▼

Only VPCs with a corresponding DB subnet group are listed.

> ⓘ After a database is created, you can't change the VPC selection.

▼ Additional connectivity configuration

Subnet group Info
DB subnet group that defines which subnets and IP ranges the DB instance can use in the VPC you selected.

> default   ▼

Publicly accessible Info

◉ Yes
   Amazon EC2 instances and devices outside the VPC can connect to your database. Choose one
   or more VPC security groups that specify which EC2 instances and devices inside the VPC can
   connect to the database.

◯ No
   RDS will not assign a public IP address to the database. Only Amazon EC2 instances and
   devices inside the VPC can connect to your database.

VPC security group
Choose one or more RDS security groups to allow access to your database. Ensure that the security group rules allow incoming
traffic from EC2 instances and devices outside your VPC. (Security groups are required for publicly accessible databases.)

◯ Choose existing	◉ Create new
Choose existing VPC security groups	Create new VPC security group

New VPC security group name

> ostock-sg

Availability Zone Info

> No preference   ▼

Database port Info
TCP/IP port that the database will use for application connections.

> 5432

For now, we'll create a new security group and allow the database to be publicly accessible.

Note the port number. The port number will be used as part of your service's connect string.

Figure 12.4 Setting up the networking environment, security group, and port number for the RDS database

the configuration files for the service located at the Spring Configuration Server. To do that, we'll navigate back to the RDS dashboard to view information about our database. Figure 12.5 shows this screen.

For this chapter, you can create a new application profile called aws-dev for each microservice that needs to access the Amazon-based PostgreSQL database. The application profile will contain Amazon database connection information.

At this point, our database is ready to go (not bad for setting it up in approximately five clicks). Let's move to the next piece of application infrastructure and see how to create the Redis cluster that our O-stock licensing service is going to use.

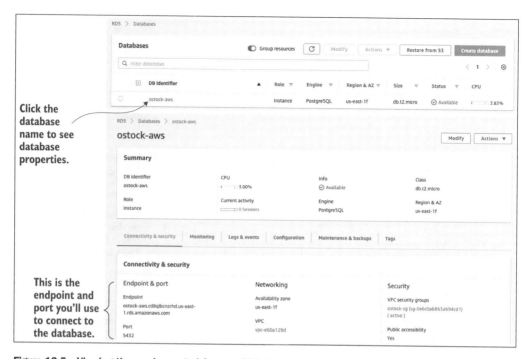

Click the database name to see database properties.

This is the endpoint and port you'll use to connect to the database.

Figure 12.5   Viewing the newly created Amazon RDS/PostgreSQL database and its properties

12.2.2 *Creating the Redis cluster in Amazon*

For the O-stock services, we want to move the Redis server we were running in Docker to Amazon ElastiCache. ElastiCache (https://aws.amazon.com/elasticache/) lets us build in-memory data caches using Redis or memcached (https://memcached.org/) data stores.

To begin, let's navigate back to the AWS Management Console's main page, then search for the ElastiCache service and click the ElastiCache link. From the Elasti-Cache console, select the Redis link (left side of the screen), and then click the blue Create button at the top of the screen. This opens the ElastiCache/Redis creation wizard (figure 12.6).

As for the Advance Redis settings on this page, let's select the same security group we created for the PostgreSQL database, then uncheck the Enable Automatic Backups option. Once the form is filled to your liking, go ahead and click the Create button. Amazon begins the Redis cluster creation process (this will take several minutes). Amazon builds a single-node Redis server running on the smallest Amazon server instance available.

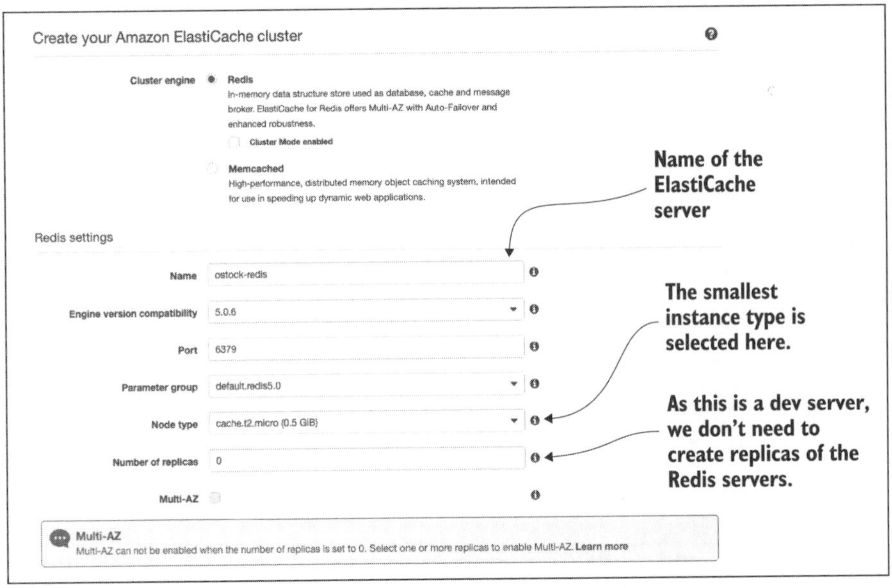

Figure 12.6   With a few clicks, we can set up a Redis cluster whose infrastructure is managed by Amazon.

Once our Redis cluster is created, we can click the name of the cluster, and it will take us to a detailed screen showing the endpoint used in the cluster (figure 12.7).

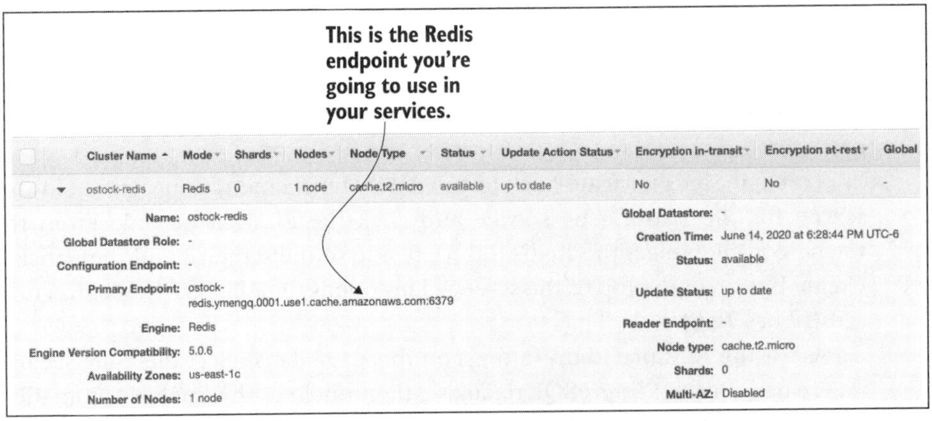

Figure 12.7   The primary endpoint is the key piece of information your services need to connect to Redis.

The licensing service is the only one of our services to use Redis. If you deploy the code examples in this chapter to your own Amazon instance, you must modify the licensing service's Spring Cloud Config files appropriately.

12.3 Beyond the infrastructure: Deploying O-stock and ELK

In this second part of the chapter, you're going to deploy the Elasticsearch, Logstash, and Kibana (ELK) services to an EC2 instance, and the O-stock services to an Amazon EKS container. Remember, an EC2 instance is a virtual server in Amazon's Elastic Compute Cloud (Amazon EC2) where we can run applications. We'll divide the O-stock deployment process into two parts as well.

The first part of your work is for the terminally impatient (like us), showing how to deploy O-stock manually to your Amazon EKS cluster. This will help you understand the mechanics of deploying the service and see the deployed services running in your container. While getting your hands dirty and manually deploying your services is fun, it isn't sustainable or recommended.

In the second part, you'll automate the entire build/deployment process and take the human out of the picture. This is your targeted end state and really tops the work you've done in this book by demonstrating how to design, build, and deploy microservices to the cloud.

12.3.1 Creating an EC2 with ELK

To set up the ELK services, we'll use an Amazon EC2 instance. Having this service separated from the ones we'll deploy to the ELK instance shows you that we can have different instances and still use the services. To create the EC2 instances, we'll carry out the following steps:

1. Choose an Amazon Machine Image (AMI)
2. Select an instance type
3. Set the default configuration for the configuration details, storage, and tags
4. Create a new security group
5. Launch the EC2 instance

To begin, navigate back to the AWS Management Console's main page, search for the EC2 service, and click the link. Next, click the blue Launch Instance button. This brings up the EC2 launch instance. This wizard contains seven different steps, and we will guide you through each of them. Figure 12.8 shows the first step in the EC2 creation process.

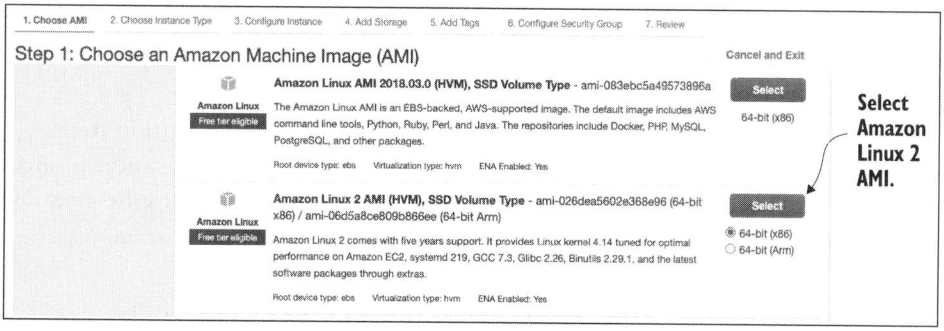

Figure 12.8 Select the Amazon Linux 2 AMI option to set up an ELK service instance.

Next, we'll choose the instance type. For this example, select an m4.large server to give us 8 GB of memory and a low hourly cost ($0.10 per hour). Figure 12.9 shows our second step.

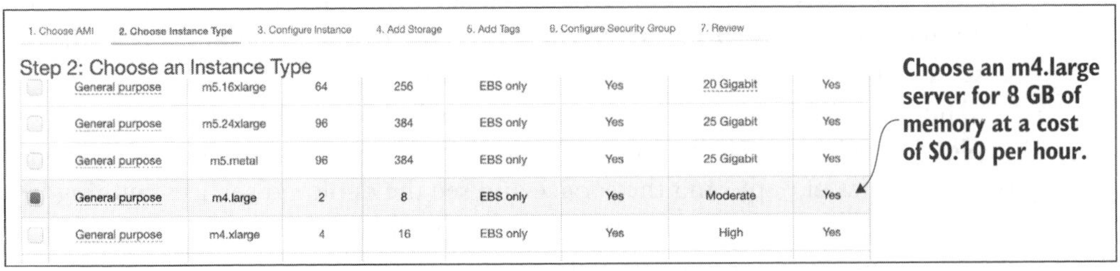

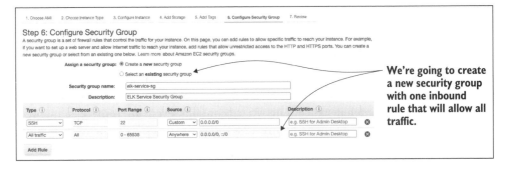

Figure 12.9   Selecting the instance type for the ELK service

Once you've selected the instance, click the Next: Configure Instance link. In the third, fourth, and fifth steps, you don't need to change anything, so just click Next through those steps, accepting all the default configurations.

For the sixth step, we need to select to create a new security group (or select an existing Amazon security group if you've already created one) to apply to the new EC2 instance. For this example, we will allow all inbound traffic (0.0.0.0/0 is the network mask for the entire World Wide Web). In real world scenarios, you need to be careful with this setting, so we recommend that you take some time to analyze the inbound rules that best fit your needs. Figure 12.10 shows this step.

Figure 12.10   Creating a security group for the EC2 instance

Once the security group is set, click the Review and Launch button to check the EC2 instance configuration. Once you're satisfied that the configuration is correct, click Launch Instances to execute the last step. The final step involves the creation of a key pair to connect to the EC2 instance. Figure 12.11 shows this process.

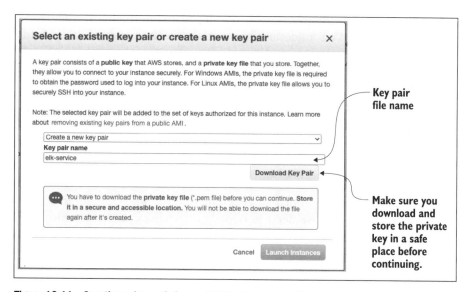

Figure 12.11   Creating a key pair for our EC2 instance security group

Now we have all the infrastructure we need to run the ELK Stack. Figure 12.12 shows the status of our EC2 instance.

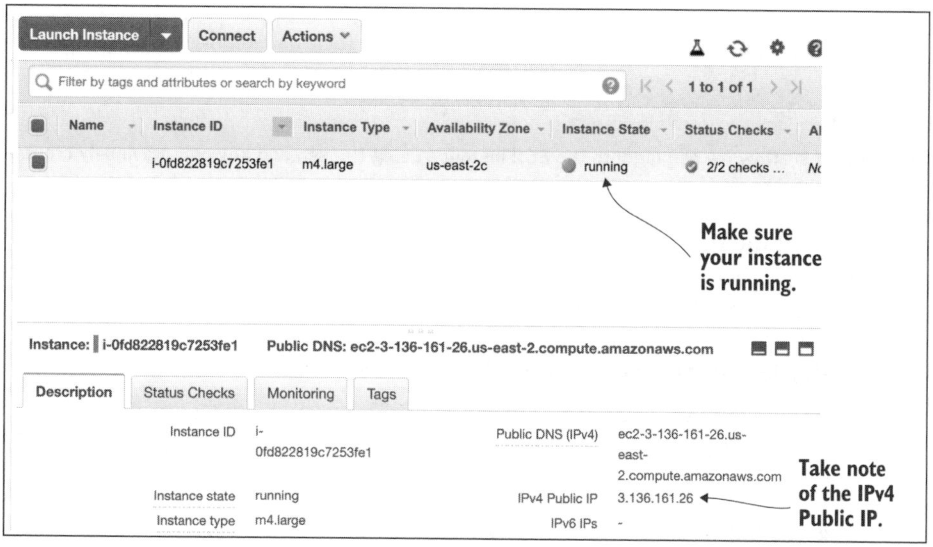

Figure 12.12   Amazon EC2 dashboard page showing the status of our newly created EC2 instance

Before moving on to the next step, take note of the IPV4 instance state. We'll need that information to connect to our EC2 instance.

NOTE Before you continue with the next part, we highly recommend you download the AWS folder from the chapter 12 repository here: https://github.com/ihuaylupo/manning-smia/tree/master/chapter12/AWS. In this repository, we've already created the service scripts in the .yaml and docker-compose files that we'll use for deploying the EC2 and EKS containers.

To continue, open a terminal console on the path where you downloaded the key-pair file and execute the following commands:

```
chmod 400 <pemKey>.pem
scp -r -i <pemKey>.pem ~/project/folder/from/root ec2-user@<IPv4>:~/
```

It's important to highlight that we are going to use a project folder that contains all of the configuration files we need to deploy our services. If you downloaded the AWS folder from GitHub, you can use that as your project folder. Once the previous commands are executed, you should see the output shown in figure 12.13.

```
Last login: Sat Jun 20 06:35:47 2020 from 186.176.131.131

    _|  _|_  )
    _|  (    /    Amazon Linux AMI
    __|\__|__|

https://aws.amazon.com/amazon-linux-ami/2018.03-release-notes/
-bash: warning: setlocale: LC_CTYPE: cannot change locale (UTF-8): No such file or directory
[ec2-user@ip-172-31-42-196 ~]$ ls -l
total 4
drwxr-xr-x 3 ec2-user ec2-user 4096 Jun 18 16:55 AWS
```

Figure 12.13 Now we can log into the EC2 instance using the ssh and key pair previously created.

If we list the files and directories of the root for our EC2 instance, we will see that the entire project folder was pushed into the instance. Now that everything is set up, let's continue with the ELK deployment.

12.3.2 *Deploying the ELK Stack in the EC2 instance*

Now that we have created the instance and logged in, let's continue with the deployment of the ELK services. To achieve this, we must complete the following steps:

1 Update the EC2 instance
2 Install Docker
3 Install Docker Compose
4 Run Docker
5 Run the docker-compose file that contains the ELK services

To execute all of the previous steps, run the commands shown in the following listing.

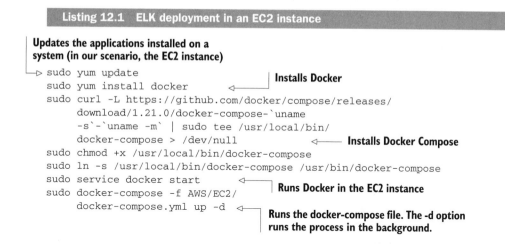

Listing 12.1   ELK deployment in an EC2 instance

**Updates the applications installed on a
system (in our scenario, the EC2 instance)**

```
sudo yum update
sudo yum install docker            ◄────── Installs Docker
sudo curl -L https://github.com/docker/compose/releases/
      download/1.21.0/docker-compose-`uname
      -s`-`uname -m` | sudo tee /usr/local/bin/
      docker-compose > /dev/null        ◄────── Installs Docker Compose
sudo chmod +x /usr/local/bin/docker-compose
sudo ln -s /usr/local/bin/docker-compose /usr/bin/docker-compose
sudo service docker start        ◄──────
sudo docker-compose -f AWS/EC2/      Runs Docker in the EC2 instance
      docker-compose.yml up -d  ◄──────
                                 Runs the docker-compose file. The -d option
                                 runs the process in the background.
```

Now that we have all the ELK services running, to verify that everything is up, you can enter the http://<IPv4>:5601/ URL. You'll see the Kibana dashboard. Now that we have the ELK services running, let's create an Amazon EKS cluster to deploy our microservices.

12.3.3 Creating an EKS cluster

The last and final step before deploying the O-stock services is to set up an Amazon EKS cluster. EKS is an Amazon service that allows us to run Kubernetes on AWS. Kubernetes is an open source system that automates deployment, scheduling, and the creation and deletion of containers. As previously discussed, managing a large number of containers and microservices can become a challenging task. With tools like Kubernetes, we can handle all of our containers in a faster, more efficient way. For example, let's imagine the following scenario.

We need to update a microservice and its image, which is propagated in dozens or maybe hundreds of containers. Can you imagine yourself manually deleting and re-creating those containers? With Kubernetes, you can destroy and re-create them simply by executing a short command. This is only one of the numerous advantages that Kubernetes brings to the table. Now that we have a brief overview of what Kubernetes is and does, let's continue.

The process of creating the EKS cluster can be done by using the AWS Management Console or the AWS CLI. For this example, we will show you how to use the AWS CLI.

NOTE   To continue with this part, make sure you have all the tools previously mentioned in the earlier sidebar entitled, "Some prerequisites for working with AWS," and that you have configured the AWS CLI. In case you haven't, we highly recommend you look at the documentation here: https://docs.aws .amazon.com/cli/latest/userguide/cli-configure-quickstart.html.

After we've configured and installed all the necessary tools, we can start creating and configuring our Kubernetes cluster. To do so, we need to

1   Provision a Kubernetes cluster
2   Push the microservice images into repositories
3   Deploy our microservices manually to the Kubernetes cluster

PROVISIONING A KUBERNETES CLUSTER

To create our cluster using the AWS CLI, we need to use eksctl. This is accomplished by using the following command:

```
eksctl create cluster --name=ostock-dev-cluster
   --nodes=1 --node-type=m4.large
```

The previous eksctl command line allows us to create a Kubernetes cluster (named ostock-dev-cluster), which uses a single m4.large EC2 instance as a worker node. In this scenario, we use the same instance type we previously selected in the EC2 ELK service creation wizard. The execution of this command takes several minutes. While processing, you'll see different line outputs, but you will know when it is finished because you'll see the following output:

```
[✓] EKS cluster "ostock-dev-cluster" in "region-code" region is ready
```

Once executed, you can now run the `kubectl get svc` command to verify that the Kubectl configuration is correct. This command should show the following output:

```
NAME           TYPE        CLUSTER-IP    EXTERNAL-IP   PORT(S)   AGE
kubernetes     ClusterIP   10.100.0.1    <none>        443/TCP   1m
```

PUSHING THE MICROSERVICE IMAGES INTO REPOSITORIES

Up to now, we've built our services on our local machine. To use these images in our EKS cluster, we need to push the Docker container images to a container repository. A *container repository* is like a Maven repository for your created Docker images. Docker images can be tagged and uploaded to it, then other projects can download and use the images.

There are several repositories such as the Docker Hub, but for this example, let's continue with the AWS infrastructure and use the Amazon Elastic Container Registry (ECR). To learn more about ECR, see https://docs.aws.amazon.com/AmazonECR/latest/userguide/what-is-ecr.html.

To push the images to the container registry, we must ensure the Docker images are in our local Docker directory. If they aren't there, execute the following command on the parent pom.xml file:

```
mvn clean package dockerfile:build
```

Once the command executes, we should now see the images in the Docker images list. To verify this, issue the `docker images` command. You should see the following output:

```
REPOSITORY                       TAG          IMAGE ID       SIZE
ostock/organization-service      chapter12    b1c7b262926e   485MB
ostock/gatewayserver             chapter12    61c6fc020dcf   450MB
ostock/configserver              chapter12    877c9d855d91   432MB
ostock/licensing-service         chapter12    6a76bee3e40c   490MB
ostock/authentication-service    chapter12    5e5e74f29c2    452MB
ostock/eurekaserver              chapter12    e6bc59ae1d87   451MB
```

The next step is to authenticate our Docker client with our ECR registry. To achieve this, we need to obtain a password and our AWS account ID by executing the following commands:

```
aws ecr get-login-password
aws sts get-caller-identity --output text --query "Account"
```

The first command retrieves the password, and the second returns our AWS account. We'll use both values to authenticate our Docker client. Now that we have our credentials, let's authenticate by executing the following command:

```
docker login -u AWS -p [password]
➡ https://[aws_account_id].dkr.ecr.[region].amazonaws.com
```

Once authenticated, the next step is to create the repositories where we will store our images. To create these repositories, let's execute the following commands:

```
aws ecr create-repository --repository-name ostock/configserver
aws ecr create-repository --repository-name ostock/gatewayserver
aws ecr create-repository --repository-name ostock/eurekaserver
aws ecr create-repository --repository-name ostock/authentication-service
aws ecr create-repository --repository-name ostock/licensing-service
aws ecr create-repository --repository-name ostock/organization-service
```

When each command executes you should see output similar to the following:

```
{
    "repository": {
        "repositoryArn": "arn:aws:ecr:us-east-2:
    8193XXXXXXX43:repository/ostock/configserver",
        "registryId": "8193XXXXXXX43",
        "repositoryName": "ostock/configserver",
        "repositoryUri": "8193XXXXXXX43.dkr.ecr.
    us-east-2.amazonaws.com/ostock/configserver",
        "createdAt": "2020-06-18T11:53:06-06:00",
        "imageTagMutability": "MUTABLE",
        "imageScanningConfiguration": {
            "scanOnPush": false
        }
    }
}
```

Make sure to take note of all the repository URIs because we are going to need them to create the tag and push the images. To create the tags for our images, let's execute the following commands:

```
docker tag ostock/configserver:chapter12 [configserver-repository-
uri]:chapter12
docker tag ostock/gatewayserver:chapter12 [gatewayserver-repository-
uri]:chapter12
docker tag ostock/eurekaserver:chapter12 [eurekaserver-repository-
uri]:chapter12
docker tag ostock/authentication-service:chapter12 [authentication-service-
repository-uri]:chapter12
docker tag ostock/licensing-service:chapter12 [licensing-service-
repository-uri]:chapter12
docker tag ostock/organization-service:chapter12 [organization-service-
repository-uri]:chapter12
```

The `docker tag` command creates a new tag for our images. If you execute this command, you should see output similar to that shown in figure 12.14.

REPOSITORY	TAG	IMAGE ID	CREATED	SIZE
819322222443.dkr.ecr.us-east-2.amazonaws.com/ostock/organization-service	chapter12	b1c7b262926e	45 hours ago	485MB
ostock/organization-service	chapter12	b1c7b262926e	45 hours ago	485MB
819322222443.dkr.ecr.us-east-2.amazonaws.com/ostock/gatewayserver	chapter12	61c6fc020dcf	45 hours ago	450MB
ostock/gatewayserver	chapter12	61c6fc020dcf	45 hours ago	450MB
819322222443.dkr.ecr.us-east-2.amazonaws.com/ostock/configserver	chapter12	877c9d855d91	45 hours ago	432MB
ostock/configserver	chapter12	877c9d855d91	45 hours ago	432MB
819322222443.dkr.ecr.us-east-2.amazonaws.com/ostock/licensing-service	chapter12	6a76bee3e40c	46 hours ago	490MB
ostock/licensing-service	chapter12	6a76bee3e40c	46 hours ago	490MB
819322222443.dkr.ecr.us-east-2.amazonaws.com/ostock/authentication-service	chapter12	f5e5e74f29c2	5 days ago	452MB
ostock/authentication-service	chapter12	f5e5e74f29c2	5 days ago	452MB
819322222443.dkr.ecr.us-east-2.amazonaws.com/ostock/eurekaserver	chapter12	e6bc59ae1d87	5 days ago	451MB
ostock/eurekaserver	chapter12	e6bc59ae1d87	5 days ago	451MB

Figure 12.14   Docker images with the Amazon Elastic Container Registry (ECR) repository URI tags

Finally, we can push our microservice images to the ECR registry repositories. To do this, we'll execute the following commands:

```
docker push [configserver-repository-uri]:chapter12
docker push [gatewayserver-repository-uri]:chapter12
docker push [eurekaserver-repository-uri]:chapter12
docker push [authentication-service-repository-uri]:chapter12
docker push [licensing-service-repository-uri]:chapter12
docker push [organization-service-repository-uri]:chapter12
```

Once all the commands run, you can visit the ECR service in the AWS Management Console. You should see a list similar to the one shown in figure 12.15.

ECR > Repositories

Repositories (6)

	↻	View push commands	Delete	Edit	**Create repository**	

🔍 *Find repositories*

⟨ 1 ⟩ ⚙

	Repository name ▲	URI	Created at ▽	Tag immutability	Scan on push
○	ostock/authentication-service	🗇 819322222443.dkr.ecr.us-east-2.amazonaws.com/ostock/authentication-service	06/18/20, 11:54:29 AM	Disabled	Disabled
○	ostock/configserver	🗇 819322222443.dkr.ecr.us-east-2.amazonaws.com/ostock/configserver	06/18/20, 11:53:06 AM	Disabled	Disabled
○	ostock/eurekaserver	🗇 819322222443.dkr.ecr.us-east-2.amazonaws.com/ostock/eurekaserver	06/18/20, 11:54:13 AM	Disabled	Disabled
○	ostock/gatewayserver	🗇 819322222443.dkr.ecr.us-east-2.amazonaws.com/ostock/gatewayserver	06/18/20, 11:53:54 AM	Disabled	Disabled
○	ostock/licensing-service	🗇 819322222443.dkr.ecr.us-east-2.amazonaws.com/ostock/licensing-service	06/18/20, 11:54:44 AM	Disabled	Disabled
○	ostock/organization-service	🗇 819322222443.dkr.ecr.us-east-2.amazonaws.com/ostock/organization-service	06/18/20, 11:55:06 AM	Disabled	Disabled

Figure 12.15   ECR repositories for the examples in this chapter

DEPLOYING OUR MICROSERVICES IN THE EKS CLUSTER

To deploy our microservices, we first need to make sure that the licensing, organization, and gateway services have the appropriate Spring Cloud Config files. Remember, the PostgreSQL, Redis, and the ELK Stack services changed.

> **NOTE** In the GitHub repository, you'll find all the changes we made to the configuration server, which also contains the configuration for the Logstash server. Here's the link to GitHub: https://github.com/ihuaylupo/manning-smia/tree/master/chapter12. Remember, we used a hardcoded value when we created the Logstash configuration.

Before deploying our microservices, let's create our Kafka and Zookeeper services. There are several ways to create these services. For this scenario we chose to create them using Helm charts. In case you are not familiar with Helm, it's a package manager for Kubernetes clusters. A Helm chart is a Helm package that contains all the required resource definitions to run a specific service, application, or tool inside a Kubernetes cluster.

> **NOTE** If you don't have Helm installed, visit https://helm.sh/docs/intro/install/ to see all the possible ways to install it on your computer.

Once Helm is installed, let's execute the following commands to create our Kafka and Zookeeper services:

```
helm install zookeeper bitnami/zookeeper \
  --set replicaCount=1 \
  --set auth.enabled=false \
  --set allowAnonymousLogin=true

helm install kafka bitnami/kafka \
  --set zookeeper.enabled=false \
  --set replicaCount=1 \
  --set externalZookeeper.servers=zookeeper
```

Once these commands execute, you should see output with some of the details of the services. To be sure that everything ran successfully, execute the `kubectl get pods` command to see your running services.

```
NAME          READY   STATUS    RESTARTS   AGE
kafka-0       1/1     Running   0          77s
zookeeper-0   1/1     Running   0          101s
```

The next step in deploying our services is to convert our docker-compose file into a compatible Kubernetes format. Why? Kubernetes doesn't support the Docker Compose files, so in order to execute these files, we need to use a tool called Kompose.

Kompose converts Docker Compose files to container implementations such as Kubernetes. Using this tool allows us to convert all the docker-compose.yaml file configurations with the `kompose convert <file>` command, run the docker-compose files with the `kompose up` command, and more. If you want to know more about Kompose, we highly recommend that you see the documentation at this link: https://kompose.io/.

For this example, you'll these files in the AWS/EKS folder in the following GitHub repository: https://github.com/ihuaylupo/manning-smia/tree/master/chapter12/AWS/EKS. But before moving on, let's review the Kubernetes service types, which allow us to expose the services to external IP addresses. Kubernetes has the following four types of services:

- *ClusterIP*—Exposes the service on a cluster-internal IP. If we choose this option, our service is only going to be visible within our cluster.
- *NodePort*—Exposes the service at a static port (the `NodePort` value). Kubernetes allocates a default port range from 3000 to 32767. You can change this range by using the `--service-node-port-range` flag in the `spec.containers.commands` section of the service.yaml file.
- *LoadBalancer*—Exposes the service externally using a cloud load balancer.
- *ExternalName*—Maps the service to the contents of an external name.

If you take a look at the files, you'll see that some of the *<service>*.yml files have a `type=NodePort` and a `nodePort` attribute. In Kubernetes, if we don't define a service type, Kubernetes uses the default ClusterIP service type.

Now that we know more about the Kubernetes service types, let's continue. To create the services using these converted files, execute the following commands on the root of the AWS/ELK folder:

```
kubectl apply -f <service>.yaml,<deployment>.yaml
```

We prefer to execute this command individually to see that everything is created successfully, but you can also create all the services simultaneously. To do this, you need to concatenate all the YAML files with the -f argument as in the previous command. For example, to create the configuration server and view the pod status and the logs, we need to execute the following commands:

```
kubectl apply -f configserver-service.yaml,configserver-deployment.yaml
kubectl get pods
kubect logs <POD_NAME> --follow
```

To test that our service is up and running, we need to add a few rules to our security group to allow all the incoming traffic from the node ports. To do so, let's execute the following command to retrieve the security group ID:

```
aws ec2 describe-security-groups --filters Name=group-name,
Values="*eksctl-ostock-dev-cluster-nodegroup*"  --query
    "SecurityGroups[*].{Name:GroupName,ID:GroupId}"
```

With the security group ID, let's execute the following command to create an inbound rule. You can also do this in the AWS Management Console by going to the security group and creating a new inbound traffic rule like this:

```
aws ec2 authorize-security-group-ingress --protocol tcp --port 31000
--group-id [security-group-id] --cidr 0.0.0.0/0
```

To get the external IP, you can execute the `kubectl get nodes -o wide` command. This command shows you output similar to the one shown in figure 12.16.

Figure 12.16 Getting the external IP address for the node

Now you can open the following URL in your browser: http:<node-external-ip>: <NodePort>/actuator. In case you need to delete a pod, service, or deployment, you can execute one of the commands listed here:

```
kubectl delete -f <service>.yaml
kubectl delete -f <deployment>.yaml
kubectl delete <POD_NAME>
```

We are almost done. If you looked at the YAML files, you may have noted that the postgres.yaml file is a bit different. In this file, we'll specify that the database service will be used with an external address. In order to make the connection work, you should specify the endpoint for the RDS Postgres service. The following listing shows you how.

Listing 12.2   Adding the external reference to the database service

```
apiVersion: v1
kind: Service
metadata:
  labels:
    app: postgres-service
  name: postgres-service
spec:
  externalName: ostock-aws.cjuqpwnyahhy.us-east-2
                .rds.amazonaws.com        ◁──────  Sets the RDS
  selector:                                         PostgreSQL endpoint
    app: postgres-service
  type: ExternalName
status:
  loadBalancer: {}
```

Make sure that you add the `externalName` endpoint of your RDS PostgreSQL instance. When you've made this change, you can execute the following command. Once the services are created and running, you can now continue running all of the other services.

```
kubectl apply -f postgres.yaml
```

While developing this chapter, we noticed that we needed to create a VPC peering connection and update the route tables of both the RDS and the EKS cluster to allow communication between them. We will not describe how to do this, but we highly recommend that you read the article, "Accessing Amazon RDS From AWS EKS," at https://dev.to/bensooraj/accessing-amazon-rds-from-aws-eks-2pc3, which contains all of the steps, and/or the official AWS documentation to understand a bit more about VPC peering at https://docs.aws.amazon.com/vpc/latest/peering/create-vpc-peering-connection.html.

At this point, you've successfully deployed your first set of services to an Amazon EKS cluster. Now, let's build on this by looking at how to design a build/deployment pipeline that automates the process of compiling, packaging, and deploying your services to Amazon.

12.4 *Your build/deployment pipeline in action*

From the general architecture laid out in section 12.1, you can see that there are many moving pieces behind a build/deployment pipeline. Because the purpose of this book is to show you things "in action," we're going to walk through the specifics of implementing a build/deployment pipeline for the O-stock services. Figure 12.17 lays out the different technologies we'll use to implement our pipeline.

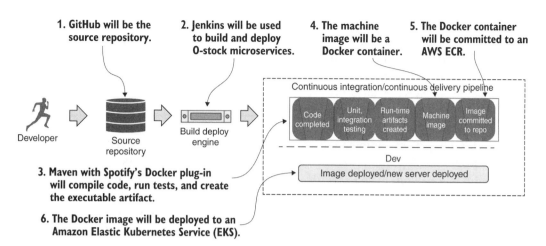

Figure 12.17 Technologies used in the O-stock build/deployment pipeline

Let's take a peek at the technologies we'll need for our build/deployment pipeline:

- *GitHub* (http://github.com)—GitHub is our source control repository for our source code. All the application code for this book is in GitHub. We chose GitHub as the source control repository because it offers a wide variety of webhooks and robust REST-based APIs for integrating GitHub into your build process.

- *Jenkins* (https://www.jenkins.io/)—Jenkins is the continuous integration engine we used for building and deploying the O-stock microservices and for provisioning the Docker image that will be deployed. Jenkins can be easily configured via its web interface and includes several built-in plugins that are going to make our work easier.

- *Maven/Spotify Docker plugin* (https://github.com/spotify/dockerfile-maven) *or Spring Boot with Docker* (https://spring.io/guides/gs/spring-boot-docker/)— While we use vanilla Maven to compile, test, and package Java code, these essential Maven plugins will allow us to kick off the creation of a Docker build right from within Maven.

- *Docker* (https://www.docker.com/)—We chose Docker as our container platform for two reasons. First, Docker is portable across multiple cloud providers. We can take the same Docker container and deploy it to AWS, Azure, or Cloud Foundry with a minimal amount of work. Second, Docker is lightweight.

  By the end of this book, you've built and deployed approximately 10 Docker containers (including a database server, messaging platform, and a search engine). Deploying the same number of virtual machines on a local desktop would be difficult because of the sheer size and speed of each image.

- *Amazon Elastic Container Registry (ECR)* (https://aws.amazon.com/ecr/)—After you build a service and create a Docker image, it's tagged with a unique identifier and pushed to a central repository. For this Docker image repository, we chose to use ECR.

■ *Amazon's EKS Container Service* (https://aws.amazon.com/eks/)—The final destination for our microservices will be Docker instances deployed to Amazon's Docker platform. We chose Amazon as the cloud platform because it's by far the most mature of the cloud providers and makes it trivial to deploy Docker services.

12.5 Creating our build/deploy pipeline

Dozens of source control engines and build deploy engines (both on-premises and cloud-based) can implement your build/deployment pipeline. For the examples in this book, we purposely chose GitHub as the source control repository and Jenkins as the build engine. The Git source control repository is extremely popular, and GitHub is one of the largest cloud-based source control repositories available today. Jenkins is a build engine that integrates tightly with GitHub. It's also straightforward to use. Its simplicity and opinionated nature make it easy to get a simple build pipeline up and off the ground.

Up to now, all of the code examples in this book can be run solely from your desktop (with the exception of connectivity out to GitHub). For this chapter, if you want to completely follow the code examples, you'll need to set up your own GitHub, Jenkins, and AWS accounts. We're not going to walk through how to set up Jenkins; however, if you are not familiar with Jenkins, you can take a look at the file that we made that walks you through (step by step) how to set up the Jenkins environment from scratch in an EC2 instance. The file is located in the chapter 12 repository at the following link: https://github .com/ihuaylupo/manning-smia/blob/master/chapter12/AWS/jenkins_Setup.md.

12.5.1 Setting up GitHub

To construct our pipeline, we must create a GitHub webhook. What is a webhook? A webhook is also known as a web HTTP callback. These HTTP callbacks provide real-time information to other applications. Usually, the callback is triggered when a process or action is executed on the application containing the webhook.

If you haven't heard about webhooks, you might be wondering why we need them. For our purposes, we'll create a webhook in GitHub so that it lets Jenkins know when a code push is made. That way Jenkins can start a specific build process. To create a webhook in GitHub, we need to do the following steps. Figure 12.18 shows this process.

1 Go to the repository containing your pipeline projects
2 Click the Settings option
3 Select Webhooks
4 Click the Add Webhook button
5 Provide a specific payload URL
6 Click the Just the Push Event option
7 Click the Add Webhook button

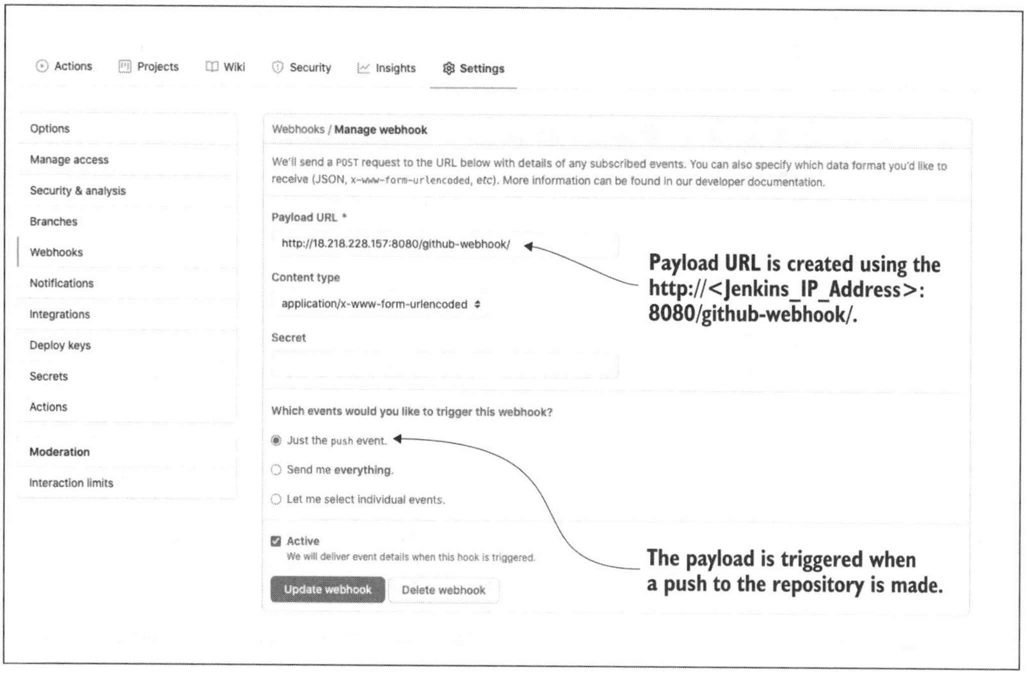

Figure 12.18 Generating a webhook for Jenkins

It's important to note that the payload URL is created using the IP address of Jenkins. This way GitHub can call Jenkins whenever a push to the repository is made. Now that we have the webhook, let's configure the pipeline using Jenkins.

12.5.2 Enabling our services to build in Jenkins

The heart of every service built in this book has been a Maven pom.xml file that's used to build the Spring Boot service, package it into an executable JAR, and build a Docker image that can be used to launch the service. Up until this chapter, the compilation and startup of the services occurred by

1 Opening a command-line window on your local machine.
2 Running the Maven script for the chapter. This builds all the services for the chapter and then packages them into a Docker image that's pushed to a locally running Docker repository.
3 Launching the newly created Docker images from your local Docker repository, by using the `docker-compose` and `docker-machine` commands to launch all the services for the chapter.

The question is, how do we repeat this process in Jenkins? It all begins with a single file called the Jenkinsfile. The Jenkinsfile is a script that describes the actions we want to run when Jenkins executes our build. This file is stored in the root directory of our microservices GitHub repository.

When a push occurs on a GitHub repository, the webhook calls Jenkins using the payload URL, and the Jenkins job searches for the Jenkinsfile to initiate the build process. Figure 12.19 shows the steps for this process.

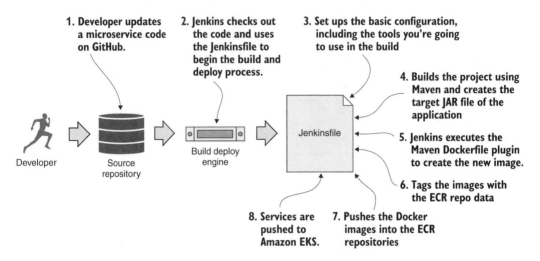

Figure 12.19   The steps taken—from developer to the Jenkinsfile—that build and deploy our software

As figure 12.19 shows:

1. A developer makes a change to one of the microservices in the GitHub repository.
2. Jenkins is notified by GitHub that a push has occurred. This notification is made by the GitHub webhook. Jenkins starts a process that is used to execute the build. Jenkins then checks out the source code from GitHub and uses the Jenkinsfile to begin the overall build and deployment process.
3. Jenkins sets up the basic configuration for the build and installs any dependencies.
4. Jenkins builds the project, executing the unit and integration tests, and generates the target JAR file for the application.
5. Jenkins executes the Maven Dockerfile plugin to create the new Docker images.
6. Jenkins then tags the new images with the ECR repository data.
7. The build process pushes the images to the ECR with the same tag name you used in step 6.
8. The build process connects to the EKS cluster and deploys the services using the service.yaml and deployment.yaml files.

A quick note

For this book, we set up separate folders in the same GitHub repository for each chapter. All the source code for the chapter can be built and deployed as a single unit. However, for your projects, we highly recommend that you set up each microservice in your environment with its own repository and independent build processes. That way, each service can be deployed independently of one another.

With the build process example, we deploy the configuration server as a single unit only because we want to push the projects to the Amazon cloud separately and to manage build scripts for each individual service. In this example, we only deploy the configuration server, but later, you can use the same steps to create other deployments.

Now that we've walked through the general steps involved in our build/deployment process with Jenkins, let's look at how to create the Jenkins pipeline.

NOTE To make the pipeline work, you need to install several Jenkins plugins such as GitHub Integration, GitHub, Maven Invoker, Maven Integration, Docker Pipeline, ECR, Kubernetes Continuous Deploy, and Kubernetes CLI. To learn more about these plugins, we recommend that you read the official Jenkins documentation for each (for example, for the Kubernetes CLI, see https://plugins.jenkins.io/kubernetes-cli/).

Once we've installed all the plugins, we need to create the Kubernetes and ECR credentials. First, let's start with the Kubernetes credentials. To create these, we need to go to Manage Jenkins, Manage Credentials, Jenkins, Global Credentials, and then click the Add Credentials file. Select the Kubernetes Configuration (kubeconfig) option and fill in the forms with your Kubernetes cluster information.

To retrieve the information from the Kubernetes cluster, connect to the Kubernetes cluster as we previously explained when we manually deployed our services and then execute the following command:

```
kubectl config view
```

Copy the returned contents and paste that into the Content text box in Jenkins. Figure 12.20 shows this step.

Now, let's create the ECR credentials. In order to do this, we first need to go to the IAM page in the AWS console, then go to Users and click the Add User option. In the Add User page, you need to specify a username, the access type, and the policies. Next, download the .CSV file with the user credentials and, finally, save the user. We will guide you step by step as we create the credentials. First, add the following data in the IAM page:

```
User name: ecr-user
Access type: Programmatic access
```

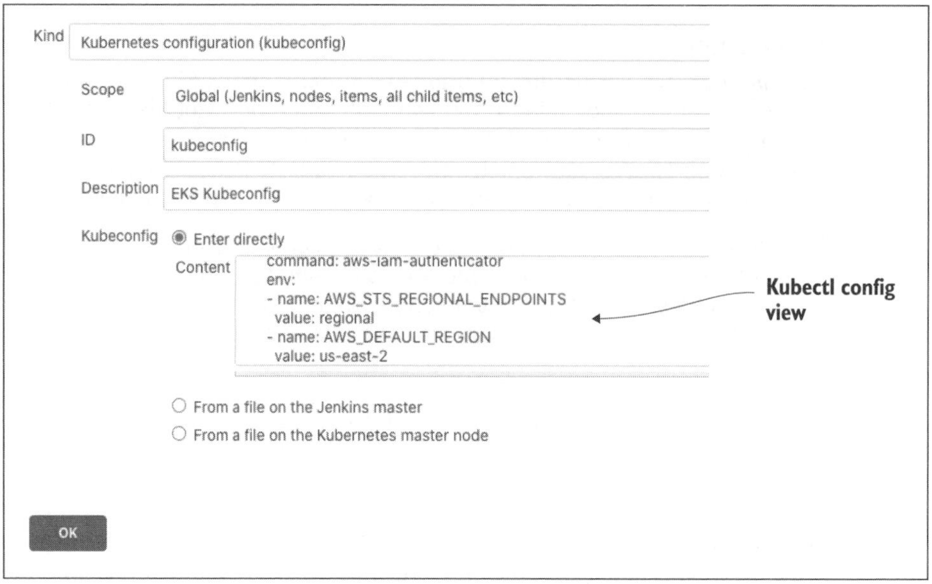

Figure 12.20   Configuring kubeconfig credentials to connect to the EKS cluster

In the second page, the Permissions page, select the Attach Existing Policies Directly option, and search for "AmazonEC2ContainerRegistryFullAccess" and then select it. Finally, on the last page, click Download .csv. The download step is really important because we'll need those credentials later. Finally, click the Save button.

The next step is to add the credentials to Jenkins, but before that, make sure you installed the ECR plugin in Jenkins. Once installed, go to Manage Jenkins, Manage Credentials, Jenkins, Global Configuration page and click the Add Credentials option. In this page, add the following data:

```
ID: ecr-user
Description: ECR User
Access Key ID: <Access_key_id_from_csv>
Secret Access Key: <Secret_access_key_from_csv>
```

Once the credentials are created, you can continue with the pipeline creation. Figure 12.21 shows the pipeline setup process. To access the page shown in figure 12.21, go to the Jenkins dashboard and click the New Item option in the top left of the screen.

The next step is to add the GitHub repository URL and select the GitHub Hook Trigger for GITScm Polling option (figure 12.22). This option enables the webhook payload we configured in the previous section.

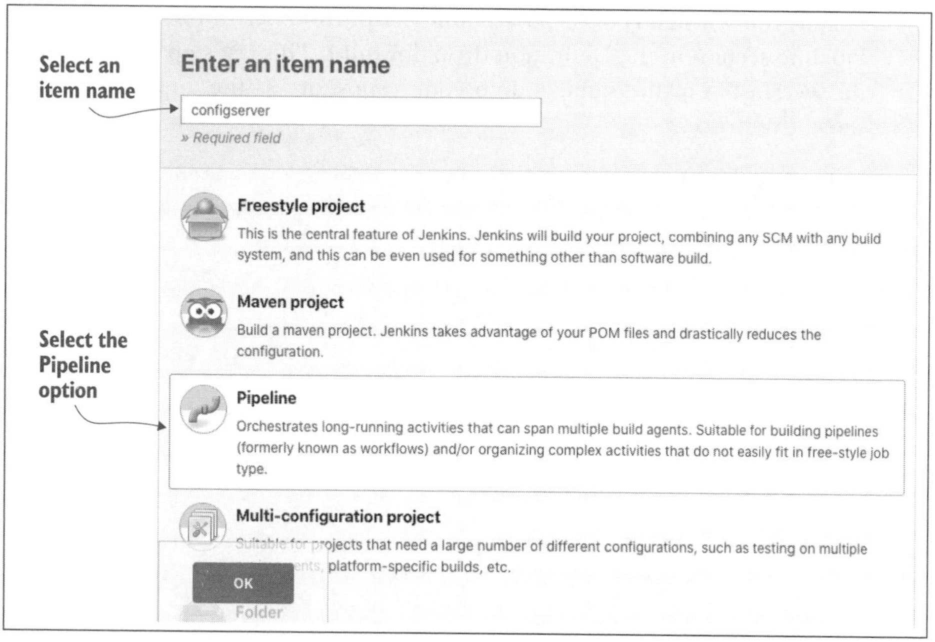

Figure 12.21 Creating a Jenkins pipeline to build the configuration server

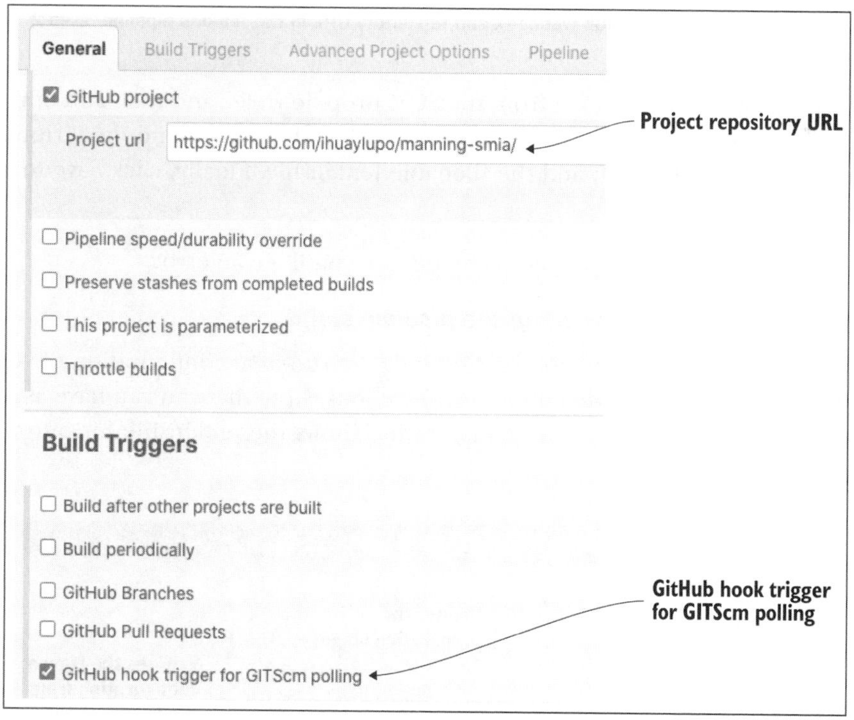

Figure 12.22 Configuring the GitHub webhook and repository URL in the Jenkins pipeline, step 1

Finally, the last step is to select Pipeline Script from SCM, which is located under the Pipeline section in the Definition drop-down list. This last step allows us to search for the Jenkinsfile in the same source code repository as the application. Figure 12.23 shows this process.

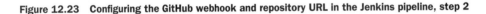

Figure 12.23   Configuring the GitHub webhook and repository URL in the Jenkins pipeline, step 2

In figure 12.23, we select Git from the SCM drop-down list and then add our pipeline-specific information such as the Repository URL, the branch and the script path that is the root (in our case), and the filename Jenkinsfile. Finally, click Save to go to the pipeline home page.

NOTE   If your repository needs credentials, you'll see an error.

12.5.3 Understanding and generating the pipeline script

The Jenkinsfile deals with configuring the core run-time configuration of your build. Typically, this file is divided into several sections. Note that you can have as many sections or stages as you want. The next listing shows the Jenkinsfile for our configuration server.

Listing 12.3   Configuring the Jenkinsfile

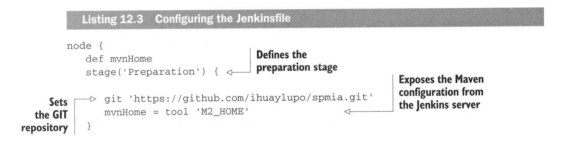

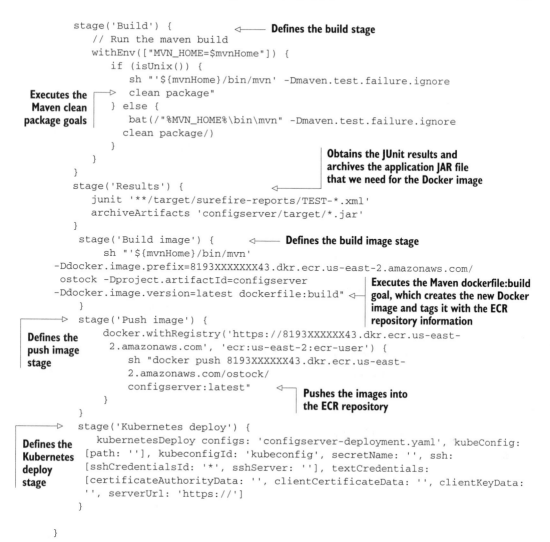

```
        stage('Build') {                    ←——— Defines the build stage
            // Run the maven build
            withEnv(["MVN_HOME=$mvnHome"]) {
                if (isUnix()) {
                    sh "'${mvnHome}/bin/mvn' -Dmaven.test.failure.ignore
                    clean package"
                } else {
                    bat(/"%MVN_HOME%\bin\mvn" -Dmaven.test.failure.ignore
                    clean package/)
                }
            }
        }
        stage('Results') {
            junit '**/target/surefire-reports/TEST-*.xml'
            archiveArtifacts 'configserver/target/*.jar'
        }
        stage('Build image') {              ←——— Defines the build image stage
            sh "'${mvnHome}/bin/mvn'
-Ddocker.image.prefix=8193XXXXXXX43.dkr.ecr.us-east-2.amazonaws.com/
ostock -Dproject.artifactId=configserver
-Ddocker.image.version=latest dockerfile:build" ←—
        }
        stage('Push image') {
            docker.withRegistry('https://8193XXXXXX43.dkr.ecr.us-east-
                2.amazonaws.com', 'ecr:us-east-2:ecr-user') {
                sh "docker push 8193XXXXXX43.dkr.ecr.us-east-
                2.amazonaws.com/ostock/
                configserver:latest"      ←—
            }
        }
        stage('Kubernetes deploy') {
            kubernetesDeploy configs: 'configserver-deployment.yaml', kubeConfig:
            [path: ''], kubeconfigId: 'kubeconfig', secretName: '', ssh:
            [sshCredentialsId: '*', sshServer: ''], textCredentials:
            [certificateAuthorityData: '', clientCertificateData: '', clientKeyData:
            ''], serverUrl: 'https://']
        }

    }
```

Annotations (from figure):

- **Executes the Maven clean package goals** → (points to `clean package"`)
- **Obtains the JUnit results and archives the application JAR file that we need for the Docker image** → (points to `stage('Results')`)
- **Executes the Maven dockerfile:build goal, which creates the new Docker image and tags it with the ECR repository information** → (points to `dockerfile:build"`)
- **Defines the push image stage** → (points to `stage('Push image')`)
- **Pushes the images into the ECR repository** → (points to `configserver:latest"`)
- **Defines the Kubernetes deploy stage** → (points to `stage('Kubernetes deploy')`)

This Jenkinsfile describes all of the steps involved in our pipeline. As you can see, the file contains the commands to execute each stage. In the first stage, we add the Git configuration. Doing this, we can remove the step where we define the GitHub URL repository in the build section. In the second stage, the second command line exposes the Maven installation path so that we can use the maven command throughout our Jenkinsfile. In the third stage, we define the command we will use to package our application. In this case, we use the clean package goals. For packing our application, we'll use the Maven environment variable where we define the Maven root directory.

The fourth stage allows us to execute the dockerfile:build Maven goal that is in charge of creating the new Docker image. If you remember, we defined the Maven spotify-dockerfile plugin in the pom.xml files of our microservices. If you take a closer look at the line with `dockerfile:build`, you'll notice that we send some parameters to Maven. Let's take a look:

```
sh "'${mvnHome}/bin/mvn' -Ddocker.image.prefix=8193XXXXXXX43.dkr.ecr.us-
east-2.amazonaws.com/ostock -Dproject.artifactId=configserver
-Ddocker.image.version=latest dockerfile:build"
```

In this command, we pass the Docker image prefix, the image version, and the artifact ID. But here you can send as many parameters as you want. Also, here is a good place to set the profile you are going to use in the deployment (for example: dev, stage, or production). Also, in this stage, you can create and assign specific tags with the ECR repository data to the new images. In this particular scenario, we use the latest version, but here you can specify different variables to create different Docker images.

The fifth stage pushes the images to the ECR repositories. In this case, we added the configuration server just created to the Docker image in the 8193XXXXXXX43.dkr .ecr.us-east-2.amazonaws.com/ostock   repository. The final stage, the Kubernetes deploy stage, deploys to our EKS cluster. This command can vary, depending on your configuration, so we will give you a tip on how to create the pipeline script for this stage automatically.

12.5.4 *Creating the Kubernetes pipeline scripts*

Jenkins offers a Pipeline Syntax option that lets us automatically generate different pipeline snippets that we can use in our Jenkinsfile. Figure 12.24 shows this process.

To use this option, we need to execute the following steps:

1 Go to the Jenkins dashboard page and select your pipeline.
2 Click the Pipeline Syntax option shown in the left column on the dashboard page.
3 On the Snippet Generator page, click the Sample Step drop-down list and select the kubernetesDeploy: Deploy to Kubernetes option.
4 In the Kubeconfig drop-down list, select the Kubernetes credentials that we created in the previous section.
5 In the Config Files option, select the deployment.yaml file. This file is located in the root of the GitHub project.
6 Leave the other values as default.
7 Click the Generate Pipeline Script button.

NOTE Remember, for this book, we set up separate folders in the same GitHub repository for each chapter of the book. All the source code for this chapter can be built and deployed as a single unit. However, we highly recommend that you set up each microservice in your environment with its own repository and with its own independent build processes.

Once, everything is set up, you can now change your code. Your Jenkins pipeline is automatically triggered.

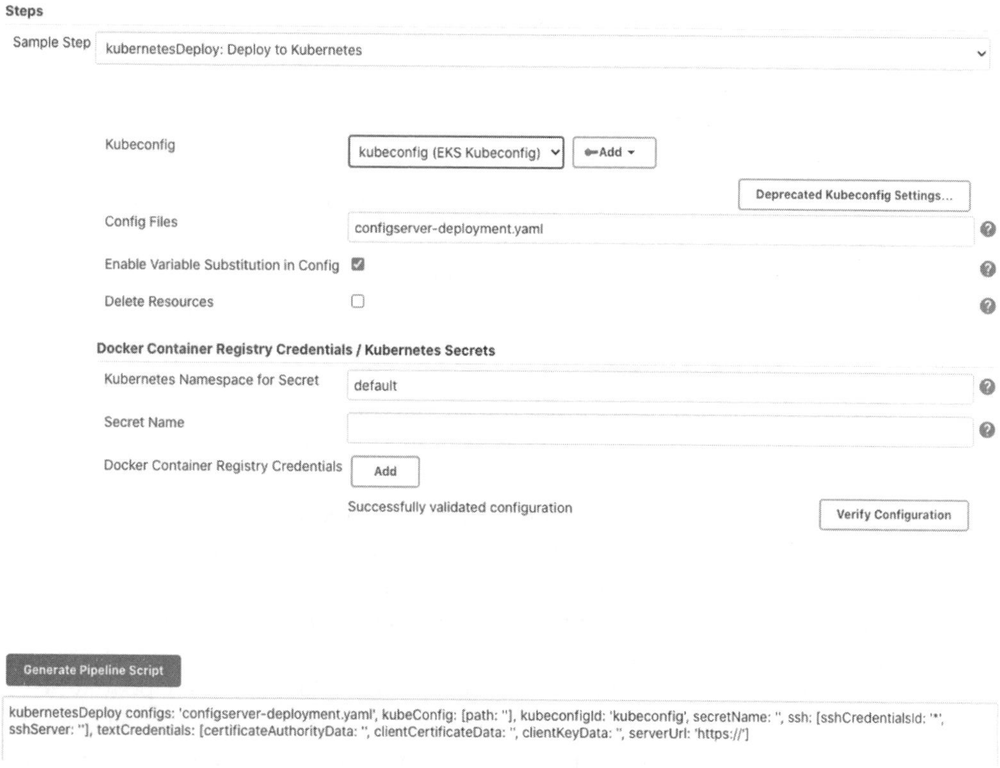

Steps

Sample Step | kubernetesDeploy: Deploy to Kubernetes | ⌄

Kubeconfig | kubeconfig (EKS Kubeconfig) ⌄ | ◆Add ⌄

Deprecated Kubeconfig Settings...

Config Files | configserver-deployment.yaml | ❓

Enable Variable Substitution in Config ☑ | ❓

Delete Resources ☐ | ❓

Docker Container Registry Credentials / Kubernetes Secrets

Kubernetes Namespace for Secret | default | ❓

Secret Name | | ❓

Docker Container Registry Credentials | Add

Successfully validated configuration | Verify Configuration

Generate Pipeline Script

kubernetesDeploy configs: 'configserver-deployment.yaml', kubeConfig: [path: '], kubeconfigId: 'kubeconfig', secretName: '', ssh: [sshCredentialsId: '*', sshServer: '], textCredentials: [certificateAuthorityData: '', clientCertificateData: '', clientKeyData: '', serverUrl: 'https://']

Figure 12.24 Using the Pipeline Syntax option to generate the `kubernetesDeploy` command

12.6 *Closing thoughts on the build/deployment pipeline*

As this chapter closes (and the book), we hope you've gained an appreciation for the amount of work that goes into building a build/deployment pipeline. A well-functioning build/deployment pipeline is critical to the deployment of services. And the success of your microservices architecture depends on more than just the code:

- Understand that the code in this build/deploy pipeline is simplified for the purposes of demonstration in this book. A good build/deployment pipeline is much more generalized. It will be supported by the DevOps team and broken into a series of independent steps (compile > package > deploy > test) that the development teams can use to "hook" their microservice build scripts into.

- The virtual machine imaging process used in this chapter is simplistic. Each microservice is built using a Dockerfile to define the software that's going to be installed on the Docker container. Many shops use provisioning tools like Ansible (https://github.com/ansible/ansible), Puppet (https://github.com/puppetlabs/puppet), or Chef (https://github.com/chef/chef) to install and configure the operating systems on the virtual machine or the container images.

- The cloud deployment topology for your application has been consolidated to a single server. In the real build/deployment pipeline, each microservice would have its own build scripts and would be deployed independently of any others to a cluster EKS container.

Writing microservices is a challenging task. With microservices, the complexity of creating applications doesn't go away; it is just transformed. The concepts around building individual microservices are easy to understand, but running and supporting a robust microservice architecture involves more than writing the code. Remember, a microservices architecture gives us a lot of options and decisions to make on how to create our application. When making these decisions, we need to consider that microservices are loosely coupled, abstract, independent, and constrained.

Hopefully, by now, we've given you enough information (and experiences) to create your own microservices architecture. In this book, you learned what a microservice is and the critical design decisions needed to operationalize them. You also learned how to create a complete microservices architecture following the twelve-factor best practices (configuration management, service discovery, messaging, logging, tracing, security), using a variety of tools and technologies that can be combined perfectly with Spring to deliver a robust microservices environment. And, finally, you learned how to implement a build/deployment pipeline.

All the previously mentioned ingredients create the perfect recipe to develop successful microservices. In closing, as Martin Fowler says, "If we don't create good architecture, then, in the end, we're deceiving our customers because we're slowing down their ability to compete."

Summary

- The build/deployment pipeline is a critical part of delivering microservices. A well-functioning build/deployment pipeline should allow new features and bug fixes to be deployed in minutes.
- The build/deployment pipeline should be automated with no direct human interaction to deliver a service. Any manual part of the process represents an opportunity for variability and failure.
- The build/deployment pipeline automation requires a great deal of scripting and configuration to get right. The amount of work needed to build it shouldn't be underestimated.
- The build/deployment pipeline should deliver an immutable virtual machine or container image. Once a server image is created, it should never be modified.
- Environment-specific server configuration should be passed in as parameters at the time the server is set up.

appendix A
Microservices
architecture best practices

In chapter 2, we explained some of the best practices that we should consider when creating a microservice. With this appendix we want to go deeper into these best practices. In the next sections, we will give you some guidelines (or best practices) to create a successful microservices architecture.

It is important to note that there isn't a well-defined set of rules to achieve this; however, Hüseyin Babal in his talk "Ultimate Guide to Microservice Architecture" presented a set of best practices to achieve a flexible, efficient, and scalable design. We consider this talk essential among the developer's community because it not only gives guidelines on how to develop a microservices architecture, but it also highlights which are the fundamental components of a microservice. In this appendix, we have selected some of the practices that we consider most important (those that we used throughout the book to create a flexible and successful architecture).

> **NOTE** If you're interested in knowing all of the best practices mentioned in the "Ultimate Guide to Microservice Architecture" talk, visit the following link that contains a video describing them: https://www.youtube.com/watch?v=CTnMUE06oZI.

The following list gives some of the best practices mentioned in his talk. We'll cover these in the following sections.

- Richardson Maturity Model
- Distributed configuration
- Monitoring
- Application performance management
- Spring HATEOAS
- Continuous delivery
- Logging
- API gateways

Richardson Maturity Model

This best practice (http://martinfowler.com/articles/richardsonMaturityModel.html), described by Martin Fowler, is a guide to understanding the main principles of REST architectures and to evaluate our REST architecture. It's important to note that we can see these levels more as a tool to help us understand the components of REST and the ideas behind the RESTful thinking rather than a kind of assessment mechanism for your company. Figure A.1 shows the different levels of maturity used to evaluate a service.

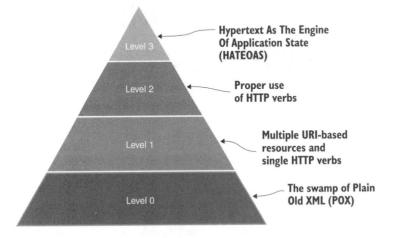

Figure A.1   Richardson's Maturity Model showing the levels of maturity

In the Richardson Maturity Model, level 0 represents the basic functionalities expected of an API. Basically, the API interaction in this level is a simple remote procedure call (RPC) to a single URI. It's mostly a back-and-forth XML sent in every request and response that specifies the action, the target, and the parameters to run the service.

For example, let's assume that we want to buy a specific product from an online store. First, the store's software needs to verify that is has the product in stock. At this level, the online store will expose a service endpoint with a single URI. Figure A.2 shows the level 0 service requests and responses.

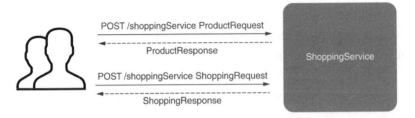

Figure A.2   Level 0: a simple RPC with a plain old XML (POX) sent back and forth between consumer and service

With level 1, the main idea is to perform actions on individual resources rather than making requests to a singular service endpoint. Figure A.3 shows the individual resources with their requests and responses.

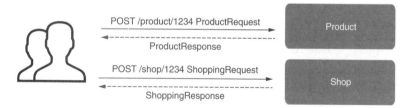

Figure A.3   Level 1: individual resource calls to perform some action

At level 2, the services use HTTP verbs in order to perform specific actions. The GET HTTP verb is used to retrieve, POST to create, PUT to update, and DELETE to remove. As previously mentioned, these levels function more as a tool to help us understand the components of REST, and REST advocates mention using all the HTTP verbs. Figure A.4 shows how to implement the use of HTTP verbs in our store example.

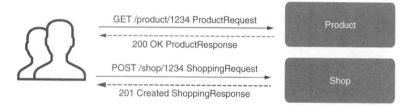

Figure A.4   HTTP verbs. In our scenario, GET retrieves product information and POST creates the shopping order.

The final level, level 3, introduces Hypertext as the Engine of Application State (HATEOAS). By implementing HATEOAS, we can make our API respond with additional information, such as link resources, to create richer interactions (figure A.5).

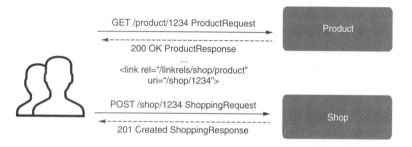

Figure A.5   HATEOAS in the retrieve product response. In our scenario, the link shows additional information on how to buy a specific product.

Using the Richardson Maturity Model, it is easy to explain that there is no definitive way to implement REST-based applications. We can, however, choose the degree of adherence that best suits the needs of our projects.

Spring HATEOAS

Spring HATEOAS (https://spring.io/projects/spring-hateoas) is a small Spring project that allow us to create APIs that follow the HATEOAS principle explained in level 3 of the Richardson Maturity Model. With Spring HATEOAS, you can quickly create model classes for links and resource representations. It also provides a link builder API to create specific links that point to Spring MVC controller methods, and more.

Externalized configuration

This best practice goes hand in hand with the configuration best practice listed in the twelve-factor app mentioned in chapter two (section 2.3). The configuration of our microservices should never be in the same repository as our source code. Why is it that important?

Microservices architectures are composed of a collection of services (microservices) that run in separate processes. Each service can be deployed and scaled independently, creating more instances of the same microservice. So, let's say that you, as a developer, want to change a configuration file of a specific microservice that has been scaled several times. If you don't follow this best practice and you have the configuration packaged with the deployed microservice, you'll be forced to redeploy each instance. Not only is this time consuming, but it also can lead to configuration issues between the microservices.

There are many ways to implement externalized configurations in a microservice architecture. But in this book, we used Spring Cloud Config as described in chapter 2.

Continuous integration (CI) and continuous delivery (CD)

Continuous integration (CI) is a series of software development practices where the team members integrate their changes to a repository within a short period of time to detect possible errors and to analyze the software's quality that they created. This is accomplished by using an automatic and continuous code check (build) that includes the execution of tests. On the other hand, continuous delivery (CD) is a software development practice in which the process of delivering software is automated to allow short-term deliveries into a production environment.

When we apply these processes to our microservices architecture, it's essential to keep in mind that there should never be a "waiting list" for integration and release to production. For example, a team in charge of service X must be able to publish changes to production at any time, without having to wait for the release of other services. Figure A.6 shows a high-level diagram of how our CI/CD process should look when working with several teams.

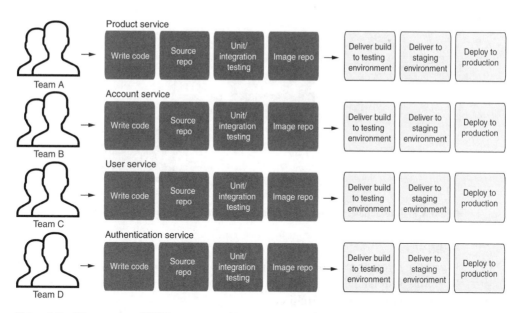

Figure A.6 Microservices CI/CD processes with a test and staging environment. In this figure, each team has its own source repository, unit and integration testing, image repository, and process of deployment. This allows each team to deploy and release newer versions without having to wait for other releases.

For the provisioning implementations, we need to make a technology shift. Spring framework(s) are geared toward application development and don't have tools for creating a build/deployment pipeline.

Monitoring

The monitoring process is critical when we talk about microservices. Microservices are part of large and complex distributed systems, and remember, the more distributed a system is, the more complicated it is to find and solve its problems. Imagine that we have an architecture with hundreds of microservices, and one of the microservices is affecting the performance of other services. How do we know which is the unstable service if we don't implement a suitable monitoring process? In order to tackle this, in appendix C, we explain how to achieve a good monitoring system in our architecture using the following tools. Figure A.7 shows the interaction between Micrometer, Prometheus, and Grafana.

- Micrometer (https://micrometer.io/) is a default metrics library in Spring Boot 2 that allows us to obtain application metrics as well as JVM metrics like garbage collection, memory pools, and so forth.
- Prometheus (https://prometheus.io/) is an open source monitoring and alert system that stores all data as a time series.
- Grafana (https://grafana.com/) is an analysis platform for metrics that lets you query, visualize, and understand data no matter where it's stored.

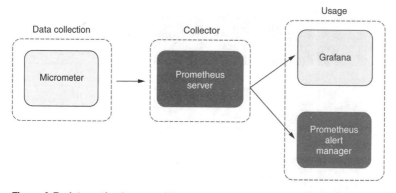

Figure A.7   Interaction between Micrometer, Prometheus, and Grafana

Logging

Every time you think about logs think about *distributed tracing*. Distributed tracing helps us understand and debug our microservices by pinpointing where a failure occurs in a microservices architecture.

In chapter 11, we explained how to achieve this with Spring Cloud. The traceability of the requests we make within our architecture is another "new" technological (Spring Cloud Sleuth) situation that comes up when speaking about microservices. In monolith architectures, the majority of the requests that reach the application are resolved within the same application. The ones not following this rule were the ones that interacted with a database or some other service. However, in microservices architectures (Spring Cloud, for example), we find an environment composed of several applications, generating a single client request that can go through several applications until it is answered.

How can we follow the path of that request in a microservices architecture? We can associate a unique request identifier that can then be propagated across all the calls and add a central log collection to see all the entries of that client request.

API gateways

An API gateway is an API REST interface that provides a central access point to a group of microservices and/or defined third-party APIs. In other words, the Spring Cloud API Gateway essentially decouples the interface that clients see from the microservice implementation. This is particularly useful when we want to avoid exposing internal services to external clients. Keep in mind that this system not only acts as a gateway, but you can also add additional features such as these:

- Authentication and authorization (OAuth2)
- Protection against threats (DoS, code injection, and so on)
- Analysis and supervision (who uses the APIs, when, and how)
- Monitoring of incoming and outgoing traffic

appendix B
OAuth2 grant types

After reading chapter 9, you might think that OAuth2 doesn't seem too compli-cated. After all, you have an authentication service that checks a user's credentials and issues a token back to the user. The token can, in turn, be presented every time the user wants to call a service protected by the OAuth2 server.

With the interconnected nature of the web and cloud-based applications, users have come to expect that they can securely share their data and integrate function-ality between different applications owned by various services. This presents a unique challenge from a security perspective because you want to integrate across different applications while not forcing users to share their credentials with each application they want to integrate with.

OAuth2 is a flexible authorization framework that provides multiple mecha-nisms for applications to authenticate and authorize users without forcing them to share credentials. Unfortunately, it's also one of the reasons why OAuth2 is consid-ered complicated. These authentication mechanisms are called *authentication grants*. OAuth2 has four forms of authentication grants that client applications can use to authenticate users, receive an access token, and then to validate that token. These grant types are

- Password
- Client credential
- Authorization code
- Implicit

In the following sections, we walk through the activities that occur during the exe-cution of each of these OAuth2 grant flows. We also talk about when to use one grant type over another.

Password grant types

An OAuth2 password grant is probably the most straightforward grant type. You'll use this grant type when both the application and the services explicitly trust one another. For example, the O-stock web application and the licensing and organization services are all owned by the same company (Optima Growth), so there's a natural trust relationship between them.

> **NOTE** To be explicit, when we refer to a "natural trust relationship," we mean that the same organization completely owns the application and services. These are managed under the same policies and procedures.

When a natural trust relationship exists, there's little concern about exposing an OAuth2 access token to the calling application. For example, the O-stock web application can use the granted OAuth2 password to capture the user's credentials and directly authenticate against the OAuth2 service. Figure B.1 shows the password grant type in action between O-stock and the downstream services.

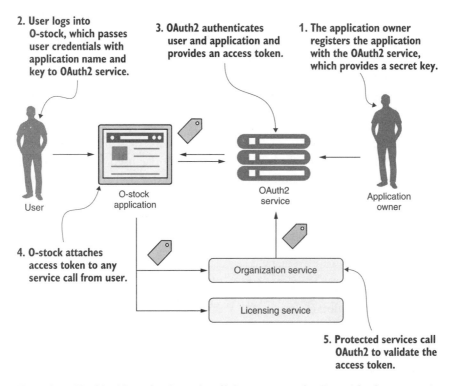

Figure B.1   The OAuth2 service determines if the user accessing the service is an authenticated user.

In figure B.1, the following actions take place. The numbers correspond to those in the figure:

1 Before the O-stock application can use a protected resource, it needs to be uniquely identified within the OAuth2 service. Usually, the owner of the application registers with the OAuth2 application service and provides a unique name for their application. The OAuth2 service then provides a secret key back to register the application. The name of the application and the secret key provided by the OAuth2 service uniquely identify the application trying to access any protected resources.

2 The user logs into O-stock and provides their login credentials to the application. O-stock passes the user credentials and the application name/application secret key directly to the OAuth2 service.

3 The O-stock OAuth2 service authenticates the application and the user and then provides an OAuth2 access token back to the user.

4 Every time the O-stock application calls a service on behalf of the user, it passes along the access token provided by the OAuth2 server.

5 When a protected service is called (in this case, one of the licensing or organization services), the service calls back to the O-stock OAuth2 service to validate the token. If the token is good, the invoked service allows the user to proceed. If the token is invalid, the OAuth2 service returns an HTTP status code 403, indicating that the token is invalid.

Client credential grant type

You'll use the client credential grant type when an application needs to access an OAuth2 protected resource, but no one is involved in the transaction. With the client credential grant type, the OAuth2 server only authenticates based on the application name and the secret key provided by the resource owner. This grant type is usually used when the same company owns both applications. The difference between the password grant type and the client credential grant type is that a client credential grant authenticates by only using the registered application name and the secret key.

For example, let's say that the O-stock application has a data analytics job that runs once an hour. As part of its work, it makes calls out to O-stock services. However, the O-stock developers still want that application to authenticate and authorize itself before it can access the data in those services. This is where the client credential grant type can be used. Figure B.2 shows this flow.

In figure B.2, the following actions take place. The numbers correspond to those in the figure:

1 The resource owner registers the O-stock data analytics application with the OAuth2 service. The resource owner provides the application name and receives back a secret key.

2 When the O-stock data analytics job runs, it presents its application name and secret key provided by the resource owner.

3 The O-stock OAuth2 service authenticates the application using the provided application name and the secret key and then returns an OAuth2 access token.

4 Every time the application calls one of the O-stock services, it presents the OAuth2 access token received with the service call.

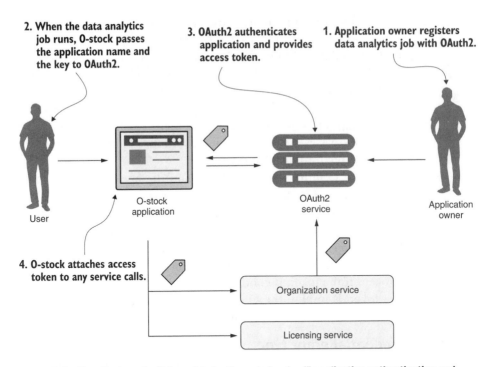

2. When the data analytics job runs, O-stock passes the application name and the key to OAuth2.

3. OAuth2 authenticates application and provides access token.

1. Application owner registers data analytics job with OAuth2.

User

O-stock application

OAuth2 service

Application owner

4. O-stock attaches access token to any service calls.

Organization service

Licensing service

Figure B.2   The client credential grant is for "no-user-involved" application authentication and authorization.

Authorization grant type

The authorization code grant is by far the most complicated of the OAuth2 grant types, but it's also the most common because it allows different applications from different vendors to share data and services without having to expose a user's credentials across multiple applications. It also enforces an extra layer of checking by not letting a calling application get an OAuth2 access token immediately, but it rather receives a "preflight" authorization code.

The easiest way to understand the authorization grant type is with an example. Let's say you have an O-stock user who also uses Salesforce.com. The O-stock customer's IT department has built a Salesforce application that needs data from an O-stock service (the organization service). Let's look at figure B.3 to see how the authorization code grant type works to allow Salesforce access to data from the organization service without the O-stock customer ever having to expose their O-stock credentials to Salesforce.

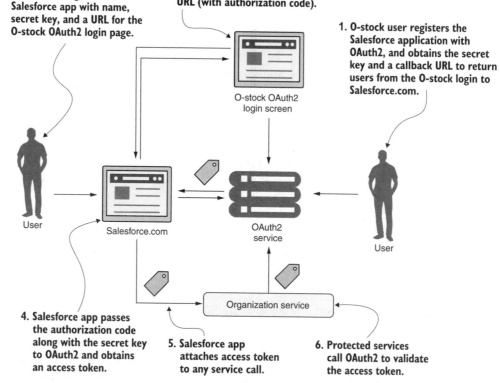

2. The user configures the Salesforce app with name, secret key, and a URL for the O-stock OAuth2 login page.

3. Potential Salesforce app users now directed to the O-stock login page; authenticated users return to Salesforce.com through a callback URL (with authorization code).

1. O-stock user registers the Salesforce application with OAuth2, and obtains the secret key and a callback URL to return users from the O-stock login to Salesforce.com.

O-stock OAuth2 login screen

User

Salesforce.com

OAuth2 service

User

Organization service

4. Salesforce app passes the authorization code along with the secret key to OAuth2 and obtains an access token.

5. Salesforce app attaches access token to any service call.

6. Protected services call OAuth2 to validate the access token.

Figure B.3   The authentication code grant type allows applications to share data without exposing user credentials.

In figure B.3, the following actions take place. The numbers correspond to those in the figure:

1   The user logs in to the O-stock application and generates an application name and application secret key for the Salesforce application. As part of the registration process, they also provide a callback URL for the Salesforce application. This Salesforce callback URL is called after the OAuth2 server authenticates the O-stock credentials.

2   The user configures their Salesforce application with the following information:

 a   The application name they created for Salesforce

 b   The secret key they generated for Salesforce

 c   A URL that points to the O-stock OAuth2 login page

Now when the user tries to use the Salesforce application and access O-stock data via the organization service, they are redirected to the O-stock login page via the URL described in step 1. The user provides their O-stock credentials. If they are valid credentials, the O-stock OAuth2 server generates an authorization code and redirects the user to Salesforce via the URL provided in step 1. The OAuth2 server sends the authorization code as a query parameter on the callback URL.

3   The custom Salesforce application persists the authorization code. Note that this authorization code isn't an OAuth2 access token.

4   Once the authorization code is stored, the Salesforce application presents the secret key generated during the registration process and the authorization code back to the O-stock OAuth2 server. The O-stock OAuth2 server validates the authorization code and then returns an OAuth2 token to the custom Salesforce application, which is used every time Salesforce needs to authenticate the user and get an OAuth2 access token.

5   The Salesforce application calls the O-stock organization service, passing an OAuth2 token in the header.

6   The organization service validates the OAuth2 access token passed into the O-stock service call. If the token is valid, the organization service processes the user's request.

Wow! We need to come up for air. Application-to-application integration is convoluted. The key takeaway from this entire process is that even though the user is logged in to Salesforce and accessing O-stock data, at no time were the user's O-stock credentials directly exposed to Salesforce. After the initial authorization code was generated by the OAuth2 service, the user never had to provide their credentials back to the O-stock service.

Implicit grant type

You use the implicit grant type when you're running a web application through a traditional server-side web programming environment like Java or .NET. What happens if your client application is a pure JavaScript application or a mobile application that runs entirely in a web browser and doesn't rely on server-side calls to invoke third-party services? This is where the implicit grant type comes into play. Figure B.4 shows the general flow of what occurs with the implicit grant type.

With an implicit grant, you usually work with a pure JavaScript application running entirely inside a browser. With the other grant types, the client communicates with an application server that carries out the user's request, and the application server interacts with any downstream services. With an implicit grant type, all service interactions

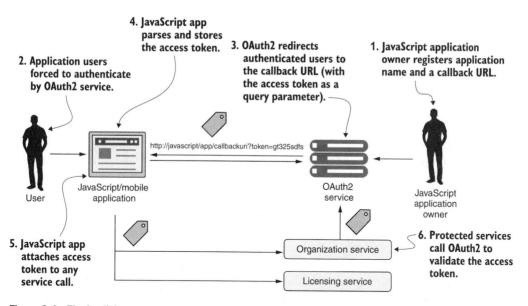

Figure C.4   The implicit grant type is used in a browser-based Single Page Application (SPA) JavaScript application.

happen directly from the user's client (usually a web browser). In figure B.4, the following activities take place. Note that the numbers correspond to those in the figure:

1 The owner of the JavaScript application registers the application with the O-stock OAuth2 server. The owner provides an application name and a callback URL that will be redirected with the OAuth2 access token for the user.

2 The JavaScript application calls the OAuth2 service. The JavaScript application must present a preregistered application name. The OAuth2 server then forces the user to authenticate.

3 If the user successfully authenticates, the O-stock OAuth2 service doesn't return a token but, instead, redirects the user back to the page the owner of the JavaScript application registered in step 1. In the URL redirected back to the user, the OAuth2 access token is passed as a query parameter by the OAuth2 authentication service.

4 The application takes the incoming request and runs a JavaScript script that parses the OAuth2 access token and stores it (usually as a cookie).

5 Each time a protected resource is called, the OAuth2 access token is presented to the called service.

6 The called service validates the OAuth2 token and checks that the user is authorized to do the activity they're attempting to do.

Keep several things in mind regarding the OAuth2 implicit grant type. First, the implicit grant is the only grant type where the OAuth2 access token is directly exposed to a public client (web browser).

With the authorization grant type, the client application receives an authorization code returned by the application server hosting the application, and the user is granted an OAuth2 access by presenting the authorization code. The returned OAuth2 token is never directly exposed to the user's browser. With the client credential grant type, the grant occurs between two server-based applications, and with the password grant type, both the application requesting a service and the services are trusted and owned by the same organization.

OAuth2 tokens generated by the implicit grant type are more vulnerable to attack and misuse because the tokens are made available to the browser. Any malicious JavaScript running in the browser can access the OAuth2 access token and call the services you retrieved the OAuth2 token for on your behalf, essentially impersonating you. The implicit grant type OAuth2 tokens should therefore be short-lived (1–2 hours). Because the OAuth2 access token is stored in the browser, the OAuth2 spec (and Spring Cloud security) doesn't support the concept of a refresh token in which a token can be automatically renewed.

How tokens are refreshed

When an OAuth2 access token is issued, it is valid for a limited amount of time, eventually expiring. When the token expires, the calling application (and user) need to re-authenticate with the OAuth2 service. However, in most of the OAuth2 grant flows, the OAuth2 server will issue both an access token and a refresh token. A client can present the refresh token to the OAuth2 authentication service, and the service will validate the refresh token and then issue a new OAuth2 access token. Let's look at figure B.5 and walk through the token refresh flow.

In figure B.5, the following actions take place. The numbers correspond to those in the figure:

1 The user logs in to O-stock but is already authenticated with the OAuth2 service. The user is happily working, but unfortunately, their token expires.

2 The next time the user tries to call a service (say, the organization service), the O-stock application passes the expired token to the organization service.

3 The organization service tries to validate the token with the OAuth2 service, which returns an HTTP status code 401 (unauthorized) and a JSON payload, indicating that the token is no longer valid. The organization service returns an HTTP 401 status code to the calling service.

4 The O-stock application gets the 401 HTTP status code and the JSON payload back from the organization service. The O-stock application then calls the OAuth2 authentication service with a refresh token. The OAuth2 authentication service validates the refresh token and then sends back a new access token.

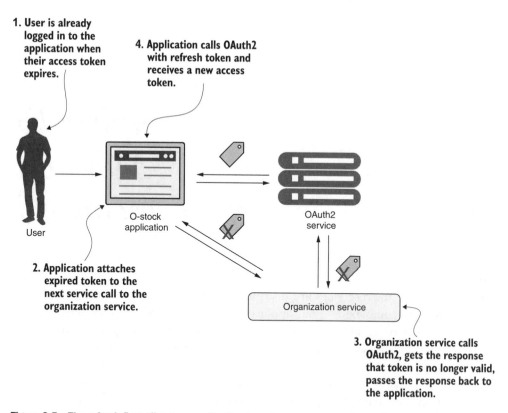

1. User is already logged in to the application when their access token expires.

4. Application calls OAuth2 with refresh token and receives a new access token.

User

O-stock application

OAuth2 service

2. Application attaches expired token to the next service call to the organization service.

Organization service

3. Organization service calls OAuth2, gets the response that token is no longer valid, passes the response back to the application.

Figure C.5   The refresh flow allows an application to get a new access token without forcing the user to reauthenticate.

appendix C
Monitoring
your microservices

Because microservices are distributed and fine-grained (small), they introduce a level of complexity to our applications that don't exist in monolithic applications. Microservices architectures require a high degree of operational maturity, and monitoring becomes a critical part of their administration. If we research service monitoring, we will see that most people agree that it's a fundamental process, but what exactly is monitoring? We define monitoring as the process of analysis, collection, and data storage such as application, platform, and system event metrics among others, that helps us visualize failure patterns within an IT environment.

Only failures? It is essential to clarify that failure is one of the most apparent reasons why monitoring is fundamental, but it isn't the only one. The microservice performance also is considered another reason and, indeed, plays a critical role in our applications. We cannot describe the performance as a binary concept that is "up and running" or "down." Service architectures can operate with a specific state of degradation that may affect the performance of one or more services. In the following sections, we show you how to monitor our Spring Boot microservices using several technologies such as Spring Boot Actuator, Micrometer, Prometheus, and Grafana. So, let's start.

C.1   *Introducing monitoring with Spring Boot Actuator*

Spring Boot Actuator is a library that provides monitoring and administration tools for our REST API in a reasonably simple way. It does this by organizing and exposing a series of REST endpoints that allow us to access different monitoring information to check the status of our services. In other words, Spring Boot Actuator provides out-of-the-box operational endpoints that will help us understand and manage our service's health.

To use Spring Actuator, we need to follow two simple steps. The first is to include the Maven dependencies in our pom.xml file, and the second is to enable the endpoints we are going to use in our application. Let's look closer at each of these steps.

C.1.1 Adding Spring Boot Actuator

To include Spring Boot Actuator in our microservice, we need to add the following dependency to the pom.xml in the microservice we are working on:

```
<dependency>
    <groupId>org.springframework.boot</groupId>
    <artifactId>spring-boot-starter-actuator</artifactId>
</dependency>
```

C.1.2 Enabling Actuator endpoints

Setting up Spring Boot Actuator is a straightforward process. Just by adding the dependency to our microservices, we now have a series of endpoints available to consume. Each endpoint can be enabled or disabled and exposed via HTTP or JMX. Figure C.1 shows all the Actuator endpoints enabled by default. To enable a specific endpoint, we only need to use the following format property:

```
management.endpoint.<id>.enabled= true or false
```

For example, to disable the beans endpoint, we need to add the following property:

```
management.endpoint.beans.enabled = false
```

For this book, we enable all the default Actuator endpoints for all our microservices, but feel free to make the changes that best fit your needs. Remember, you can always add security to the HTTP endpoints by using Spring Security. The following code shows the Spring Boot Actuator configuration for our licensing and organization services:

```
management.endpoints.web.exposure.include=*
management.endpoints.enabled-by-default=true
```

With this configuration, if we enter the http://localhost:8080/actuator endpoint in Postman, we'll see a list like the one shown in figure C.1, with all the endpoints exposed by Spring Boot Actuator.

```
{
  "_links": {
    "self": {↔},
    "archaius": {↔},
    "beans": {↔},
    "caches-cache": {↔},
    "caches": {↔},
    "health": {
      "href": "http://localhost:8080/actuator/health",
      "templated": false
    },
    "health-path": {↔},
    "info": {↔},
    "conditions": {↔},
    "shutdown": {↔},
    "configprops": {↔},
    "env": {↔},
    "env-toMatch": {↔},
    "integrationgraph": {↔},
    "loggers": {↔},
    "loggers-name": {↔},
    "heapdump": {↔},
    "threaddump": {↔},
    "metrics-requiredMetricName": {↔},
    "metrics": {↔},
    "scheduledtasks": {↔},
    "mappings": {↔},
    "refresh": {↔},
    "restart": {↔},
    "pause": {↔},
    "resume": {↔},
    "features": {↔},
    "service-registry": {↔},
    "bindings-name": {↔},
    "bindings": {↔},
    "channels": {↔},
    "hystrix.stream": {↔}
  }
}
```

Figure C.1   Spring Boot Actuator default endpoints

C.2   Setting up Micrometer and Prometheus

Spring Boot Actuator offers metrics that allow us to monitor our application. However, if we want to have more precise metrics for our application, and we want to obtain those metrics, we will need to use additional tools like Micrometer and Prometheus.

C.2.1   Understanding Micrometer and Prometheus

Micrometer is a library that provides application metrics and is designed to add little or no overhead to the metrics collection activity in our applications. Micrometer also allows metrics data to be exported to any of the most popular monitoring systems.

Using Micrometer, the application abstracts the metric system used and can be changed in the future if desired. Alternatively, one of the most popular monitoring systems is Prometheus, which is responsible for collecting and storing metrics data exposed by the application. It offers a data query language with which other applications can visualize the metrics in graphs and control panels. Grafana is one tool that allows you to view the data provided by Prometheus, but Micrometer can also be used with other monitoring systems like Datadog, SignalFx, Influx, New Relic, Google Stackdriver, Wavefront, and more.

One of the advantages of using Spring Boot for our microservices is that it allows us to choose one or more monitoring systems containing different views to analyze and project our results. With Micrometer, we will be able to measure metrics that allow us to understand the performance of our systems as a whole; through several components of a single application or instances of clusters; and so forth. The following list contains some of the metrics we can obtain with Micrometer:

- Statistics related to garbage collection
- CPU usage
- Memory usage
- Threads utilization
- Data source usage
- Spring MVC request latencies
- Kafka connection factories
- Caching
- Number of events logged in Logback
- Uptime

For this book, we chose Prometheus as the monitoring system because it integrates with Micrometer and Spring Boot 2 simply. Prometheus is an in-memory dimensional time series database and also a monitoring and alert system. When we talk about storing time series data, we refer to storing data in chronological order and measuring variables over time. Time series–focused databases are exceptionally efficient for storing and querying this data. Prometheus's main objective is to work as a pull model, scraping the metrics from the application instances periodically. Some of the main characteristics of Prometheus are these:

- *Flexible query language*—It contains a custom query language that allows us to query data straightforwardly.
- *Efficient storage*—It efficiently stores the time series in memory and on a local disk.
- *Multidimensional data models*—All time series are identified by a metric name and a set of key-value pairs.
- *Multiple integrations*—It allows integration with third parties like Docker, JMX, and more.

C.2.2 *Implementing Micrometer and Prometheus*

To export the data to Micrometer and Prometheus using Spring Boot 2, we need to add the following dependencies. (Note that Prometheus comes with the Micrometer package.)

```xml
<dependency>
    <groupId>io.micrometer</groupId>
    <artifactId>micrometer-registry-prometheus</artifactId>
</dependency>
<dependency>
    <groupId>io.micrometer</groupId>
    <artifactId>micrometer-core</artifactId>
</dependency>
```

For this book, we enabled all of the default Actuator endpoints for all our microservices. If you only want to expose the Prometheus endpoint, you should include the following property in the licensing and organization service application properties:

```
management.endpoints.web.exposure.include=prometheus
```

By executing these steps and by entering the http://localhost:8080/actuator URL in Postman, you should now be able to see a list of Actuator endpoints like the ones shown in figure C.2.

```
{
  "_links": {
    "self": {↔},
    "archaius": {↔},
    "beans": {↔},
    "caches": {↔},
    "caches-cache": {↔},
    "health": {
      "href": "http://localhost:8080/actuator/health",
      "templated": false
    },
    "health-path": {↔},
    "info": {↔},
    "conditions": {↔},
    "shutdown": {↔},
    "configprops": {↔},
    "env-toMatch": {↔},
    "env": {↔},
    "loggers": {↔},
    "loggers-name": {↔},
    "heapdump": {↔},
    "threaddump": {↔},
    "prometheus": {
      "href": "http://localhost:8080/actuator/prometheus",
      "templated": false
    },
```

Figure C.2   Spring Boot Actuator endpoints including the `actuator/prometheus` endpoint

There are several ways to set up Prometheus. In this book, we use a Docker container to run the Prometheus services using the official images that are ready to use. But feel free to use the one that best suits your needs. If you want to use Docker, make sure you have the service defined in the Docker Compose file as shown in the following listing.

Listing C.1   Setting up Prometheus in the docker-compose file

```yaml
prometheus:
    image: prom/prometheus:latest
    ports:
```

```
      - "9090:9090"
    volumes:
    - ./prometheus.yml:/etc/prometheus/prometheus.yml
    container_name: prometheus
    networks:
      backend:
        aliases:
          - "prometheus"
```

For the Prometheus container, we've created a volume for the Prometheus configuration file, which is called prometheus.yml. This file contains the endpoints that Prometheus uses to pull the data. The following listing shows the content of this file.

Listing C.2   Setting up the prometheus.yml file

Sets the scrape interval to every 5 seconds

```
    global:
      scrape_interval:     5s
      evaluation_interval: 5s
    scrape_configs:
      - job_name: 'licensingservice'
        metrics_path: '/actuator/prometheus'
        static_configs:
        - targets: ['licensingservice:8080']
      - job_name: 'organizationservice'
        metrics_path: '/actuator/prometheus'
        static_configs:
        - targets: ['organizationservice:8081']
```

Sets the evaluate rules time to every 5 seconds

URL for the actuator/prometheus endpoint that exposes metrics information in the format that Prometheus expects

⟵ **URL for the licensing service**

⟵ **URL for the organization**

The prometheus.yml file defines the configurations for the Prometheus service. For example, with the previous values, the service scrapes all the /Prometheus endpoints every 5 seconds and adds the data to its time series database.

Now that we have the configuration set up, let's run our services and verify that the scraping was successful. To confirm this, visit the URL http://localhost:9090/targets to see a page similar to the one shown in figure C.3.

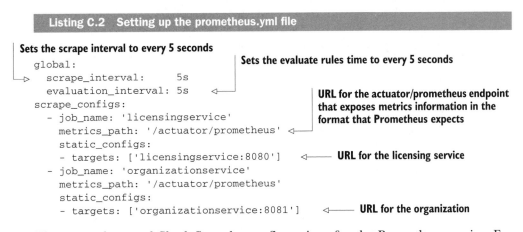

Figure C.3   Prometheus targets configured in the prometheus.yml file.

C.3   Configuring Grafana

Grafana is an open source tool that displays time series data. It offers a set of dashboards that lets us visualize, explore, add alerts, and understand the application data. Grafana also enables us to create, explore, and share dashboards. The main reason we chose Grafana in this book is that it is one of the best options for displaying dashboards. It contains incredible graphics and multiple functions, is flexible, and most important, it is easy to use.

There are several ways to set up Grafana as well. In this book, we use the official Grafana Docker image to run the service. But feel free to use the one that best suits your needs. If you want to use Docker, make sure you have the service defined in the docker-compose file as shown in the following listing.

> **Listing C.3   Configuring Grafana in the docker-compose file**

```
grafana:
    image: "grafana/grafana:latest"
    ports:
      - "3000:3000"
    container_name: grafana
    networks:
      backend:
        aliases:
          - "grafana"
```

Once the configuration is added to the docker-compose file, you can execute the following command to run your services:

```
docker-compose -f docker/docker-compose.yml up
```

When it finishes, Grafana should be up and running on port 3000, as set in listing C.3. Visit the http://localhost:3000/login to see the page shown in figure C.4.

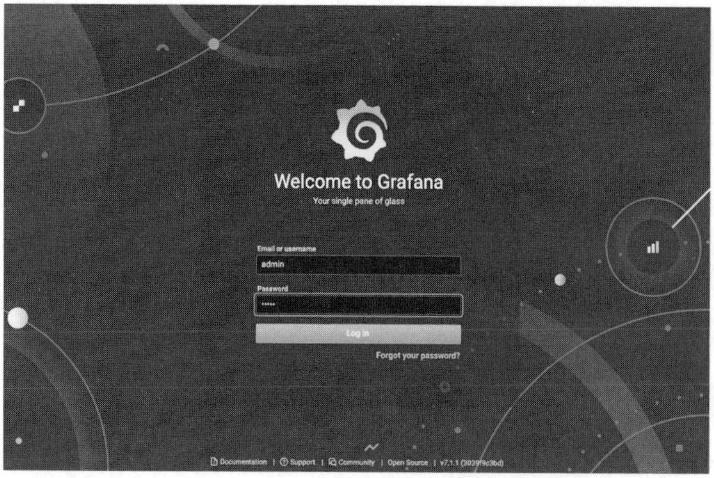

Figure C.4   Grafana login page showing the default username and password (admin admin)

Figure C.4 shows the default username and password for Grafana. We can change this default once we log in, or we can define a username and password in the docker-compose file. The following listing shows how to do this.

Listing C.4   Configuring the admin username and password for Grafana

```
grafana:
    image: "grafana/grafana:latest"
    ports:
      - "3000:3000"
    environment:
      - GF_SECURITY_ADMIN_USER=admin          ◁───── Sets the admin username
      - GF_SECURITY_ADMIN_PASSWORD=password    ◁───── Sets the admin password
    container_name: grafana
... rest of the file removed for conciseness
```

To finish the configuration in Grafana, we need to create a data source and a dashboard configuration. Let's start with the data source. To create the data source, click the Data Sources section on the main page in Grafana, click the explore icon on the left, and select Add Your First Data Source, as shown in figure C.5.

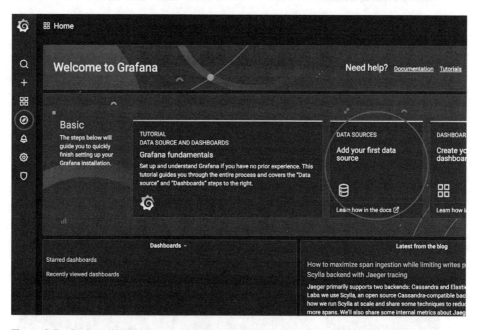

Figure C.5   Grafana Welcome page. This page shows the links to set the initial configuration.

When you are at the Add Data Source page, select Prometheus as the time series database as shown in figure C.6.

The final step is to configure the Prometheus URL (http://localhost:9090 or http://prometheus:9090) for our data source. Figure C.7 shows you how.

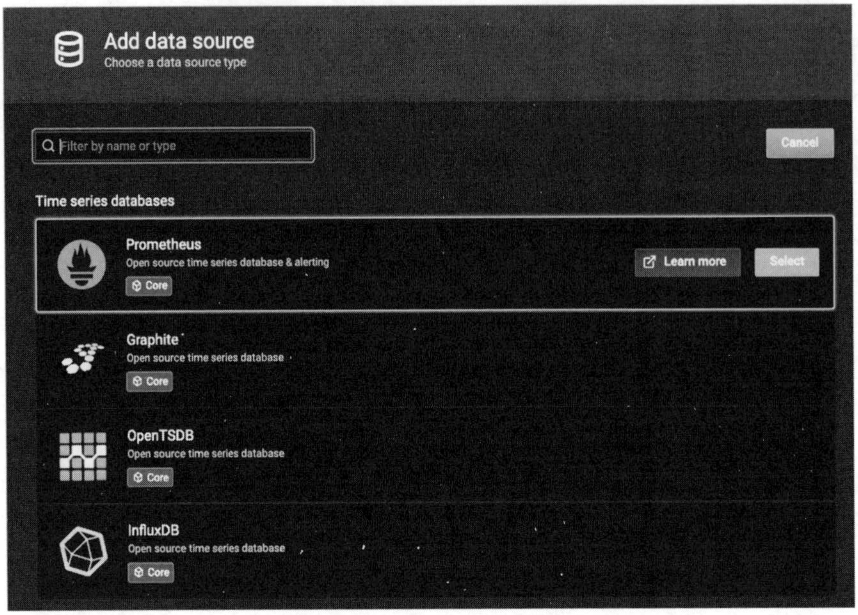

Figure C.6 Selecting the time series database for Prometheus in Grafana

NOTE We use localhost when we run the services locally, but if we run the services with Docker, we need to use the Prometheus service backend alias we defined in the docker-compose file. For the Prometheus service, we defined the prometheus alias. You can see this in listing C.1.

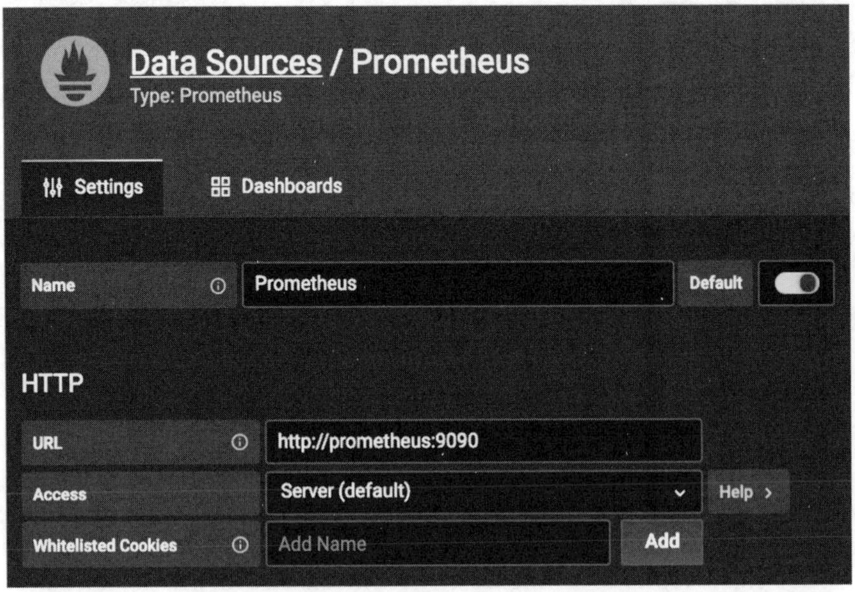

Figure C.7 Configuring the Prometheus data source using a local or a Docker Prometheus URL

Once filled, click the Save and Test button at the bottom of the page. Now that we have our data source, let's import a dashboard for our Grafana application. In order to import a dashboard, in Grafana click the Dashboard icon on the left menu, select the Manage option, and click the Import button.

On the Import page, you will see the following options:

- Upload a JSON File
- Import Via grafana.com
- Import Via Panel JSON

For this example, we'll select Import Via grafana.com to import the following dashboard: https://grafana.com/grafana/dashboards/11378/. This dashboard contains the Spring Boot 2.1 statistics by Micrometer-Prometheus. To import this dashboard, copy the URL or the ID to the clipboard, paste it into the Import Via grafana.com field, and click the Load button. Clicking the Load button redirects you to the Dashboard Configuration page where you can rename, move to a folder, or select a Prometheus data source. To continue, select the Prometheus data source and click the Import button.

If the configuration is successful, you should now see your dashboard page with all the Micrometer metrics. Figure C.8 shows the Spring Boot 2.1 System Monitor dashboard.

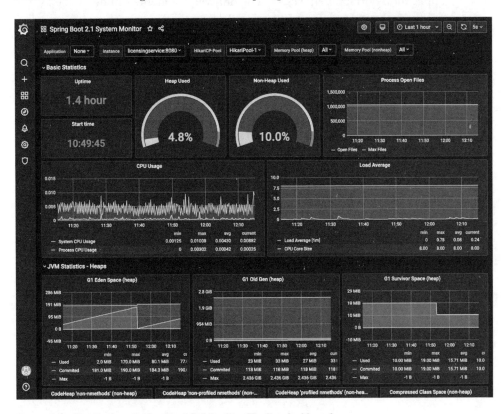

Figure C.8   The Grafana Spring Boot 2.1 System Monitor dashboard

We recommend that you visit the official documentation if you want to know more about Grafana and Prometheus at these links:

- https://grafana.com/docs/grafana/latest/
- https://prometheus.io/docs/introduction/overview/

C.4   *Summarizing our discussion*

Our microservices architecture needs to be monitored for the same reasons as any other type of distributed system. The more complex our architecture gets, the more challenging it is to understand the performance and to troubleshoot the issues.

When we talk about monitoring an application, we often think of failure, and yes, failure is one of the most common reasons why adequate monitoring is essential. Still, it is not the only reason. Performance is another excellent reason for monitoring. As we mentioned in the first chapters, services are not only up or down; they can also be up and running but with a degraded state that can damage our best intentions.

With a reliable monitoring system like the one we explained in this appendix, you can prevent performance failures and can even visualize possible errors in your architecture. It is essential to note that you can add this monitoring code to any of your application development stages. The only requirements you need to execute the code in this book are Docker and a Spring Boot application.

index

MANNING

A new online reading experience

liveBook, our online reading platform, adds a new dimension to your Manning books, with features that make reading, learning, and sharing easier than ever. A liveBook version of your book is included FREE with every Manning book.

This next generation book platform is more than an online reader. It's packed with unique features to upgrade and enhance your learning experience.

- Add your own notes and bookmarks
- One-click code copy
- Learn from other readers in the discussion forum
- Audio recordings and interactive exercises
- Read all your purchased Manning content in any browser, anytime, anywhere

As an added bonus, you can search every Manning book and video in liveBook—even ones you don't yet own. Open any liveBook, and you'll be able to browse the content and read anything you like.*

Find out more at www.manning.com/livebook-program.

*Open reading is limited to 10 minutes per book daily

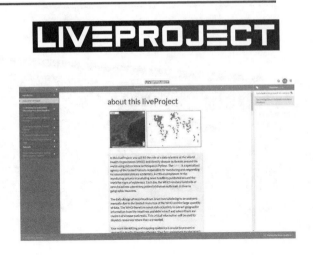

Hands-on projects for learning your way

liveProjects are an exciting way to develop your skills that's just like learning on-the-job.

In a Manning liveProject you tackle a real-world IT challenge and work out your own solutions. To make sure you succeed, you'll get 90 days full and unlimited access to a hand-picked list of Manning book and video resources.

Here's how liveProject works:

- **Achievable milestones.** Each project is broken down into steps and sections so you can keep track of your progress.

- **Collaboration and advice.** Work with other liveProject participants through chat, working groups, and peer project reviews.

- **Compare your results.** See how your work shapes up against an expert implementation by the liveProject's creator.

- **Everything you need to succeed.** Datasets and carefully selected learning resources come bundled with every liveProject.

- **Build your portfolio.** All liveProjects teach skills that are in-demand from industry. When you're finished, you'll have the satisfaction that comes with success and a real project to add to your portfolio.

Explore dozens of data, development, and cloud engineering liveProjects at www.manning.com!